Research Methods in Child Welfare

Research Methods in Child Welfare

AMY J. L. BAKER

WITH

BENJAMIN J. CHARVAT

Columbia University Press *New York*

Columbia University Press
Publishers Since 1893
New York   Chichester, West Sussex
Copyright © 2008 Amy J. L. Baker and Benjamin J. Charvat
All rights reserved
Library of Congress Cataloging-in-Publication Data

Baker, Amy J. L.
  Research methods in child welfare / Amy J. L. Baker with
Benjamin J. Charvat.
     p.   cm.
  Includes bibliographical references and index.
  ISBN 978-0-231-14130-7 (cloth : alk. paper)—ISBN 978-0-231-14131-4
(pbk. : alk. paper)—ISBN 978-0-231-51214-5 (ebook)
  1. Child welfare—Research—United States.   I. Charvat,
Benjamin J. II. Title.

HV741.B294 2008
362.7072—dc22   2007044173

Contents

Contents

Figures

viii

Figures

Tables

Tables

Foreword

This book is a welcome addition to the field of child welfare. The past several decades have seen an increased emphasis on research and evaluation in both public and private child welfare settings. This research and evaluation on child welfare issues is occurring in academic as well as public and private child service agency settings. It is incumbent on those of us who seek to improve the lives of children and their families to seek empirical evidence to support our practice. With limited resources, we must identify promising and evidence-based practices to serve as a basis for effective assessment, interventions, and policies. Whether information collection involves simple client satisfaction surveys, analysis of data in administrative databases, or more complex randomized control studies, certain processes and procedures are important to follow to know that the information produced is valid and reliable.

Research Methods in Child Welfare by Amy Baker with Benjamin Charvat is a well-written and comprehensive book that discusses the underlying philosophy of research, offers important considerations regarding research ethics, and provides easily understandable information related to different aspects of the conduct and dissemination of research and evaluation data. Early chapters provide an overview of the child welfare context within which research is conducted; later chapters provide step-by-step coverage of research issues on problem formulation, design, measurement analysis, and dissemination of research findings. The authors identify the advantages and disadvantages of different approaches and contexts within which research and evaluation in child welfare is conducted, providing useful guidance on the implementation of future research.

Evaluation and research in child welfare settings is not as straightforward as research in a laboratory setting. In the social sciences, many factors influence both how data may be gathered and how that data may be understood. The Child Welfare League of America supports the goal of this book—to inform child welfare practitioners, researchers, and policymakers about issues related to research in a child welfare–specific context. This book will be of value to both the private and public child welfare sectors and will assist us all in better serving vulnerable children and families.

Christine James-Brown, president and CEO
Child Welfare League of America

Acknowledgments

The authors gratefully acknowledge the foresight and dedication to research of Mr. Bill Baccaglini and Dr. Mel Schneiderman of the New York Foundling Hospital, as well as of Nan Dale, formerly of the Children's Village. We are also indebted to our team at Columbia University Press, including Lauren Docket, our editor. We gratefully acknowledge the many child welfare researchers who have taught and inspired us over the years, especially Trudy Festinger and Fred Wulczyn. Their groundbreaking work and lifetime commitment to high-quality child welfare research has set the standard for the rest of us. And, finally, we acknowledge the contributions of child welfare program staff and the clients themselves, for whose benefit child welfare research is conducted.

Research Methods in Child Welfare

[1]

Introduction to Child Welfare Research

In this chapter the following topics will be covered:

- The purpose of and audience for this book
- A brief overview of philosophy of science
- A brief history of child welfare policy and research

The Purpose of and Audience for This Book

Welcome to the world of child welfare research. The purpose of this text-book is to provide a thorough discussion of the theory and practice of conducting social science research in a child welfare setting or with a child welfare population. Much of what is known about how to conduct child welfare research is based on basic research principles that apply to any social science field of study. However, these principles will be described in the context of child welfare research, consistent with the mission and purpose of this book. In addition, conducting research in a child welfare setting or with a child welfare population often carries with it additional considerations or nuances, and these will be highlighted throughout the book as applicable.

There are four primary audiences for this book: (1) social work and psychology students who need a comprehensive overview of how to conduct social science research, (2) graduate students and child welfare professionals who need to acquire research method skills in order to better understand published research so that they can integrate the findings into their practice, (3) professional researchers working in a child welfare context who need to understand how to apply the basic tenets of research practice into this particular setting, and (4) professional clinicians and administrators in child welfare settings who want to conduct their own research and need a thorough and practical guide for doing so. It is also quite likely that child welfare administrators, both public and private, will consult this book in order to sharpen their understanding of the research being conducted in their agency or under their auspices.

To set the stage for the book, this chapter begins with a brief discussion of the book's philosophy of science, followed by a brief history of child welfare research.

A Brief Overview of Philosophy of Science

All research is conducted within a particular worldview about the nature of reality and the ability of scientific inquiry to discover and predict that reality. The worldview—also known as an epistemology—of social science researchers has evolved over the course of social science research and shapes the general paradigm that guides the researcher's projects. A paradigm is a basic model or schema that organizes the way a researcher views his or her world (Kuhn 1970).

The French writer and philosopher Auguste Comte (1798–1857) is widely credited with being the first to apply the methods of the physical sciences to the social sciences, an approach he termed "positivism." This approach became the dominant epistemology for scientific inquiry beginning in the middle of the nineteenth century. As a philosophical system of thought, positivism maintains that the goal of knowledge is to describe systematically observed phenomena. In a positivist view of the world, scientific "truths" exist and the scientific method is the appropriate means for discovering these truths in order to understand the world well enough so that events and experiences can be predicted and perhaps controlled. Thus, the "objective" world exists independently of the perspectives of or measurements by researchers, and the goal of research is to disclose these "objective" facts. A distinguishing feature of positivism is the absence of any distinction between reality (as things that exist) and knowledge of reality (as things that are recognized). The universe is viewed as deterministic and controlled by the laws of cause and effect, which can be discerned through the application of the scientific method.

Described more fully in chapter 2, the scientific method is the accepted framework for conducting social science research. This entails conducting studies in such a way as to ensure that empirical observations are systematic, samples are representative, and data collection methods are clearly specified, so that the project can be replicated (i.e., the same methods repeated would produce the same results). Replication is of great importance in social science research, as it can reduce both error and the misinterpretation of findings (Rosenthal 1991). The results of studies conducted with these guidelines can be used to confirm or revise theory in order to better describe and predict reality. In this way, the positivist approach is empirical, with observation and measurement (ideally through controlled experimentation and manipulation) as the core of the scientific endeavor.

By the middle of the twentieth century, positivism came under criticism for its assumption and acceptance of an independent reality that can be uncovered as long as the scientific method is correctly applied. In response to such criticism, postpositivism emerged as an alternative epistemology, one accepting the basic premise that there is an external, objective reality but recognizing that its complexity often defies accurate description and explanation. In addition, postpositivism acknowledges the limitations of human observers, which often preclude researchers from developing anything more than a partial understanding of reality. In this view, the goal of science is to achieve consensus to the highest degree possible regarding the nature of reality.

There have been several specific forms of criticism of positivism, each of which has led to the articulation of a more distinct "postpositivistic" epistemology and research methodology. A few will be noted here. The first criticism is that, in general, scientists and their work are more fallible than previously acknowledged. This is considered to be so for several reasons, including the fact that humans are only equipped to perceive certain aspects of reality, which can either be limited (i.e., humans cannot perceive the full range of lights, colors, and sounds) or in fact faulty (i.e., it appears to most humans that the sun is revolving around the earth when in fact the earth is rotating around the sun, and it appeared to many that the earth was flat when in fact it is round). A branch of science based on this tenet is known as critical rationalism (Popper 1971). It assumes that all knowledge is tentative and conjectural as opposed to definitive. In this view, the most that science can offer is guesses as to effective solutions to social problems based on the accumulated ability of the evidence to withstand falsifiability, the active attempt to demonstrate that the theory is not correct. Falsifiability stands in contrast to the goal of conducting research in order to confirm theory, an approach that is subject to what is known as confirmatory bias. The trial-and-error approach proposed ultimately results in the acceptance of a few theories that remain unfalsified and represent the best knowledge available at any given point. Currently accepted theories are viewed as always open to correction or replacement in the future.

A second criticism of positivism is that it fails to acknowledge that knowledge and reality are socially constructed and, therefore, do not exist as separate entities to be discovered by the researcher. From this idea came the school of thought known as social constructivism. Adherents of social constructivism believe that reality is constructed through human activity and that members of a society together invent the properties of the social world (Kukla 2000). For the social constructivist, social reality cannot be discovered per se, as it does not exist prior to its social invention (Ernest 1999; Gredler 1997; Prawat and Floden 1994). Individuals create meaning through their interactions with one another and with the environment in which they live. Intersubjectivity is the term used to describe the shared understanding among individuals whose interactions are based on common interests and assumptions that form the basis for their communication (Rogoff 1990). Within social constructivism there are a range of positions regarding social science methods. For example, Lincoln and Guba (1985, 75) advocate multiple socially constructed realities that, "when known more fully, tend to produce diverging inquiry." They argue that reality cannot be studied "in pieces" (for example, as variables) but only holistically and in a larger context. In addition, they reject the traditional relationship between knower (the scientist) and known (the object of a research study) and endorse instead the belief that scientists and their "subjects" develop a joint understanding through a process of dialogue and negotiation. There are no external objective truths that can be generalized from one setting to another, because all human behavior is bound by its specific context. This approach is also known as interpretivism. Interpretive researchers start out with the assumption that access to reality (given or socially constructed) is possible only through social constructions such as language, consciousness, and shared meanings. Interpretive studies generally attempt to understand phenomena through the meanings that people assign to them.

Positivism has also come under fire for not being sufficiently critical of social realities such as class, race, and gender bias. Some have argued that social reality is historically constituted and, although people can consciously act to change their social and economic circumstances, their ability to do so is constrained by various social, cultural, and political barriers. The main task of research, according to this perspective, is to provide a critique of existing social realities. As such, studies are conducted in order to identify and bring attention to the limitations and constraints that prevent certain classes or groups of individuals from rising above their circumstances. This approach draws on the works of Karl Marx and is most closely associated with the Frankfurt School and the Institute for Social Research.

The epistemological perspective of this book is squarely within the post-positivistic framework. That is, we recognize that there are limits in the human endeavor to uncover scientific truths. This process is viewed as a flawed and imperfect enterprise due to the fallibility in a human's ability to perceive and measure reality. It is also recognized that often what is most of interest is not an objective reality (should that exist) but rather the *experience* of reality from the perspective of specific "others," such as clients and consumers and staff in the field of child welfare. At the same time, the book does not endorse a purely relativistic approach either. That is, we believe that some measures are better than others and that some truths can be converged upon. Thus, a humble approach is taken, in which the scientific method is used as the best approximation to capturing a version of truth and reality at any given time.

A Brief History of Child Welfare Policy and Research

Although there may be other definitions of child welfare in use, the one used for the purpose of this review and for the book as a whole is the set of services put into place (abuse investigations, prevention services to maintain families, out-of-home placement when children are deemed unsafe at home, and all efforts to achieve safe and permanent homes for these children) that are activated when government and voluntary agencies become involved in the concern about the safety of children in a home.

Initially, the work of child welfare was supported through charitable organizations offering informal assistance to vulnerable children and families, such as the Ursuline Convent in New Orleans. Prior to the mid-nineteenth century, poor and indigent children were routinely placed in almshouses alongside adults, with no recognition of their distinct needs. Eventually, there was a public demand to remove children from almshouses and place them in institutions in order to protect and care for them apart from adults. The first private agency to care for children in family settings or placing-out services was the New York Children's Aid Society (NYCAS), led by Charles Loring

Brace. This organization was created in the 1880s in order to address the increasing problem of juvenile delinquency and the "moral degradation of society" that might result from poor youth who were abandoned. Brace and NYCAS began the now infamous transportation of inner-city children out west via the "orphan trains." The children were placed with farming families as a means of removing them from the dangers of the city and improving their morale and work ethic. It was also a way of providing free labor to families pioneering the American West. Other agencies joined this placing-out effort, including the New York Foundling Hospital.

Eventually, several seminal events converged to highlight the need for society to address the problem of abandoned children, the numbers of which had increased dramatically by the end of the Civil War. In 1889, the American Pediatric Society was formed to address the medical needs of children, and in 1904, Robert Hunter published his groundbreaking work, *Poverty*, in which he argued that poverty not only degrades adults but also hinders child development and thus has a long-term detrimental impact on society. In the same year, G. Stanley Hall (1904) published his influential book on youth development, *Adolescence: Its Psychology and Its Relation to Physiology, Anthropology, Sociology, Sex, Crime, Religion, and Education*. President Theodore Roosevelt, in response to pressure from child advocates, most notably James E. West, Jane Addams, and Lillian Wald, convened the White House Conference on Dependent Children in 1909. One eventual outcome of this conference was the formation of the Children's Bureau in 1912 by President Taft. The oldest government agency devoted to the needs of children, the Children's Bureau has the primary responsibility for administering federal child welfare programs. Its original mission was to investigate and report on infant mortality, birth rates, orphanages, juvenile courts, and other social issues of the time. Currently, its mission is to "provide for the safety, permanency, and well-being of children through leadership, support for necessary services, and productive partnerships with States, Tribes, and communities."

Thus three important benchmarks related to the needs of children were established in the early part of the twentieth century: (1) the debate regarding dependent children was raised to a national level; (2) a federal agency was established, acknowledging that the government had a responsibility to care for children in need; and (3) the government also acknowledged the utility and need for research-based knowledge about dependent children. To this day, much of the funding available to conduct child welfare research and efforts to compile data regarding the problem of child abuse and neglect is provided by the federal government.

Over the years, research, legislation, and public opinion about the needs of children and families have intertwined to move the field forward and shape specific areas of concern and emphasis. In 1959, Maas and Engler published their account of the lack of stability of out-of-home placements, coining the term "foster care drift" to describe children who stay too long in the foster care system without any plan for a permanent home. These findings were echoed and expanded upon in other seminal works (e.g., Fanshel 1971; Fontana 1968), which, along with public support, led to the enactment by the United States government of the Child Abuse Prevention and Treatment Act (CAPTA) in 1974. CAPTA provided additional federal dollars for increased child abuse prevention and created a legal mandate for states to track and report the number of suspected and confirmed cases of abuse and neglect. A primary goal was to prevent as many children from entering the system as possible and, ideally, avoid the problem of foster care drift.

In 1980, the United States government enacted the Adoption Assistance and Child Welfare Act (AACWA), which established the need for preventive services as a means of avoiding placement. In addition, AACWA legislated that children who were in the child welfare system were to be placed in the least restrictive setting possible and were to receive casework, documented with a detailed case plan, aimed at achieving permanency. Reporting requirements were expanded to include a statewide information system to account for children in foster care. AACWA also allowed for subsidized adoptions in order to increase the number of children with special needs (i.e., medical and/or mental health needs) adopted by families, by providing financial assistance and support.

The concerns of the public and federal policymakers about length of stay in the system and lack of permanency have been echoed in the efforts of researchers in the field of child welfare. In response to this legislation, research in child welfare turned to uncovering why children remain in foster care for a longer period of time than necessary. Gibson, Tracy, and DeBord (1984), for example, studied the effects of various types of contacts between the family, child, and agency providing foster care services. They found that intensive and frequent contact, especially in the initial month of foster care placement, could potentially reduce the amount of time a child was in care. Testa (2001) examined whether kinship placements (with relatives) were more likely to achieve permanency than nonkinship foster care. He found that kinship placements were more stable than nonkinship placements but that these differences diminished over time. Also as a result of the 1980 legislation requiring the collection of administrative data, large-scale data sets were created and became available to researchers for multistate studies of the dynamics of foster care (Vogel 1999). For example, Wulczyn (1996) applied newly developed statistical techniques such as survival analysis and the use of entry cohorts to a multistate study of the length of stay in foster care. By using survival analysis and an entry cohort, all data can be used—even if some of the children in the sample had not yet exited care—to document length of stay in care and to link reductions in stays to program or policy changes. Building on this work, Baker, Wulczyn, and Dale (2005) used survival analysis to examine factors associated with rate of discharge from a residential treatment center. For youth who were transferred or reunified, mental health issues were the strongest factor that slowed down the rate of discharge.

Beyond questions related to length of stay, researchers have also focused on placement stability and its relationship to permanency, in response to evidence that multiple placements while in foster care negatively impact the likelihood of a child being reunified (Landsverk, Davis, Ganger, Newton, and Johnson 1996). For example, Wulczyn, Kogan, and Harden (2003) found that the initial six months in care were crucial for a child in foster care to make a connection with his or her foster family.

Level of care was also examined as a factor affecting length of stay and stability of placements. Using data from the state of California, Berrick, Barth, Needell, and Reid (1998) found that younger children in group care settings had less stability, lower rates of adoption, and longer stays in care.

Other researchers have focused on the impact of reunification and the potential for recidivism back into foster care. Festinger (1996) studied 210 children in New York City who exited foster care (either foster boarding home or group care). For those children who returned within twelve months (12.9 percent of the sample), the strongest predictors of reentry were four characteristics/experiences of the biological parents: lower parenting skills (as rated by caseworkers), less social support, more unmet needs (as rated by caseworkers), and less organizational participation in community groups.

Legislation and research has also been concerned with preventing out-of-home placement of children. The 1980 Adoption Assistance and Child Welfare Act required states to make "reasonable efforts" to prevent children from entering foster care and to reunify children who were placed out of the home. As part of the legislation, the Department of Health and Human Services (DHHS) was authorized to set aside funds to evaluate a range of family preservation and family support programs.

Several related but distinct models of prevention have emerged as the focus of research, policy, and practice (Nelson and Landsman 1990). One particularly well-known model is crisis intervention, of which the Homebuilders

Program is the most prominent example. The program calls for short-term, time-limited services provided in the home to families with children at imminent risk of foster care placement. Key program characteristics include contact with the family within twenty-four hours of the crisis, caseload sizes of one or two families per worker, service duration of four to six weeks, and provision of both concrete services and counseling, up to twenty hours per family per week. Several evaluations of the Homebuilders Program model have been conducted, most but not all of which have produced generally positive results, that is, low rates of placement of the children served (e.g., Fraser, Pecora, and Haapala 1991). Summaries of other research on Homebuilders can be found at http://www.institutefamily.org/programs_research .asp. The principles of Homebuilders are largely incorporated into what is now referred to as Intensive Family Preservation Services. Other models of family preservation provide longer-term and more family systems–focused services or services with a specific emphasis on substance abuse or delinquency in the children. In reality, many states and agencies offer an eclectic mix of program elements in their prevention efforts.

In sum, child welfare research has both spurred and been guided by various public concerns and federal legislation. A review of the current body of policy- and practice-related research reveals seven major tenets. The first is concern for children's safety. The child welfare system was developed primarily to ensure that when a child is at risk for maltreatment, services can be brought to bear to determine whether the family and child can remain together safely (Pecora, Whittaker, Maluccio, Barth, and Plotnick 1993). This is accomplished by a child protective services (CPS) investigation of a family based on a call made to a state central registry from an anonymous person or a mandated reporter who suspects child abuse. It is important to understand that these reports of child abuse are made based on suspicion, as opposed to evidence. This policy ensures that the largest possible safety net is created to protect children.

The second tenet is to keep families together whenever possible. Thus, if the CPS investigation substantiates the abuse, attempts are made to maintain the child safely and appropriately in the child's home so that familial and community bonds can be maintained and strengthened and out-of-home placement avoided. This is done by offering preventive service to the child and family in the community in which they live. (In addition, a family may request prevention services on their own based on their perception of need or as advised by professionals, friends, or neighbors). In all cases, maintaining the child in the home and in the community is the preferred option for families and children that come into contact with the child welfare system.

If the CPS investigation determines that the child cannot be maintained in the home, the child is placed into out-of-home care. The third tenet of child welfare practice is that children should be placed in the least restrictive level of care necessary to maintain the child's safety. The least restrictive setting is family foster care and kinship care, in which children live in families and attend schools and receive services in the community in which they live. Therapeutic and specialized foster homes are somewhat more restrictive, because children are provided with a structured behavioral management program and may attend specialized schools. Nonetheless, they are still living with a family and are cared for by parent figures. Group homes are more restrictive, in that children live in a group setting, are cared for by rotating shifts of professional staff, and are typically subject to a series of "house rules" and restrictions regarding their activities and movement in the community. Even more restrictive are diagnostic reception centers (DRCs) and residential treatment centers (RTCs), in which children receive a regimen of treatment and often participate in behavioral management reward and punishment systems to control and shape their emotions and behaviors. It is important to bear in mind that even at the highest level of restrictiveness, DRC and RTC facilities are not secured (i.e., locked), and children are able to leave the premises at any time (although it is likely that there will be consequences for leaving without permission).

The fourth tenet of the child welfare system is that once a child is placed in care, the length of time a child remains in foster care should be as short as possible in order to maintain family-child bonds. As noted above, considerable research has focused on identifying factors associated with length of stay, and several legislative initiatives have spurred efforts to shorten stays for children in care.

A fifth tenet is that children in foster care should achieve permanency, either by reunifying them with their family of origin or through adoption into an alternative permanent family. The early research on foster care drift highlighted the problem of children spending too many years in the system, moving from one foster home to another with no efforts made toward achieving a permanent home. In response, concurrent planning, which involves the simultaneous pursuit of reunification and adoption options, is now mandated casework practice.

The sixth tenet is the emphasis on placing children with relatives whenever possible. This is known as kinship care. Although figures vary by agency, nationwide approximately 30 percent of all children in family-level foster care are currently being cared for by relatives (United States Department of Health and Human Services 2000). Kinship care represents the fastest growing category of foster care (Wulczyn and Goerge 1992). The push for utilization of kinship care was shaped largely by a 1979 Supreme Court ruling that encouraged greater use of kinship care by allowing government payments to be allocated for the support of children cared for by relatives.

And finally, the seventh tenet is that children should be prepared for life after foster care, regardless of their permanency plan. A spate of studies conducted with foster care alumni documented their difficulty in achieving self-sufficiency following emancipation from the foster care system (Courtney, Piliavin, Grogan-Kaylor, and Nesmith 2001; Festinger 1983). Currently, states must provide training in independent living skills to all youth in the system who are fourteen years of age or older in order to help prepare them for adulthood.

All of these major principles of child welfare practice are dynamic, meaning that they occur at the same time and interact with one another. This necessarily complicates research efforts aimed at isolating the effects of one principle on outcomes for children and families. The complexity of child welfare research will be considered throughout the remainder of the book.

PART 1

Planning and Developing Research Studies

[2]

The Philosophy and Logic of Research

In this chapter the following topics will be discussed:

- Child welfare research: similarities to and differences from social science research
- Overview and principles for planning a research study
- The blessings and the curses of agency-based child welfare research
- Tensions in the field of child welfare research

In this chapter, an outline of planning a research study in a child welfare setting is provided, along with the enumeration of some overarching principles. These principles are **bolded** in the text for easy reference. From the outset, it is essential to clarify the ways in which child welfare research is similar to and different from other social science research.

Child Welfare Research: Similarities to and Differences from Social Science Research

Most importantly, like other empirical research endeavors, research conducted within a child welfare setting or on a topic related to child welfare is based on the scientific method. Social science research—regardless of setting—adheres to the conventions of the scientific method, which contains the shared wisdom about how to conduct research that will result in reliable and valid findings. The scientific method represents the closest approximation to a systematic, disciplined, logical, and unbiased search for knowledge obtained by examination of the best available evidence, although theory is always subject to correction and improvement based on subsequent research findings. The scientific method has historical roots in the philosophy and teaching of Roger Bacon (1214–1292), Francis Bacon (1561–1626), and Al-Biruni (972–1048). This method contains the blueprint that scientists use when conducting research, and it comprises the following components:

- Observation of a phenomenon of interest
- Development of theory to explain the phenomenon
- Creation of testable hypotheses
- Implementation of an experiment/study to test the hypotheses
- Analysis of data in order to reach a conclusion (accept, revise, or discard the theory)

From this outline, two key points should be noted. The first is that hypotheses (and theories) are never proven. All research is based on recognition of the fallibility of both theory and measurement, and thus the method acknowledges that rarely are there definitive answers to research questions. At best, social scientists can conclude that the findings confirm the hypotheses with a certain degree of confidence and that such confirmation supports the theory. The second point is that knowledge-based theory is continually being revised and elaborated upon. There is rarely a definitive endpoint in the scientific study of a particular phenomenon, and it is recognized that the search for truth is a continuous process. Monette, Sullivan, and DeJong (2005) highlight five key aspects of the scientific method: (1) it is empirical (based on observation), (2) it is systematic (using an organized methodology recognized by colleagues), (3) it seeks to identify and understand causal relationships, (4) it is provisional (all conclusions are tentative and subject to revision or rejection upon further evidence and knowledge), and (5) it is objective (scientists aim to avoid bias and judgment).

Despite a shared utilization of the scientific method, there are also ways in which child welfare research—especially agency-based research—differs from other social science research. The first difference is that many child welfare research samples are composed of individuals who are mandated to participate in the services that make them eligible for the research. Two key implications flow from this fact. First, most child welfare research samples involve highly vulnerable individuals and families who are dealing with economic and emotional and psychological hardship. All of the ethical issues involved in conducting research with vulnerable populations are magnified, because the stakes are unusually high (removal of a child, lack of family reunification, harm to the child). Second, the family's relationship with the researcher is likely to be affected (positively or negatively) by the family's experience with the child welfare service programs. Even under the best of circumstances, child welfare clients are likely to have conflicted feelings about the child welfare agency by which they are being served. The families (and children) may resent anyone associated with the agency and may resist involvement in the research as a form of (conscious or unconscious) protest. Another possibility is that they may decline to participate out of concern that the results might create additional obstacles to treatment and reunification goals. On the other hand, they may feel compelled to participate in research out of a (hopefully) misguided concern that lack of participation could result in negative consequences for their treatment. Issues of informed consent and avoidance of coercion must be uppermost in the researcher's mind at all times. These and related ethical considerations are elaborated further in chapter 3.

A second way that child welfare research is set apart results from the complexity of the child welfare system itself. In child welfare, variation exists within and among agencies and within and among programs even within a single agency. Certain aspects of the system are determined federally (timelines for termination of parental rights, need for concurrent planning), some are determined at the state level (e.g., funding streams and resources for aftercare and independent living), and others are set by local social service agencies (mandates of city and county accountability systems).

Even the placement of child welfare services within the governmental bureaucracy varies across states. For example, in some but not all states, mental health, child welfare, and juvenile justice systems are situated within one umbrella agency. Even within the same state there is variation across agencies. Each child welfare agency offers its own unique blend of services. Some offer different levels of care within the child welfare system (foster homes, group homes, residential treatment centers) and others provide services across different systems (child welfare, mental health, office of mental retardation and developmental delay, juvenile justice). Other sources of variation include the philosophy, staffing structure, and mix of actual services offered. For example, Baker, Fullmore, and Collins (forthcoming) found that the type of mental health services offered to youth in residential treatment centers varies across programs (which staff offers such services, the philosophical orientation of these services, the role of the mental health providers within the treatment team, and so forth). It is also possible that a sample within a single program may be heterogeneous in unexpected ways. For example, within a child welfare agency's maternity shelter, a significant portion of the girls served by the program may have had no prior child welfare involvement; in a residential treatment center, a portion of youth may be referred from the juvenile justice system; and within a prevention program, not all families may be mandated for services. These are the kinds of differences that—if not understood and addressed—can seriously compromise the integrity of the results and the generalizability of the findings.

This variation can affect the types of families served and the types of programs agencies can offer, and it needs to be understood from the outset, as it affects the sociopolitical context within which any study can be conducted and interpreted. In some cases, certain questions would be absurd, such as studying the socioeconomic backgrounds of families served by a program mandated to provide services to only families from a particular socioeconomic background. Likewise, it would not make sense to study the continuum of care in an agency that only offers family-level programs. Variation across agencies is also important to understand, given that some findings can only be generalized to other agencies (geographic areas) that operate under the same opportunities and constraints relevant to the issue at hand.

What this means for the child welfare researcher is that each agency and each program needs to be understood prior to the development of any research plan. No assumptions should be made about the sample or the service. There is simply no shortcut to getting to know the agency and its programs prior to planning a research study.

Overview and Principles for Planning a Research Study

Problem Formulation

Research is the search for truth or an answer to a question (or the best approximation of truth or an answer that is available given existing knowledge and methods). Thus all research starts with a problem or a question—something that needs clarification, explication, or elucidation. Research questions come from a variety of sources, including prior research (all studies raise more questions than they answer), from a gap in theory or the knowledge base, or from practice experience. Questions can be asked about processes (for example, why and when do children who move from an institution to a group home return to the institution?), about change over time (for example, how does the impact of sexual abuse express itself in therapy over the course of treatment?), about differences between groups (for example, are youth who were placed into care as teens more likely to age out of care than youth who were placed into care as infants?), about effects of interventions (for example, is therapeutic foster care an effective program for aggressive teens?), and about various combinations of all these types of questions.

Ideal questions for agency-based child welfare research are those that address a pressing need of the agency staff (administrative or program) and that make a significant contribution to the scientific knowledge base. **Principle 1: There are two primary audiences for agency-based child welfare research (the agency and the field), and studies should be designed to simultaneously address the needs and concerns of both.** Adhering to this principle increases the likelihood that an agency will approve and support the study (i.e., allocate staff time and other resources) and that the findings can be submitted to a peer-reviewed publication. If the researcher works within a child welfare agency (is an employee of the agency), it is quite likely that only those studies that address pressing agency needs will be approved. Even if this is not the stated condition for agency approval, studies that address the needs and concerns of the agency will certainly be more likely to garner staff support. If the researcher is not an employee of the agency (that is, he or she is employed by a university or an independent research center) it is also highly likely that only those proposed studies that are consonant with acknowledged agency concerns will be approved.

At the same time, the researcher needs to be cognizant of the concerns and interests of the field in general (outside the needs of any one agency) in order to craft a study that is designed to make a contribution to the scientific knowledge base. In this way the findings can be submitted to a peer-reviewed publication, garnering significant benefits for the agency and for the researcher. One benefit of the peer-review process is that it screens out studies that are ill conceived and/or poorly executed. Thus, acceptance by the panel of peer reviewers of a journal offers the researcher increased confidence that the findings should be considered sufficiently reliable for the agency (and the field) to make changes based upon them. In this way, the peer-review process offers the agency-based researcher access to professional colleagues who can provide assurance that the work merits consideration by the agency. Without this screening process, the agency-based researcher risks providing the agency with findings that are theoretically or methodologically flawed. Thus, **Principle 2 is: Clinical and practical implications of agency-based research should only be considered after professional colleagues have had the**

opportunity to provide a thorough critique—and ultimate approval—of the work. Ideally, this is achieved through the peer-review process of a journal but could also be provided by professional colleagues in the field.

Publication in a peer-reviewed journal also confers benefits to a sponsoring agency by garnering prestige and credibility for their support of research and can assist the researcher and the agency in attracting future research colleagues and funding. Thus, in designing agency-based research it is important to begin with a set of research questions that—all else being equal—will be sufficiently unique and important to result in a paper that can be submitted to a scholarly peer-reviewed publication. Note the twin criteria of unique and important. Both are necessary for submission of an article to a scholarly journal. A study must produce findings that have not been published before (i.e., are unique), because, unfortunately, it is the rare replication study that is published, and the study must also produce knowledge that has scientific weight/import (i.e., is of significance to the field).

Several avenues exist for the identification of research questions that will result in unique and important findings. The first avenue is related to **Principle 3: Determine whether data exist within the agency that lends itself to a research study.** This is an unorthodox approach and stands in contrast to the traditional avenue of question development via literature review and discussion with practitioners. These other avenues are described below (and at length in chapter 4). However, one should not discount the fact that an agency-based researcher has access to a large and varied preexisting database that could be mined for possible research studies—prior to developing studies that entail collection of new data. Existing data in child welfare agencies are composed of two primary sources: paper records (charts) and electronic data files. Most agencies have both. Records entail paper data produced over the course of a client's participation in the agency. They typically include a form from the referring agency explaining why the client is receiving services, an intake form summarizing the client's psychosocial history, medication and psychiatric history, and family history. The record also might include progress notes from therapy sessions, family visits, and treatment planning meetings, as well as an account of medications, hospitalizations, criminal activity, court hearings, and perhaps summaries of participation in other services such as special education, substance abuse treatment, and mental health counseling. Most agencies also have an electronic administrative database tracking "movements" within the agency of the clients served. These data are relatively accurate, especially when tied to the agency's payment/reimbursement systems, and, although not broad, have great specificity regarding each client's movement through the agency (admission date and dates of all running away episodes, hospitalizations, vacations, home visits, discharges, and reentries). For agencies that provide services along a continuum of care (such as foster homes, group homes, residential treatment centers, diagnostic reception centers, and so forth), clients can be tracked across this continuum. Although imperfect, these agency databases can be mined for research purposes and it is well worth the researcher's time to consider conducting studies with these data. Benefits of doing so include it being virtually cost free, immediately available, and unconstrained by the limits of ethical concerns related to consent (since the data already exist). One caution in doing so is that the researcher must demonstrate complete competence in retrieving and interpreting data from the agency data systems/charts. These data and systems can be idiosyncratic and inconsistent in ways not at all obvious. Specific discussions with the agency staffpeople who operate and manage these systems should precede any data retrieval and/or analysis to ensure that the researcher has a thorough grasp of the meaning and coding of the variables (more detailed information about using existing data can be found in chapter 8).

In the event that a researcher decides to conduct a study that is outside the scope of the existing database, one avenue for identifying meaningful research questions is prior research conducted by the researcher. **Principle 4: Child welfare researchers should develop a series of related studies.** This principle recognizes the economy involved in conducting more than one study on the same general topic. To begin with, only one literature review and analysis of available assessment tools is required in order to identify viable measures and develop a thorough understanding of the existing knowledge base. Further, a series of related studies affords the researcher the opportunity to become recognized as an expert on the topic and brings prestige to the sponsoring agency as a leader in that area.

A third avenue for developing research questions is collaborations with researchers in other agencies, universities, and research centers. **Principle 5: Collaborations with other agencies and other researchers can extend the generalizability and enhance the credibility of child welfare research.** Although collaborations are notoriously difficult to do well, the value for an agency-based researcher may outweigh the challenges. One way to reduce the likelihood of friction is to resolve "hot-button" issues in advance, such as ownership of the data and order of authorship on published papers and reports. Professional guidelines developed by the American Psychological Association (APA) can be used to guide these discussions.

The fourth avenue for developing research questions is discussion with key program staff who have developed practice wisdom and deep knowledge of the client base and know what they need to know in order to improve their practice. This is especially true for program staffpersons who attend professional conferences and participate in collaborations with practitioners at other agencies. They have a keen sense of the burning questions for the field. One way to tap into this practice wisdom is to schedule a meeting at which staffpeople working at different levels of a program's operation are invited to brainstorm possible research questions. It might be advisable to ask them, "What do you really wish you knew about your clients?" or "What keeps you up at night when you are thinking about your program?" or "What do you need to know in order to better serve your clients and meet your program's objectives?" It is important that these discussions are not perceived as a criticism or an implication that the staff must be doing something wrong. It is quite likely that, if handled tactfully, such a discussion will generate several possible research topics.

Program participants themselves can also constitute a source of inspiration and ideas about possible research questions. Inclusion of the clients in the development of a research study is part of a model of research in which all stakeholders who have a vested interest in the study play an equal role in the development of the study and in the interpretation and dissemination of the findings. Traditional roles of researcher as expert and client as merely a subject in the study are reshaped into more equitable and collaborative relationships in which each partner is viewed as having something valuable to contribute to the research process.

After the researcher has engaged program staff (and possibly clients as well) in brainstorming sessions that identify potential research questions, it is important to confirm that the questions are in fact unique. A review of the existing literature in the field will reveal whether previous studies have addressed the same question. If so, either new questions will have to be identified or the proposed study will need to be modified in order to take into account the existing knowledge. That is, even if the same study has already been done, it is possible that it would be important for the field (and the agency) to know whether the same results could be obtained with a different sample (ethnicity, age, type of abuse experience, and so forth), in a different geographic location (e.g., urban as opposed to rural), or in a different service context (one kind of program participation as opposed to another). It is usually possible to frame a research question to be unique and significant regardless of the existing knowledge base.

For this reason, a literature review is a necessary part of the process for question development and refinement and should be conducted on the "front end" of the study. Although rarely done, it is advised here that the researcher utilize what is learned in the literature review to draft the introduction section of the manuscript that will eventually be submitted for publication to a peer-reviewed journal. Usually the paper is written *after* the study is completed. However, writing the introduction *prior* to the study will help illuminate inconsistencies in the logic of the study and should clarify the links between existing theory—as offered in the literature review—and the research questions developed for the study. Solidifying these links prior to data collection can spare the researcher considerable inconvenience later: it is considerably more difficult to fix this kind of problem after the data have been collected.

Once the primary research question has been identified, a series of hypotheses can be generated. These are the prediction statements about the nature of the relationships between the variables that will be tested in the study. The development of these statements will also begin to flesh out the necessary design of the study. Taking one of the questions suggested above as an example ("Is a therapeutic foster boarding home [TFBH] a more effective program for aggressive teens than residential treatment?") the primary hypothesis might be: "Youth who were placed in a TFBH will exhibit greater improvement in social skills and affect regulation than youth placed in a residential treatment center (RTC)." From this primary hypothesis, a series of specific hypotheses follow, based on how the construct of "social skills" is operationalized (turned into measurable phenomena) and whether the hypotheses are directional (one group is hypothesized to be different than the other group and the nature—direction—of that difference is specified in advance) or nondirectional (the two groups are hypothesized to be different from each other but the nature—direction—of that difference is not specified). Whenever possible, directional hypotheses should be developed, as they demonstrate a thorough knowledge of the theory underlying the study. If the hypotheses for the study of therapeutic boarding homes are all directional in that it is expected that the youth in a TFBH will have better social skills than the youth in a RTC, and if the construct of social skills is operationalized as the number of peer conflicts, caretaker perception of youth as cooperative, teacher ratings of youth aggression, and youth-demonstrated social cognitive skills, then the following specific hypotheses could be tested: (1) youth placed in a TFBH will show greater reduction in peer conflicts than youth placed in an RTC, (2) youth placed in a TFBH will show greater improvement in teacher ratings of cooperativeness than youth placed in an RTC, (3) youth placed in a TFBH will show greater improvement in teacher ratings of aggression than youth placed in an RTC, and (4) youth placed in a TFBH will exhibit a greater degree of improved social cognitive skills than youth placed in an RTC.

Sample

These hypotheses logically lead to the identification of a series of decisions that will need to be made about the sample, such as (1) How will youth be "placed" in an RTC versus TFBH, randomly or not? (2) What is the age group of interest (how will "teen" be defined)? (3) Are there some youth who would not be appropriate for the study (i.e., have psychosis, are too old at the start of the placement, have cognitive deficits)? Fleshing out these and related questions about the study will lead to the development of the sampling plan. There are three main considerations pertaining to sampling: (1) who specifically is the study about, (2) how will they be found and identified, and (3) how many subjects are needed.

The first issue, who the study is about, is theoretical in nature and can be answered by considering the population to whom the study findings will be generalized. Most research involves the collection of data on a sample, which is then deemed to be useful for making inferences about the population. In the study of youth in therapeutic foster homes, sampling issues could revolve around age of the youth, length of time in the foster care system, gender, ethnicity, type of emotional problems, type of TFBH programs, and city in which the program is located. Once the population has been identified (i.e., all youth in TFBHs in New York City in 2001 who are between ten and fourteen years of age), then sampling strategies can be developed, including random selection of a sample from a list of all members of the population, a convenience sample of youth from TFBHs operated by cooperating agencies, a purposive sample of the highest and lowest functioning youth, or a snowball sample in which TFBH families are asked to nominate other TFBH families to participate in the study. The advantages and disadvantages of these different sampling strategies are described in chapter 5, which also discusses how to determine the desired size of the sample for conducting analyses likely to reveal meaningful statistical effects should they exist.

Design Strategies

There are two main types of designs utilized in child welfare research: within-group correlational designs and between-group quasi-experimental or experimental designs. In a study that is correlational in design, both the independent and dependent variables are naturally occurring and are measured on a single sample, usually at the same point in time. A key requirement for such a design is that there is sufficient variation on both variables. If one or both are constant (all cases in the study have the same value on the variable), then the appropriate analyses cannot be conducted. Assuming sufficient variation on both variables, questions about associations between two or more variables can be answered with a correlational design. Of course, conclusions about causation cannot be made regardless of the strength of associations found. That is, even if two variables (e.g., severity of abuse and length of stay in foster care) are found to be statistically related, it cannot be concluded that one actually caused the other. This is so for at least two reasons. First, a third and unmeasured variable may actually be "causing" both. For example, in the above example, it is possible that younger children were more severely abused and more likely to stay longer. Such a pattern would produce a significant correlation between severity of abuse and length of stay although the real explanatory variable is age of the child. That being said, it might still be of interest for agencies to know that youth with greater severity of abuse stay longer regardless of whether such an effect is actually caused by a third variable, in this case, age.

The second reason for caution regarding causality pertains to the directionality of the findings. In a correlational design, the measure of the two variables is taken at the same time. While the research question may be framed in such a way that one variable is the presumptive independent variable (cause) while the other is the presumptive dependent variable (effect), in actuality, the relationship might be in the other direction. As an example, take a study in which an association was found between the number of social workers a youth has and length of stay in an RTC. Researchers may be tempted to conclude that youth with more social workers have longer stays, perhaps because turnover in social workers slows down the work of treatment and reunification. On the other hand, it is equally plausible that youth who stay longer (for other reasons) will have more social workers because they are in the system longer and have more opportunity for social workers to leave and new ones to be assigned. Despite these cautions regarding correlational designs, they are often used in child welfare research as a means of establishing associations among variables.

Correlational designs do not necessarily require that statistical correlations be conducted. The statistic correlation is appropriate only when the independent and dependent variables are both continuous (and meet the assumptions underlying the use of continuous variables, such as being normally distributed and having a linear association). In this case, a Pearson product moment correlation would be conducted to determine whether variation on one variable is associated with variation on the other. Results range from −1.0 to +1.0, with positive correlations (.01 to 1.0) indicating that individuals ranked high on one are also ranked high on the other, while negative correlations (−.01 to −1.0) indicate that individuals ranked high on one are ranked low on the other. More than two variables can be measured at the same time in a correlational design, in which case multivariate analyses can be conducted to determine the combined association among the set of variables. This is still considered a within-subject correlational design because all of the variation is naturally occurring (i.e., none of the variables are manipulated). Another variation of the correlational design is when one or more of the variables are categorical or dichotomous rather than continuous. In this case, different statistical tests are conducted (chi-squares, t-tests, or logistic regressions), but the design per se is still considered correlational because none of the variables were manipulated.

The second frequently utilized design is quasi-experimental. This design involves the comparison of two groups, one of which received an intervention of some sort while the other group did not. The "quasi" nature of the design refers to the fact that participation in the intervention was not randomly assigned. For this reason, the study does not qualify as a "true" experiment. There are many variations of this design depending upon the number of groups compared and the timing of data collection (for example, before and after the intervention or only after the intervention). Program evaluations, a special class of quasi-experimental and experimental designs common in child welfare research, are explored at length in chapter 17.

The key to a good quasi-experimental design is consideration of ways in which the two groups might be different that could affect the measure of the dependent variable other than involvement in the intervention. These variables are called plausible alternative explanations for the findings. By way of example, consider the hypothesis that families who participate in a voluntary prevention program will—after participation—have better attitudes toward parenting than families who do not participate in the prevention program. The key to this study will be the identification of the group of families who do not participate. If it is composed of families who were recommended to the program but chose not to participate, then if the intervention group scores better on parenting attitudes it is possible that they were already more positive parents because they chose to participate in such a program. Thus, it is possible that initial differences rather than the program itself accounted for the differences between the groups on the measure of the dependent variable (in this case, parenting attitudes). Likewise, if the group that did not participate in the program is composed of people on the waiting list, then it is possible that they would score worse simply because they were not as positively inclined toward the program or as organized or committed as the people who signed up for the program early. It is also possible that the groups might vary on race or age or proportion of single-parent mothers or teen mothers or any other number of variables that might be associated with differences in the dependent variable. All of these potentially important variables need to be identified (based on theory and prior research) and measured in both groups to establish that the two groups are similar on these variables or to allow for the statistical control of any differences between the groups that are identified. Using the example of a study of improvement in TFBH youth as compared to RTC youth, it would be vital to know the ways in which the two groups differed at the time of placement. Of relevance might be studies showing that RTC youth are more likely to have serious mental health and behavioral problems as compared to TFBH youth (Baker, Kurland, Curtis, Papa-Lentini, and Alexander, forthcoming). Theory and practice underlying use of quasi-experimental and experimental designs are described in greater detail in chapter 7.

Measurement Strategies

Once the design is selected, the researcher must then identify the data collection strategies to be employed. Key questions to consider when making these decisions include: Who will be providing the data (the youth themselves using self-report, or other reporters such as foster parents, teachers, or staff in the program)? Will data be standardized (using norms from population-based studies)? Will the data be objective or opinion based? Answers to these questions will lead to the selection of one or more measurement strategies. While some textbooks propose a dichotomy between quantitative and qualitative methods and suggest that some designs are necessarily qualitative while others are quantitative, we reject that perspective and propose the sixth principle. **Principle 6: Child welfare research can draw on both qualitative and quantitative methods and measures in the same study.** Although some designs lend themselves to qualitative as opposed to quantitative data (such as a case study), we suggest that there is no definitive one-to-one correspondence and that many designs can accommodate both data collection approaches. Such a "mixed method" approach offers multiple perspectives and the best of both worlds. The primary options for data collection include: existing structured measures, surveys, field observations/case studies, focus groups, and interviews.

Sometimes the constructs of interest in a particular study have been studied extensively by other researchers. This is particularly true for some of the key constructs of interest to child welfare researchers, including parenting attitudes, stress, and skills; parent-child relationships; child behavioral problems; child sexual behavior problems; child cognitive skills; adult depression; child self-esteem; and so forth. For these and other constructs, there are existing measures that have been used in populations similar to those of many child welfare program participants (poor, minority, English as a second language) and have demonstrated reliability and validity. It is advisable for child welfare researchers to explore the possibility of using existing measures. In addition to having known validity and reliability, additional advantages include the availability of norms for comparing sample data against and preexisting manuals for clarity of use and interpretation of findings. The primary disadvantage is cost, as often these measures must be purchased from the publisher or measure developer. In addition, many are tailored for a specific age group that may be outside the scope of the current study.

When the primary focus of the study is the opinions of the individuals in the sample, a survey is the ideal data collection instrument. Surveys are often developed on a study-by-study basis in order to ensure that they are tailored specifically to the study's goals and population of interest. Surveys contain primarily closed-ended items that produce quantitative data (although a few well-chosen open-ended questions that produce qualitative data can add depth and richness to the study). Surveys can be mailed or e-mailed to people, conducted via computer or over the telephone, or administered to individuals or groups in a face-to-face format. Surveys are one of the most common data collection tools available to the child welfare researcher and are appropriate for correlational and quasi-experimental and experimental designs. Surveys are easy to develop but difficult to obtain an adequate response rate for. Chapter 10 presents guidelines for developing survey questions and strategies for increasing participation rates.

Case studies provide qualitative data about the interactions among program participants (staff and parents, parents and children, teachers and students, and so forth) and data about the provision of services. This methodology is well suited for studies that aim to describe a program holistically as it operates in the real world. Data collected for case studies should be systematically recorded in order to allow for data analysis and description that is accurate and detailed. This measurement strategy is described in detail in chapter 11.

An interview aims to understand in a focused way an individual's everyday life as it relates to a specific topic of interest, in a qualitative rather than quantitative format and with an emphasis on the description of real-life experiences. This information is obtained through a sensitively conducted interpersonal exchange between the interviewer/researcher and the person. In practical terms, a selected group of individuals, all of whom have experienced the same event or process and/or share a similar belief or attitude, are individually interviewed about their beliefs, attitudes, and experiences. Typically, a semistructured protocol is developed, composed primarily of openended questions in which participants are guided through an exploration of their feelings and expression of their beliefs with specificity and detail. Individual interviews—conducted in person or on the telephone—typically last between one and three hours and are audiotaped. Audiotapes are transcribed verbatim and submitted to a content analysis in which major themes and issues are identified, typically in a qualitative format (although under certain conditions quantitative data can be obtained from interviews). The findings can be used to answer research questions and to generate hypotheses for future studies. This topic is explored in depth in chapter 13.

A focus group is a research paradigm in which a trained facilitator leads a group discussion about attitudes and beliefs among a set of individuals who share a particular experience or characteristic. The premise underlying the group nature of the data collection (the reason that the individuals are asked the questions as a group) is that the synergy of the group dynamic produces richer and more authentic and meaningful information than would be produced by individual interviews or quantitative means. In practical terms, a selected group of six to ten individuals, all of whom have experienced the same event or process and/or share a similar characteristic, are brought together to discuss and share their ideas, beliefs, attitudes, and experiences. It is important that they do not already know one another and that they are not likely to interact with each other following the focus group. Similar to the individual interview format described above, a structured protocol is developed that is composed primarily of open-ended questions guiding participants through a detailed exploration of their feelings and beliefs. Several focus groups are conducted in order to capture the full range of experiences and beliefs about the topic. Focus group sessions typically last between 1.5 and 2.5 hours and are audiotaped. The tapes are transcribed verbatim and submitted to a content analysis in which major themes and issues are identified, typically in a qualitative format. However, systematic quantitative data can also be collected from the participants to create a mixed-method approach. The findings can be used to answer research questions and to generate hypotheses for future studies. Chapter 12 presents the theory and practice of conducting focus groups.

Taken together, the sampling plan, the design strategy, and the measurement strategy compose the proposed methods of the study. Prior to finalizing the study methods, it is suggested that the researcher write a draft of the methods section of the manuscript that will eventually be submitted to a peer-reviewed journal. In writing about the sample, design, measures, and procedures of the proposed study, any flaws in the logic of the plan should become apparent and can be addressed prior to implementation of the study. Of course, key agency staff will need an opportunity to offer input and suggestions to the proposed plan and suggest ways to ensure that it is appropriate for the agency and sensitive to the needs of the staff and clients.

Once the methods section has been explicated, the researcher should write a draft of the results section of the paper that will eventually be submitted to a peer-reviewed journal (without inserting any actual numbers). This exercise will force the researcher to think through the logic of the analyses planned and ensure that the statistics proposed will actually allow the researcher to answer the study questions. At this point, of course, it is not too late to revise the methods to bring them more in line with the questions and necessary analyses. In this way, the introduction (leading up to the study questions), the methods, and the results section should be tightly woven together into a seamless and logical tapestry of theory and method. Chapter 14 provides detailed information about analyzing different types of data, while chapter 15 describes methods for writing up and disseminating the findings to different audiences.

One thread that should run through the entire planning of the study is the ethical considerations of the project. The researcher (along with agency staff) should be considering at every stage of the planning possible ethical considerations. These are described fully in chapter 3 and are touched on briefly here. The primary ethical considerations include: (1) Will participation in the research be voluntary and, if so, how will it be obtained in a noncoercive, respectful, and honest manner? (2) Will the individual's responses remain anonymous and, if so, how will confidentiality be maintained? (3) What, if any, limits to confidentiality will exist and how will these be explained to potential participants? (4) Will the study include a service or treatment to a subset of agency clients and, if so, what are the ethical implications of doing so? And (5) will payment be made to the research participants and, if so, how will it be determined that the payment is appropriate and noncoercive? All of these issues need to be resolved prior to finalization of the research plan.

The Blessings and the Curses of Agency-Based Child Welfare Research

Conducting research in a child welfare setting offers its own specific set of advantages and disadvantages. These "blessings" and "curses" are described below. There are at least four significant drawbacks to conducting agency-based child welfare research. With some forethought, they can each be mitigated, if not neutralized. The first is lack of credibility in the eyes of the professional community. There is no denying the reality that professors at universities and prestigious research centers have a better reputation than researchers situated within an agency. This is at least in part because the people who hire agency-based researchers are not necessarily knowledgeable about the criteria for selecting a rigorous scientist and may not be able to offer the kinds of salary and resources that would attract a top researcher. The primary strategy by which an agency-based researcher can counter this perception is to develop collaborative relationships with researchers at more prestigious institutions and to publish in peer-reviewed journals.

The second "curse" is that, because of the lack of prestige and credibility, many funding opportunities are closed to agency-based researchers. Developing collaborations and publishing in peer-reviewed journals is the best antidote to this. Creative use of existing funds and existing data can also mitigate the problems inherent in not winning external funding awards.

A third "curse" relates to pressure that agency staff might place on the researcher to suppress findings that could place the agency in a poor light. Understandably, an agency will seek to protect its reputation with colleagues, funders, clients, and related professional and giving communities. Many research studies—even descriptive and qualitative—carry the risk of producing results that are unflattering to the agency. Although there is no simple solution to resolving this issue, honest and detailed discussion with key staff within the agency prior to commencing a study can reduce the likelihood of conflict later. Agency staff should be apprised of the nature of expected findings (e.g., proportion of group home youth who go AWOL, effects or lack thereof of a model program, client attitudes about staff, prevalence of substance abuse problems in teens). It is better to have studies rejected by the agency in the planning stages than to conduct the research and have a conflict over reporting and disseminating the findings afterward. With creativity and integrity, a good researcher can craft a study that will be acceptable to the agency—regardless of the findings.

Finally, agency-based researchers are "cursed" with the lack of professional resources such as an academic library (literature reviews, in particular, can be challenging in the absence of access to a full-text library), graduate students for collecting and entering data, and a pool of colleagues available for ad hoc consultations and inspiration. The agency-based researcher tends to work in relative professional isolation when compared to researchers situated in universities and research centers. One solution to many of these shortcomings is adjunct teaching at a nearby college or university. This typically confers rights to the library and may attract research interns as well. Absent this option, the agency-based researcher will simply have to be especially diligent in gaining access to relevant literature (paying for articles, requesting them from authors, developing a lending/sharing library with other similarly situated researchers) and in developing relationships with colleagues who are available (for a fee perhaps) on a consultancy basis.

Despite these many challenges, agency-based research offers several "blessings" that should not be overlooked. Three are mentioned here. The first is that the researcher has ongoing access to a wealth of practice wisdom and clinical experience. The ability of the knowledge that program and agency staff have honed over years of agency-based clinical work to enhance the meaning and relevance of research cannot be overestimated. This practice wisdom can be drawn on at all stages of research, notably during problem formulation, interpretation of findings, and development of clinical and programmatic implications of findings.

The second "blessing," as noted above, is that agency-based researchers have immediate access to rich and interesting data (both paper records and electronic files), which—with the right theoretical framework—can be mined for utilization in several related studies. Important questions can be asked with these existing data, allowing an agency-based researcher to develop a series of studies and publishable papers at less expense and in less time than would otherwise be possible.

The third "blessing" is the opportunity to improve practice and influence policy. Findings from research studies can be presented to agency staff (once approved for publication) with an eye toward improving and refining practice. In this way, the researcher can have the satisfaction of seeing knowledge utilized in an immediate and practical way.

Tensions in the Field of Child Welfare Research

In addition to the above set of advantages and disadvantages, there are four areas of tension for agency-based child welfare researchers. The first is the tension between qualitative and quantitative research methodologies. Agency and program staff often want the kinds of findings that can only be obtained with quantitative research (i.e., does a program "work"?), while a researcher may prefer to conduct a study that illuminates individual perspectives and experiences in a rich and textured fashion. On the other hand, the researcher may prefer to conduct a quantitative study that addresses a narrow niche in the knowledge base while agency staffpeople yearn for findings that speak to the complexity of service delivery and reflect the holistic reality of staff and client experiences. While there is no right or wrong approach, it is important for the goals of a study to be agreed upon by all "stakeholders" in advance. As noted above, it is quite possible to develop a study that results in both quantitative and qualitative findings.

A second tension relates specifically to program evaluations. Researchers who have working relationships with child welfare agencies may be called on to conduct program evaluations (to cover the cost of the researcher's salary, to address agency needs, and so forth). In some cases, program evaluation is not particularly interesting work for a researcher (unless the study can go beyond the black box of determining whether or not a program "works"). Program evaluations can also place the researcher in an adversarial relationship vis-à-vis program staff in terms of monitoring program fidelity and tracking client participation. Another difficulty with program evaluations is that in light of small samples, lack of reliable measures, no additional staff for data collection, and lack of random assignment (or even a comparison group), the program evaluation conducted will not produce the type of results the agency staff thinks it wants. Good program evaluations require considerably more money and resources than most agencies are able to allocate to that endeavor. The researcher may be placed in the difficult position of having to explain to the agency why they cannot do what they think they want to do. Often, a less ambitious "evaluation" can be designed that can answer some important intermediate questions regarding a program such as: (1) Are clients satisfied with the program? (2) Do staff believe that they are making a difference in the lives of clients? And (3) what proportion of clients stay in the program until its end? But if the prevailing interest is the establishment of evidence of program effectiveness, the researcher may have to take a hard-nosed approach and decline to participate unless certain conditions are met (creation of a control group or access to a viable comparison group, a team of independent data collectors, sufficient time to follow the clients through program completion).

A third source of tension is between the practitioner and the researcher. Practitioners have developed practice wisdom honed from years of program and service delivery. It sometimes happens that the results of a study are not consonant with what practitioners believe to be reality and truth. It might be that they developed their understanding of "truth" based on a biased sample that is not reflective of the larger population of clients and that, in fact, the study is a more accurate representation of the average experience of clients. It is equally possible that the measures used were not adequate for capturing real differences between families or real improvements in families over time. In other cases, the results of the analyses are so qualified or complex that they are not translatable to the frame of reference of program staff. Researchers will need to be creative in their efforts to translate research findings into statements that are both accurate and accessible to the typical program staffperson (and perhaps client as well).

A fourth tension revolves around the role of the agency in the development and ownership of the project. This is particularly relevant for researchers who are not on salary at the agency but work on a consultancy basis. Issues regarding ownership of the data, rights to publish findings, and the extent to which each party will help develop and craft the study need to be negotiated in advance to avoid misunderstanding about roles, responsibilities, and rights. Unlike university-based researchers, who own their data, the agency and not the researcher owns the data collected on agency clients.

Conclusion

Conducting a study in the field of child welfare follows the scientific method and is composed of the same steps in project development as other social science research studies, including problem formulation and development of hypotheses, identification of a sample, selection of measures, development of a design and collection of data, data analysis, and reporting and dissemination of the findings. Conducting agency-based child welfare research offers a unique set of opportunities and challenges. In addition, the agency-based researcher is likely to contend with at least one, if not all, of the four tensions identified above. That being said, conducting high-quality child welfare research is of the utmost importance, as the program staff deserves access to the most accurate and useful knowledge possible in order to best meet the needs of the highly vulnerable population of children and families they serve.

[3]

Ethical Considerations

In this chapter, the following topics will be discussed:

- A brief history of ethics in human subjects research
- The institutional review board (IRB)
- Oversight of human subjects research in a child welfare setting
- Conducting ethical research in a child welfare setting

Overview of the Topic

Until the middle of the last century, research with human subjects was not bound by any legal constraints regarding the ethical treatment of study participants. However, in response to the Nuremberg Trials and several other high-profile incidents, the United States government developed standards for research practice with human subjects. In addition, several membership organizations (for example, organizations for social workers and psychologists) have developed their own guidelines regarding the treatment of human subjects in research. The child welfare researcher should be cognizant of all legal and moral guidelines that apply to research in the child welfare setting and ensure that every aspect of a research study is fully consistent with both the letter and the spirit of these guidelines.

Brief History of Ethics in Human Subjects Research

Prior to the 1970s, no guidelines existed for the ethical treatment of human subjects participating in medical research. Consideration of the effects of participation in research was sparked during the Nuremberg Trials after World War II, when it came to light that doctors had performed painful and often fatal medical experiments on concentration camp inmates, such as studies of the length of time it takes to lower the temperature of the human body to the point of death and whether it was possible to resuscitate someone who was near death due to hypothermia. In 1946, following the revelations at the Nuremberg Trials, the first code of medical research ethics was created to protect the rights of subjects and to articulate the obligations of researchers. This code marked the first and perhaps most important contribution to the development of ethics related to research (Shuster 1997).

It took another thirty years for the U.S. federal government to require that the ethical principles guiding medical research be applied to social science research as well. In 1974, the National Research Act (Public Law 93-348) was passed, creating the National Commission for the Protection of Human Subjects of Biomedical and Behavioral Research. One of the commission's charges was to identify the basic ethical principles that should underlie the conduct of biomedical and behavioral research involving human subjects and to develop guidelines to assure that such research is conducted in accordance with those principles. The result of this commission's efforts was the Belmont Report, which summarized basic ethical principles that should be followed when conducting research with human subjects. This report can be obtained on the Internet at http://www.hhs.gov/ohrp/humansubjects/guidance/belmont.htm. The Belmont Report presents three unifying ethical principles that form the basis for the National Commission's topic-specific reports and the regulations that incorporate its recommendations: (1) respect for persons, (2) beneficence, and (3) justice. Since the creation of the Belmont Report, over ten other federal departments and agencies have joined the United States Department of Health and Human Services (DHHS) in adopting a uniform set of rules for the protection of human subjects, identical to those of DHHS regulations (which can be found on the Internet at: http://www.hhs.gov/ohrp/humansubjects/guidance/45cfr46 .htm#subparta). This uniform set of regulations is the Federal Policy for the Protection of Human Subjects, informally known as the "Common Rule."

Professional associations have also weighed in on the ethical treatment of human subjects participating in social science research. Two that are particularly relevant for the child welfare researcher are those developed by the National Association of Social Workers (NASW) and those developed by the American Psychological Association (APA). The NASW explicates sixteen principles related to ethical conduct in research and evaluation. Social workers should: (1) monitor and evaluate policies, programs, and practice interventions; (2) promote and facilitate evaluation and research to build knowledge; (3) critically examine and keep current with emerging knowledge relevant to social work practice; (4) carefully consider possible consequences of research and should follow guidelines developed for the protection of evaluation and research participants and should consult institutional review boards; (5) obtain voluntary and written informed consent from research participants; (6) provide an appropriate explanation to the participants, obtain the participants' assent to the extent that they are able, and obtain written consent from an appropriate proxy when informed consent is not possible; (7) never design or conduct an evaluation or research study that does not use consent procedures unless rigorous and responsible review of the research has found it to be justified; (8) inform participants of their right to withdraw from an evaluation and research study at any time without penalty; (9) take appropriate steps to ensure that participants in evaluation and research have access to appropriate supportive services; (10) protect participants from unwarranted physical or mental distress, harm, danger, or deprivation due to research; (11) discuss data collected from research only for professional purposes and only with people professionally concerned with the information; (12) ensure the anonymity or confidentiality of participants and of the data obtained from them and clarify any limits of confidentiality; (13) protect participants' confidentiality when reporting research results; (14) report evaluation and research findings accurately; (15) avoid conflicts of interest and dual relationships with participants of research; and (16) educate themselves, their students, and their colleagues about responsible research practices. The complete NASW code of ethics can be found on the Internet at http://www.socialworkers .org/pubs/code/code.asp. Social workers should consult the complete and—when necessary, updated—text rather than rely solely on the synopsis provided here.

Likewise, the American Psychological Association (APA) has identified eight guiding principles of ethical conduct for psychologists (whether conducting research, providing clinical services, consulting, or conducting other professional actions and services): beneficence, nonmalfeasance, fidelity and responsibility, integrity, justice, and respect for people's rights and dignity. Research-specific guidelines are offered as well, specifying that psychologists (1) should provide accurate information to an internal review board about proposed research, obtain approval prior to conducting the research, and conduct the research in accordance with the approved protocol; (2) when obtaining informed consent, should provide all necessary information and an opportunity to ask questions and receive answers, and, in addition, psychologists conducting intervention research involving the use of experimental treatments should clarify the experimental nature of the treatment, the services that will or will not be available, how assignment to groups will be made, treatment alternatives, and compensation for participating; (3) should obtain informed consent from research participants prior to recording their voices or images for data collection; (4) when conducting research with clients/patients, students, or subordinates as participants, should protect them from adverse consequences of declining or withdrawing and, if students, should provide them with an equitable alternative activity; (5) may dispense with informed consent only under certain circumstances; (6) should avoid offering excessive or inappropriate inducements for participation and should clarify the risks, obligations, and limitations associated with any services offered as an inducement; (7) should not conduct a study involving deception unless justified by the study's significant prospective scientific, educational, or applied value, should not deceive prospective participants about research that is reasonably expected to cause physical pain or severe emotional distress, and should explain any deception that is an integral feature of the design and conduct of an experiment to participants as early as is feasible; and (8) should provide debriefing in order for participants to obtain appropriate information about the nature, results, and conclusions of the research and take reasonable steps to correct any misconceptions that participants may have of which the psychologists are aware. More information about the APA's ethical guidelines can be found at the following Web address: http://www.apa.org/ethics/history.

The overarching principle is that child welfare researchers should be knowledgeable about all guidelines for ethical research practice and should consider the ramifications of all sampling, design, measurement, data analysis, and reporting choices in that context.

The Institutional Review Board (IRB)

The Code of Federal Regulations, Title 45, Public Welfare Department of Health and Human Services Part 46 Protection of Human Subjects also specifies that certain research projects must be approved by an institutional review board (IRB). The APA and NASW, as well, suggest and/or mandate that certain research projects conducted with human subjects be reviewed by such a board. Therefore, it is advisable for all child welfare agency-based research to be reviewed by an IRB. According to federal government guidelines, an IRB should have at least five members, with varying backgrounds, to promote complete and adequate review of all research activities. It is also required that the members of the IRB should have the necessary professional competence to review research proposals and to evaluate the research in terms of agency requirements, applicable law, and professional standards. If an IRB regularly reviews research that involves a vulnerable category of subjects, such as children, prisoners, pregnant women, or handicapped or mentally disabled persons, the regulations require that consideration be given to the inclusion of one or more individuals who have specific experience and expertise in working with these subjects. In addition, every appropriate effort should be made to ensure that the IRB is not biased in terms of gender and professional backgrounds of its members. Additional requirements are that each IRB include at least one member whose primary concern is the scientific merit of the research as well as least one member whose primary concerns are in nonscientific areas, and that each IRB include at least one member who is not otherwise affiliated with the institution or is a family member of someone affiliated with the institution. In addition, no IRB may have a member participate in the IRB's initial or continuing review of any project in which the member has a conflicting interest (except to provide information requested by the IRB). An IRB may, at its discretion, invite individuals with competence in special areas to assist in the review of issues that require expertise beyond or in addition to that available to the members of the IRB. However, these individuals may not vote with the IRB. It is strongly recommended that an agency-based researcher assist the agency in developing an IRB to review all research. The noninstitutional member(s) could be professional researchers at nearby universities, in order to help establish collegial relationships with these individuals and organizations (an advisable action, as noted in chapter 2).

The IRB should meet on an as-needed basis, reviewing all research proposals (prepared by individuals internal and external to the agency). Some proposals, according to most ethical guidelines, qualify for what is known as an expedited review (as opposed to a full review by the IRB). There are several types of studies that can qualify for an expedited review. Most relevant for child welfare research is the following statement in the U.S. CFR 45 Part 46:

"Research involving the collection or study of existing data, documents, records, pathological specimens, or diagnostic specimens, if these sources are publicly available or if the information is recorded by the investigator in such a manner that subjects cannot be identified, directly or through identifiers linked to the subjects." This means that a child welfare agency researcher can conduct a study with expedited review if the study involves the utilization of existing data and the confidentiality of the participants is protected. An expedited review usually entails a subset of the IRB reading the proposal and providing written or oral feedback to the chair of the committee about the acceptability of the proposal. A full meeting and discussion is not necessary.

Any research that requires a full (as opposed to expedited) review will most likely need to be approved by the appropriate city and state agencies that provide oversight to the child welfare services. Each city and state governing office has its own guidelines for submitting proposals and the researcher will need to become familiar with those relevant to the agency at which he or she is conducting the research study. In addition, any studies involving collaborations with university professors may also need to be approved by the university's own IRB.

Conducting Ethical Research in a Child Welfare Setting

Every phase of research is touched by moral and ethical issues. A hypothetical research study on successful trial discharges is discussed below, with a detailed explication of the ethical concerns that should be uppermost on the minds of a child welfare researcher as such a study is planned and implemented. It is possible that a researcher hired by a child welfare agency will be the only person on staff with a thorough knowledge of research standards and practice. As noted in chapter 2, this is one of the "curses" of being an agency-based child welfare researcher. It is unlikely that anyone else on staff will be able to adequately judge the methods and procedures proposed. The agency-based researcher (unless working with professional colleagues outside the agency) stands as both judge and jury of his or her own work prior to the work being approved by the IRB—and the sole judge, if an expedited review is permissible. This confers a special onus on the researcher to examine the study in light of the following two questions: (1) Is the research being conducted with scientific rigor and in accordance with standards of excellence in the field? And (2) are the participants in the research being treated with honesty, dignity, and respect? These twin concerns should shape every aspect of research, from problem formulation to analyzing the data and presenting the findings.

Problem Formulation

From the outset, the researcher should ensure that she or he has a thorough knowledge of the field—in this case, successful trial discharges—prior to selecting a topic or conducting a research study in a topic of interest to the agency. The researcher has an ethical obligation to not waste the agency's resources by conducting a study that is superfluous to the field, ill conceived, or irrelevant. The researcher may have to advocate strongly for access to books and articles and time in the library and on the Internet in order to conduct the necessary preliminary work to determine whether a study has merit and import. A staffperson within an agency might have a burning interest in conducting a study that has in fact already been conducted or for some reason has been demonstrated to be not feasible to conduct. For example, it is possible that a definitive single study or set of related studies has been conducted on trial discharges, which fully explicate the factors associated with successful as opposed to failed discharges. On the other hand, it is possible that a review of the literature reveals that it is not possible to conduct such a study because of the extraneous sources of influence on this event or because most of the variance is accounted for by administrative and policy regulations that determine when and who can return to care following a trial discharge. It is also possible that a review of the literature would reveal that each agency defines the construct so differently or that too few agencies even use this procedure to make a study of this of interest to the larger field of child welfare. In this case, the researcher must bring this to the attention of the administrators within the agency and help agency staff develop studies and research questions that will produce meaningful and interpretable data.

Problem formulation can also touch on ethical guidelines by considering whether individuals and groups with less power and voice within an agency have an opportunity to participate in the formulation of the research problem. This is not only ethically sound but good science as well, in that often the clients/consumers and front-line service delivery staff—those who typically do not participate in problem formulation—have a unique and valid perspective and a vested interest in various research topics (Alpert 2005; Curran and Pecora 1999). Their insight and input can enhance both the quality and the integrity of most agency-based research. At a general level, this might mean inviting consumers and front-line staff to suggest topics for research. More specifically, this could mean purposefully seeking out staff involved with cases in which the trial discharge was successful as well as when the discharge failed, and any staff with special responsibility for working with families on trial discharge, in order to involve them in research development discussions once a topic has been identified. For example, if the general topic of trial discharge has been designated as being of interest and a literature review has indicated only minimal knowledge of the range of factors that are associated with failed and successful trial discharges, preliminary discussion with staff and families might be useful for developing a model of possible correlates.

A third ethical issue related to problem formulation is that the researcher should understand from the outset of a study what the chain of command is and who has the right/need to approve of various aspects of the study. It is quite likely that the executive director/president of the agency will want to review all manuscripts prior to submission to a peer-reviewed journal or distribution outside the agency. This is a necessary part of working within an agency. What may become problematic is if the paper or report is shelved simply because the findings are unflattering to the agency. To the extent that this can be anticipated it is wise for the researcher to explain to the people who have the power to approve or disapprove of a paper prior to the study being conducted what the likely data will reveal (based on the research questions). It is better to not conduct a study likely to be refused distribution. Ideally, important and timely research questions can be identified that will produce data of interest to the agency regardless of the direction of the findings. For example, a study on trial discharges could aim to identify factors associated with successes as well as documenting the number of discharges that fail. However, if the agency is only interested in supporting research that will put the agency in a positive light, this could be difficult for the researcher, as it violates the spirit of ethical guidelines. For example, the preamble of the APA's guidelines states: "Psychologists are committed to increasing scientific and professional knowledge of behavior and people's understanding of themselves and others and to the use of such knowledge to improve the condition of individuals, organizations, and society." Withholding from the professional community research findings hinders the pursuit of knowledge and should be avoided. Another potential disadvantage to only publishing "positive" findings is that colleagues will avoid future collaborations, and professionals who would otherwise join the IRB might decline involvement with the agency's research endeavors because of the lack of a spirit of knowledge building or the fear that a subsequent paper could be refused distribution.

Selecting Research Partners from Outside the Agency

As noted in chapter 2, working with professional colleagues is one way to enhance both the prestige and quality of the research. It might also bring in additional resources (interns, students, access to literature, and so forth). There are many advantages to working with research partners for the agency-based researcher. There are also some ethical pitfalls. Ownership of the data, access to individual case data, and authorship are three primary concerns. These must be discussed in advance of the formalization of any research partnership. Data collected from and about clients in a child welfare agency belong to the agency solely. Thus, for example, if an agency-based researcher conducted a qualitative study of interviews of families in which a trial discharge failed, when the researcher leaves his or her post, the data stay at the agency. Unlike university-based research, in which the researcher can take his or her data at the end of employment, the data from child welfare research belongs to the agency. This holds true for external partners as well; this must be explained in order to avoid later misunderstandings. There are also ethical issues revolving around the sharing of individual-level data with a research partner who works outside the agency. For example, if an agency conducts a survey of all child welfare agencies in the city about trial discharges and partners with the city's child welfare administration, it must be made clear that the administration will not have access to raw data (either paper or electronic), because it is quite likely that—even if the names of the agencies are not included in the database—the child welfare administration could link the data with the agency. This would violate the confidentiality promised to the participants in the informed consent for the study.

The third issue pertains to which actions on the part of a research partner qualify for authorship. The decision-making guidelines regarding authorship should be understood and agreed upon in advance. For example, using the above example of working with a governmental agency as a partner, it is possible that their input would be minimal and primarily administrative. That is, they could be asked to supply the researcher with mailing labels of all agencies that meet the inclusion criteria for the study, and they could be asked to sign a cover letter endorsing the project, as a strategy to improve participation rates. These actions alone would not qualify for authorship. According to the APA, authorship is appropriate for those individuals who make a substantive scientific contribution to the project, including conducting the literature review, helping design the study and select the measures, developing the statistical analytic plan, or helping write or make significant edits to the report/paper. One way to ensure that all partners have the opportunity to become authors is to provide them with information about the project on an interim basis (for example, drafts of the measurement tools, drafts of the introduction of the paper, drafts of the results, the draft of the full paper) and allow them to offer insight and input, which if substantive would ultimately warrant authorship.

Selecting Research Partners from Inside the Agency

Often, agency-based researchers will develop working relationships with staff within the agency, which will result in collaborations on research projects. Ideally, staff involved in the particular field of interest will be involved in the problem formulation stage and in the development of the study's design (to ensure that it will work well within the specific configuration of the agency). The types of involvement that meet the criteria for authorship should be explained to such partners at the beginning of the collaboration in order to avoid any misunderstandings. As noted above, one approach is to invite all relevant staff to read a draft of various portions of the paper/report and provide substantive feedback. Anyone who makes a substantive contribution should be included as an author (this could entail suggesting another way to understand the findings, shedding additional clinical light on the findings, developing clinical implications, and so forth).

Sampling

Once a topic has been identified and the necessary literature review has been conducted, the next step is to develop inclusion and exclusion criteria for the study; that is, who will be invited to participate? At every step of the sampling process, ethical issues need to be considered. There are two main issues related to ethics and sampling: withholding treatment and informed consent.

WITHHOLDING TREATMENT

In between-group designs, in which one group of individuals receives a treatment or intervention while another does not, the agency needs to consider how placement into the groups will be determined. There are many aspects of treatment and services within the child welfare system that are mandated, and no agency is allowed to withhold these services to any clients (nor would they want to). Thus, if a child and his or her family has been designated as ready for trial discharge, the agency is required to make certain efforts on behalf of the child and family to expedite the process. No research can be conducted in which individuals who receive mandatory services are compared to individuals who do not. That being said, there are many aspects of service delivery that are not mandated and therefore could be the subject of a study in which those who receive it are compared to those who do not. This is possible as long as those receiving the program (treatment, intervention) do so on a voluntary basis and can cease their participation in it at any time, with no consequences to their receipt of mandated services.

Unfortunately, although providing service in such a fashion is consistent with ethical practice, it does not always feel comfortable for program staff. Sometimes when a new program or treatment is developed, staffpeople within the agency become so enthusiastic about it that they have difficulty accepting that some families will not receive it. Some discussion might be necessary to explain the need for a rigorous evaluation of these services because, in the long run, this will ensure that a greater number of families will have access to the program (to the extent that positive results of the evaluation will increase funding and support for the program). It is vital that staff endorse the between-subjects design, otherwise they could undermine the integrity of the research. This is particularly relevant for studies in which random assignment is used to determine who will receive the program and who will not. Although by logical standards random assignment is the fairest approach (no favoritism or bias is at play), it can seem cruel or arbitrary to withhold a program from families the staff believe are likely to need it or deserve it the most (should they not be randomly assigned to be in the program group). Working with program staff around these ethical considerations will be an important part of the development and implementation of the research project. And, of course, random assignment is only ethical if it is explained to the participants that they will be randomly assigned into either a treatment or no-treatment group.

INFORMED CONSENT

The second ethical issue pertaining to sampling is informed consent. This means that those who meet the inclusion criteria for the study are provided with enough information about the project (the program component and the research component) that they can make an informed decision about whether or not to participate in the project. Informed consent is the cornerstone of ethical guidelines in human subjects research and is designed to protect the rights of the potential participants. Informed consent must be obtained prior to every data collection session (but not every measure within the same data collection session). There are several steps involved in obtaining informed consent: (1) reading out loud a prepared written statement presenting a detailed description of the project to each potential participant, (2) allowing the participant to ask and have answered all questions about the project, and (3) asking the participant if he or she wants to participate and, if so, having the consent form signed and dated. Each of these steps is described in more detail below. In this way, "informed consent is a process, not just a form," as noted by the United States Department of Health and Human Services, Office for Protection of Research Risks (1993).

A detailed written description of the project must be provided to the potential participants. There are ten major points that need to be included in any informed consent form. The first is that there must be a statement about which agency(s) is sponsoring and/or funding the project. The potential participant has a right to know who the sponsors are and make decisions accordingly. It is possible that a drug company might sponsor a study of the utilization of a new psychotropic medication that has been made available to children in an agency. The parents have a right to know this. Even if there is no actual conflict of interest, the parent has a right to decide for him or herself that there is the appearance or feel of one and choose not to participate for that reason.

Second, the stated purpose of the project must be included. For a study of trial discharges in which some but not all families will have failed discharges and it cannot be known in advance which ones will fail, the stated purpose could be something like: "The purpose of this study is to follow families through the trial discharge process and to learn about how things work for the children and parents." Thus, the description does not have to include the hypotheses or the list of variables, just a general overview of the goals of the project. This is an important safeguard against the utilization of deception, which had been an acceptable practice in human subjects research prior to the development of guidelines prohibiting it.

Third, exactly what participation entails must be described. This means the number of data collection visits, the probable location, and the likely materials to be covered during the visit. As an example, the following statement could be written: "Participation in this project will involve six monthly home visits following the trial discharge, at which time several paper-and-pencil measures will be completed by you." Again, it is not ethical to mislead participants about the extent of their commitment to the project by, for example, implying or stating that the participation will require less time and inconvenience than it really does.

Fourth, the risks and benefits of participation must be clearly spelled out. Risks include the physical, emotional, social, and psychological ramifications of the research as well as of the services provided and treatment offered. Thus the informed consent has to explain whether completing the measures, interviews, surveys, etc. will be stressful to the participants in any way and whether receiving the services themselves could involve any risks. The anticipated level of distress of the research and the program must be explained, such as: "Some parents may experience some mild discomfort in completing the research forms." The procedures in place to help the participant manage these responses must be described as well (e.g., that a clinician is available from Monday–Thursday 12:00 to 3:00 pm to discuss any feelings or thoughts about the project). In addition to describing the risks, the benefits of participation should be described as well. One potential benefit is that additional services could be offered if the data on a particular measure warrant it. For example, in a correlational study in which all data are collected at a single point in time, parents could be provided with immediate feedback about their responses and offered additional services if such services are of interest to the family. This might serve as an inducement to participation. To the extent that this is the case, the specific nature of the service needs to be described. There is a large difference between a "service" that involves a summary report mailed to a family and a service that entails weekly home-based supplemental parenting skills training.

Fifth, the informed consent must describe how the information provided by the participant will be managed so as to protect his or her confidentiality. One option is to offer anonymity. That is, no names or IDs will be used and all data will be completely anonymous. In a longitudinal study in which data collected at one point in time needs to be linked to data collected at another point in time, this would not be feasible. Anonymity also would prohibit keeping track of who participated in a survey and who did not, preventing the researcher from following up to ensure participation. Thus a more standard approach is to utilize an ID system that prevents anyone without access to the master list linking the IDs to the individuals to determine which data belong to which participant. But because the same ID is used for all data collected from the same person, the researcher is able to link data across measures. If this is the case, it must be explained to the participant that a unique ID will be assigned to his or her data such that no names will appear on any of the forms. It should also be explained who has access to the master ID code (typically, only the researcher and his or her staff) and how that list will be stored (typically, in a locked filing cabinet to which only research staff have access).

Sixth, limits to confidentiality, if any, must be described. In most human subjects research in which confidentiality is offered, there are usually exceptions or situations under which the researcher must notify someone else about the information provided. In these cases, the participant's confidentiality is breached. These limits must be explained in advance. Typically, limits involve some indication of harm to self or others. Examples of information that should not be kept confidential include a youth revealing that he or she is being sexually abused by another youth or staffperson in an agency program, a foster parent admitting to abusing a child, and a parent in a prevention program revealing that he or she is using drugs or alcohol. All three of these scenarios represent situations in which clinicians must be apprised of this information in order to prevent further harm being caused by or to the research participants. It is necessary that participants understand—prior to agreeing to participate in a research project—what the specific limits to confidentiality are. It is advised that this list of limits be developed in consultation with clinicians and an ethics committee within the agency. These limits will vary on a study-by-study basis, as the measures will vary as will the sample. For example, the endorsement of corporal punishment by a youth in a group home has a different set of legal and clinical ramifications for the agency than does a foster parent endorsing the same beliefs. There are some data that would not represent an ethical concern regardless of sample. For example, a study of literacy in group home youth is not likely to produce any limits in confidentiality. At the same time, there is some data that are likely to almost always introduce ethical concerns, such as a study of childrearing beliefs in foster parents. For each study, the researcher must know what the limits to confidentiality will be and must state them clearly in the informed consent form.

Seventh, whether there will be payments for participation must be explained in the informed consent materials. Many studies provide some monetary compensation for a participant's time and effort. Whatever the payments are, they must be explained (how much money and in what form, such as cash, check, or coupon). In addition, the payment should be large enough to indicate the value of the person's time but small enough so as not to sway someone to participate who would otherwise truly not want to do so.

Eighth, the voluntary nature of participation must be explained. The potential participant must understand that he or she is not obligated to participate simply because of receipt of services at the agency. It must be explained that participation is strictly voluntary and that this means that the person can change his or mind about participation at any point. A person can agree to participate and then change his or her mind and decide not to answer any questions in a research protocol, a person can complete one form but refuse to complete another form, a person can agree to participate in one session but decline participation in the next, or any other combination of agreeing but not fully participating. It is usually acceptable in such situations to ask the person if he or she would like to explain why their participation has ceased. But it is not acceptable to pressure the person or try to induce guilt for the decision. As inconvenient and frustrating as it is for the researcher to "lose" a participant, it is not acceptable to convey that to the individual.

Ninth, the potential participant must understand that there will be no consequences for not participating in terms of receipt of mandated services by the agency. In fact, no one at the agency should even be aware of which clients are and are not choosing to participate in a research study.

Finally, information must be provided to the participant in written form about whom to contact for more information or if upset by the participation. A name, job title, and phone number must be provided.

Once the informed consent form is read out loud to the participant, he or she must be asked whether there are any questions about the project. This must be posed in a tone and style that conveys genuine interest and concern for the thoughts of the potential participant. It cannot be asked in a cursory tone of voice that conveys that this is perfunctory and that the expectation is that the person will not actually ask any questions. All questions asked must be answered to the satisfaction of the participant. Often the answer is in the informed consent form, which can be reviewed for the desired information. It is possible that the research assistant conducting the data collection session does not know the answer to the question and should be honest in saying so. For example, if the participant asks how many people are participating in the project or where the results will be published, the assistant cannot know the answer to those questions at that point in the process. The assistant should say that he or she does not know the answer and then ask the person whether he or she wants to participate even without that information. Once all the questions have been asked and addressed, the person should be asked to sign and date the consent form. The assistant should sign it as well.

Consent and Assent with Children

Children cannot legally make the decision about whether to participate in a research study. This right resides with the child's legal guardian or with an advocate appointed on behalf of the child should the child be a ward of the state. In addition, if the IRB deems it feasible, assent from the child must also be obtained. Child assent does not replace parental consent; it supplements it to ensure that the child is being treated with dignity and respect. Federal guidelines for human research protection for children can be found in the Code of Federal Regulations, Title 45, Public Welfare Department of Health and Human Services Part 46, Protection of human subjects, subparts .406, .407, .408, and .409. The basic premise is that that once consent has been obtained but prior to the administration of measures, the project should be described (in child terms), the child should be asked whether he or she has any questions, and then the child should be asked if he or she wants to participate.

Measurement

As noted in chapter 9, there is often more than one measure available for any given construct of interest in a research study. The experience of data collection from the perspective of the participant should be a primary concern when selecting one measure over the other. Specifically, measures that take less time to complete, are less intrusive, and are less likely to be experienced as judgmental by the participant are to be preferred. In light of the vulnerability of the population of families served by child welfare agencies (minority status; low income; limited education; suffering from alcohol, substance abuse, and mental health problems; multiple life stressors; and so forth), extreme caution should be taken prior to selecting a measure that could introduce additional stress into their lives. Any measures that are deemed to be more than a little emotionally disturbing to complete should be considered absolutely vital to the study or be eliminated. At all times, the needs of the clients should supersede the desires of the researcher.

Data Collection

The individuals hired to collect the data (e.g., administer the surveys, interviews, or focus groups) must be trained to be respectful and honest at all times. The message should be conveyed that it is an honor and a privilege to be able to spend time with the participants and conduct the data collection session with them. At no time should the participants have the experience that the person collecting the data is annoyed, put out, disgusted, or negatively judging them in any way. This means hiring people who are mature, flexible, and are able to develop rapport with individuals who might be quite different from the data collectors. It also means that extensive training and supervision will need to be offered to them in order to ensure consistency in data collection across data collectors and to help them process and cope with anything disturbing that they might encounter during the data collection sessions. As with the subjects, the data collectors deserve to be treated with the utmost respect and honesty as well. Thus, the risks and benefits of working on the project should be clearly explicated to them (will they have to travel to dangerous neighborhoods and enter other people's homes? Are they expected to work on the weekends and evenings? Are they likely to encounter individuals with mental health and substance abuse problems?). To the extent that they are treated with respect and care, they will convey those same attributes to the study participants.

Data Analysis

Ethical considerations in data analysis primarily involve strict adherence to standards in the field for the management and interpretation of data. The researcher has an obligation to ensure that data are collected in a consistent and appropriate manner (measures are administered properly following guidelines established and with samples for whom the measure is appropriate). The researcher must ensure that every effort is made to obtain a complete data set and that the data entered into the computer are free from error. And, most importantly, the researcher must be familiar with the full range of statistical techniques to ensure that the appropriate analyses are conducted. The following five specific rules should be followed.

First, cases should not be excluded from any analyses unless one of two criteria are met. The first is that the cases are statistical outliers. A statistical outlier is a case that is plus or minus three standard deviations away from the mean. This should be established empirically, not just by examination of a scatter plot or frequency distribution. The second rationale for excluding cases from the sample is if the final sample is so skewed on a critical characteristic that some cases should be removed in order to address this imbalance. For example, if a study of substance use in group home youth at a particular agency results in a final sample of fifty-three males and three females, then it probably makes sense for the three females to be excluded and to consider the study a study of group home males. This is allowed because prior research has demonstrated that gender is an important factor is substance use attitudes and behaviors, but too few females are in the sample to allow for statistical control of gender. Thus the only remaining option is to remove the females. Because often one or two cases can make the difference between a statistically significant effect and not, it is vital that all cases be included unless a valid reason can be offered for removing any cases. In other words, it is not acceptable to exclude a case (or a few cases) in order to move the statistical significance from above to below the alpha level.

Second, comparability between two (or more) groups should be established prior to conducting any analyses that compares them on outcomes or performance. Groups that are not comparable to begin with are likely to also not be comparable on outcome comparisons. Misattributions could easily be made about causes for such differences in outcomes unless all other plausible explanations can be ruled out. The best way to do this is to establish comparability (on all relevant measures) prior to the administration of the outcome measures. That is, it could be concluded that a program was effective at improving some behavior because the treatment group outperformed the comparison group on the post-test assessment. However, it is possible that the two groups were different to begin with on the behavior, indicating that it was not the treatment that accounted for the differences on post-testing. This is an especially relevant concern in studies that do not utilize random assignment.

Third, no statistical tests should be conducted if the assumptions underlying the procedures are violated. The researcher needs to be thoroughly familiar with the assumptions underlying all tests and knowledgeable about how to assess whether the assumptions have been violated.

Fourth, unless a priori hypotheses have been developed, two-tail tests of statistical significance should be used. When a paper is submitted for publication, the editors and reviewers have no way of knowing whether the hypotheses presented were developed a priori or whether they were developed after the fact to support findings that emerged over the course of exploratory analyses. It is up to the researcher to uphold ethical standards in the field that dictate when one-tail and two-tail hypotheses can be utilized.

Likewise, it is not considered ethical to conduct multiple exploratory analyses in the hopes of finding some interesting results around which a paper can be built. The reason why this violates standards in the field is that if enough tests are conducted, it is likely that something will eventually turn up statistically significant by chance alone. Thus, fishing for a statistically significant effect will ultimately produce one, but it cannot be known if it is spurious or not because of the methods used to identify it. Such an action represents a disservice to the field of science, to the field of child welfare, and to the agency at which the study was conducted.

Writing the Report

From an ethical standpoint, writing the report must include input from the program staff and the agency that sponsored the research. This is good practice as well, so it should not pose a significant burden on the researcher, although it may represent a more collaborative approach than the researcher is comfortable with or used to. Often the clinical staff has a keen eye for clinical insight and administrative staffpeople have a deeper understanding of the policy context of certain research findings. Therefore it is quite likely that a final report or research paper will be much improved for having been shaped in part by these nonresearchers within the agency and/or field.

Disseminating the Findings

The researcher has an obligation to share the findings within the agency and with the larger child welfare community. This means that the researcher should be familiar with standards in the field for writing up research findings and shepherding the writeup through various stages of publication. This might include summarizing the findings for nonprofessional program staff, describing the findings in an agencywide newsletter, and writing a manuscript for submission to a peer-reviewed journal. At all stages, the researcher should be familiar with who at the agency needs to sign off on these various dissemination products and what to do should conflict ensue (i.e., someone in the agency objects to findings that put the agency in a poor light or simply does not agree with the researcher's interpretation of the findings).

The researcher also has an obligation to share the findings with staff within the agency and with the clients who participated in or are affected by the research. Obviously, the style and format of a report to these "stakeholders" will be quite different from a writeup for an academic or professional community. Sharing the findings in a manner that is accessible and meaningful to clients and staff is an important ethical obligation that should not be overlooked, despite the fact that it does not advance the researcher's career in the same way that a professional publication can. In addition, such a presentation requires great sensitivity, creativity, and tact and should not be put off as a way of avoiding dealing with the tricky issues of explaining research to a client population.

Conclusions

From the above discussion, it can be seen that every aspect of a research study can touch upon ethical dilemmas and considerations that must be explored and appropriately resolved in order for the study to meet the spirit and the letter of both federal guidelines for research with human subjects and whatever guidelines the individual researcher is subject to based upon professional affiliation. In the area of child welfare, these ethical guidelines are even more important to follow because the children and families in the child welfare system are some of the most vulnerable members of our society. The researcher needs to be cognizant of the fact that most if not all of the potential participants of child welfare research studies have already experienced multiple traumas and adopt as a guiding principle the goal that all research should be conducted in such a way as to avoid introducing any additional harm or trauma into their lives.

[4]

Problem Formulation

In this chapter, the following topics will be discussed following the introduction of the chapter scenario and the brief literature review:

- Formulating a research problem
- Ensuring that the topic is unique and of importance to the field
- Formulating research questions
- Formulating study hypotheses

CHAPTER SCENARIO

A second-year master's of social work student has been placed in the adoption unit of a foster care agency for an internship. The adoption unit works exclusively with children and youth who will not be reunified with their parents and are available for adoption. As part of the internship, the caseworker has been working with a thirteen-year-old boy living in an adoptive home. As per the Adoption and Safe Families Act (ASFA) of 1997, a termination of parental rights (TPR) petition has been filed for him because he has been in care for fifteen of the most recent twenty months and there is no compelling reason not to

(continued)

do so. However, his preadoptive parents decided not to adopt him because they are moving to Florida in order to be closer to their own parents. The youth was recently placed in another foster boarding home awaiting a new adoptive family. Devastated by this turn of events, his schoolwork has suffered: his attendance has been spotty and he has performed poorly on some important tests.

In a recent team meeting, the caseworker expressed concern about the boy's problems in school. Another member of the team mentioned that the same thing had happened to a girl on his caseload who also experienced an adoption disruption (that is, adoption plans did not work out after being placed in an adoptive home). The caseworker started to wonder about how often adoptions disrupt in the agency and whether school problems were a common response in children, and the topic eventually became the focus of a master's thesis.

BRIEF LITERATURE REVIEW:
THE IMPACT OF FAILED ADOPTION ON CHILDREN

The Adoption and Safe Families Act of 1997 changed the timelines within which child welfare workers operate in terms of filing for termination of parental rights (TPR) and pursuing adoption of children. This legislation has resulted in an increase in the number of adoptive families recruited and in the number of children being adopted from the foster care system. For example, in 1995, 25,000 children were adopted, while by 2004, that number had almost doubled (Children's Bureau 2006). Interestingly, the number of children classified as waiting to be adopted had not changed during that same time period, with about 120,000 children having parental rights terminated and a goal of adoption in both years (Children's Bureau 2006).

What these numbers do not speak to is the fact that some portion of planned adoptions disrupt. That is, the adoption process ends after the child has been placed in an adoptive home and before the adoption is legally finalized, resulting in the child's return to (or entry into) foster care or placement with new adoptive parents. Individual studies of dif-

(continued)

ferent populations throughout the United States have consistently found adoption disruption rates ranging from about 10 to 25 percent, depending upon the population studied, the duration of the study, and geographic and other factors(Festinger 2002; Goerge, Howard, Yu, and Radomsky 1997).

Professionals have expressed concern that recent public and private initiatives to increase adoptions and decrease time to adoption (the length of time between the child having a goal of adoption and the actual finalization of the adoption) might lead to inadequate selection and preparation of adoptive homes, which could in turn increase rates of adoption disruptions. These concerns have often focused on the shortened legal timeframes to file for termination of parental rights in the absence of an exception allowable by ASFA. The U.S. Government Accounting Office (2002, 2003) explored the question of the impact of ASFA but concluded that it was not possible to determine whether the increase in adoptions reported after ASFA reflects changes in data collection systems or in actual changes in numbers of adopted children. On the other hand, the Evan B. Donaldson Foundation (2004) conducted a fifteen-state study of adoption disruption and found rates no higher than 8 percent per state.

Regardless of the actual rates (only 8 percent or higher), they translate into large numbers of children who are experiencing the disruption of their potential adoptive home. For these children, the impact is likely to be negative, although the specific responses to adoption disruption have not been the focus of systematic empirical investigation. To date, most adoption disruption research has focused on identifying the characteristics of youth and families most likely to experience a disruption and/or on the services adoptive families need in order to prevent a disruption (Barth and Berry 1988; Barth, Gibbs, and Siebenaler 2001; Berry and Barth 1990; Dance and Rushton 2005). Some studies have looked at the experience of adoption from the perspective of adoptive parents, such as McDonald, Propp, and Murphy (2001), who interviewed 159 families eighteen to twenty-four months following an adoption to learn about the experience of this significant family transition. Similarly, Schmidt, Rosenthal, and Bombeck (1988) conducted in-depth interviews with a small sample of adults whose adoptions of special-needs children disrupted. However, to date, the actual and perceived impact of disruption on the children has not been the focus of much research attention.

Overview of the Topic

The journey in the development of a research project begins with an idea or topic of interest. This idea or topic can come from any number of sources, but it must meet the twin criteria of being unique and having the potential to make a contribution to the scientific knowledge base in the field. Once a topic has been selected and found to be unique and of importance, the researcher—through a series of steps—develops general research questions and then specific testable hypotheses that form the basis of the research study. This process will elucidate for the researcher the ultimate goals of the study (describe or explain/predict) and the need for a qualitative and/or quantitative approach.

Formulating a Research Problem

Choosing a topic for a research study may not initially seem like a particularly difficult task. However, as a researcher starts the journey, the first thing that he or she might notice is that the world is filled with problems that need answers. In the area of child welfare, due to the relatively small amount of research conducted compared to other fields, there are many topics from which to choose. Because of the seemingly unending list of issues that could be researched, one could become overwhelmed and deterred from even considering conducting research. As such, the problem formulation process requires patience, the willingness to see things in a different light, and a touch of originality and imagination. From the outset it is important to be aware of the fact that all research problems must have the potential to produce new information likely to be meaningful to clinicians, other researchers, program developers, or policymakers. These are the twin criteria of good research problems: uniqueness and importance. One without the other renders any study useless. A study that produced highly unique information that was of interest to no one would be pointless to undertake. Equally useless would be a study in which the topic was of great interest but the particular questions had already been thoroughly answered by prior research. Thus the first step in the problem formulation process is the identification of a topic that is likely to be unique and of importance (Light and Pillemer 1984). The problem formulation phase of any research project is crucial to the success of the entire project (Carter 1955; Sacks 1985). The idea for such a study can come from many different sources, several of which are described below.

Researcher's Personal Interest and Experience

Ideas for a research project can emerge from one's own personal life experience. For example, individuals who have overcome daunting obstacles or have been close to those who have done so may be curious as to what the source of their resilience was. Likewise, individuals who endured certain stressful or traumatic experiences may wonder about the influence of these factors on their own development. A researcher may have been in foster care him- or herself as a child and, as a result, may be driven to further his or her own understanding of that experience. Similarly, a researcher may have a friend whose family received prevention services (services offered to the family while the child remains in the home, which are designed to prevent out-of-home placement), and so has a personal interest in researching the effectiveness of such programs.

The goal of research—all research—is to describe or to explain/predict. The research process does not exist to satisfy one's own personal interests. If the topic selected is generated from a researcher's personal experience or interest, then the researcher must be prepared to develop for the scientific community a convincing argument as to why the problem is of value beyond that personal interest. Failing to do so can result in a project that never gets off the ground or, worse, a project that is completed but never published due to its scientific unworthiness. In this case, not only is any knowledge derived from the project lost to the child welfare field (as it is not published), but also, if the project entailed the participation of staff, parents, or children, their participation would have been for naught.

Job Experience

Certainly, working in the field of child welfare can provide an individual with many opportunities to develop ideas for research, as was the case for the social worker in the chapter scenario. Her own experience with the adoption disruption of the boy who had academic problems led to a general question about adoption disruptions and school performance. She thought about the issue and then upon hearing that the same phenomenon (school problems following an adoption disruption) had happened to another child in her agency, began to expand her interest to encompass children whose adoptions disrupted in general. Keen observation of child, family, staff, and agency problems can develop many ideas for interesting research projects from daily work-related experiences.

Schoolwork

Another source of inspiration for research ideas can be found in coursework (if the researcher is also a student). Many professionals in the field of child welfare are currently enrolled simultaneously in an academic program to further their training, education, and credentials (such as a master's degree in clinical social work, doctorate in social work administration, master's degree in counseling psychology, and so forth). Discussions with classmates can often lead to identification of interesting dilemmas in the field of child welfare, especially because professors often aim to elicit divergent points of view during classroom discussions in order to enhance critical thinking skills. Through lively classroom debates, a researcher could easily formulate ideas for future research.

Current Events

One can also draw on sociopolitical issues of the day to select a topic for a research project. The local newspapers and daily televised news reports are filled with discussions of social and political issues from which to choose a topic, such as homelessness, oppression, poverty, racism, war, terrorism, health problems, immigration, domestic violence, substance use, or, regrettably, a child's death in the child welfare system. All of these issues, and the many others that exist, can have significant implications for child welfare services. For example, if there were a change in immigration law that would make providing social services to a person who is undocumented a felony (an option that has been proposed by the United States Congress), an interesting research question would be to determine what happens to the children and families receiving child welfare services who are undocumented. Another fruitful area of research would be to track children who leave the foster care system in order to understand their long-term life course outcomes (e.g., how many graduate from high school and attend college, how many become homeless, how many obtain medical insurance, and so forth).

Research in child welfare is subject to many influences, including changes in law, fiscal issues, and the emergence of substance abuse epidemics. For example, the crack/cocaine epidemic caused a rise in the number of children entering the foster care system in the late 1980s, and, more recently, the use of crystal methamphetamine in certain areas of the United States has also brought a large number of children into the child welfare system, due to parental substance use that impacts their ability to care for their children. Fiscal issues are always at play in child welfare, such as when Congress considers reducing funding for child welfare services, potentially impacting service provision to children and families. Also, as Congress increases the number of required activities (i.e., mandated services and reporting requirements), staff satisfaction may decline as job demands become more cumbersome.

Thus, reading the newspaper and watching the local and national news can certainly indicate important and possibly unique areas of research. Stories about the child welfare system appear in the newspaper on a regular basis, especially when something goes terribly wrong, such as when a child dies, either while in out-of-home placement or within the home, in the event that a placement was not made. In either case, the article is likely to highlight the gaps in the knowledge base and emphasize the importance of answering certain questions before additional children suffer similarly tragic outcomes.

A current event could form the basis of a research study in several different ways. First, a study could set out to chart changes in state and national policies regarding some aspect of child welfare over time. Second, a study could aim to measure the impact of a recent sociopolitical development on subsequent service delivery or outcomes for children and families. A third approach would be to help develop a program that aims to ameliorate an identified societal problem affecting children in the child welfare system and then conduct a program evaluation in order to determine the impact of the new service. All of these areas are excellent sources for a research topic.

Prior Research

Another source of inspiration for a research topic is prior research. Prior published research is particularly useful as a source of inspiration, because the studies published in peer-reviewed journals are composed of research conducted on topics that the field has already deemed worthy. The peer-review process of writing up the findings of a completed study, submitting the manuscript to a panel of peers, and having that manuscript accepted by the panel ensures that only research producing unique and important findings will be published. This process adds further confidence in the research findings, as other objective and well-informed eyes have looked at the project and deemed it scientifically acceptable. In terms of identification of a research problem, this means that any topic (generally speaking) that has already been the subject of a published study is likely to be considered of interest to the field.

Although these prior research studies have been completed and the results have been published, this does not mean that the topic is closed for future researchers. In fact, quite the opposite is likely to be true. Most research projects answer some questions about the research topic under investigation and at the same time raise additional as yet unanswered questions about the topic as well. Thus the researcher can fashion a research problem based on these unanswered questions about a topic of interest. Using the chapter scenario as an example, a researcher might read an article about the incidence of adoption disruptions in an agency but note that the article did not report on the academic experiences of the youth when an adoption disruption occurred. Thus the researcher could design a project to look at the incidence of adoption disruptions (already done) and investigate youths' academic experience as a result of that experience (not yet done).

In addition, as the context of child welfare practice changes due to federal, state, or local regulations and polices, prior findings need to be periodically reexamined in order to determine the impact of those regulatory and policy changes on the published results. A good example would be a study of the length of time it takes for a child to be adopted. Data could be compared before and after the implementation of the federal ASFA legislation, which was designed to shorten the time to adoption. In addition, many prior studies have one or more methodological limitations (issues that may have impacted the integrity of the results or the generalizability of the findings to the population of interest). Thus new studies could be conducted that are designed to examine the same issue with one or more of these methodological limitations addressed. An example might be a prior researcher using a small sample of children ($n=20$) in a foster care setting and finding that older children (16+ years) who had at least one special need had higher rates of adoption disruption than older youth who did not have a special need. The small sample size (for more about sampling, see chapter 5) poses a limitation, as there were only ten children over the age of sixteen in the first study (five with a special need and five without a special need). The researcher interested in working on the same topic could design a similar study with a larger sample size in order to determine whether the results can be replicated. Research can also be replicated with different populations (gender, age, language, ethnicity), in different service settings (regular foster home, therapeutic foster home, kinship foster home), or in different regions of the country or in different types of community settings (large northeastern urban city as compared to a southern rural town). In this way, prior research on the same topic can inform future research.

Agency Program Evaluation

Another area that provides ideas for potential research topics is agency program evaluations. Within the field of child welfare, there is a strong push for accountability, which has led to a renewed interest in funding evaluation projects. This push has been driven both by internal agency interest and by changes in the federal, state, and local governmental child welfare administrations that oversee the voluntary agencies providing child welfare services. For example, in 1986, Congress amended Title IV-E of the Social Security Act, which provided directives to implement a mandatory reporting system, the Adoption and Foster Care Analysis and Reporting System (ACFARS). In 1993, the Omnibus Budget Reconciliation Act (PL 103-66) provided funding for individual states to develop their own reporting systems, known as the Statewide Automated Child Welfare Information System (Federal Register 1993a, 1993b). The Adoption and Safe Families Act of 1997 (PL 105-89) provided a further push for accountability in the child welfare arena by requiring that the federal government design and implement Child and Family Services Reviews (CFSRs), which provide a report card to Congress on the performance of child welfare services within each state. The CFSRs were established in 2000 and include assessments of state-level child welfare programs in the core domains of safety, permanency, and child and family well-being. With this strong accountability push coming from the federal government, the amount of evaluation underway in local agencies has increased. These evaluations can provide ideas for some interesting research topics. For example, a researcher could review the Child and Family Service Reviews for his or her state in order to determine which areas were identified in the report as in need of improvement. Doing so for New York revealed under the heading of mental health services for children and families that "according to the many participants who contributed to the self assessment, increased and improved mental health services would prevent foster placements, better address the needs of children and youth in foster care, and better prepare children for adoption" (New York State Office of Children and Family Services 2001, 141). With this information, a researcher could convene a team of clinicians in the agency to develop a targeted intervention to address this issue. This could potentially result in a whole program of research focusing on the mental health needs of children and families served by the foster care system, an important and timely issue (Dale, Kendall, and Schultz 1999).

Program evaluations might also be developed in response to the city and state governmental agencies that provide oversight and funding to local child welfare entities. Child welfare services including adoption services are frequently offered by voluntary (nongovernmental) agencies as opposed to state or local governmental agencies. Voluntary agencies offering child welfare services for the government are under contract by the government to provide services and to receive payment for doing so in the form of a per diem rate per child. The contract not only indicates the rate at which a voluntary agency is reimbursed for services rendered to children and families but also stipulates the need for regular evaluations of the agency to ensure that quality services are being offered. Areas in which the agency does not receive top scores could form the basis of an idea for a research study that aims to document the extent of the problem and identify some causal pathways.

Even projects or services that are funded by a private foundation (i.e., a grant) as opposed to the government often require some form of evaluation that provides the funder with assurance that the program is achieving its intended outcomes. These evaluations could be overseen by the researcher and/or be built upon in subsequent studies that aim to enhance and document services delivered and outcomes achieved (see chapter 17 for a detailed discussion of program evaluations).

Accreditation Process

Finally, there is a push within child welfare for agencies to become accredited by national organizations such as the Council on Accreditation (COA) or the Joint Commission on Accreditation of Healthcare Organizations (JCAHO). The actual process of accreditation creates the impetus for a social agency to ensure that its vision, mission, strategic plan, and operating principles correspond to the actual services offered by the agency (Seelig and Pecora 1996). It is important to know the vision and mission, as these will impact the type of research performed at the agency level. Accreditation by either group certainly adds prestige to the agency, as the accreditation indicates that an agency has met standards for management and service provision. Accreditation also generates a good deal of evaluation work within the agency (see chapter 16 and chapter 17 for further details), and with that evaluation many good research ideas can be found.

All of the above mentioned areas offer excellent starting points for the problem formulation phase of a research project. Once the general topic has been formulated, the next step is to ensure that the information gleaned from such a study would in fact be unique and of importance.

Ensuring the Topic Is Unique and of Importance to the Field

Once the general topic has been identified (in this case, adoption disruption), it must be determined that the topic is unique and of importance to the field. This is most easily accomplished through (1) discussion with program and administrative staff within the agency and (2) a review of the existing literature on the topic. As noted in chapters 2 and 4, there is no shortcut from problem formulation to data collection. The following steps must be conducted.

Discussion with Program and Administrative Staff Within the Agency

One important audience and partner for agency-based child welfare research is the agency itself. This means that key personnel within the agency should be involved in the selection of a study topic. These individuals have honed their practice wisdom over years of working in the field and should be consulted at an early stage of problem formulation in order to ensure that they believe that the topic has value. There should be a recognition from them that studying such a problem would help the agency in some way do a better job of serving children and families. In the chapter scenario, it was the caseworker's discussion with colleagues that allowed her to gain confidence in the relevance of the topic beyond her single case experience. Often, staffpersons within an agency attend cross-agency meetings, conferences, and committees (citywide, statewide, and multistate) and have a clearer understanding of what the field in general needs to know. In addition, they may be informed about trends and upcoming systemic changes that would increase or decrease the relevance of a particular topic.

Literature Review

The literature review must be conducted once the general idea has been selected and prior to designing the actual study (Locke, Silverman, and Spirduso 1998). Only in this way can the researcher be assured that what will be learned will be unique and important. The literature review can speak to both of these concerns. Uniqueness can be established by determining what other specific research questions have already been addressed on the selected topic and then developing specific research questions that are fresh in some way (a different population, a different type of program, a different measure of the same construct, and so forth). Importance can be achieved by clarifying what the clinical, research, programmatic, and policy implications of various studies would be and then developing research questions that would produce findings that would have clear and compelling implications for the field.

The literature review is a valuable aspect of any research project (Light and Pillemer 1984). This process reveals to the researcher the current knowledge base about the topic of interest. It will also provide the researcher with potential theories that others have developed to frame their studies. Finally, the literature review highlights potential research designs that could be employed and clarifies design limitations others have encountered while studying the same topic. The literature review will also expand the knowledge base of the researcher about the topic to be studied. Generally speaking, the more a researcher knows about the topic, the better his or her study will be. The literature review, as summarized in the introduction section of the final report or paper, is also the researcher's best argument that the project is scientifically worthy and that the answers to the questions will make a contribution to the scientific knowledge base. After a comprehensive literature review has been conducted, the researcher should have a real sense of mastery of the topic of the research project.

In order to conduct a literature review, access to a library to execute a search of the database system is needed. This can take place on site at the library or off site though an Internet connection to a library's database (if one is on faculty or a current student). It is also important to remember that not all of the material that a researcher will need can be found in published journal articles. Books, government reports, reports prepared by for-profit and not-for-profit research centers, and other materials are all valuable sources of information that a researcher must access in order to obtain the full scope of the literature in the topic area. Therefore, a researcher should plan to spend considerable time in the library to access books, documents, and other materials. In addition, a researcher can usually request articles/ books through interlibrary loan if the material cannot be located in the available library, usually at no cost. Other places to access research are the Web sites of government and research centers. Many government agencies (such as the Children's Bureau) and private research organizations (such as the Chapin Hall Center for Children) provide links to research reports that can be downloaded free of charge. The ease with which a literature review can be performed adds a new level of responsibility to the researcher. Today's researcher has no excuse not to access the extant literature on the topic that he or she wishes to study.

In general, a literature review follows a series of logical steps. First, a search engine must be selected. Useful search engines for child welfare researchers include PsychInfo and Social Work Abstracts. To begin the search, the researcher must select a word or key phrase that identifies the general topic the database should be searched for articles about. Narrowing criteria can also be selected, including publication source (such as a specific journal, or only journals but not books) or date (only for a certain period of time). Using the chapter example, a researcher might begin a search in PsychInfo using the keywords "adoption disruption" and with the date set for the past twenty-five years, to start with the broadest possible reach. Such a search would produce fifty-nine records. The search could also be refined to narrow the results (e.g., using "school" as an additional keyword). If the search returns too few citations (in this case, only twenty-six records were produced), it would be advisable to access all items that were found in the initial search. This search should be repeated with Social Work Abstracts. Once an initial list of articles has been identified, they should be obtained and read. The researcher should make note of all relevant studies referenced in these articles and access them as well. This becomes an iterative process in which sources are found, articles are read, additional sources are found, these are read, additional sources are found, and so on until the researcher has read as many articles as possible on the topic. As the researcher becomes engrossed in the literature, certain authors and specific works will be cited repeatedly, indicating that they are seminal studies within the topic area. Even if these were published more than twenty-five years ago, they should be read and referenced in the final report or paper. In the area of adoption disruption, there are few seminal works, as it is a relatively new area of research, although the topic is currently on the agenda of many child welfare jurisdictions (Barth, Berry, Yoshikami, Goodfield, and Carson 1988). The literature review ends when the researcher believes a solid understanding of the topic has been achieved.

Formulating Research Questions

Assuming that the literature review and discussions with agency staff have confirmed the value of a particular general topic, it is time to move further into the process and begin to define the phenomenon under investigation. The next step is for the researcher to take the general topic (adoption disruption) and formulate some specific research questions. In general, a research question asks a question—as opposed to a topic, which identifies a general area of interest. The research questions can be viewed as an intermediary stage between problem formulation and the arrival at a testable hypothesis; they explicate in more detail the general areas of concern but are not specific enough to compose a statement about expected associations among variables.

Examples of research questions that could be developed from the general topic of adoption disruption include: (1) What proportion of adoptions disrupt? (2) What is the general time frame of adoption disruptions? (3) What are the youth and family characteristics associated with adoption disruption? And (4) what are some of the common responses in children whose adoptions disrupt? These questions represent an explication of, in general, what the researcher wants to know about the topic. Through the development of the research questions, two design issues will be clarified: (1) Will the study entail collection of qualitative data, quantitative data, or both? And (2) is the purpose of the study to describe, explain/predict, or both? Each of these issues is addressed in turn.

Determining a Quantitative and/or Qualitative Approach

The issue of qualitative versus quantitative research has preoccupied the field of social science research for decades. Often researchers will take one "side" or the other as the preferred way to perform a research study (Corbetta 2003). It is proposed here that each has its place in the toolbox of child welfare researchers and that some studies can employ a combination of the two methodologies and data collection strategies.

Quantitative research is best understood as a search for objective description or explanation of events that can be observed and quantified with standardized measures in an, ideally, statistically representative sample. The objective of the data analysis is to explain variance in the dependent variable in order to confirm or refute hypothesized associations. Quantitative research represents the positivist or postpositivist paradigm, in which the world is considered to be independent of the observations of it (Durkheim 1938).

On the other hand, qualitative research aims to understand a phenomenon from the subjective lived perspective of the individual or group in a particular social context, using unstandardized measures in a—usually—nonrepresentative sample. It is understood that the subject is constructing his or her social reality in the context of the study and that the researcher is actively engaged in that process. Theory building and analysis are integrated and ongoing (as opposed to using data to test preexisting hypotheses based on already explicated theory). Data tend to be text rich and are rarely reduced to a simple acontextual numeric format. Qualitative data are analyzed in such a way as to provide the reader with the felt experience of the participants in relation to the topic of the study.

These opposing world views of researchers, objective or subjective, have created a lively discussion especially in the social work literature. For example, Hudson (1978, 65) adamantly argued that "if you cannot measure the client's problem, it does not exist" and "if you cannot measure a client's problem, you cannot treat it." From the opposing point of view, Weick (1987) attempted to change the philosophical orientation of the profession and move it away from the objective model of research. Striking a balance, Hartman (1990, 3) wrote a seminal editorial in the journal *Social Work*, which stated that "there are many truths and there are many ways of knowing. Each discovery contributes to our knowledge, and each way of knowing deepens our understanding and adds another dimension to our view of the world." The discussion and debate among social scientists regarding the most appropriate paradigm continues to this day.

More recently, Corbetta (2003) outlined three positions vis-à-vis whether one approach is better than the other. In the first position, quantitative and qualitative methodologies represent incompatible paradigms (neopositivist versus social constructionist) regarding how one understands the social world. Within this position are people who champion one approach while holding little or no regard for the other. The second position is a preference for the neopositivist perspective without denying the value of the social-constructionist perspective. However, qualitative methods are usually relegated to the exploratory and descriptive stages of research. The third position, ascribed to by Corbetta (2003, 50) himself, "upholds the legitimacy and dignity of each," with the hope that each will be utilized as necessary on a study-by-study basis. He concludes with a metaphor of painting a portrait and the value of multiple perspectives of the same subject (different angles, different distances, different media). "There is no absolute portrait, just as there is no absolute 'true' representation of reality" (Corbetta 2003, 51).

Beyond the philosophical concerns of research, the questions asked in a study in large measure determine the type of data collected. Some questions naturally lend themselves to quantitative data while others are best answered with qualitative data. Questions about quantity, frequency, and duration, for example, are best answered with numeric data. On the other hand, questions about feelings and related subjective experiences are more suited to qualitative data and analyses. Some questions can be answered by either approach. For example, questions about associations among variables can be addressed with statistical analyses conducted to determine whether statistically significant associations are found or by content analysis of an individual's perception of associations. It primarily depends upon the research questions developed by the researcher and other "stakeholders" in the research project, including staff within the agency, colleagues in the field, policymakers, and program developers.

Another factor that will be clarified through the process of developing the research questions is the desired purpose of the study. All research can be divided into the following two primary goals: (1) to describe, and (2) to explain/predict. The specific research questions developed for a study will have implications for these two purposes.

Determining Purpose of Study

The purpose of a study can be to describe a phenomenon or to explain/predict associations among two or more variables. A descriptive study asks about what something looks like as it naturally occurs. No associations among variables are asked about. Examples for the chapter scenario could include: (1) How many adoptions disrupt? (2) What is the timetable of disruptions? And (3) what do the children and families report feeling about the disruption? As can be seen, the data from descriptive studies can be quantitative or qualitative. To answer the first question, quantitative data would be used, probably a frequency distribution of the number of adoptions that disrupted from a total sample of adoptions finalized in a given time period. The second question would also be addressed with quantitative data, in which the length of time between two points is described. For example, the number of weeks or months between placement in the adoptive home and removal from the home (due to disruption) could be charted to see how many times the removal occurred within three months of placement, six months of placement, nine months of placement, and so forth. However, sometimes what needs to be described cannot be understood with quantitative data. For example, if what is of interest is the phenomenological experience of adoption disruption, then it is likely that at least some of the data presented will be qualitative rather than quantitative. The findings would include rich textual statements by the individuals themselves, organized into a thematic structure. The primary distinguishing characteristic of a descriptive study is that associations among variables are not assessed.

On the other hand, some studies have as a stated goal explaining or predicting the association between two or more variables. Examples of possible research questions from the chapter scenario include: (1) Which child characteristics are associated with adoption disruption? And (2) what adoptive parent characteristics are associated with adoption disruption? In both cases, data from two or more variables (such as a characteristic of the child, on the one hand, and whether or not the adoption disrupted, on the other hand) are examined for associations between them.

The difference between explanatory and predictive purposes relate to whether the study is correlational or experimental. In a correlational design, associations between naturally occurring phenomena are examined after they have occurred. The researcher's job is to uncover the associations in an effort to explain the nature of them. In contrast, an experimental (or even quasi-experimental) study aims to manipulate the environment in some way (usually through offering a new program or service) in an effort to create an expected outcome, which is predicted to be the result of the intervention. An example of a correlational study of adoption disruptions would be an examination of whether the age of the child is associated with whether or not an adoption will disrupt. An example of an experimental study of adoption disruption would be an examination of whether additional support for adoptive parents—offered to a randomly selected subgroup of families—is associated with a decrease in disruptions. Typically, quantitative data are utilized to determine whether associations between variables are statistically significant. However, some qualitative data have been used in explanatory/predictive studies. As an example, a group of adoptive parents could be interviewed to determine what child-level factors they believed were associated with the disruption of the adoption.

In sum, once the general research questions have been developed, it will be clear whether qualitative data only, quantitative data only, or a combination of both will be collected in order to answer the questions. It should also be clear whether the purpose of the study is descriptive only, explanatory/predictive only, or a combination of both. In either case, the next step is to formulate the specific hypotheses that will be tested in the study. One way to think about these two dimensions is that they represent a two-by-two matrix in which research questions can be associated with studies that aim to (1) describe with qualitative data, (2) describe with quantitative data, (3) explain/predict with qualitative data, and (4) explain/predict with quantitative data. This is presented in figure 4.1, with examples of research questions on the topic of adoption disruption in the appropriate cells. As can be seen, the same topic can be approached with questions represented by each of the four possible cells, and many studies simultaneously involve more than one purpose or method.

Figure 4.1
Purpose of study crossed with methodological approach

	Qualitative	Quantitative
Describe	What feelings do children whose adoption disrupted report having?	How many adoptions disrupt? How quickly do adoptions disrupt?
Explain/Predict	What do caseworkers believe are the primary factors associated with disrupted adoptions?	Is age of child at placement associated with rate of disruption?

Formulating Hypotheses

The hypotheses represent the specific testable statements about the distribution of a single variable (univariate hypotheses) or about the associations among two or more variables (multivariate hypotheses). Examples of hypotheses for the issue of adoption disruption and school performance could be: (1) fewer than 20 percent of all adoptions will disrupt, (2) youth will experience a decline in school grades as a result of an adoption disruption, (3) youth will experience a decline in their school test scores as a result of an adoption disruption, and (4) youth will experience a decline in their school attendance as a result of an adoption disruption. The univariate hypothesis (hypothesis 1) makes a prediction about the expected distribution of a single variable, while hypotheses 2, 3, and 4 are bi- or multivariate hypotheses, making a prediction about an expected association between two (or more) variables.

Causality

In bivariate or multivariate hypotheses, there is often a presumed causal relationship between two or more variables. In these cases, the presumed causal variable is referred to as the independent variable and the presumed effected variable is referred to as the dependent variable. Causality is a central issue in the field of research methods and is particularly relevant for the development of hypotheses (Kenny 1979). Hypotheses predict associations among variables between which a causal relationship is presumed to exist. However, even when a statistically significant association is revealed between two or more variables, it cannot be concluded that they are actually causally related to each other. It is commonly accepted that a researcher can never definitively establish causality—that one variable (the independent variable) produced the other variable (the dependent variable)—empirically. Causality really only belongs at the level of theory. At the same time, if variation in the independent variable reliably and predictably is followed by variation in the dependent variable—especially when all other possible known causes of the dependent variable have been controlled—then there is strong evidence for a causal association between the two variables. However, at all times, interpretation of significant effects in terms of causality must be made with caution, because it is rare that any single study can make such a claim. It is usually only with the accumulated knowledge developed over a series of related studies that it can be concluded that variation in one variable predictably follows variation in the other variable while controlling all other sources of variation. Every single other possible source of variation may not be known at the time of a study, or ever.

Directionality of Hypotheses

Bi- or multivariate hypotheses can be either nondirectional or directional. Nondirectional hypotheses state that there will be a statistically significant association among the specified variables, but the nature of that association is not stated. As an example, a nondirectional hypothesis related to adoption disruption might be that age is associated with likelihood of adoption. The hypothesis does not make a prediction about whether younger or older children will have more disruptions, just that some association is expected. A nondirectional hypothesis might be proposed in cases where the theory is not fully explicated or in which prior research has produced contradictory findings regarding the possible association between the two variables.

Nondirectional hypotheses are tested with two-tail significance tests. For example, if a correlation was calculated between age of child at placement into adoptive home and time to disruption, it is expected that there will be a statistically significant correlation. It is not stated in advance whether the correlation will be negative (older children take less time to disrupt) or positive (older children take more time to disrupt). A two-tail test of significance with a t-test of an association between child's age and whether or not an adoption

Figure 4.2
Relationship between directionality and alpha level

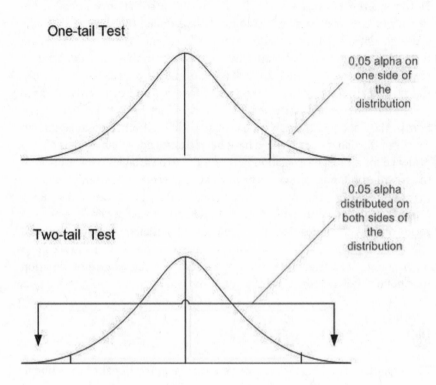

disrupted would test the hypothesis that the mean age of the two groups (those who disrupted and those who did not) will be statistically significantly different, but it is not stated which group will have the higher mean age.

The reason that a nondirectional hypothesis requires a two-tail test of significance is that the researcher is seeking to find an effect at the end of either tail of the distribution, while a directional hypothesis is only seeking an effect at one tail of the distribution. Figure 4.2 presents this pictorially. All statistical tests produce a statistic that represents the size and direction of the effect. A correlation produces an r (either positive or negative), a t-test produces a t (either positive or negative), and so forth. This statistic is plotted against a normal curve in order to determine whether it is statistically significant. The further away from the center of the normal curve, the more likely it is that the statistic is considered significant. With an alpha of .05 and a two-tail test, the statistic needs to be large enough to be in the top 2.5 percent of the normal distribution (2.5 percent on either end of the distribution), but in a one-tail test, in which it is predicted that the effect will be in one direction, the statistic only needs to be in the top 5 percent of the normal distribution (5 percent on the one side of the distribution where an effect is expected). It is obviously easier to be in the top 5 percent than the top 2.5 percent, and thus it is easier to achieve significance with a one-tail test based on a directional hypothesis. However, this also means that if an effect is found in the direction not predicted, the researcher cannot use that finding in the study (except as an interesting note that the hypothesis was not borne out and that, in fact, the association was statistically significant in the opposite direction).

A directional hypothesis, on the other hand, states not only that there will be a statistically significant effect but also in what direction that effect is expected to be found. A one-tail test of significance can be conducted—enhancing the likelihood that an effect will be statistically significant. Thus, when it is possible to do so, it is always better to offer a directional hypothesis. A directional hypothesis using a correlation would state that it is expected that youth at one end of the spectrum on one variable will also be at a particular end of the spectrum on the other variable. For example, a directional hypothesis about the association of age and time to adoption could be that it is expected that older youth have adoptions that take longer to disrupt than adoptions involving younger youth. A directional hypothesis with a t-test would state that it is expected that the mean age of one group (either disrupted or nondisrupted) is expected to be different (either higher or lower) than the mean age of the other group. For example, it is expected that the mean age of the group of youth who disrupted will be statistically significantly higher than the mean age of the youth who did not disrupt. In both directional and nondirectional hypotheses, a relationship is expected between two or more variables. The only difference is whether the nature of the relationship is specified.

Implications of Hypotheses for the Research Endeavor

Once the hypotheses have been developed, many other aspects of the research project will become illuminated. To begin with, the operationalization of the concepts into measurable variables will have to occur in order for the general research topic to be framed as hypotheses. This means that the specific set of variables that need to be measured will be explicated at this point. The hypotheses also generally point to the design of the study, in that the number of groups and the number of testing sessions will become clear. Some hypotheses are framed as a single-sample correlational study, in which data are collected at a single point in time, while other hypotheses require two or more groups and two or more data collection sessions. The hypotheses also provide a general blueprint of the analyses that will need to be conducted to test the hypotheses. Thus the general plan of the entire study is reflected in the hypotheses. The researcher should be aware of this as the hypotheses are developed and should take into account several practical matters in selecting to test some hypotheses rather than others.

Finances

Research is an expensive proposition, with some studies being more expensive than others. Studies that require the collection of many measures in a large sample over several data collection points will usually cost more than a study drawing on existing data or requiring the collection of only a few measures on a small sample at a single point in time. Thus some hypotheses can only be tested in studies that are likely to cost a significant amount of money while other hypotheses can be tested in less costly studies. Therefore, as the hypotheses are being developed, the researcher should have a general idea of the budget for a study and work within that constraint. This may require conversations with agency administrative staff (or the funder of a program that is asking for an evaluation to be conducted) about the fact that certain hypotheses cannot be tested under certain financial conditions.

Timing

Likewise, certain hypotheses imply a longitudinal design with multiple data collection points, while other hypotheses can be tested with data collected at a single point in time. Plans for a longitudinal design need to be consistent with agency staff (and/or funder) expectations. If key agency staffpeople are expecting results within a six-month period, it would not make sense to develop hypotheses that require assessments over a several-year period of time. The hypotheses need to be consistent with the scope and expectations of the staffpeople within the agency with whom the researcher is working. Another timing issue is the need for a literature review and the selection of measures. This effort can take several weeks, if not longer, and should not be forgotten in the development of a timetable. Likewise, if measures such as surveys, interviews, or focus group protocols will be developed, time needs to be allocated for their development, pilot testing, and revision. There is no reason that clinical and administrative staff would be aware of all of the technical and preparatory aspects of research that can slow down the process.

Approval by the IRB

Unless a project meets the criteria for expedited review (only existing data will be used and the confidentiality of the cases can be protected), the study will need to be approved by the agency's institutional review board (IRB). This committee will review the plan for the proposed study, including the hypotheses and proposed design, and will assess it for both scientific merit and its ability to address ethical constraints associated with conducting research with human subjects. Therefore, when developing a study's hypotheses it will be important to consider all of the ethical issues involved in human subjects research to ensure they can be addressed. For example, it would not be permissible to test the hypothesis that families that receive mandated services for adoptive families have fewer disruptions than families who do not receive mandated services, because ethical guidelines prohibit withholding mandated services for research purposes. Likewise, it would not be permissible to test a hypothesis that families who are led to believe that their adoptive child has a history of sexual abuse when he or she does not are more likely to have a disrupted adoption than families who do not believe this about their child, because research with human subjects is not allowed to involve deception, except under very rare situations. Therefore, awareness of all the ethical constraints involved in human subjects research will be a necessary precursor to the development of study hypotheses (see chapter 3).

Endorsement by the Agency

When all is said and done, key agency staff must be comfortable with the hypotheses or they will not support the project. At the extreme, this could mean simply not permitting the researcher to move forward with the research plan or refusing to allow the researcher to publish the findings once the study has been completed. Lack of support could also be more subtle, such as agency staff not doing the kinds of things that could and need to be done to ensure that the research plan can be effectuated (such as providing time for the researcher to conduct the literature review, facilitating access to records if necessary, and providing the researcher with the space and tools to successfully complete the project). For these and many other reasons raised throughout this book, staff within the agency should be a part of the research process, especially during the phase of problem formulation and hypothesis development.

At the end of the day, the researcher wants to have a set of testable hypotheses reflecting the research problem of interest, the answers to which will make a unique contribution to the knowledge base and that staff within the agency have endorsed. At this point, the researcher can turn his or her attention to issues of sampling (chapter 5) and study design (chapter 7).

Conclusion

All research begins with a topic about which someone has formed a research question. Sources of ideas for possible topics to study are plentiful and include the researcher's own experience, prior research, and current events. Once the topic has been selected, a question is formed that identifies the general area of inquiry. From this a set of testable hypotheses are developed. These hypotheses then guide the design of the study.

[5]

Sampling Theory

In this chapter, the following topics will be discussed following the introduction of the chapter scenario and the brief literature review:

- Sampling theory for quantitative data
- Determining sample size
- Identifying the population from which to sample
- Probability sampling strategies
- Nonprobability sampling strategies
- Sampling from administrative data

CHAPTER SCENARIO

A child welfare agency operates a shelter for girls who are pregnant. As a nonsecure facility located in the heart of a major city, the program experiences its share of runaway incidents among its clients. Certain staff members in the program have become concerned about this behavior because they believe that when girls run away, they place themselves and their pregnancies at risk. Staffmembers have shared with the program supervisor that they worry about the girls when they

(continued)

leave the program. The agency decides to conduct a study in order to document exactly how many girls are running away and how many times each one does so over the course of her stay in the shelter.

BRIEF LITERATURE REVIEW: RUNAWAYS FROM TEEN PROGRAM

The extant literature on runaway youth has identified four primary ways in which running away from home may be associated with negative outcomes and experiences. To begin with, adolescents who run away from home have been found to be more likely to engage in high-risk sexual activity, substance abuse, and delinquent behavior than their same-age peers (Allen, Lehman, Green, Lindegren, Onorato, Forrester, and the Field Services Branch 1994; Bailey, Camlin, and Ennett 1998; Rotherman-Borus and Koopman 1991; Rotheram-Borus, Mahler, Koopman, and Langabeer 1996). A second negative outcome of adolescent running away is increased mental health problems such as hypervigilance, anxiety, and a sense of vulnerability (Goodman, Saxe, and Harvey 1991; Kipke, Simon, Montgomery, Unger, and Iverson 1997; Rohr 1996; Rotheram-Borus 1993; Whitbeck, Hoyt, and Bao 2000; Yoder, Hoyt, and Whitbeck 1998). Third, adolescent runaways are more likely to be exposed to higher levels of crime than same-age peers. This occurs through increased proximity to offenders combined with a lack of protective resources (Hoyt, Ryan, and Cauce 1999; Tyler, Hoyt, Whitbeck, and Cauce 2001; Whitbeck et al. 2000; Kipke et al. 1997). Finally, adolescent runaways experience negative developmental outcomes associated with education and health care (Whitbeck et al. 2000). For example, it was found that at least four in ten adolescents who ran away from home did not attend school during the runaway episode (Kurtz, Jarvis, and Kurtz 1991).

Each of these four negative outcomes of running away may be especially problematic if experienced by pregnant teens who have run away from a group care facility, most likely compounding their preexisting vulnerabilities and/or worsening their treatment outcomes. For example, as Kurtz, Jarvis, and Kurtz (1991) argued, adolescents who run away from a group care facility may suffer additional trauma from be-

(continued)

ing "doubly homeless." That is, not only did they run away from home, but they also left the treatment program. As Guest, Baker, and Storaasli (forthcoming) argue, victimization experienced by AWOL shelter youth may trigger post–traumatic stress disorder symptoms from prior abuse histories and threaten the sense of safety the treatment facility is trying to establish. Further, some shelter residents take psychiatric or other types of medication, which require consistent dosage and monitoring of blood levels in order to maintain effectiveness and avoid problems associated with abrupt discontinuation. Such monitoring is not possible while on the run. Similarly, when adolescents are AWOL from a group care facility, their therapy and treatment is interrupted. Going AWOL and the high-risk behaviors adolescents may engage in while away from treatment can also threaten the feasibility of a resident's discharge plans and indicate a need for greater supervision once they are returned to placement. In addition, running away from a group care facility might result in negative feelings on the part of staff, also affecting the quality of care the youth receives upon return. Needless to say, running away while pregnant is likely to put the pregnancy and the fetus at risk for complications and negative outcomes as well. For all these reasons, it is important to identify the factors associated with youth runaway behaviors from treatment facilities in order to develop more effective targeted prevention and intervention efforts.

Overview of the Topic

Research is the search for truth: usually the truth about a particular population. A population is the universe of units to whom the researcher aims to generalize research findings. Examples of child welfare populations include parents in prevention programs, teens in maternity shelters, former foster care youth, and social work interns. However, it is rarely possible to collect data on every member of the population of interest, as the cost and time would be prohibitive (unless the entire population is relatively small and easily accessible). Instead, procedures are utilized in order to identify a subset of the population from whom data will be collected. This subset is known as the sample. When sampling strategies are properly implemented, inferences about the population can be made based on the data collected from the sample. There are two primary sampling strategies: probability and nonprobability. In probability sampling, the entire population can be identified in advance, and from a list of members of the population (the sampling frame) a sample can be selected in such a way that each member of the population has an equal probability of being selected into the sample. By doing so, it is highly likely that the sample will resemble the population sufficiently to allow for inferences about the population to be made from the sample. When the members of the population (or a subset thereof) cannot be identified in advance (i.e., there is no known sampling frame), a variety of nonprobability sampling strategies can be used. With certain caveats, researchers can still make inferences about the population from nonprobability samples, albeit with less precision. In all cases where statistical inferences will be made, sample size should be calculated in advance by determining the statistical significance level, the power, and the desired effect size of the results of the study.

Sampling Theory for Quantitative Data

In any population, there is variation on the dimension of interest. Using the chapter scenario, there is variation in the number of times teens run away from a maternity shelter. For example, using a hypothetical population of one thousand pregnant teens in a maternity shelter, the distribution of the number of times a teen ran away can be examined. Table 5.1 presents the frequency distribution of number of times teens ran away in this hypothetical population. In this hypothetical population, one teen did not run away at all, two teens ran away one time each, eight teens ran away two times, and, at the other end of the spectrum, one teen ran away 24 times. If the entire population of 1,000 clients could be measured on this variable, the mean would be found to be 12 runaway episodes per teen. However, if a sample of teens is selected from the population of 1,000, it is likely that the mean number of times that the sample ran away would not be exactly 12.0, as it is in the population. In fact, if multiple samples were drawn from this population, the mean for each sample would vary. Using the hypothetical dataset, 10 random samples of 50 cases each were drawn, which produced the following 10 sample means: 12.6, 11.4, 12.9, 11.9, 12.5, 11.8, 12.6, 11.3, 11.6, and 10.8. Not one of these means is exactly the same as the population mean, although all are close.

When researchers collect quantitative data from a sample, what they really want to know is how close the population mean is to the sample mean. If the sample was randomly selected from the population, statistical infer-

Table 5.1
Frequency distribution of number of runaway episodes of teens in a maternity shelter

	N	%
0	01	0.1
1	02	0.2
2	08	0.8
3	12	1.2
4	20	2.0
5	30	3.0
6	40	4.0
7	45	4.5
8	50	5.0
9	60	6.0
10	80	8.0
11	97	9.7
12	110	11.0
13	100	10.0
14	77	7.7
15	60	6.0
16	50	5.0
17	45	4.5
18	40	4.0
19	30	3.0
20	20	2.0
21	12	1.2
22	08	0.8
23	02	0.2
24	01	0.1
Total	1000	100%

ences can be made about the population from the sample data. Using the sample mean as a starting point, the researcher can conclude with a certain degree of certainty (usually 95%) that the population mean is the same as the sample mean plus or minus the error associated with sampling. Thus, for the first random sample selected from the population, the mean was 12.6. It can be concluded with 95% confidence that the population mean is 12.6 plus or minus the sampling error. Figure 5.1 presents the formula for calculating sampling error.

Figure 5.1
Formula for calculating sampling error

Z (sd/√n)

Terms:

Z=level of confidence. If 95%, z=1.96; if 98%, z=2.58

S=standard deviation of the variable in the sample

N=sample size

Using the hypothetical sample of 50 cases in which the mean was 12.6 runaway episodes and the standard deviation was 4.0 episodes, figure 5.2 makes a calculation of sampling error. It can be concluded with 95% certainty that the population mean is 12.6 runaway episodes plus or minus 1.1, thus, between 11.5 and 13.7. If 98% certainty is desired, z would be set at 2.58 instead of 1.96. This would result in a sampling error of 1.46 instead of 1.1. Thus, one could conclude with 98% confidence that the population mean is 12.6 runaway episodes plus or minus 1.46, that is, between 11.14 and 14.0 runaway episodes. The greater the confidence (from 95% to 98% certainty), the larger the range is around the estimated mean (from 1.1 sampling error to 1.46 sampling error).

One way to increase the precision in the estimate of the population mean—without reducing the degree of confidence—is to increase the sample size. Using the same data as above but with a sample of 100 instead of a sample of 50, the sampling error would be .78 instead of 1.1, and it could be concluded with 95% confidence that the population mean is between 11.82

Figure 5.2
Calculation of sampling error: 50 cases, mean of 12.6,
standard deviation of 4.0

Sampling error   =1.96 (4.0/√ 50)

Sampling error   =1.96 (4.0/7.07)

Sampling error   =1.96 (.57)

Sampling error   =1.1

and 13.38. The bracket (confidence interval) around the estimate of the population mean decreases as the sample size increases.

Because sample size affects the likelihood of detecting statistical effects, it is important in designing a study to determine in advance how large the sample should be. As noted above, the larger the sample is, the more precise the estimates of the population statistics from the sample statistics are. If the goal of the study is to estimate parameters in the population based on the sample, the larger the sample, the closer the estimate of the population can be to the sample. In the example above, doubling the sample from 50 to 100 increased the precision with which the population mean could be estimated from a range of 1.1 points to .78 points (the smaller the range, the greater the precision).

However, typically researchers in the field of child welfare want to do more than estimate population means. Testing for relationships between measured variables in the sample is often the primary interest. For example, using the chapter scenario about teens in a maternity shelter, perhaps researchers want to determine whether the age of the girls or the number of weeks pregnant the girls are at entry to the shelter is associated with the number of runaway episodes. Perhaps the focus is on determining whether programs in urban settings have higher runaway rates among clients than programs in rural settings. It also might be of interest to ask whether girls with prior child welfare histories have higher runaway rates than girls entering the shelter from outside the child welfare system. In these scenarios, the focus is not on estimating population means but on determining whether relationships exist among the variables being measured in the sample. Sample size is extremely important here as well. A simple rule is: the larger the better. However, real-life budgetary and time constraints and limits in the availability of clients in child welfare programs to participate in research often means that samples should not be any larger than they need to be. Thus it is critical to calculate the necessary sample size in advance in order to ensure that the sample of the study is large enough to detect relationships among variables should they actually exist but not unnecessarily large so as to place an undue burden on the program or the researcher. This is a necessary but complicated undertaking (Kraemer and Thiemann, 1987).

Determining Sample Size

Two factors affect the calculation of sample size: (1) level of statistical significance/power and (2) size of effect.

Level of Statistical Significance/Power

In every study that examines the association between two (or more) variables, a statistic is calculated (such as t, f, r, X^2) that determines whether associations can be said to exist between the variables. If associations between the variables are found to exist, the null hypothesis, which states that no relationship exists, can be rejected. If no associations between the variables are found to exist, then the null hypothesis is not rejected.

Two results of a statistical test in a sample are possible: (1) it is concluded that an association exists, or (2) it is concluded that an association does not exist. At the same time, there are two possible truths in the population: (1) there really is no association between the variables, or (2) there really is an association between the variables. Thus, each research study results in one of four possible conclusions about observed associations in the sample studied: (A) the conclusion that there is an association (reject the null hypothesis) when there really is no association (the null hypothesis is true), (B) the conclusion that there is no association (accept the null hypothesis) when there really is no association (null hypothesis is true), (C) the conclusion that there is an association (reject the null hypothesis) when there is an association (null hypothesis is false), and (D) the conclusion that there is no association (accept the null hypothesis) when there is an association (null hypothesis is false). In two of these options (B and C), the correct conclusion was made, and in the other two options (A and D), an erroneous conclusion was made. Figure 5.3 depicts the relationship between these four possible outcomes and the types of scientific error associated with them.

Power represents the balance between Type I and Type II errors and can be thought of as the strength of a study to detect true effects if they exist; that is, to not make a Type II error. Type II error is represented by the bottom right cell in figure 5.3 and occurs when a researcher concludes that an association does not exist (accepts the null hypothesis) when an association really does exist (the null hypothesis should be rejected). For example, in a study of the association between prior child welfare histories and runaway rates, a t-test is conducted to compare mean runaway rates for two groups of girls: those with and those without a prior child welfare history. If the t statistic is 1.81, the probability of this size statistic occurring by chance is seven times in a hundred (p<.07). This does not meet the predetermined alpha level of .05 and thus the hypothesis of a relationship between prior child welfare history and runaway rates is rejected. It is not concluded that girls with prior child welfare histories have higher runaway rates than girls with-

Figure 5.3
Type I and Type II errors

	Reject null hypothesis	Accept null hypothesis
Null hypothesis is true	A: Type I error	B: Correct decision
Null hypothesis is false	C: Correct decision	D: Type II error

out such histories. If in fact there really were an association between prior child welfare history and runaway rates in the population, a Type II error would have been made. The convention in the field is to set the likelihood of Type II error (called beta) at no more than 20 times in a 100 (beta=.20). The power of a study is calculated as 1−beta. Thus, when beta=.20, the power of a study is said to be .80.

Type I error is represented in the top left cell of figure 5.3 and occurs when a researcher concludes that an association exists when one does not. Take for example the study of association between prior child welfare history of youth and number of times youth ran away. A hypothetical t statistic of 1.97 has a probability of occurring 5 times in 100 by chance (p<.05). The mean number of runaway episodes for the girls with prior welfare histories is 12.5, while for the girls without child welfare histories the mean is 10.7. Thus, it can be concluded with 95% confidence that in the population being studied girls with prior child welfare histories have higher runaway rates than girls without prior child welfare histories. The likelihood of concluding this when it is not true is only 5 times in 100. But if in fact there really were no association between prior child welfare history and runaway rates, then concluding that there is one entails a Type I error.

Setting alpha (the likelihood of making a Type I error) at .05 is the convention in social science. That is, the researcher should be able to conclude with 95 percent confidence that an association does exist, that is, that such a size statistic would only be found five times in one hundred by chance. That is, if one hundred versions of the same study were conducted and there really were no association between two variables, then that size statistic would be produced in only five of the one hundred studies. With an alpha level of .05, the researcher can have 95 percent confidence that the findings were not due to chance. (One exception to the .05 convention pertains to conducting multiple tests in the same study. If several tests are being run and the alpha remains at .05, the likelihood of a Type I error increases. Methods for reducing Type I error when calculating multiple tests are discussed in chapter 14.)

Most computer-generated statistical printouts provide information about the level of statistical significance of every test calculated. One need only review the output to determine whether the statistical test meets the alpha level. It must be remembered, however, that the formula for determining statistical significance is strongly affected by sample size. For example, in a study of age at intake to a maternity shelter and number of runaway episodes, a correlation of $r=.25$ in a sample of 25 girls would not be statistically significant, while in a sample of 125 girls a correlation of the same size would be. And in a sample of 1,000, a correlation as small as $r=.06$ would be statistically significant at an alpha of .05. In large-sample studies, almost all statistical tests will be statistically significant. At the other end of the extreme are small sample studies in which some effects might be quite large but not statistically significant. For example, in a sample of 25, a correlation of $r=.39$ would not be statistically significant. If a definition of meaningful is used, then the researcher can decide to attend to such a finding even if it is not statistically significant (perhaps as something to be considered in the future with larger samples).

For this reason, researchers need to guard against treating all statistically significant effects as if they were meaningful and ignoring all effects that are not statistically significant. One way to avoid this common pitfall is to decide in advance what size of effect will be considered meaningful.

Effect Size

Meaningfulness is a concept developed to determine whether a statistical effect should be considered as having importance. Cohen's (1969) seminal work on effect size is still considered the standard in the field. He proposed that an effect size of .20 should be considered small, an effect size of .50 moderate, and an effect size of .80 large. These standards are still used today, with two caveats. The first is that in some fields of research or in studies with a particular measure the conventions might be different. Researchers should be familiar with their field of study and the particular measures being utilized in order to gauge the effect size normative for that area of study, if such a standard can be determined. Second, the meaning of meaningfulness changes depending upon the context. For example, if the effect signifies lives saved at no risk or no cost, then a much smaller effect size would be considered meaningful. In general, an effect of .50 is considered mean-ingful and is a respectable goal if no other information is available to esti-mate the effect size in advance.

Calculating Sample Size

Once the power, alpha level, and desired effect size have been determined, these numbers can be entered into the formula presented in figure 5.4 for calculating the necessary sample size. Take as an example a study of two groups of girls in teen maternity shelters, some of whom have prior child welfare histories and some of whom do not. If the following parameters are applied, the sample size can be determined as seen in figure 5.5. The desired sample size is 63 girls in each group, for a total sample size of 126 girls. A shortcut to remember is that the numerator of the formula will al-ways be 15.68 (which can be rounded to 16) for the conditions of .80 power with alpha of .05. Thus, a shortcut to the formula for sample size for each group is $16/d^2$. If there is a one-group study, such as a correlational design in which the sample cannot be grouped based on their belonging to one or another category of the independent variable, then the results of the calcu-lation should be doubled for the total sample size needed. Table 5.2 pres-ents the required sample sizes under varying conditions of statistical significance, confidence, power, and desired effect size.

As can be seen in table 5.2, when confidence increases from 95% to 98% (and alpha decreases from .05 to .01), the required sample size increases. For example, under the same conditions of alpha=.05, power=.80, and effect size=.20, the sample necessary increases from 400 to 585 when the confidence increases from 95% to 98%. It can also be seen that when the desired power increases from .80 to .90 so does the necessary sample size.

Figure 5.4
Formula for calculating sample size

$$\frac{2\,(Z\acute{\alpha}+Z\beta)^2}{\dfrac{(M_1 - M_2)\,2}{\sigma}} = \frac{16}{d^2}$$

Figure 5.5
Calculation of sample size

Alpha=.05

Beta=.20

Z for alpha=1.96

Z for beta=.84

Power=.80 $(1-\beta)$

Desired effect size (d)=.50

Sample size= $\dfrac{2\,(1.96+.84\,)^2}{50^2}$

Sample size=15.68 / .25

Sample size=63 per group

Under the same condition of 95% confidence/alpha=.05 and effect size=.50, the required sample increases from 63 per group to 84 per group. Increasing the estimated effect size, however, decreases the required sample (as smaller samples are needed to detect large effects). Thus, a .20 effect size with 95% confidence and .80 power requires a sample of 400, while the same conditions with a .80 effect size requires a sample of only 25 per group.

It is also important to remember that this calculation produces the size of the needed sample on whom data will be collected, not the size of the sample to be invited to participate in the study. If surveys are being mailed, individuals are being invited to participate in a program, or records are being found to be coded, it should be assumed that there will be some loss of the sample size due to refusal to participate, inability to find the person/record, and so forth. Once the desired sample size is determined, then the sample can be selected, taking into account some loss of size. Experience is the best judge of how many extra cases to select to be in the sample due to potential loss. An excellent text to further a researcher's knowledge of sampling is *Applied Sampling* (Sudman 1976).

Table 5.2

Required sample sizes under varying power, effect size, and confidence intervals

Confidence	Power	Alpha	Z alpha	Beta	Z beta	D	N per group
95%	.80	.05	1.96	.20	.84	.20	400
95%	.90	.05	1.96	.10	1.29	.20	528
98%	.80	.01	2.58	.20	.84	.20	584
98%	.90	.01	2.58	.10	1.29	.20	749
95%	.80	.05	1.96	.20	.84	.50	63
95%	.90	.05	1.96	.10	1.29	.50	84
98%	.80	.01	2.58	.20	.84	.50	93
98%	.90	.01	2.58	.10	1.29	.50	119
95%	.80	.05	1.96	.20	.84	.80	25
95%	.90	.05	1.96	.10	1.29	.80	33
98%	.80	.01	2.58	.20	.84	.80	37
98%	.90	.01	2.58	.20	1.29	.80	47

Identifying the Population from Which to Sample

The first step in any study is to identify with as much precision as possible the population of interest (see chapter 4 for more discussion of this). In doing so, it is important to remember that the population is composed of units. If the research question is "do case records document runaway episodes in teens residing in a maternity shelter?" then the unit is the record, and the data collection would focus on whether the record documents runaway episodes (regardless of whether someone actually ran away). If the question is how many or why girls run away, then the girls represent the unit of analysis. If the question pertains to program factors such as staff opinions, then the staffperson is the unit of analysis. If the research question pertains to program characteristics such as size or location, then the program is the unit of analysis. It is important to clarify what the unit of analysis is in order to determine what the population is (all records, all staff, all programs, all girls, and so forth).

Once the unit of analysis has been determined, the population can be identified and a plan implemented for selecting a subset of the population from whom to collect data. These data can then be used to draw inferences about the population. Using the chapter example, if the unit of analysis is the girls themselves, it must be asked whether the agency wishes to understand runaway behavior in the current group of girls being served at one agency's teen maternity shelter or whether the agency is interested in knowing more generally about the population of girls that tend to be served in this kind of program over time. Even broader, it is possible that the agency wishes to learn about girls served in teen maternity shelters in urban locations (as runaway behaviors may vary by rural/urbanicity) or perhaps about runaway behaviors in all teen maternity shelters across the country or throughout the world. The first option can be ruled out as too narrow to be of interest. Most research aims to understand something about a population as opposed to a particular group of people in a particular program at a particular point in time. Likewise, the last option is too broad to be feasible for an agency-based study, as it would involve multistate or multinational data collection efforts. Typically, research generated within an agency is geared toward learning something about the types of individuals who tend to be served in its programs and similar ones.

Thus, it is most likely that the population of interest would be girls served in an agency's—and similar agencies'—teen maternity shelters. However, it is possible that even this population is too large to include in a single study (every participant in every similar program). For this reason, a subset of the population is used in the study and serves as a stand-in for the whole population. If sampling is implemented correctly, a researcher can collect data on a subset of the population and use that information to generalize the findings to the whole population, in order to be able to say something of interest to the field.

The most important feature of the sample, therefore, is that it is representative of the population to which generalizations will be made. For example, if the population of teens in maternity shelters in New York City tends to be on average sixteen years of age, then the sample should be on average sixteen years of age. The reason for this is that if age affects the phenomenon under investigation (older youth are more likely to run away or have different reasons for running away), then studying a sample that differs from the population on this important variable will mean that the findings from the study can probably not be used to make generalizations about the population. There are several strategies for selecting a sample representative of the population.

Probability Sample Selection Procedures

Probability sampling represents the ideal, as every member of the population has an equal chance of being selected into the sample. This is achieved through random selection. There are several versions of random sampling. What they have in common is that the researcher has access to a list of every individual in the population (the sampling frame) and uses a random selection process to identify those members of the population who will be in the sample. In many cases, the sampling frame is a close approximation but not an exact replica of the population. For example, if the population comprised every teen who entered a maternity shelter during a particular period of time, it is possible that if such a list were compiled from each agency's roster of clients or from a city listing there would be some error on the list (some names might be included although they never actually participated in the program, some names might be misspelled or duplicated, and so forth). Nonetheless, random selection from the sampling frame represents the best chance of creating a representative sample.

Single-Stage Simple Random Selection

A simple random selection procedure can be used to select a subset of the sampling frame in such a way that each unit on the list has an equal probability of being selected. There are at least three ways to do this. If the sampling frame comprises about one hundred units or less and the list is written on paper (not in a computer file), then each name on the list can be separated from the other names by cutting little strips of paper with the names on it. Each piece of paper with one name on it should be placed into a container. The researcher should select from that container—one at a time—as many pieces of paper as corresponds to the number of people in the desired sample. It is important to select them one at a time so that each piece of paper has the same chance of being selected as every other piece of paper.

The second method of random selection is advisable in situations where the list of members of the sampling frame consists of well over one hundred units/names written on a piece of paper (not in a computer file). Clearly, it would be too time consuming to cut up all the little strips of paper for random selection from a container. A table of random numbers can be used to identify those members of the sampling frame that will be in the sample. A table of random numbers is a compilation of single- and multidigit integer numbers whose frequency and sequence of occurrence have been determined entirely by chance. Table 5.3 presents a sample table of random numbers.

The first step in using the table of random numbers is to determine the size of the sampling frame and assign a unique number to each unit/name

Planning and Developing Research Studies

Table 5.3

Table of random numbers

10385	75110	61726	54021	98637	72631	14147	75121	94512	01602
04351	47573	46157	18729	57389	89198	56132	44381	11965	45095
44331	28068	56129	78567	13678	64809	56812	12519	49450	67881
54162	30067	44432	15789	78953	16376	76404	67813	74541	71304
65510	02275	11463	16653	75211	91782	56781	76183	16684	60172
00161	14707	88047	64531	76318	67451	16471	34513	89655	14893
84165	62300	32160	86749	98872	11456	50814	60123	15813	33440
26501	12967	89457	78461	18876	45671	58595	56860	69564	58875
49379	05339	34906	74631	74553	53781	61740	14830	25121	89016
65371	53837	57381	00756	53060	67813	17867	56137	12558	56812
34118	35174	67428	32567	70997	31249	52735	77812	43906	68316
56541	90401	11639	15106	49626	76545	23581	89395	16540	69012
90439	54469	19644	86014	88974	33478	56156	14577	35605	57832
30545	54129	87531	67481	48237	56735	08909	76394	15911	56712
25139	79136	11048	90731	77233	12149	60124	40156	77685	85977

on the sampling frame. For example, if the sampling frame comprises a list of all 359 girls in one city's maternity shelter programs on a given day, then one number between 1 and 359 should be assigned to each name on the list. The order of the items on the list is of no consequence. As the total sampling frame comprises 359 names, three-digit numbers from the table of random numbers will be used. Each number randomly selected from the table should represent an individual in the sampling frame that can be selected into the sample. Take as an example a situation in which there are 359 girls currently in one of the city's teen maternity shelters and it has been determined that the sample for a study of these girls should consist of one hundred girls. A number from the table is selected at random and the last three digits of the number are used to select the first case from the population. For example, if the random number selected is 75211, the last three digits (211) could be used, and the name on the list that corresponds to 211 would be the first person selected into the sample. Using the table of random numbers horizontally or vertically, the last three digits of the next number would identify the next person selected for inclusion in the sample.

A third method of simple random selection can be used if the list of individuals in the population is available in an SPSS data file (or other statistical software, or can be converted into an SPSS data file from an Excel spread-sheet or Access database). The sequence of commands in SPSS for selecting a random sample from a list is as follows: (1) choose the "data" tab, (2) choose "select cases" from the drop-down menu options, (3) click the circle by the option "random," (4) click on the "sample" tab, then (5) choose either the "approximately" or the "exactly" option. In the "approximately" option, type in the percentage of cases that should be selected, then click on the "ok" tab and then click on the "ok" tab again to initiate the process. For example, if it is known that 15 percent of a sample is of interest, then "15" would be typed in and then "ok" would be clicked twice to select 15 percent of the population. If the "exactly" option is selected, then two numbers are required: (1) the number of cases to be selected and (2) the total number from which to select from, such as twenty cases from the first hundred. The option is always to select from the top of the list unless the full list is used. For example, if the list contains 359 names of girls and the sample-size cal-culations have determined that a final sample of 130 girls is needed, the command would be to select 130 from the first 359 cases.

Single-Stage Systematic Random Sampling

In systematic random sampling, the sampling frame consists of a list (prob-ably on paper, otherwise a computer program would be used to employ a simple random selection) of units/names. In this procedure, the total sam-ple frame (say, 500 girls) is divided by the desired sample size (say 100) to produce a number (500/100=5) that is then used to guide the systematic se-lection of units from the list. Using the list of 500 names as an example, it is determined that if every fifth name is selected from the sampling frame, then the total sample will be the desired size of 100. The final step is to ran-domly select a number between 1 and 500 from which to begin the selection process. For example, if the number 123 is randomly selected, then the 123rd name on the list is the starting point, and every fifth name is selected from there, until 100 names are selected. A drawback of systematic random selec-tion is that if the order of the list is not random to begin with, then the final sample will not be a probability sample. For example, if the list of names is in alphabetical order, then siblings will be next to each on the list and once the first sibling has been selected the second sibling has no chance of being selected. However, in a true random selection, once one sibling is selected the second sibling has the same chance of being selected as every other name on the list not yet selected.

Single-Stage Stratified Random Sampling

In stratified random selection, the final sample is created in order to ensure that it has the same proportions on a key variable as the sampling frame. For example, if the sampling frame consists of girls in a teen maternity shelter and the known ratio of girls already within to those not within the child welfare system is known to be 80:20, it is likely that with a simple random selection process the sample would be different on this variable (due to chance in the selection process). If it is important that the final sample be close to 80 percent and 20 percent on this variable, then the selection process can be designed to produce the desired result. The sampling frame can be divided into two groups (those entering the shelter from a child welfare program and those not). From the group with prior child welfare histories, 80 percent of the desired sample size can be selected, and from the second list of girls with no prior child welfare history, 20 percent of the final sample can be selected. By way of example, if the desired sample is 200 cases, 160 can be selected from the first list (80%) and 40 (20%) can be selected from the second.

Multistage Probability Sampling

In multistage probability sampling, a sampling frame is not available from which to select the sample. However, it is possible through consecutive stages to create a sampling frame of a subset of the population. The classic example is based on area clustering. If the goal is to sample former foster care youth living in a certain city, all of the neighborhoods of a city can be listed, a subset of which can be randomly selected. From this list of selected neighborhoods, it will be possible to list all of the residential units. A subset of the residential units is then randomly selected and each one is canvassed to identify which contain former foster care youth. From this list, a random selection of study participants can be made.

Response Error in Random Selection

Response error occurs when not every randomly selected case actually participates in the study. Some selected cases are not included due to failure to contact the case (the record is missing, the individual moved, the program is too costly or inconvenient to reach) or due to refusal of the individual to participate once reached. In both instances, the sample's representativeness can be compromised. For example, if the government agency provides the researcher with a list of all teens in city maternity shelters and the researcher uses a table of random numbers to select twenty-five girls to be in the study but only fifteen participate (five refused to participate and five could not be reached after several visits and calls to their residence), it is quite likely that the fifteen who chose to participate will vary from the population in ways that make the sample no longer representative. Random selection works perfectly only in cases where (almost) every unit that is selected is actually included in the study (such as when files are being selected to be reviewed). When individual people represent the unit of analysis, participation rates can affect the size and representativeness of the sample. One strategy for dealing with this is to collect some data even on those who decline to participate and then compare the decliners to the participators. If there are no differences (assuming the sample size is large enough to detect such differences), then the researcher can have greater confidence that the random selection process did in fact produce a representative sample. If there are ways in which the sample is different than the known population, then these variables should be used as statistical covariates in all analyses. Alternatively, cases in the actual sample can be weighted to bring it back into alignment with the population.

Nonprobability Sampling Strategies

Obviously, the procedures described above for random selection are only feasible if the researcher has access to the sampling frame—or some portion of it—from which to select a sample. This is not always the case in child welfare research. Using the chapter scenario, it is not likely that the city (or other agencies) will provide a list of all program participants in teen shelters throughout the city. Fortunately, there are viable strategies for planning research in the absence of random selection.

Convenience Samples

Convenience samples consist of members of the population who are selected into the sample based on their easy access and availability. Examples include a study of clients in one's own agency, people who are selected from postings on the Internet, or clients at agencies that happen to belong to the same larger group. What these strategies share is that the sampling frame is not identified in advance and that members of the population are selected in such a way that it is not likely that each member has an equal chance of being selected. However, if the argument can be made that collecting data on such a convenience sample would produce a sample that is—in all important ways—representative of the population, then there is no need to identify the known population prior to collecting data. Thus, if one can reasonably conclude that the sample is representative of the population, then one can proceed with generalizing the findings of the research to the population. In order to make this case, one needs to know something about the population to which generalizations will be made. For example, if a list of all youth in a city's teen maternity shelter cannot be obtained, knowledge of the referral system could be used to argue that the sample in any one agency is comparable to the sample across all agencies. If, for example, the city makes referrals to agencies on a random basis, then the sample in any one agency would be comparable (in theory) to the population. If there is published data available (city reports, published studies) describing the population, that data can be used also to argue that a sample is comparable to the population.

One complicating factor in child welfare research is when the program itself changes the variable of interest. For example, if the focus of a study is the beliefs and attitudes of girls in a maternity shelter about running away, and all the girls in one agency's maternity program are interviewed or surveyed during their first week of being in the program, it is likely that what is learned from this sample can be applied to the population of such teens in other programs as well. However, over time the program itself may change the girls' ideas about running away and their inclination to actually run away. These factors—unless they are identical across programs—may decrease the likelihood that the findings will be applicable to other agencies. In such situations, it probably makes sense to collect data early in the girls' stay in the program to reduce the impact of the program on their beliefs.

Purposive Sampling

A departure from random and convenience sampling is to select cases (individuals, programs, records) not because they are likely to be representative of the population but because they will be particularly illustrative of a phenomenon of interest or likely to produce data that are particularly rich in detail. For example, teens with histories of extensive running-away behaviors might be selected to participate in a focus group or in-depth interviewing in order to understand the factors—from their perspective—that account for their behavior. They may have the most to say about the pressure to run away or the ways in which the program failed to prevent their behavior. Likewise, if certain teen shelters are known to have problems with high rates of running away, then they could be selected as the site of case studies, field observations, or interviews. Purposive sampling does not aim to produce a representative sample and in no way can data collected from such a sample be used to make generalizations about the population in full. At best, generalizations can be made about the population of particular interest (i.e., girls with high running-away rates).

Quota Sampling

This is a variation on purposive sampling. Instead of aiming to identify cases at one extreme end of the sample for analysis, the aim is to identify a certain number of cases (programs, records, clients) that represent a range of positions on the variable of interest. For example, a program with a high runaway rate and a program with a low runaway rate could be invited to participate in a case study. Likewise, interviews would be conducted with a sample of girls known to be repeat runners and a sample of girls who have never run away in order to identify the important areas of difference between the two groups. Such a study is more likely to function as a hypothesis-generating study rather than an hypothesis-testing study. For example, in such a study several factors might appear to differentiate youth with high runaway rates from youth with low runaway rates. The next step would be to test out these differences using standardized measures and a representative sample that included youth with both high and low runaway rates. Additionally, an intervention could be developed that aims to change the girls on the dimension identified to differentiate the two groups. However, at no time can generalizations be made to the population as a whole from a quota sample, as the sample is by definition not representative of the population.

Snowball Sampling

This technique is used when a hard-to-find population is of interest (such as teen prostitutes, criminals, illegal immigrants, and so forth). Snowball sampling is what Denzin (1989) terms "interactive sampling," meaning that the sample is drawn from people who know one another in the same social network. In this procedure, one informant is found and asked to identify additional possible members of the group to be included in the study. If each participant identifies at least one additional participant, eventually a sufficient sample will be developed. There will be no way to determine whether the sample is representative of the population because it is quite likely that there is a certain segment that remains unknown even to other members of the group (those who operate outside the social network).

Sampling Cases in Child Welfare Agency Databases

A special case of sampling applies to working in a child welfare agency in which there is an administrative database from which cases can be drawn for a retrospective study (the events have already happened). Many important questions for a child welfare agency can be answered using available administrative data, including questions about the length of stay of children and families in various programs, the proportion of children discharged home/reunified, the number of children who have foster home disruptions, and so forth. Assuming that the data from a single agency will be of use to the field or that the study is only being conducted for internal agency purposes, the next step is to construct the sampling frame. In many cases, every member of the sampling frame can be included in the study (when no data collection in required, there is no need to limit the sample size). There are three possible means of identifying the sampling frame: point-in-time cohort, exit cohort, and entry cohort.

Selecting the Sampling Frame

POINT-IN-TIME COHORT

In this sampling strategy, everyone in care on a certain day (at a certain point in time) is considered to be "in the study." This might include all 654 cases in care in an agency's foster home program, 315 cases in an agency's residential treatment center, or ten girls in an agency's maternity shelter. This seemingly simple approach carries several drawbacks. First, while data collected on such a sample provides information about the current census and thus is timely, every member of the sample will still be in care and, therefore, the data is subject to change. For example, if the focus of the research is number of runaway episodes, individuals still in care at the time of data collection might run away again in the future, thus adding to the total number of runaway episodes in the population. Thus, a point-in-time sample can only provide information about what has occurred in the sample as of the date of data collection, recognizing that as each day passes the data may change as new runaway episodes occur. A second drawback is that point-in-time samples are particularly unhelpful for studying length of stay, not just because everyone in the sample will stay longer but because this sampling strategy overrepresents youth with long stays (Wulczyn 1996). Finally, defining "in care" will need to be thought through. For example, are youth who are on trial discharge, on AWOL status, or on vacation/in the hospital to be included in the study or not? There is not necessarily a right or wrong approach, but decisions will have to be made.

EXIT COHORT

In exit cohort sampling, all youth who were discharged from the agency within a certain time period (on a given day, within a certain month, during a quarter or year) are included in the study. This is particularly helpful for learning about why staff leave an agency or for learning about client attitudes and feelings about leaving the agency (as it is fresh in their mind), but exit cohort sampling is not advisable for learning about behaviors such as running away or length of stay. An exit cohort is likely to overrepresent short-stayers (as more leave within a year than long-stayers) and thus is not representative of the population (Wulczyn 1996). Another limitation with exit cohort sampling is that clients enter the program at different points in time and thus might have experienced different staff or programmatic features within the program. Some clients in an exit sample may have entered the program within the prior month (those with one-month stays), while others in the sample might have entered the program several years ago (those with multiyear stays). Therefore, generalizations based on exit cohorts are problematic.

ENTRY COHORTS

In light of the limitations associated with exit and point-in-time sampling, entry cohort sampling is considered to be the most appropriate for studying length of stay as well as behaviors that can occur over the course of a client's stay in a program. Using the chapter example, in an entry cohort all girls who enter the agency's teen maternity shelter within a specified time period (a day, a month, a quarter, a year) will be included in the sample. When possible, time periods should be organized by calendar or fiscal year for ease of interpretation of the data (that is, results will say something about everyone who entered the program within the same calendar year). It is also important to start the cohort far enough back in time that the vast majority of girls have been discharged from the program, so that the total number of events of interest can be counted. At the same time, one should not use data that is too old, in the event that historical changes have occurred in the agency (e.g., new director of the program, change in structure of program, change in population served), because then the data collected will no longer be relevant. Determining what the time period should be is based on desired sample size and the length of typical stays in the program. In programs with typically short stays (such as a weekend respite program for developmentally delayed adults, a short-term shelter for runaway teens, a crisis nursery for mothers at risk of abusing their children), the time period can begin as recently as six months prior, as everyone who entered six months ago will have left already. For programs with longer stays (foster homes, group homes, residential treatment centers), the time period should begin at least three years prior, as most likely at least half the sample will have left already. It is not necessary for everyone to have left (especially with studies of length of stay where only half of the sample needs to have been discharged).

Defining Admission and Discharge

Once the sampling strategy has been selected and the specific time frame has been identified, the researcher will still need to define with specific detail what constitutes an admission and what constitutes a discharge.

DEFINING ADMISSION

Agency administrative databases usually identify the date that a client entered the agency. Obviously, those cases admitted to the agency from outside the agency during the time period of interest should be included in the sampling frame. If the agency only offers one specific program, then all admissions to the agency will coincide with all admissions to the program of interest and the definition of admission is complete. However, many child welfare agencies offer more than one program (foster homes, group homes, diagnostic reception centers, and so forth), and the study may focus only on clients in a specific program within the specified time period. For example, the research may aim to understand a client's experience in a particular program, such as the number of times youth run away from the maternity shelter, length of stay in a residential treatment center, or number of times youth are hospitalized while in a group home. Selecting a sample based upon admission to the agency would include some clients who belonged in the sample but would also result in two types of sampling errors.

The first type of error is that the sample would include some clients who did not belong because they were admitted to the agency in the time frame of interest but did not enter the program of interest until later. For example, a youth might have been admitted to an agency's residential treatment center during the sampling time frame (January 1, 2003, through December 31, 2003) but did not enter the program of interest (maternity shelter) until after the sampling frame (say, in February 2004). This client should not be included in the study but would be if all admissions during 2003 were included.

The second type of sampling error that would result from using "admissions" is that some youth who should be in the sample would be excluded because they were admitted to the agency prior to the sampling frame but did in fact enter the program during the sampling frame. For example, a youth was admitted to the agency in 2001 (prior to the sampling frame), into a group home program, and moved to the maternity shelter in March 2003 (during the sampling frame). Selecting the cohort based on admissions in 2003 would exclude this youth, who really does belong in the study.

In order to avoid these two sampling errors, the researcher will need to work with the information technology/data management department of the agency in order to determine how to identify the appropriate cases. Typically, the database will have to be queried with a multistage series of commands that selects exactly the sample of interest.

Another conceptual issue to be thought through is how to handle cases that had been in the program of interest prior to the time period of interest, left the program, and then returned during the time period of interest. For example, suppose that admission to the maternity shelter in calendar year 2003 is of interest and a youth was admitted in 2001, then left on trial discharge from December 2002 through February 2003, and then came back to the maternity shelter in February 2003. Does this move to the program constitute "entering" the program in calendar year 2003 or is it a continuation of a stay that actually began in 2001? One rule to follow is that if the departure was in the form of a final discharge, then any return should count as a new admission. However, if the departure was for a trial discharge (a situation in which the agency is still considered responsible for the youth but the youth is living outside the agency on a trial basis to determine whether the current discharge plan is viable) or move to a foster home that did not work out, then length of time away from the program should be taken into consideration. In one study (Baker, Wulczyn, and Dale 2005), six months away from a program was considered the cutoff. Thus, a youth who was admitted to the program prior to the sampling time frame, left the program not on final discharge, and came back in less than six months was not considered as entering the program and therefore was not included in the study. A youth who was in the program, left for more than six months, and came back during the time period of interest was included in the study. There are no hard and fast rules about this, so discussion with agency staff and thorough knowledge of the conventions in the field should be used as guides. Describing these decision rules in the paper or report will be very important. These decision rules constitute the inclusion and exclusion criteria for the study.

DEFINING DISCHARGE

Defining discharge from the program will also entail some consideration. Discharge could be defined as final discharge only, trial and/or final discharge out of the program, transfer to another agency, and, in some cases, a move to another setting within the same level of care (from one group home to another or from one foster home to another). The purpose of the study should help guide these decision rules. For example, if the focus of a study is on foster home disruption, then a move from one foster home to any other residence other than reunification should count as disruption, while if the focus is on the length of stay in foster care, moves from one foster home to another should not be considered relevant.

A timeframe needs to be considered in defining discharge as well, because some youth who leave a program return; thus, rules will need to be developed to determine how long a youth should have to be away from the program for it to count as the end of the stay. For example, if length of stay in a residential treatment center is the focus and a youth moves from the center to a foster home and only stays there one day and then returns to the center, that probably should not count as the end of the stay. The youth should have to stay out of the center for a predetermined length of time in order to consider that as the end of the stay. Using the same timeframes for defining discharge as were used for defining admission probably makes sense.

An additional discharge issue needs to be resolved, one that relates to events that occur on one date but result in an official decision to consider the youth discharged on a much later date. This can occur when a youth runs away from an agency's program for six months or more and is eventually considered "discharged to AWOL status." This decision date can occur as much as six months after the youth has left the agency. The same holds true for trial discharges. The youth might have left the program on trial discharge on a certain date and six or more months later the youth is considered to be final discharged. In each case, the researcher will need to develop a consistent rule determining whether the last date the youth was in care counts as the end of a stay or whether the date the discharge decision was made should be considered the end-of-stay date. Previous research has used the date the child left (Guest, Baker, and Storaasli, forthcoming).

Conclusion

Sampling is the procedure by which the researcher selects from the population of interest a subset to participate in a study. If the selection process follows certain guidelines, inferences can be made about the population based on the data collected in the sample. Using agency administrative data holds special promise for the agency-based child welfare researcher but poses special challenges in terms of sampling. The most important issue for the researcher is defining the decision rules, uniformly applying the decision rules, and explaining the decision rules (and any limitations to them) in the final report/paper. Using administrative data is discussed in greater detail in chapter 8.

PART 2

Design Strategies

[6]

Single-System Design

In this chapter the following topics will be discussed:

- Deciding when to use a single-system design
- Identifying the system
- Articulating and implementing the treatment
- Selecting a design
- Collecting data
- Analyzing the data
- Writing the report

CHAPTER SCENARIO

A caseworker is providing standard casework practice to children in a large city's child welfare agency that provides child protection, prevention, and foster care services. Her primary goals are to help children and families adjust to foster care placements and work with biological families to expedite reunification with their children. The caseworker employs an eclectic mix of approaches in order to help children adjust

(continued)

to their placement and learn better coping skills so that foster home disruption can be avoided and reunification achieved. Over time, the caseworker notices that many of the children in the program are exhibiting severe emotional disturbances that appear to be related to the abuse and neglect that led to their placement in out-of-home care.

The caseworker recently attended a training conference on abuse-specific treatment for children in foster care and wonders whether this is an approach that should be integrated into casework practice. This becomes the question for a single system–design study and a case that represents a good candidate for abuse-specific treatment is identified.

BRIEF LITERATURE REVIEW:
ABUSE-SPECIFIC TREATMENT FOR YOUTH IN FOSTER CARE

The vast majority of youth served in the United States foster care system have been removed from their homes due to abuse and neglect. Given the trauma of the separation from their family coupled with a history of maltreatment, it is unsurprising that foster care youth have elevated rates of mental health problems (e.g., dosReis, Zito, Safer, and Soeken 2001). High rates of emotional and behavioral disorders have been documented among foster care youth, including depression, anxiety, and aggression (Clausen, Landsverk, Ganger, Chadwick, and Litrownik 1998).

Despite the overwhelming need, mental health services are not routinely available to children in the foster care system. According to a recent Federal Child and Family Service Review (CFSR), most states failed to meet the psychological and behavioral treatment needs of child abuse and neglect victims (Huber and Grimm 2004). The child welfare system is mandated to first and foremost ensure children's safety and, whenever possible, preserve families. Child welfare workers assess the safety of children, provide in-home services to preserve families, and remove children from their home when their safety cannot be assured. Once in the "system," caseworkers work toward permanency, ideally with the biological family but also with an eye toward

(continued)

adoption or independent living in the event that the biological family cannot safely care for the child (known as concurrent planning).

Addressing the mental health and emotional problems of youth in the system is conceptually related to safety and permanency yet in reality is left to the discretion of child welfare agencies (working in coordination with state and city regulations and expectations). Outside the core mandate, the provision of mental health services is cobbled together by each foster care agency, using a mix of in-patient care when necessary, in-house providers when on staff at an agency, and referrals to community-based clinics.

Even when receiving treatment, foster care youth may be at a disadvantage in not receiving the most up-to-date treatment modalities, such as abuse-specific treatment. Abuse-specific treatment is based on theory and clinical experience regarding the impact of various forms of abuse on social, emotional, and cognitive functioning over the course of an individual's development. Examples of abuse-specific mental health treatment include models developed by Herman (1997), Kolko (1996), Pearce and Pezzot-Pearce (1997), Urquiza and Winn (1994), and Deblinger and Heflin (1996), as well as the integrated model developed by Friedrich (2002), which is based on the core concepts in the field of developmental psychopathology (Cicchetti 1984; Rutter and Sroufe 2000). In Friedrich's model, the therapist aims to promote the abused child's feelings of security and to help the child develop emotion regulation and an accurate self-perception. These models share an acknowledgement that developing rapport with the abused child is particularly challenging because issues of trust and betrayal are paramount, and they also share the recognition that early abuse affects memory and information processing in such a way as to cause emotion dysregulation and distorted relational styles (Perry 2000). Also common is a planned incremental exposure to and discussion of the abuse event(s) in the context of the therapeutic relationship as a way of integrating the memories and making new meaning of the experience. In addition, issues of repression, denial, and self-hatred may be exhibited as a means of avoiding the painful reality of the abuse. Regardless of the specific model favored, there is consensus in the field that abuse-specific treatment is the best option for maltreated children. In this framework, the foster care child's processing

(continued)

of the abuse is a necessary step toward learning new relational and coping styles that would ideally result in reduction of symptoms, which is necessary for achieving stabilization of placement and, ultimately, permanency, either through reunification or adoption.

Unfortunately, foster care youth may not actually be receiving abuse-specific treatment. In fact, Friedrich (2002, 143) concluded that most abused children receive mental health services by therapists who may not "appreciate the unique and differential impacts of physical and sexual abuse, have little broad-based clinical training, and are not aware of empirically validated treatment techniques."

Overview

The single-system design (SSD) is a set of empirical procedures used to observe change in an identified target following a specific intervention (Bloom, Fischer, and Orme 2003). It is a quasi-experimental research method that measures the impact of an independent variable on a dependent variable. In child welfare, a SSD study typically examines the effects of an intervention or treatment (such as casework practice) on a single case. In most SSD studies there is an assessment of the case at baseline, an administration of a time-limited intervention, and an assessment of the case following the removal or completion of the treatment. In an SSD in child welfare, the independent variable is usually a program or model of casework and the dependent variable is a measure of casework success, typically a measure of family functioning. When possible, standardized measurements are made at multiple points at baseline and at post-testing in order to allow for a visual inspection of change in the family or child's functioning or performance of the case over time. This methodology bridges the worlds of casework practice and research by allowing practitioners to systematically observe and monitor a single case in order to make an informed and objective conclusion regarding the impact of the casework (Gibbs 1991).

SSD has two hallmark features. The first is that there is one only one system under analysis (a system could be an individual, a family, a program), and the second is that measurement of the dependent variable is repeated over the course of the study in order to establish a stable baseline and to measure change following the treatment. The acceptance of SSD as a research method has been increasing over the years as graduate and undergraduate programs have begun to teach SSD as part of their research curriculum.

Deciding When to Use Single-System Design

Child welfare is in the midst of creating its own research knowledge base to demonstrate its credibility as a profession and to remain accountable to its many funding sources, typically, a government entity that provides the funding to continue providing child welfare services (Wells 2006). The issue of accountability in human services is important because funding sources, consumers, practitioners, and policymakers would like to know if the services provided to children and families are effective and worth continuing. The National Association of Social Workers has made part of its code of ethics both the evaluation of one's own practice and the review of the literature to keep abreast of new knowledge to enhance practice (NASW 1999). However, these types of questions about overall service effectiveness tend to involve aggregate-level views of the service provided (i.e., group designs) to demonstrate effectiveness. But what happens at the practitioner level? How can individual practitioners (e.g., therapists, caseworkers) know if the services they provide are effective for a particular family or if they should be altered to improve service delivery?

SSDs are ideally suited for situations in which a therapist, caseworker, and/or administrator wants to determine with quantitative data whether improvements have been made in a single case in response to a targeted intervention. An SSD study can be implemented with almost any intervention model as long as the model and goals of the intervention are clear and measurable. SSD can be performed on one client or on a series of clients. When performed on a number of clients receiving the same services, the results can be aggregated to allow for inferences about the replicability of the treatment for different families and in different contexts. SSD also allows practice knowledge to be built and recorded for future use. Practice wisdom, or learned practice, is an important part of casework, and having the ability to record the effectiveness of specific practices is one component of establishing and sharing this wisdom. Thus, SSD not only has the ability to improve practice outcomes for a specific case but also contributes to the development of a knowledge base for practice in child welfare that is accessible to other clinicians and caseworkers as well. SSD can be employed not only to gain valuable insight into the issues that families present, but to bring research methodology and rigor to the front line of child welfare practice. In this way, SSD offers a way to join practice, such as casework practice, and research.

Prior to SSD, the standard method for assessing casework practice was the qualitative methodologies of a case study or a case history, both of which generally produce rich, descriptive, contextual qualitative data that can be difficult to summarize, interpret, and replicate. In addition, in neither case studies nor case histories are reference groups available to indicate that change occurred in response to a specific intervention. SSD methodology was developed for just this purpose, and as a method of assessing casework practice it has much to recommend it.

In particular, there are many advantages of SSD in comparison to group designs, which also utilize quantitative data to assess the effectiveness of various treatments. Traditionally, group research methods have been employed, as they allow the researcher to understand the impact of one treatment (say a model of casework) over another treatment (i.e., does the enhanced model perform better in terms of outcomes for clients than the usual method of service already in place at the agency?). However, group designs may not always be the method of choice in child welfare agencies. For several reasons, SSD may be preferable.

One advantage of SSD is that data are collected and available on an ongoing basis and can be shared with clients and used as a component of supervision with the caseworker as the case unfolds. A related benefit is that in SSD, data are available at the case level. In contrast, in group designs, the results are in aggregate form and not available as an individual result. Individual caseworkers, whose cases are included in a group design study, would only be able to learn whether the treatment was effective programwide. They would not have access to individual case data and thus would have no information about practice outcomes for specific cases.

Another advantage to SSD is that it provides objective evidence to the client and the agency staff about the improvements (or lack thereof) of a particular case. For example, it might appear to a family or to the caseworker that no improvements are being made, but examination of the SSD data might reveal otherwise. Thus, SSD has the ability to objectively clarify the actual, as opposed to perceived, changes in a case. Likewise, a caseworker might falsely believe that a client is improving while the data do not support such claims. Examination of the data from an SSD might identify for the caseworker the need to change the direction of casework practice.

Thus the most transparent benefit of the use of SSD is its ability to guide and/or improve casework practice on a case-by-case basis. In this respect, SSD stands in contrast to longitudinal group designs that are administered over time such that results are only available after all of the data have been collected and analyzed. Often, this is too late to have an impact on any single case. The SSD provides research data that is immediately available to the caseworker and other decision makers on the team.

Another advantage pertains to cost. Group methods are expensive to plan and implement. Often participants are paid for participation in data collection. Many measures need to be purchased from the author or publisher. Research assistants are hired and trained to collect data. Staffpeople are sometimes needed to oversee the logistics of data collection and analysis (e.g., tracking subjects, copying multiple measures, entering data). An SSD study, on the other hand, incurs minimal if any cost. Typically, the sample is a single client and thus all the costs associated with managing a large-scale sample are eliminated.

Group designs can also be difficult and time consuming to plan and implement. Often, a caseworker aims to understand the impact of an intervention but lacks training in conducting large-scale studies and access to a researcher with such training. In such a scenario, SSD is clearly the preferred method.

Another advantage of SSD over group designs is that the ethical and logistical constraints involved with a "no-treatment" group are eliminated. In a child welfare agency that is charged with the protection of children, there are some services that simply cannot be withheld from clients (which would be necessary for certain group designs). In an SSD study, the case itself serves as a control.

Another impediment to group design for a caseworker is the need to analyze the results with inferential statistics. In many graduate social science programs, students learn how to be "informed consumers" of research as opposed to learning how to select and utilize a range of advanced statistical approaches. As a result, the level of statistical understanding may be limited or lost over time due to lack of use. A potential result in this scenario is that the information learned from a group design, although sound in terms of method and statistics, may not be presented in a context readily accessible for a caseworker to take advantage of and integrate into practice. SSD allows the caseworker to conduct the entire study without the aid of a trained researcher.

Despite these many advantages, there certainly are instances in child welfare practice and research when SSD may not be practical or advisable to implement. To begin with, some cases require immediate attention and there is simply no time for the collection of baseline data prior to implementation of the treatment or intervention. In cases where risk of abuse or neglect is imminent, the needs of the child and family take precedence over data collection and research.

A second limitation is that the family may not agree to participate. However, this only poses a problem when the data collected for the study are over and above whatever data are collected routinely for casework practice. That is, if the SSD entails data collection from a child's classroom teacher, the parent (and perhaps the child, depending upon age) will need to sign an informed consent agreeing to the data collection plan.

The other limitation related to SSD is the difficulty in generalizing the results. One successful SSD project is clearly not sufficient to conclude that a casework model is effective—beyond its effectiveness with that particular case. The results of one SSD relate solely to that one case. In order to "build" generalizability, multiple SSDs must be implemented with the same intervention and the same measures. If the data are consistent across several cases, knowledge can be built to increase the generalizability of the data to inform child welfare practice more generally.

Identifying the System

Single-system design (Bloom, Fischer, and Orme 2003) is a research design involving one system ($N = 1$). The system, or unit of analysis, can be a child, a family, a group, an agency; in fact, just about anything could be the focus of an SSD as long there is only one system and the data are collected on that system as the "unit of analysis." A typical scenario for implementing SSD in a child welfare setting is one in which the unit of analysis is a single case and the goal is to determine whether casework practice is effective for that case. In this context, casework refers to the mechanism employed in child welfare to help ensure that children and families remain safe from abuse and neglect. In the chapter scenario, the system is a foster care child with mental health problems who will receive abuse-specific casework.

Articulating and Implementing the Treatment

In order to conduct an SSD study, the treatment being evaluated must be fully articulated in order to ensure that (a) the treatment was implemented as planned and (b) specific measurable goals and outcomes can be identified. Using the chapter scenario, the model of casework being implemented could be an intensive abuse-specific module of treatment aimed at enhancing child-family functioning in order to reduce the likelihood of placement disruption due to the child's emotional and behavioral problems. The intervention model should be clearly specified (what happens during each session, length of program, and so forth), as should the specific outcomes (enhanced family functioning, maintaining the child in the foster home until reunification is feasible).

However, if a caseworker is not using a defined model of practice, this phase will push the caseworker to clearly define his or her goals for the case. This can be an intimidating task for a caseworker who is not used to thinking about measurement. At times, a caseworker might feel that his or her casework results are too complex and subtle to be amenable to a research project. This is certainly a consideration, but with the need to demonstrate positive outcomes, this phase is an important aspect of the research project and cannot be overlooked. Clearly, the more structured a casework model, the easier it becomes to implement an SSD. Conversely, the less structured a casework model, the more complex it becomes to implement an SSD.

In addition, with an SSD, it is vital to administer a single intervention at a time. For example, if a child welfare caseworker administers a variety of casework methods, there will be no way of determining which casework method or model was successful and which was not. The point of SSD is to link a specific casework model to measurable improvement. In addition, the casework model that is introduced must have clear and precise interventions (so the casework model can be replicated if found to be successful) that can be implemented across families with consistency. To that end, an SSD is an experiment, and so the casework setting and caseworker should be consistent throughout the life of the SSD project. As the casework selection needs to be clearly defined, utilization of this design by caseworkers who do not use a manualized model of treatment has been modest (Nelson 1981).

Determining the Design

In SSD, as in group designs, there are many variations in the timing of data collection. In SSD, the notations of "A" and "B" are used to delineate different design phases. "A" refers to no treatment and "B" refers to treatment.

The basic SSD follows an A-B model in which A is the assessment of baseline functioning when no specific casework intervention is provided. In the chapter scenario, when a child first exhibits emotional and behavioral problems, an assessment period begins and several child and family assessments are administered to establish their baseline functioning. This is the

A phase of the design. Then the B phase begins, in which the intervention is provided. Once the intervention is complete, there are additional measures of functioning. In this respect, the data collection follows the classic OXO of the one-group pre-test and post-test design as discussed in chapter 7. The A and B refer to the phases of treatment (no treatment followed by treatment), whereas the OXO refers to the timing of data collection and implementation of an intervention (pre-test, treatment, post-test).

There are other models of SSD available to the caseworker. In an ABA design, there is a pretreatment phase during which initial baseline data are collected. This is followed by the implementation of the treatment (in this case casework practice). The last A in this design refers to the withdrawal of the casework practice (reverting back to a no-treatment condition) in order to investigate whether the family maintains functioning independent of casework.

A further modification is the ABAB, design in which the treatment is administered, withdrawn, and then readministered. The same treatment could be administered a second time in order to determine whether it is effective in a second dose. Alternatively, a second treatment could be administered in order to determine its effect on the case following the first treatment. Using the chapter scenario as an example, the caseworker might have noticed that many of the youth coming into the program are at risk for placement disruption but also have significant educational deficits. In order to work with both issues, an ABAB model is utilized. First is the no-treatment condition A, in which baseline data are collected. Casework is implemented in order to prevent placement disruption (B). Casework is then withdrawn (A) and a second set of treatment activities are introduced (B), in order to address the educational performance of the youth. An ABAB single-system design employs the positive results of the primary goal (prevent placement disruption) in order to build on the successful completion of a secondary goal (improved educational attainment).

These are the basic SSD model choices amenable to child welfare settings. There are several other designs that have been well documented (Bloom, Fischer, and Orme 2003). In general, the more complex the SSD, the stronger the validity of the study.

Collecting Data

Typically in an SSD project, measurement of the key outcome/construct of interest is made at several points prior to the administration of the intervention and at several points following the intervention. The multiple measures prior to the treatment allow for the determination of a more stable pretreatment baseline functioning. Multiple measures following the treatment allow for identification of subtle changes over time that can be visually recognizable. Ideally, an established scale will be employed to add reliability and validity to the project. Chapter 9 outlines the many benefits of using a measure that has been demonstrated in prior studies to be reliable and valid for the population in question. However, if there is no established scale to use to measure the outcome of the SSD, a measure can be developed for the specific study. This adds flexibility to the study. If a measure needs to be developed for the purpose of the study, at a minimum face validity can be established by showing the draft of the measure to key stakeholders (the family, other caseworkers, etc.) in order to obtain feedback about improving the measure.

One measure that has gained acceptance in the field of child welfare and that is ideally suited for SSD is the North Carolina Family Assessment Scale or NCFAS (Kirk, Kim, and Griffith 2005). The NCFAS was specially designed by research practitioners and state policymakers to evaluate the effectiveness of family preservation models or models that primarily prevent placement into foster care. The measure could also be used for assessing family functioning in other contexts as well. The NCFAS measures the family along the following five domains: environment, social support, family interaction, family/caregiver characteristics, and child well-being. Both reliability and validity have been established for the NCFAS (Reed-Ashcraft, Kirk, and Fraser 2001).

In order to control for threats to internal validity, the NCFAS is administered at the beginning stages of the assessment and then reviewed and updated for the next two weeks so that a valid baseline can be established. Barlow and Hersen (1973) argue that at a minimum three separate measurements should be taken of the dependent variable in an SSD study in order to establish a valid baseline. The NCFAS, due to its robust nature and the "built-in" ability to adjust the ratings as new material surfaces (Kirk, Kim, and Griffith 2005), can achieve a solid baseline. At the end of the treatment phase, the NCFAS is implemented again one to two weeks after the end of the casework cycle. In this example, there is a baseline and a post-test taken on the dependent variable—family functioning—to gauge the improvement of child and family functioning based on program participation. There could also be another post-testing some time later, after the program has ended, in order to assess whether program effects held up after removal or completion of the program.

Analyzing the Data

Data from an SSD can be analyzed via visual inspection or advanced statistical techniques. It is recommended here that visual inspection be utilized, as the software necessary for SSD is not typically available to the caseworker (or even many seasoned researchers). To determine if a model of casework is effective using visual inspection of the data, the data collection points are plotted on a graph, with a clear indication of the introduction of the treatment. Ideally, there will be a visually recognizable improvement in scores between the multiple baseline assessments and the multiple post-treatment testing assessments.

When using the NCFAS, scores are available on five scales ranging from -3 (serious problem) to +2 (clear strength), with 0 indicating that a domain is adequate. The baseline can be determined to demonstrate one of four possible forms: unstable, decreasing, increasing, or stable. If the baseline is unstable, the graph of the scores across the multiple baseline measurements will be erratic, with a combination of high points and low points across the multiple assessments taken prior to treatment. A decreasing baseline can indicate that the client's condition (i.e., family functioning) is worsening on its own over time prior to treatment. An increasing baseline indicates an improvement in the client's condition (i.e., family functioning) even prior to the treatment. Finally, the baseline data can indicate a stable pattern of behavior (consistent across the multiple assessments prior to treatment). Figure 6.1 presents an example of unstable baseline data. The unstable baseline indicates that family functioning is inconsistent prior to treatment. As casework is introduced, the points on the graph increase and cross over the 0 point, indicating that family functioning has improved during casework intervention.

The form that the baseline takes can also help determine if the proposed model of casework is appropriate. Using the chapter example, families with foster children who have severe emotional and behavioral problems can present with any of the four baseline readings. A family with a decreasing baseline (i.e., decreasing family functioning) can hopefully change course once the abuse-specific intervention has begun. A family with a stable baseline (i.e., a stable pattern of family functioning) may be a good candidate for a new model of casework, as improvement could be observable based on the stable baseline. A family that has an increasing baseline (i.e., improved family functioning) without the benefit of a new model of casework may not need services, as the family seems to be improving without any modifications in casework practice.

Figure 6.1
NCFAS AB design data (hypothetical)

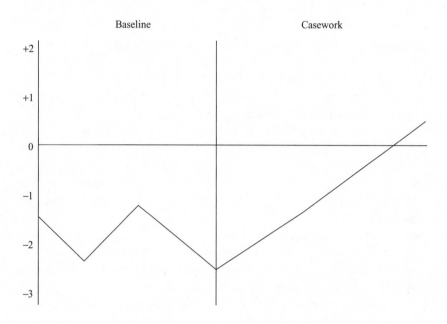

Unfortunately for the caseworker, families that come to the attention of supervisors as needing a novel approach because they are currently not doing well may have unstable baseline readings due to the very event (increasing behavioral problems of the youth that are jeopardizing placement) that brought them to the attention of the caseworker. This is unfortunate, as it makes it more difficult to discern an identifiable improvement from baseline to post-treatment assessments. One option proposed by Barlow and Hersen (1984) is to prolong the baseline recording period to achieve a more stable baseline.

In such a scenario, a caseworker can define success of the case as therapeutic significance (TS); that is, did the client achieve the goals set out in the casework plan? In the chapter example, a family with a child at risk for placement improves to the point that a local child protective case can be closed. The caseworker can conclude that the case achieved therapeutic significance even if the unstable baseline precludes more systematic analysis of the case.

Additionally, TS can be concluded to have occurred in the event of some level of goal attainment even when there is less than 100 percent achievement. For example, in a foster home, the child's behavior and/or the family functioning can be seen to improve somewhat but the placement may still be viewed as at risk and needing respite or additional services in order to prevent disruption. These mixed results can be considered to have therapeutic significance.

Alternatively, the caseworker could employ advanced statistical techniques in order to detect improvement from an unstable baseline to post-treatment assessments (such effects might be discernable with statistics although they are not visually apparent on the chart). However, the need for statistics may deter caseworkers from using SSD methodology. If statistics are utilized, statistical significance (SS) is sought, meaning that a conclusion about the case is made based on the results of statistical analyses that detect subtle changes that may not be visually observable but are in fact significant at the $p < .05$ level.

With these different definitions of significance (therapeutic, statistical), the caseworker may have a statistically significant result even though the client does not appear to the caseworker to have changed at all. In child welfare, it is recommended that the caseworker rely on visual inspection to analyze the results of casework practice as opposed to implementing a statistical analysis. Caseworkers are trained in their profession, providing casework services and accessing the literature to improve their casework practice; they are not necessarily trained to perform statistics. There are researchers who have developed advanced statistical techniques for SSD studies (see Bloom, Fischer, and Orme 2003) and there are computer applications that can produce graphs as well as statistics for SSD (see Conboy, Auerbach, Schnall, and Laporte 2000), but these go beyond the scope of this chapter.

Report Writing

After the project is completed and the data have been analyzed, the results of the project are written up in such a way as to be accessible to other caseworkers as well as other interested parties, such as program directors in the agency. The main focus of SSD is to inform practice at the casework level. Additionally, in a larger project, the data collected can be written up for the agency as well as for publication. Once data are published about a specific casework model with a specific population, child welfare can then begin to build on its existing knowledge base by documenting casework practice that is effective.

Conclusion

A single-system design study is an appropriate option for situations in which the goal is to document on a case-by-case basis improvement of an individual system as a result of the implementation of a highly specified and replicable intervention. The quantitative results are immediately available to both the caseworker and the client and can shed light on and provide feedback about progress made. SSD can allow for the integration of practice with research in order to determine which treatments or interventions produce the best results as well as building a knowledge base for the profession (Kirk and Reid 2002).

[7]

Group Designs

In this chapter, the following topics will be discussed following the introduction of the chapter scenario and the brief literature review:

- Correlational designs
- Quasi-experimental and experimental designs
- Threats to internal validity
- Components of the data collection session

CHAPTER SCENARIO

A child welfare agency operates a series of group homes for adolescents who are in out-of-home placement. A recent death of a teen in another agency due to drug-related causes has increased awareness throughout the system about the problem of substance use and abuse among group home youth. In response, an agency receives a grant from the city's child welfare administration to conduct a study of the problem within its various group homes. The agency asks the director of research to plan such a study. The researcher puts together a team

(continued)

of agency staff to develop the research questions for the project. The following questions are identified: (1) What proportion of youth meet the criteria for having a substance abuse disorder? (2) What youth characteristics, if any, are associated with having such a disorder? And (3) what programmatic characteristics, if any, are associated with youth having a substance abuse disorder? The agency also decides to develop a peer-based intervention for reducing substance abuse and aims to evaluate the effectiveness of the intervention. Thus, the final question of the project is: (4) Do youth who receive the intervention reduce their substance use?

BRIEF LITERATURE REVIEW: SUBSTANCE USE AND ABUSE IN GROUP HOME YOUTH

Substance abuse among adolescents is a longstanding concern of practitioners and policymakers. This concern is based, in part, on the magnitude of the problem. In 2004, researchers found that almost 11 percent of adolescents, or over two million youth, between the ages of twelve and seventeen used substances in the previous month, not including alcohol and cigarettes (Office of Applied Studies 2005b, table 1.28B). The concern over adolescent substance use also grows out of awareness of the negative short- and long-term consequences associated with the use of alcohol and illicit drugs in teens. Teens who use substances are at heightened risk for involvement with the criminal justice system (Guy, Smith, and Bentler 1994). They are also more likely to drop out of school and/or not complete a GED (Krohn, Lizotte, and Perez 1997; McCluskey, Krohn, Lizotte, and Rodriguez 2002). They have been found to be more likely to engage in sexually risky behaviors that may lead to sexually transmitted diseases, HIV/AIDS, and unintended and unwanted pregnancies (Guo, Chung, Hill, Hawkins, Catalano, and Abbott 2002; Krohn et al. 1997; Tapert, Aarons, Sedlar, and Brown 2001).

In response to the severity of this problem, researchers have focused on identifying risk and protective factors for substance use in

(continued)

adolescents. Factors found that heighten the risk of teen substance abuse include low educational attainment and aspirations (Bryant and Zimmerman 2002; Diego, Field, and Sanders 2003; Hawkins, Catalano, and Miller 1992; Newcomb and Felix-Ortiz 1992), a history of victimization and abuse (Edmond, Auslander, Elze, McMillen, and Thompson 2002; Kilpatrick, Acierno, Saunders, Resnick, Best, and Schnurr 2000; Perez 2000), and several "milieu" factors such as perceived and/or actual use of substances by family members (Andrews, Hops, Ary, Tildesley, and Harris 1993; Hawkins et al. 1992; Kilpatrick et al. 2000; Newcomb and Felix-Ortiz 1992), perceived support for substance use by peers (Bryant and Zimmerman 2002; Hawkins et al. 1992; Newcomb and Felix-Ortiz 1992; Wills, Resko, Ainette, and Mendoza 2004; Rodgers-Farmer 2000), and availability of substances (Hawkins, Catalano, and Miller 1992; Newcomb and Felix-Ortiz 1992; Office of Applied Studies 2004).

Adolescents in the child welfare system have many of these risk factors. Therefore it is not surprising that they have been found to be more likely than same-age peers to use substances during adolescence and more likely than other young adults to be drug dependent during their lifetime. For example, a report from the National Survey on Drug Use and Health (Office of Applied Studies 2005a) found that one-third of youth with prior child welfare histories had used illicit drugs, compared to one in five youth with no child welfare experience. Likewise, Pecora et al. (2005) found that among former foster care youth, substance abuse was five times as likely as in adults who had not been in child welfare.

Despite the severity of the problem, not enough is known about the specific factors associated with substance use among group home teens. Especially understudied is the impact of specific "milieu" factors such as the attitudes and behaviors of the peers and staff in the group home program.

Overview

The design of a study explicates what constructs will be measured, when and by whom, in order to obtain data that can answer the study's questions. As noted throughout this book, every study entails the measurement of con-

structs, either to describe the phenomenon or to assess associations between two or more constructs. Which constructs are of interest in any given
study is determined by the research questions. Once the constructs have
been identified, they are operationalized. That is, exactly what manifestation of each construct will be measured is determined, and then appropriate
measures of the constructs are selected (see chapter 9). The next step is
to determine when the data will be collected. The timing of data collection
provides the structure—or design—of the study. There are two main design options for collecting quantitative data: (1) within-group correlational
designs and (2) between-group designs that are either experimental or
quasi-experimental.

Correlational Designs

In a correlational study, both the independent and dependent variables are
naturally occurring and are measured on a single sample, usually during a
single data collection session. There is no manipulation of variables and no
classification of individuals into a treatment group and a no-treatment group.
Using the chapter scenario, the first three study questions could all be answered with a correlational design. There are three constructs of interest: (1)
youth characteristics, (2) youth substance abuse, and (3) program characteristics. These are all preexisting and naturally occurring. Youth are either using substances or not, they either possess various background characteristics
or not, and either the group homes have various attributes or they do not.

In a correlational study, measures of all three constructs would be administered to a sample of group home teens at a single point in time. Analyses would entail calculation of the proportion of youth who meet the criteria
for a substance abuse disorder (question 1); calculation of associations between youth characteristics such as age, gender, pregnancy status, and so
forth and having a substance abuse disorder or not (question 2); and calculation of associations between characteristics of the program such as size,
youth/staff ratio, youth perception of staff attitudes toward drugs and youth
having a substance abuse disorder or not (question 3).

Questions 2 and 3 pertain to associations between two or more variables
(such as youth reporting having friends who use drugs and having a substance abuse disorder). It is important to bear in mind that even when statistically significant associations are found between two or more variables,
conclusions about causation cannot be made. That is, even if two variables
are associated with each other, it cannot be concluded that one has caused

the other. For example, youth with and without a substance abuse disorder could be compared on the mean number of friends in the group home who also use drugs. If an association is found such that those with a substance abuse disorder report knowing statistically significantly more friends who also use drugs, there are at least two possible explanations for such an association. On the one hand, it is possible that using drugs draws one closer toward peers who also use drugs. On the other hand, it is also possible that having friends who use drugs increases the likelihood that one will also eventually use drugs. Thus, it cannot be determined which variable influences (is the cause) the other variable (the effect).

There are several reasons why causality cannot be determined (Kenny 1979). The first reason for caution regarding causality pertains to the directionality of the findings. In a correlational design, measurement of the independent and dependent variables are taken at the same point in time. While the research question may be framed in such a way that one variable is the presumptive independent variable (cause) and the other is the presumptive dependent variable (effect), the nature of reality may be reversed, as in the example above. As an additional example, take a study in which an association was found between the number of caseworkers a youth had while at a residential treatment center and length of stay at the center. Researchers may be tempted to conclude that youth with more caseworkers have longer stays because turnover in caseworkers slows down the work of treatment and reunification. On the other hand, however, it is equally plausible that youth who stay longer (for other reasons) will have more caseworkers because the youth is in the system longer and has more chances for caseworkers to leave and new ones assigned.

A second reason for caution regarding causation is that a third and unmeasured variable may actually be "causing" both of the other two variables. For example, in the chapter scenario about substance abuse in group home teens, it might be the case that the staffpeople in the group home are not competent at preventing drug abuse in the home such that both the youth and his or her peers use drugs. Such a pattern would produce a significant association between reporting to have friends who use drugs and using drugs oneself, while the real explanation is related to the attitudes and behaviors of staff in the home. That being said, it might still be of interest for agencies to know that youth with more friends who use drugs also are more likely to use drugs themselves regardless of whether such an effect is actually caused by a third variable, in this case staffing.

It should be obvious from the above examples that correlational designs do not necessarily require that statistical correlations be conducted. The statistic correlation (known as r) is appropriate only when the independent and dependent variables are both continuous (and meet the assumptions underlying use of continuous variables, such as being normally distributed and linearly related). In this case, a Pearson product moment correlation is conducted to ascertain whether ranking on one variable is associated with ranking on the other variable. However, if the variables are not continuous, a different statistical approach will be conducted but the design per se is still correlational. In addition, more than two variables can be measured at the same time in a correlational design, in which case multivariate analyses would be conducted to determine the combined association among the set of variables. This is still considered a within-subjects correlational design because all of the variables are naturally occurring and measured at a single point in time (i.e., not manipulated).

If age is an independent variable in a correlational study, a cross-sectional approach can be utilized. If the hypothesis is that age is associated with drug use, the sample could be grouped into cross-sections based on age, such as under 13 years of age, 13–15 years of age, 16–18 years of age, and over 18 years of age. Each of these cross-sections of age could be compared on the proportion meeting the criteria for having a substance abuse disorder. In this way, data collected at a single point in time could be used to test associations about how things change over time. That is, if the youth in the older age groups had a high proportion of a substance abuse disorder, it could be concluded that over time younger youth develop a substance abuse disorder as they age (either due to a change in attitudes, a change in access, or some other reason). However, cross-sectional designs are only feasible when certain plausible alternative explanations cannot account for why the age groups would differ. For example, if all the younger youth were in a home with staffpersons who were very strict about abuse of drugs while the older youth were in a home with staffpersons who were less strict about drugs, then the age differences would not be attributed to age per se but to some other variable. In order for the cross-sectional design to be considered valid, all possible competing explanations need to be ruled out.

In reality, the cross-sectional design is something of a shortcut to the more rigorous method of establishing change over time (in this case, change in drug use): a longitudinal design in which the same individuals are assessed at two or more points in time. In this way, it can be assessed whether the younger youth actually turn into drug users as they become older. Longitudinal designs resolve many of the plausible alternative explanations for change over time, but the researcher will still need to think about what else—other than age and time—could account for the change over time.

For example, if the younger children ended up moving into a new group home in a neighborhood with greater access to drugs, perhaps that would account for the change over time rather than age per se.

The above example represents a longitudinal design, which would determine whether something changed over time in the absence of any intervention. It is much more likely in child welfare research that the interest will be in assessing change over time as a result of some program, intervention, or treatment. Often in social science research there is interest in documenting whether some event (program, intervention, treatment) has an effect on the client's behavior. For example, program staffpeople might want to determine whether attitudes about drugs change as a result of a new staff training program or—as in the chapter scenario—a peer intervention. In these cases, the design moves away from correlational and becomes quasi-experimental or experimental.

Quasi-Experimental and Experimental Designs

In these types of designs, there is an intervention, and the goal is to assess whether the intervention had an effect on the group of individuals who received it. For example, an agency developed a peer intervention in order to reduce substance abuse in group home youth. There are many possible research designs that could be implemented to determine whether the independent variable (participation in the intervention) had an effect on the dependent variable (attitudes about substance use). In the next section, each design will be described along with its limitations.

The simplest design would entail introducing the intervention and then measuring youth attitudes and behaviors regarding substances. Figure 7.1 depicts such a design. In this figure, the X represents the independent variable (participation in the treatment) and the O represents the observation (measurement of youth attitudes about substance use). Thus, the youth participate in the intervention and then are administered a measure of attitudes about substances. This is known as the one-group post-test-only design.

Figure 7.1
One-group post-test-only design

X   O

This is not considered a strong design. To begin with, in such a study it cannot be known what the youths' attitudes and behaviors would have been in the absence of the treatment and it is, therefore, quite difficult to draw any conclusions from the data. For example, if all the youth indicated appropriately negative attitudes about drugs ("using drugs is bad"), it is possible that this was the case all along and the intervention had nothing to do with these attitudes measured at the testing session. On the other hand, perhaps all the youth tested quite poorly (indicating inappropriate attitudes such as "using drugs is not so bad"), but they would have tested even worse had the intervention not been introduced—but this also cannot be known, because the only testing was the one session after the intervention. For both these reasons, the one-group post-test-only design is not considered methodologically strong. In any given research design, there are often several alternative explanations—other than the independent variable—that could have caused the observed outcome. The ideal research study is one in which every plausible alternative explanation is ruled out (through the structure of the design), leaving as the only likely explanation the independent variable. There are several different designs that improve upon the one-group post-test-only design, each of which aims to control for some of these plausible alternative explanations.

An improvement on the one-group post-test-only design depicted in figure 7.1 is to obtain measurements of the construct of interest both before and after the intervention. This is known as the one-group pre-test post-test design. Such a design is shown in figure 7.2. The first O (on the left) is the pre-test assessment of the dependent measure (attitudes about substance use), taken prior to the intervention. The X represents participation in the intervention (the independent variable), and the second O (on the right) represents the second (post-test) assessment of the dependent variable, taken following the participation in the intervention. In this case, the teens in the group homes would be administered a measure of their substance use, provided with the peer intervention, and then measured for attitudes about substance use again. The goal would be to establish that there were changes on the measure of substance use (ideally, improvement) and to conclude

Figure 7.2
One-group pre-test post-test design

O   X   O

that these changes are attributable to the intervention. This design addresses the issue of not knowing whether the teens all started off with "good" attitudes or whether they all started off with "poor" attitudes and improved. However, while this design represents an improvement over the one-group post-test-only design (figure 7.1), it still leaves open several plausible alternative explanations for changes from pre-test to post-test on the measure of substance use. For example, perhaps the youth matured over time and their attitudes changed, regardless of the intervention. Perhaps television stations aired a particularly compelling antidrug campaign at the same time that the intervention was implemented, or perhaps a teen died of an overdose, shaking up the group home teens and reducing their substance abuse. Each of these—and other plausible alternative explanations—represents possible reasons other than the intervention for improvements from the pre-test to the post-test. Therefore, the agency would not really have compelling data as to whether the intervention per se had an effect on the substance abuse of the group home teens or whether the change from pre-test to post-test was due to some other factor.

There are several alternatives to the one-group post-test-only and the one-group pre-test post-test designs, all of which involve inclusion of two groups and all of which involve the attempt to rule out alternative explanations for the observed changes from pre-test to post-test measures on the dependent variables, so that it can be concluded that the intervention itself (the independent variable) was the likely causal agent. There are two variations of between-group designs, quasi-experimental and experimental. In each case there are two groups, one of which receives some intervention, program, or treatment and one group that does not. The two groups are compared at various points in time in order to determine whether the group that received the intervention performed better than the group that did not. Thus, unlike correlational designs, there are two groups, data collection can take place at more than one point in time, and there is manipulation of the variables (one group received some intervention while the other group did not). The difference between the quasi-experimental and experimental variations pertains only to the placement of the individual cases into the two groups that are compared. When it is a result of random assignment, the study is a true experiment, and when the placement into groups is preexisting or based on some other purposeful event that is not random (i.e., first-come-first-served for those in a program and the rest end up on the waiting list), the design is considered quasi-experimental.

Thus the major difference between correlational and between-group designs is that the independent variable is usually a dichotomous variable that is manipulated: the individuals in one group receive an intervention while the individuals in the other group do not receive the intervention. The primary purpose of the study is to determine whether the intervention led to an outcome or had a desired effect, which is determined through a comparison with the individuals who did not receive the intervention. There are several variations of the quasi-experimental/experimental design, depending upon the timing of the data collection. The first is the two-group post-test-only design. This is presented in figure 7.3. In this design, there are two groups (leaving aside whether the groups were randomly assigned or not), one of which receives an intervention and one of which does not. Following the intervention, both groups are administered a post-test measure, and scores on this measure of the dependent variable are compared. Thus, the difference in post-test scores between the two groups can be seen as an estimate of the impact of the intervention.

This design represents an improvement over the one-group designs in that it allows for some estimate of what the post-test would be in the absence of the intervention. However, it cannot be known whether the two groups were comparable to begin with, as there is no pre-test administration of the measure. For example, if teens in one group home receive an intervention while teens in another do not and both are given the post-test, it cannot be known whether the teens who did receive the intervention were comparable to the teens who did not receive the intervention. It is possible that the teens who did receive the intervention had worse attitudes to begin with, improved due to the intervention, but still tested worse on the post-testing session than the youth who did not receive the intervention. In this case, the intervention would have been effective but would have appeared to not be so. On the other hand, perhaps the teens who received the intervention had better attitudes to begin with and, therefore, tested better on the post-test measure. In this case, the intervention would appear to be effective while not actually being so. Figure 7.4 presents an improvement over this design. In the two-group pre-test post-test design, teens in both groups are adminis-

Figure 7.3
Two-group post-test-only design

X   O

        O

Figure 7.4
Two-group pre-test post-test design

    O   X   O

    O   X   O

tered the pre-test and post-test measure of the dependent variable. This design—especially when random assignment is used to determine who receives the intervention and who does not—represents the classic "true experiment." In such a design, it is possible to rule out most if not all seven of the threats to internal validity.

The Seven Threats to Internal Validity

The major consideration in designing a study in which the goal is to be able to conclude that a relationship exists between an independent and dependent variable is ruling out alternative explanations for such a relationship. These alternatives are threats to the internal validity of the study, the ability of the study to "hold together" as valid. There are seven categories of threats to internal validity (Campbell and Stanley 2005). These will be discussed using the chapter scenario of peer intervention designed to reduce drug use in group home teens.

History

In this category are events that occur between the beginning and end of the research project that could affect the measure of the dependent variable regardless of the treatment. In a one-group design it cannot be known whether such an event caused the outcome scores to improve (or decline) rather than the treatment. Examples of such an event would include if the city launched a major drug abuse awareness campaign at the same time that the intervention was taking place or the neighborhood witnessed a particularly lethal form of a drug that harmed people known to the individuals in the two groups. Typically, a two-group pre-test post-test design controls for this as long as the event affected individuals in one group the same as the individuals in the other group. However, if the effect of such an event is differential (affecting the treatment group more or less than the no-treatment group) then there is still a problem. For example, if a teen died from a drug overdose in the home of the intervention group, which subsequently altered the attitudes and the behaviors of the intervention group, there would be no way to determine whether improvements in the intervention group from pre-test to post-test were due to the program or to this "historical event."

Maturation

Maturation refers to physical or mental growth in the individuals that occurs between the beginning and end of the project that could account for changes in performance on the measures. The threat of maturation is very real, especially in research with children. For example, in a one-group design it is possible that the teens simply matured over time and changed their attitudes about drugs regardless of the treatment. In a two-group design, presumably maturation occurs at the same rate in the individuals in the treatment group as in the individuals in the no-treatment group and therefore does not pose a threat.

Testing

Being administered a measure at the beginning of the project could affect scores on the administration of the same measure at the end of the project. Thus, the testing itself could affect the outcome scores regardless of the impact of the program or intervention. Perhaps being administered an assessment about drug attitudes actually changes the attitudes such that post-testing scores are better. If this were the case, it cannot be concluded that the treatment itself was the cause of such improvements. In a two-group design, as long as testing affects the individuals in the two groups to the same degree, then testing does not introduce a threat into the study.

Instrumentation

This threat refers to the changes in outcome measures (from pre-test to post-test) that would be due to changes in the measurement instrument itself regardless of any actual changes in performance. A classic example is a weight scale in which the springs wear down between the pre-test and post-test sessions. A more relevant example for social science research could include changes in the research assistants who administer the measures of substance abuse to the teens from the pre-test sessions to the post-test sessions. For example, if the research assistants at post-test elicited more honest responses, it is possible that the outcome scores would appear worse in the absence of any real change over time. If the two groups have different research assistants, a real threat to the validity of the design would be introduced, because differences between the groups could be due to differences in data collection techniques irrespective of real differences between the teens.

Statistical Regression

If the treatment group is selected based on low scores on the pre-test, it is quite likely that improvement will be revealed in the post-test session simply due to a statistical artifact known as regression to the mean. This is based on the knowledge that all scores on a measure represent both the individual's true score plus some portion of error (actual score=true score+error). Error can come from a number of sources, including checking the wrong answer box, mishearing or misreading the question, data entry mistakes, and so forth. It is a given in social science research that there is always some error in every score. Low scores in general represent poor performance plus error that pulled the person's score down (that is, the person knew the right answer but checked the wrong answer box by mistake), while high scores represent good performance plus error that pulled the score up (that is, the person did not know the right answer but checked the right box by mistake). Error is known to be random and thus tends to even out over time. In general, if error helped a person (brought the score up) one time, the next time, error is likely to hurt the person (bring the score down). Thus, individuals who are selected based on low scores are likely to perform better the next time even if no real change takes place because error will pull up their scores. For this reason, selecting cases based on low scores on a measure is likely to cause improvement from pre-test to post-test. If such a design is used with two groups—selecting two groups based on low scores and providing one with an intervention—some of the problems associated with regression to the mean are addressed because presumably both groups will be affected by error in the same way. The question then must be whether the individuals in the treatment group improved more than those in the no-treatment group.

Differential Selection

In the absence of random assignment, it is likely that the individuals in the treatment group are different than the individuals in the no-treatment group. These differences might account for improved performance on the outcome measure regardless of the effectiveness of the intervention. For example, if the teens who received the intervention were older to begin with or if the group had more girls than the group of teens that did not receive the intervention, perhaps the improved outcome scores would be due to older youth or to girls being more likely to change their attitudes. For this reason, if random assignment is not used, every effort must be made to identify and measure all variables on which the groups might differ and that could affect the scores on the dependent variable.

Mortality

Not everyone who begins involvement in a study (is pre-tested) stays until the end (is post-tested). If those who leave (are not post-tested) are more likely to perform worse on the dependent variable, it will appear as if the group improved over time when in fact the only change is in the sample from pre-test to post-test. Even in a two-group design, if mortality (attrition) from the study is different between the two groups, then the data could appear as if the intervention had an effect when it did not, or it could appear as if the intervention did not have an effect when it actually did. To address this concern, the sample from each group with post-test data must be determined to be comparable.

Additional Threats

In addition to these seven threats to internal validity, there are also threats created by the interaction of two or more of these. For example, "maturation by selection" is a situation in which the groups are selected in such a way that one is likely to mature at a different rate than the other. Research studies must systematically consider every possible influence on the dependent variable—other than the independent variable—and explain why those variables do not pose threats to internal validity.

Components of Data Collection

Chapters 10 through 13 describe in detail data collection techniques for surveys, case studies, focus groups, and interviews. What follows is a discussion of the procedure for collecting data when research assistants (or the researcher him- or herself) individually administer one or more constructed measures to the participants in a quantitative study. Data from constructed measures (surveys, tests, scales) are usually collected by a research assistant in an individually administered data collection session. The session has the following six components: (1) scheduling the session and reminders, (2) introduction of the session, (3) obtaining informed consent, (4) administration of the measures, (5) payment to the participant, and (6) debriefing.

Scheduling the Session

Data collection sessions need to take place in a private, quiet space accessible to the participant and that can comfortably seat two adults. The location should not be intimidating for the participant (e.g., an upscale coffee shop), as that could affect the responses to the data collection instruments. The sessions should be the same for all participants (e.g., all held in client's home, all held at an agency office) so as not to introduce any differences into the data collection procedures. When scheduling the sessions, the participant needs to be provided with clear expectations regarding length of time, whether children can come and will be cared for, whether refreshments will be served, whether reimbursement for transportation will be provided, and so forth. There should be no surprises on either side. However, if the sessions are held in the client's home, the data collection person will need to be skilled at handling unexpected events such as children running around unsupervised while the session is taking place, external noise and interruptions, and so forth. There should also be a policy of whether or not to accept refreshments from the participants (should they be offered) in order to avoid offending someone who has prepared a snack (even one that is unappealing). In other words, perhaps the researcher will decide to have participants told in advance not to prepare refreshments in order to avoid any awkwardness or discomfort. If the session is held in a neutral place such as an office, the person administering the measures (referred to as the "data collector" henceforth) can arrive early and ensure that the space is clean and organized (arrange the chairs, set up a small table for refreshments, put the phone on forward or mute to prevent interruptions, and so forth). If the session is to take place in the participant's home, there is no such opportunity to prepare the environment, and the data collector will have to "roll with the punches," so to speak. The data collector should carry a tote bag containing all necessary materials, including several blank copies of each measure, several pens and pencils and erasers, blank payment forms, exact change for payments, refreshments—if that is included in the plan—and so forth. Things should be arranged in the tote bag for easy access and storage.

Introduction of the Session

When the data collector first arrives (at the home or the appointed location), the data collector should introduce him- or herself and remind the participant of the purpose of the visit. The two should settle themselves into seats (ideally sitting diagonally across from each other) and there should be a brief introduction, such as, "My name is XXX and I work for the XXX agency. As you may know, the XXX agency is conducting a study of (insert brief and neutral overview). You have been asked to participate in this study but you do not have to. What I want to do right now is tell you what is going to happen during this visit and then you will have a chance to ask any questions you have and then I will ask you to sign a consent form that says you agree to participate. After that we can get started. We are going to go through XXX forms, which should take about XXX in all. When we are done you will have another chance to ask any questions and then we can wrap up. For the entire time we will need to have some quiet and it would help if you do not have interruptions from your children." Such an introduction should provide the person with a road map for what to expect. In addition, Fowler and Mangione (1990) recommend reading a prepared statement that explains that the items on the forms will be read word for word, so that each participant is answering the same question, and that there will be two kinds of questions, those in which the participant can answer questions in his or her own words and those in which a list of possible answers are provided and the participant should select the one that fits best. This information should help the participant feel prepared for what is to follow.

Informed Consent

Prior to any research, informed consent must be obtained. This means that the prospective research participant has the project explained to him or her, then the person has an opportunity to have his or her questions answered, and then the person decides whether or not to participate. Information about the project needs to be both written down and handed to the person and read out loud. The major points that need to be included are the following: (1) that their participation is strictly voluntary, (2) the names of the agencies/organizations that are sponsoring and funding the project, (3) what the overall purpose of the project is, (4) what their participation entails, (5) whether data will be anonymous or not, (6) how confidentiality will be maintained, (7) any limits to confidentiality, (8) whether there will be payment for participation, and (9) whom the person can contact if she or he has additional questions about the study. This needs to be read slowly out loud and then the person needs to be asked if he or she has any questions. Once all questions have been asked and answered and the person has agreed to participate, the person will be asked to sign the consent form.

Administration of the Measures

Once informed consent has been obtained, the measures can be administered. If there is more than one measure, they should always be given in the same order or should be administered in a predetermined random order. If there is any reason to believe that one measure will affect another, then the order should be predetermined to always have the one that could be influenced by the other come first so that it cannot be influenced. The participant should know how many forms there are to be filled out and should be able to see how many have been completed and how many are left to be done.

It should be decided from the outset whether the measures will be read to the person or whether the person will complete the measures on his or her own. This must be consistent throughout the entire data collection process across all participants and all data collection sessions. It is quite likely that having the measure read out loud and having to say the answers out loud could affect the responses (people may be less likely to admit something out loud than they would if they were filling out a form themselves) and, therefore, it is imperative that the effect of this is consistent across all data collection. If there is reason to believe that the participants will not be able to read or follow the directions for the measures to be self-administered, then the items and response choices will have to be read out loud to the person.

If this is the chosen methodology, then seating arrangement and tone of voice/style of delivery will be very important. In order to avoid creating the impression that the participant is being judged or tested, the data collector should sit next to or diagonally from the participant and hold the measures in such a way that the participant can see everything (and read along if she or he chooses to do so). Under no circumstances should the data collection person hold the measures behind a clipboard and appear to be withholding information from the participant.

Fowler and Mangione (1990) provide a detailed analysis of the ways in which error can be introduced into the data collection process when the items on a measure are read out loud to the participant, and they give detailed suggestions for eliminating these sources of error. In general, they favor a word-for-word reading of the items and the response choices. They have found that very subtle changes in wording (for example, replacing "not allow" with "forbid") can dramatically affect participant responses. Even seemingly minor changes can affect the study's findings and can be avoided through verbatim reading of all items. They all suggest probing when the answer is not adequate. For example if the respondent is asked to rate something as "good, fair, poor, or very poor" but actually responds "not very good," Fowler and Mangione recommend that all of the response choices be offered again and not just the negative ones, which might seem warranted based on the initial answer of "not very good." This technique is generally recommended when the answer provided is in some way not responsive to the question asked.

Tone of voice is also very important when administering measures out loud to the participant. For this reason, there should be extensive training and practice of all data collection staff on the project in order to create a consistent tone of voice and delivery style that is warm but unintrusive. There should be equal phrasing and emphasis on all possible response options to avoid giving the impression that certain answers are desired or expected. Under no circumstances should the answers that are provided lead to discussion or comment on the part of the data collection person.

As each measure is administered, the ID number should be placed on every page, so that all the papers can be slipped back into the tote bag at the end, with no concern for losing track of which data belongs to which participant.

Payment

At the end of the session, the participant should be given the payment (usually cash, but it could be a coupon or gift certificate) and asked to sign a receipt. A copy of the receipt should also be given to the participant (and one kept for the study's records).

Debriefing

At this point, the participant should be asked if he or she has any questions about the project now that the data collection session has been completed. The participant should be thanked sincerely for participating. If the participant appears upset or distraught for any reason, the visit should be extended so that the participant is not left alone while upset. Sometimes simply making small talk can lighten the mood. If the participant is so upset that a more trained clinical response is necessary, the participant should be encouraged to make contact with the person who is named on the consent form. This should be pointed out to the participant. Also, if additional data collection sessions are to be scheduled in the future, the participant should be reminded that he or she will be contacted again. In some studies participants are given postcards to mail back with updated address or phone number information, which allows for uninterrupted access. Sometimes the name, phone number, and address of a friend or family member is asked for in the event that the project loses touch with a participant. If necessary, this "collateral contact" can be asked for updated information. As noted above, attrition from the study can affect the comparability of the groups and create statistical problems best avoided if possible. Obtaining the participation of as many study participants as possible in all data collection sessions is the surest way to achieve that goal.

Conclusion

The research questions for a study determine the number of groups and the timing of the data collection. Correlational designs entail one group with data collected at one point in time, while quasi-experimental and experimental designs involve more than one group and data collected usually at more than one point in time. In all cases, the research needs to rule out alternative explanations (known as threats to the internal validity of the study) for any associations found between the independent and the dependent variables. All research studies that involve the collection of new data (as opposed to using existing data) follow a series of steps, including scheduling the session, obtaining informed consent, and collecting data. Systematic use of these steps can help eliminate error in the data collection phase of a study.

[8]

Using Existing Data

In this chapter the following topics will be discussed, following the introduction of the chapter scenario and the brief literature review:

- Using agency administrative data
- Using third-party data and reports

CHAPTER SCENARIO

An agency-based researcher is hired as a consultant to help an agency develop a program of research on the topic of adoption of older and special needs children. After a series of meetings with administrative staff about resources, the researcher concludes that a good place to start would be to identify possible research studies that could be conducted with data that already exist.

BRIEF LITERATURE REVIEW:
CHILDREN WAITING TO BE ADOPTED

According to federal statistics (U.S. Department of Health and Human
Services 2006), there were 118,000 children in the foster care system
waiting to be adopted as of June 30, 2005. Each year, some twenty thousand children age of out of care without having been placed into permanent homes. Until the 1970s, adoption most commonly connoted
domestic adoptions of healthy Caucasian newborns. In 1980, the federal government aimed to reshape that concept by promoting adoption
of children previously deemed "unadoptable"; that is, they were older
and/or had special needs. There are four categories of children who are
the most difficult to adopt: (1) older children, (2) children in sibling
groups, (3) children with special needs, and (4) minority children.

Of the waiting children, half are over the age of nine. According to
the National Child Welfare Resource Center on Adoption (2004), there
are several barriers to the adoption of older children, including caseworker attitudes about the adoptability of older youth and about the
suitability of nontraditional adoptive homes (such as single mothers),
the youth's own reluctance to become adopted, and foster parents' lack
of information about financial assistance and subsidies available
should they adopt older foster children currently in their care. The federal government has sponsored both legislation and public service an-
nouncements to promote and support the adoption of older children
waiting for adoption in the foster care system, such as bonuses to
states with adoptions of older children that exceed the baseline (United
States Department of Health and Human Services 2004).

Many of the children in foster care waiting for adoption are also
members of sibling groups. Although there are no current statistics,
data from 1998 estimated that one in five special needs adoptions was a
child in a sibling group (United States House of Representatives 2000).
Children in sibling groups pose a special difficulty for adoptions because prospective adoptive parents may not want or be able to accommodate the needs of all the children in a sibling group. Nonetheless, child
welfare professionals now recognize the importance of sibling bonds and
often try to identify adoptive families that will keep brothers and sisters
together. The goal of maintaining sibling groups is based on research

(continued)

demonstrating the unique and important role siblings can play over the course of an individual's lifetime (e.g., Bank and Kahn 1982). These bonds may be particularly salient for children in foster care who have already suffered the loss and separation of parents, home, community, possessions, and friends. They may experience their siblings as their only link to their past and to their identity. The National Child Welfare Resource Center on Adoption (2002) has identified a set of tasks for child welfare caseworkers to perform in order to increase the chances that siblings will be placed together whenever possible and, when not possible, that sibling groups sustain their emotional connection through consistent and frequent meaningful contact.

Children with special needs are also overrepresented in the pool of waiting children. Although definitions vary by states, a common element across definitions is the presence of a physical disability or emotional disturbance. Families willing to adopt these children are eligible for additional financial support (known as adoption subsidies) to cover the increased costs associated with caring for such children. However, even with these enhanced avenues for assistance, not all families are up to the challenge of parenting a child with severe emotional or physical handicapping conditions. A recent development in the field is the call for including children who are at risk of developing a special need due to presence of risk factors such as mental illness in a parent or known drug and alcohol exposure in utero (North American Council on Adoptable Children n.d.). Inclusion of this new category of risk could encourage families to adopt children who do not currently show any signs of disabilities that would make them eligible for current subsidies by reassuring the families that such subsidies would be available in the future with minimal additional paperwork or bureaucratic involvement should the need arise.

Almost two-thirds of the children in foster care who are waiting to be adopted are children of minority races or ethnicities. African American children are vastly overrepresented within the child welfare system compared to their proportion within the population as a whole. For example, minority children represent about 20 percent of the overall U.S. population yet represent close to 80 percent of the child welfare population (Groza, Roberson, Brindo, Darden-Kautz, Fujimura, Goode-Cross, and Prusak 2002). They also constitute more than half

(continued)

of the children legally free for adoption, and they wait significantly longer than other children for adoptive placement. A multistate survey project identified several barriers to the adoption of minority children, including lack of recruitment of minority foster and adoptive parents, institutional racism and bias against minority families seeking to adopt, and lack of information about minority children waiting to be adopted (Gilles and Kroll 1991). In response to the growing ranks of minority children waiting to be adopted, the Multi-Ethnic Placement Act was passed in 1994 and reauthorized in 1996 in order to decrease the length of time that children wait to be adopted, facilitate the recruitment and retention of foster and adoptive parents who can meet the distinctive needs of children awaiting placement, and eliminate discrimination on the basis of the race, color, or national origin of the child or the prospective parent.

Overview of the Topic

Agency-based researchers in the field of child welfare have access to two additional sources of data in addition to collecting their own data in a research study. The first source is an agency's own administrative data (case records and electronic files) and the second is preexisting data compiled by other organizations/researchers. As long as the necessary cautions are heeded, both of these can prove to be quite useful either as a source of raw data for a study in its own right or as a source of comparison or contextual data that can enrich the interpretation and relevance of a study.

Using Agency Administrative Data

There are two sources of agency data: agency records and electronic administrative data.

Agency Records

Agency records are composed of paper documentation compiled sometimes prior to and always over the course of a child and family's involvement in an agency. These records vary in depth and breadth according to the level of care the family is involved with and according to the reporting requirements and standards of each agency (which is determined by local, state, and federal guidelines and by accreditation organizations). If the goal is to obtain information about youth prior to admission to the agency (based on information in the referral packet), it is important to bear in mind that, in general, youth entering a foster boarding home for the first time will have far less written documentation available in the record at referral than youth entering higher levels of care, for example, a residential treatment center (RTC), or then youth entering an agency after already having at least one prior spell in the system. Youth entering an RTC usually have had prior placements (such as foster homes, group homes, psychiatric hospitals, juvenile justice facilities) from which there will be summary reports and assessments available in the referral packet. Youth entering the system for a second time usually have records that contain information from the previous spell. Thus, agency records are less useful for some purposes than others.

A researcher will also find that there is variation by level of care and by agency in the extent and nature of the documentation compiled about a youth while receiving services. In addition, the information in records might vary depending upon whether the case is active or not. For example, if data are to be collected from closed cases (the youth or family has been discharged from service), some data may have been expunged from the record after a certain period of time. Closed records also may be difficult to obtain because some agencies seal them and send them offsite to a warehouse for long-term storage. These records may be quite difficult (as well as costly and time consuming) to locate and retrieve.

That being said, preexisting agency records can provide the basis for a study if important and meaningful research questions can be developed. Studies utilizing such data typically qualify for expedited review (as opposed to a full review) by an institutional review board (IRB) because the data have already been collected. However, it is still possible that an IRB could decide that the clients need to give permission for the use of the records. In such a case, the complications of conducting the research may be insurmountable. This issue should be addressed early in the development of such a project.

Data from records can also be useful for providing background data on children and families (number of prior placements, abuse history, age at first placement) that might be important for describing the sample, determining comparability between groups, and as predictors of outcomes (such as timeliness to adoption for older children).

Timing is a very important consideration in coding data from agency records, because some data in the records apply to information that is known about the child and family prior to admission to the agency while other information is collected about the child and family over the course of their involvement in the program. It is very important for a decision to be made for each variable about what the timeframe should be. For example, in coding age, it could be age of the child at admission to the agency or age of the child at the time of the data collection (or at some other point in time, such as termination of parental rights or change of permanency goal to adoption).

One common timing rule is to code presence or absence of certain characteristics at the time of admission to the agency or to the program. Examples include whether the child was ever physically abused up until the time of admission to the agency, whether the child was ever sexually abused up until the point of admission to the agency, and so forth. This is particularly relevant for describing a sample and for predicting participation in a program or outcomes of the program. For example, in a study of length of stay of youth in residential treatment, Baker, Wulczyn, and Dale (2005) coded each case in the sample from records as to legal status at the time of admission to the program (abuse/neglect, PINs, etc), age at admission to the program, age at admission to the system, whether the child had ever been psychiatrically hospitalized prior to admission to the program, and so forth. Such information was used to determine whether characteristics of the youth at the time of admission to the program were associated with length of stay in the program. This approach makes more sense than collecting information about a child or family over the course of the program, because the length of time in the program will vary on a case-by-case basis. Therefore, some cases will have had more opportunity to experience an event than others.

A third option is to link the coding of child characteristics or child behaviors to a particular key event (such as a specified time prior to a particular event). As an example, if there is interest in measuring youth behavioral problems, this could be done within the first two months of placement in order to describe youth as they enter care (Baker, Archer, and Curtis, forthcoming), at the beginning of placement in order to predict a critical event such as discharge disposition (Piotrkowski and Baker 2004), prior to a critical event such as admission to a psychiatric hospital (Baker, Piotrkowski, and Mincer 2003), or return from a transfer to a group home (Baker and Calderon 2004).

Depending upon how the data are to be used, it might be important for the researcher to establish inter-rater reliability among more than one coder. If the data being collected from the records are routine and not likely to be subject to interpretation, then one coder will suffice and establishing inter-rater reliability is not necessary. Examples of this type of variable include gender, age, ethnicity, birth date, and the like. However, if the data to be collected from the records require interpretation or judgment on the part of the person collecting the data, then it is best for the researcher to hire coders, develop coding forms and coding guidelines, and establish inter-rater reliability.

Coders

A team of coders may be required if the amount of coding is excessive (more than the researcher him- or herself or a single assistant can reasonably be expected to manage). It is also possible that the researcher should not conduct the coding because it is important for the person doing the coding to be "blind" to the hypotheses of the study and the status of the youth. For example, in a study of whether youth with sexual offending conduct disorders are more likely to have histories of family secrecy than youth with nonsexual conduct disorders, it would be important that the person coding the records for the extent of family secrecy not be aware of the hypotheses of the study (association between sexual offending and family secrecy) nor which youth have sexual offending histories, so that the coder cannot unconsciously make coding decisions based on endorsement (or rejection) of the hypothesis. For this reason, it is often necessary to find people to code records who are not intimately involved with the research project. Training will need to be provided to these coders, ranging from a single training session to a several-month "seminar" of training sessions in which sample cases are coded and discussed in such a way that eventually the coders not only agree with one another but also with the person who is providing the training. The training process should begin with a discussion of the variables and a review of a typical record. Perhaps everyone codes a record together and begins to discuss some of the "art" and nuance involved in making coding decisions. Eventually the coders are given homework assignments involving independently (each on his or her own) coding one or more records, the results of which are submitted in advance to the trainer. The team session would then involve a presentation of the areas of agreement and disagreement with the trainer explaining why the correct response is one way and not another. This continues until the coders are deemed to be reliable (see below).

When coding data from records, it will be very important to emphasize with the coders the rules governing confidentiality of both the records and the information in them. Thus, the records cannot be taken off premises (for at-home coding) nor can portions be copied or removed from the record unless all identifying information is concealed. At the end of the day, the records should be stored in a locked filing cabinet. At no time should records be left unattended or out for others to see. In addition, information gleaned from the record should not be discussed outside of the research offices. It is probably a good idea to type up a confidentiality pledge, a statement about protecting confidentiality of information, which all coders are asked to sign prior to being trained. Formalizing the process can convey the gravity of the situation to them. Various scenarios should be highlighted in which it would be possible to breach confidentiality. For example, talking to a person on a city bus about an interesting case being coded when unbeknownst to the coder someone who knows the case is within earshot. It must be emphasized that under no circumstances should a coder discuss a case with someone who is not on the coding team.

An additional consideration when other people code data from records is that the material confronted can be quite disturbing. Often the records of children and families being served in the child welfare system contain detailed information about multiple traumatic events in the lives of these individuals. Sometimes the records provide graphic and descriptive information about traumatic events and the child's response to them. Reading several records in one sitting can be particularly overwhelming and stressful for the coder. Some warning and support may be called for if it is likely that this will occur. A portion of each training session can be devoted to processing the feelings of the coders in order to ensure that they do not experience vicarious traumatization. It will be important to remind the coders that the youth are receiving services and treatment to address their victimization. At all times, sensitivity to the needs and experiences of the coders is important, as they deserve and require ethical treatment and prevention from harm. It is important to remember that they represent the next generation of child welfare researchers and should be provided with a model of conducting research that is careful, rigorous, and sensitive to the needs of all who are touched by the research endeavor.

The Coding Form

A coding form is a formatted document in which the coder can answer questions about the case based on information available from the records. It may resemble a survey in that there are questions typed onto the form and then spaces provided for the coder to write down the answer. Sometimes the questions will be open-ended, but in most cases the possible response choices are predetermined and provided on the form for the coder. The coding form may be a single page or may be several pages in length, depending upon how many variables are coded from each record. The form should have the unique ID of the case, the name of the coder, and the date the information was obtained from the record. The name of the project or study should also be on the form, to distinguish it from data collected for other studies. The form should be designed for ease of data collection and data entry. Thus, the form should have each item numbered consecutively and should be laid out on the page in such a way that there is no confusion about the questions being asked and the possible answers to be provided. Chapter 10 (surveys) should be consulted for ideas about developing questions for the coding form, as many of the issues of question development and response choice options apply to the coding form as well. The form will most likely need to be piloted by the researcher and several versions will probably be created before a final one is ready for utilization by the coding team. However, it is often the case that issues will be raised by one or more members of the coding team that will result in modification of the form in order to clarify ambiguities in the questions and response options.

Eventually, data collected from the paper records will need to be transferred to an electronic data file from the coding form. Therefore, some thought should be given in advance as to how to design the coding form for ease of both data collection and data entry. Rules about missing data will need to be developed, and it is likely that a few different types of missing data will exist. For example, sometimes the coding form might not have a question answered because the information was missing from the record. That is one type of missing data. However, it is also possible that the information in the record is ambiguous or contradictory. For example, the child's birthdate is written as one date on one form but a different birthdate is indicated on another form. Unless there is a way to resolve the confusion (for example, the child is still in care at the agency and someone can be consulted as to the child's actual birthdate), the information cannot be transferred to the coding form from the chart. In this case, the item could be coded as "missing" or as "don't know." There should probably be a "missing" and a "don't know" response option for almost every item on the coding form.

Coding Guidelines

Coding guidelines can be embedded right on the form or can constitute a separate document that is referred to by the coder as the records are reviewed. The guidelines are organized item by item as they are on the coding form and provide all the ancillary information the coder needs in order to make accurate and reliable coding decisions. For example, if the item on the coding form asks whether the youth has a history of juvenile delinquency prior to admission to the agency (coded as 0=no, 1=yes), the coding guidelines would explicate what constitutes a juvenile delinquency history. This could mean having been ajudicated in court, having exhibited one or more of certain behaviors, or some other definition. The definitions should be based on theory and prior research and should be used consistently from record to record and coder to coder.

Inter-Rater Reliability

Prior to allowing the coders to code actual data, it will need to be established that the coders have achieved inter-rater reliability: agreement between themselves and agreement with an expert. This means that regardless of who coded each record, the data would essentially be the same. The simplest form of inter-rater reliability is the proportion of coding decisions in which two coders agree with each other when the variable is dichotomous. If there are ten variables per case and ten cases are coded, the denominator is one hundred coding decisions. If the two raters agree on eighty-five of them, the rate of agreement is 85 percent. However, this method is viewed as giving too much credit to chance agreement—especially when the decision is that something is absent (a tendency to follow the rule of when in doubt decide "no" and code as "0" might lead to chance agreement on the scores of "0"). Thus, a Kappa statistic is considered a more rigorous test of inter-rater reliability when the data decisions are 0 or 1. The conceptual formula for the Kappa is: total agreement minus chance agreement divided by 1 minus chance agreement. For the above scenario of 100 coding decisions with 85 agreements and 15 disagreements, the Kappa would be .70 instead of .85. Standards in several fields of research suggest that a Kappa of .81 is considered strong agreement (e.g., Viera and Garrett 2005).

The formula for Kappa is understood in the context of the four-cell distribution of possible responses when two coders are making ratings of presence/absence, as presented in figure 8.1. In cell A, the two coders agree (both coded 0). In cell B, the two coders disagree (the first coded 0 and the second coded 1). In cell C, the two coders disagree (the first coded 1 and the second coded 0), and in cell D the two coders agree (both coded 1). The statistical formula for Kappa is presented in figure 8.2.

Figure 8.1
Four-cell distribution of responses with two coders and two coding options

	Coder 2 codes 0	Coder 2 codes 1
Coder 1 codes 0	Cell A	Cell B
Coder 1 codes 1	Cell C	Cell D

Figure 8.2
Formula for Kappa

$$Kappa = \frac{observed\ agreement - chance\ agreement}{(1 - chance\ agreement)}$$

Figure 8.3
Calculation of Kappa

	Coder A codes 0	Coder A codes 1	N
Coder B codes 0	41	07	48
Coder B codes 1	10	42	52
N	51	49	100

Observed agreement = 41+42 / 100 = .83
Chance agreement = (.48 * .51) + (.52 * .49) = .245 + .255 = .50
Kappa = .83 − .50 / (1 − .50) = .33 / .50 = .66

Figure 8.3 presents an example of calculating Kappa using data from the hypothetical case of one hundred coding decisions. The issue of inter-rater reliability is more complicated when the variables are scored with values other than 0 or 1. In the case of ordinal scales, disagreement can be close (off by just one category) or far (off by more than one category). In order to take this into account, a weighted Kappa can be calculated, although SPSS does not yet have this option (SAS does). If the variable is continuous, a Pearson correlation can be conducted, which also takes into account the degree of disagreement. If there are more than two raters, one option is to calculate the Kappa for each pair of raters and determine whether any single rater is below a Kappa of .81 with any other rater and to provide more training to that rater until his or her Kappa is above .80 with all other raters.

Once inter-rater reliability has been established for all coders, the data can be collected from the records. However, it may be necessary to assess inter-rater reliability at various intervals over the course of the data coding process in order to prevent what is known as "coder drift." If too much time elapses after establishment of inter-rater reliability, each coder may slowly drift away from the coding rules established over the course of training and no longer be a reliable coder. There is no hard and fast rule about whether or when to assess inter-rater reliability once it has been established, but one rule of thumb is if the actual coding of data will take more than a month, it probably makes sense to establish reliability at a midpoint and provide a training booster if necessary.

Agency's Electronic Database

A researcher might find that coding data from agency records requires too much preparation time, especially if the agency is eager to launch one or more research studies immediately. If this is the case, the researcher would be well advised to consider learning about and utilizing the agency's electronic database for such a study.

Most, if not all, child welfare agencies operate an administrative database, which is the record of service that captures child-level data from the point of admission to the agency through the point of discharge. Typically, these data are stored in electronic relational databases that are accessed either table by table or through an interactive query and report-writing programming system that manages the data. The programs that allow the researcher to query the tables and access the raw data vary from agency to agency, although they share certain features. The names of the variables, the structure of the variables, and the value labels all vary by agency (unless a group of agencies have worked together to create a multiagency system); thus, the specific system must be learned prior to making any use of the data.

As noted elsewhere in this book, these systems are notoriously idiosyncratic and can be seemingly illogical or internally inconsistent. Often knowledge about them and how to access them is compartmentalized throughout the agency. The line staff may understand how paper forms are completed, someone in the data entry department understands how the data are entered into the database, while yet a third person who works in the information technology (IT) or management information systems (MIS) department understands how the data are stored, backed up, and accessed. Even research staff within an agency might have great facility with one portion of the data system but be completely unfamiliar with other portions of it.

One common issue with these systems is that child-specific data may or may not refer to a particular point in time. For example, in some systems if a child's data are accessed along with information about "program," then the program will be the current program that the child is in. However, if there is a table that presents every movement of the child across different programs, then all the programs the child has been in will be listed along with dates of entry and exit. It is very important that the researcher understands whether the data being presented change over time or whether they are static.

Another issue is that some data are updated and written over while other data are fixed and historical. As an example, a child's permanency goal can change over time. Most children enter foster care with a goal of reunification (which could be assigned a value of 01). Over time, a particular child's goal might change to adoption (assigned a value of 04) or independent living (assigned a value of 03). In some systems, the original goal might be overwritten, while in other agencies every goal the child ever had and the date of change is noted.

A third issue is that often data from two or more tables can be linked and the data will be different depending upon the joining variable. The researcher should experiment with linking the same tables in different ways in order to develop an understanding of what happens to the data as a result of such linkages.

It is possible that, in addition to the primary data system, there are also secondary databases that function independently. These may be as simple as spreadsheets compiled by line staff or as complex as relational databases that coexist within the agency. A researcher should try as much as possible to develop a comprehensive understanding of all the data collected routinely within the agency.

For all these reasons, a dedicated researcher will make it his or her business to identify all of the databases that exist within the agency and, as much as possible, develop a deep understanding of the variables within them. Often, the knowledge about the variables and values are institutional and not written down or documented formally. It is quite likely that no codebook exists and that one person understands the coding of some variables while another person has knowledge about other variables. The researcher will have to be patient, thorough, and persistent in order to understand a particular agency's database system.

A final note of caution must be made about these databases regarding human error, which can cause incomplete or incorrectly completed forms and data entry mistakes (the forms are completed properly but the person transferring the information from the paper form to the electronic database makes a mistake). Like all databases, the agency's administrative database can have some error associated with it. A researcher newly learning about the agency's database should ask about checks and balances in the system for identifying and rectifying different sources of error.

All that said, these databases are often rich and detailed and can be quite fruitful for developing a program of research. At a minimum, the data contain information necessary for the agency to receive payment from the governmental entity that provides oversight to child welfare programs in the city or state. This typically includes variables such as date of admission, date of moves to all different types of care within the agency, dates of all absences (vacations, home visits, running away episodes, hospitalizations, and so forth), and dates and types of discharge. Supplementing these basic movement files can be progress notes about ongoing behavior and treatment of youth, detailed background information about families served, and information about services provided (number and type of contacts).

Coding Progress Notes

Progress notes represent a specific type of data (stored either in the paper record or in an electronic database) that are a particularly fruitful source of information for research studies. Progress notes are mandatory for all child welfare programs and constitute brief written summaries of caseworker visits, child care observations of youth in a group home or RTC, reports of visits between youth and biological parents, and discussions with foster parents. Each agency develops its own culture of what these progress notes should look and sound like, and so a study across agencies may not be feasible. But within any one agency, there should be enough consistency about what type of information is considered relevant for the data to be usable for research purposes. Regardless of format (paper or electronic), these data are usually textual, and making use of them will involve coding the content of the notes. Coding could entail a count of how many times a certain behavior is mentioned (such as youth violence) or could involve an overall rating of the youth's behavior (e.g., home visit went well). Exactly what is coded depends, of course, on the constructs of interest in a particular study. Baker, Piotrkowski, and Mincer (2003) offer an example of coding behavioral problems of youth in a residential treatment center. In that study, social workers' and child care workers' computerized progress notes were coded for emotional and behavioral problems exhibited by the youth. Coding was conducted by the first author and the third author (who was blind to the purposes of the study and the status of the youth). Inter-rater reliability was established with a Kappa above 85 percent. The progress notes were doctored to hide the identity of the youth and to delete any references that indicated the time period (two months prior to admission to a psychiatric hospital or comparable two-month period for youth in the comparison group).

The occurrence of sixteen possible emotional and behavioral problems described in the progress notes was coded as present (1) or absent (0) for each youth during the two-month time period. These sixteen problems were designated as "not too serious," "moderately serious," or "very serious" based on expert clinician ratings. The "not too serious" category consisted of four items (oppositional defiance, academic problems, provoking peers, and being disruptive), the "moderately serious" category consisted of five items (running away or is not where supposed to be, fighting with peers, using substances, depression, and theft), and the "very serious" category consisted of seven items (violence, sexual acting out, suicidal talk, suicidal attempt, bizarre behaviors, fire setting, and destruction of property). Three index scores were created for each youth by summing the total number of behaviors present within each of the three categories. These scores were found to be a significant predictor of psychiatric hospitalization of the youth. This coding scheme represents just one of many possible ways to use progress notes in child welfare research.

Existing Databases for Secondary Analysis/Companion Data

In addition to an agency's own data sources, researchers in the field of child welfare also may have the opportunity or need to access additional external databases compiled by other organizations. All of them provide statewide and or national statistics for indicators of child and family well-being and/or involvement in the child welfare system. Some also offer the researcher the opportunity to access data in order to compile more customized charts and reports. A child welfare researcher could also use the data and reports to place agency-level findings in a broader context. What follows is a brief description of eight databases that might be of interest.

Annie E. Casey's Kids Count

Kids Count is a project of the Annie E. Casey Foundation, which was created in 1948. The original purpose was to provide grants to organizations serving at-risk children and families. The agency also operates foster care programs designed to reduce placement and promote permanency through its Casey Family Programs. Kids Count, one of many projects of the foundation, is a compilation of comparative information about children's well-being across the United States and on a state-by-state basis. Data from the 2006 annual Kids Count data book are currently available online at http://www.aecf.org/kidscount/sld/databook.jsp. This database provides state-level and cross-state data aggregated by year (1999 to 2003) that can be used to create custom graphs, maps, rankings, and state profiles. The database includes data on ten key measures of child well-being: low-birth rates; infant mortality; child deaths; teen deaths from all causes; teen deaths by age group; teens who are high school dropouts; teens who are not attending school and not working; children living in families where no parent has full-time, year-round employment; children in poverty; and children in single-parent families. Data can be compared within and across states. For example, selecting New York State for the indicator of low birth rates reveals that the rate was 7.8 percent in the year 1999 compared to a national rate of 7.6 percent. Raw data are also available in a zipped file that can be downloaded free of charge.

CWLA's National Data Archives System

The Child Welfare League of America (CWLA) is an association of more than nine hundred public and private nonprofit agencies that reportedly serves more than 3.5 million abused and neglected children and their families each year with a range of services. The Child Welfare League of America is the nation's oldest and largest membership-based child welfare organization. Its stated goal is to engage people in promoting the well-being of children, youth, and their families and protect every child from harm. The National Data Analysis System (NDAS) is part of CWLA's National Center for Research, Data, and Technology program. NDAS makes child welfare data and statistics available to Internet users with the hopes of promoting discussion around state and federal data issues and promote effective integration of research, policy, and practice.

NDAS allows Internet users to create customized tables and graphs and provides information and links necessary to understand the data. NDAS can be found at http://www.cwla.org/ndas.htm.

Using NDAS requires selection of preexisting topics (adoption, agency administration, child care, out of home care, and so forth). Once the topic is selected, the user must select the year of interest and whether the data should be presented for all states or just a subset of states. For example, if the topic of adoption is selected and then the subtopic of adoptive family structure and the year 2003 for all states is selected, it can be found that in Alabama there were 329 adoptions in 2003, 72.6 percent of which were by a married couple. This compares to the national average of 60.7 percent of adoptions by married couples in 2003.

The Children's Bureau of the Administration of Children and Families' AFCARS

The Children's Bureau provides state and national data on adoption and foster care, child abuse and neglect, and child welfare. The Adoption and Foster Care Reporting and Analysis System (AFCARS) collects case-level information on all children in foster care for whom state child welfare agencies have responsibility for placement, care, or supervision, and on children who are adopted under the auspices of the state's public child welfare agency. It can be found at http://www.acf.hhs.gov/programs/cb/stats_research/index.htm #afcars. AFCARS reports are available for the years 1998 through 2003, and include the following information: number of children waiting to be adopted, number of children adopted in the current year, number of children in foster care (by type of care, length of stay, permanency goal, ethnicity, and gender), number of children entering foster care, number of children exiting care, and number of children whose parental rights have been terminated. In addition to the AFCARS reports, there is more detailed information about the gender, ethnicity, and age of the youth who were adopted and in foster care.

The Web site also provides summary data from the National Child Abuse and Neglect Data System (NCANDS), which presents information by year (1995 through 2004) and by state derived from child protective services reports (the number of reports, who makes the reports, the number that result in investigations, the number that are substantiated), about the child victims (types of maltreatment, age and gender, type by gender, and so forth), about fatalities (number, by age and gender, status of perpetrators, etc.), about perpetrators (relation to victim), and about services offered (preventive, postinvestigation, funding, by victim, and so forth).

Another component of the Web site is related to seven outcomes: (1) reducing recurrence of child abuse and neglect, (2) reducing the incidence of child abuse and/or neglect in foster care, (3) increasing permanency for children in foster care, (4) reducing time in foster care without increasing reentry, (5) reducing time in foster care to adoption, (6) increasing placement stability, and (7) reducing placements of young children in group homes or institutions. These data are presented in aggregated percentages (across states) by year (1999 to 2002).

Cornell University's National Data Archive on Child Abuse and Neglect (NDACAN)

A resource since 1988, this archive aims to promote scholarly exchange among researchers in the field of child maltreatment. NDACAN acquires data from leading researchers and national data collection efforts and makes these datasets available to the research community for secondary analysis. NDACAN supports information sharing through a variety of communication and training efforts, including an annual summer training institute.

The National Child Abuse and Neglect Data System (NCANDS) Child File dataset consists of child-specific data of all investigated reports of maltreatment to state child protective service agencies. The NCANDS is a federally sponsored national data collection effort created for the purpose of tracking the number and nature of child maltreatment reporting each year within the United States. The Child File is the case-level component of the NCANDS. There is also an NCANDS state-level component, known as the Agency File, but those data are not part of this collection. The Child File data are collected on an annual basis through the voluntary participation of states. Participating states submit their data after going through a process in which the state's administrative system is mapped onto the NCANDS data structure. Submitted data consist of all investigations or assessments of alleged child maltreatment that received a disposition in the reporting year. Records are provided at the level of each child on a report, also known as the report-child pair. Data elements include the demographics of children and their perpetrators, types of maltreatment, investigation or assessment dispositions, risk factors, and services provided as a result of the investigation or assessment. The database is available online at http://www.ndacan.cornell.edu/.

In addition, the site provides links for ordering and/or being trained to use other datasets from several large-scale studies of children and youth including:

(1) Longitudinal Pathways to Resilience in Maltreated Children, dataset Number 110. Primary investigator: Cicchetti, D. This dataset consists of information on over 250 maltreated and nonmaltreated children at a follow-up assessment of their adaptation and current symptomatology in the context of a summer camp program and home visits.

(2) Longitudinal studies of abuse and neglect, dataset number 108, primary investigator: LONGSCAN Consortium. LONGSCAN is a consortium of research studies operating under common bylaws and procedures. It was initiated in 1991 with grants from the National Center on Child Abuse and Neglect to a coordinating center at the University of North Carolina at Chapel Hill and five data collection sites. Each site is conducting a separate and unique research project on the etiology and impact of child maltreatment. While each project stands on its own merits, through the use of common assessment measures, similar data collection methods and schedules, and pooled analyses, LONGSCAN is a collaborative effort designed to be greater than the sum of its parts.

(3) The National Longitudinal Survey of Child and Adolescent Well-being, dataset number 111, primary investigator: Research Triangle Institute. The Administration on Children, Youth, and Families and the Office of the Assistant Secretary for Planning and Evaluation have undertaken the National Survey of Child and Adolescent Well-Being (NSCAW). NSCAW makes available, for the first time, nationally representative longitudinal data drawn from first-hand reports of children and families or other caregivers who have had contact with the child welfare system. Data from service providers are also collected. NSCAW is the first national study to provide detailed information on the experiences of children and families with the child welfare system and to collect measures of well-being for this population.

Children's Bureau of Administration for Children and Families Child and Family Service Reviews (CFSR)

The Child and Family Services Reviews (CFSR) are designed to enable the United States Children's Bureau to determine whether state child welfare agency practice is in conformity with federal child welfare standards, to document what is actually happening to children and families as they are involved with state child welfare services, and to assist states in enhancing their capacity to help children and families achieve positive outcomes. The CFSR reports do not provide data per se but rather the results of assessments of child welfare services on a state-by-state basis. Strengths and weaknesses of state systems regarding all aspects of child welfare practice are described along with a program improvement plan designed to address any notable weaknesses. These reports are available by state and by year (2001 to 2004). The Web site for accessing these reports is http://www.acf .hhs.gov/programs/cb/cwmonitoring/index.htm.

Center for Social Service Research at the University of California, Berkeley, Child Welfare Services Reports

This site provides ongoing analysis and reporting using California state-wide and county-specific child welfare administrative data, along with data from other sources. Under an interagency agreement with the California Department of Social Services (CDSS), quarterly extracts from the Child Welfare Services Case Management System (CWS/CMS) are received. With CDSS funding and additional support from a private foundation, the Performance Indicators Project has the stated aim of creating and presenting timely data about children who are involved in California's child welfare system. The system involves creation of custom tailored charts by year (1998 through 2005) and by county for the following topics: child abuse referrals (counts, rates, and recurrence), foster care entry cohorts, point-in-time cohorts, and foster care dynamics (entry and exit cohorts). For example, it can be found by selecting October 1, 2004, through September 30, 2005, for all of California that there were 483,560 referrals, 108,765 (22.4 percent) of which were substantiated. The reports can be obtained at http://cssr .berkeley.edu/CWSCMSreports/.

Chapin Hall Center for Children at the University of Chicago Multistate Foster Care Data Archive

Located at the University of Chicago, Chapin Hall is a research and development center that was developed with the express purpose of bringing standards of scholarship and the resources of an established research university to bear on real-world challenges faced by policymakers and service providers working with vulnerable children and families. Using a cohort-sequential design, thirteen successive entry cohorts of children admitted to foster care in seven states from 1990 to 2002 have been studied. Several reports are available from this multistate foster care data archive, which present detailed analyses of the movement of these cohorts through the foster care system. They can be found at http://www.chapinhall.org/category_editor.aspx?L2=66.

Child Defense Fund National and State Data

Since 1973, the Children's Defense Fund (CDF) has worked toward reducing the numbers of neglected, sick, uneducated, and poor children in the United States. According to CDF, their research, public education campaigns, budget and policy advocacy, and coalition building have contributed to millions of children receiving immunizations, health care, child care, Head Start, a right to education, adoptions, a chance to escape poverty, and protections in the child welfare, mental health, and juvenile justice systems. More than four hundred CDF publications have provided educational materials to millions of Americans about child conditions and what can be done individually and collectively to make improvements. Some of the data available at this Web site is ideologically driven and designed to make a particular point. For example, under the heading "Where America Stands," the following piece of "data" is available: America is first in military technology and last in protecting children against gun violence. And under state data it can be found that in Virginia a child is born into poverty every forty-four minutes. There is also some raw data pertaining to income, poverty levels, and jobless rates. These data are available at http://www.childrensdefense.org/data/default.aspx.

Conclusion

Taken together, agency records, the agency-level administrative databases, and state and national data available from governmental and private organizations offer the agency-based child welfare researcher a wide range of options for developing (or enriching) one's own child welfare research endeavor.

PART 3

Measurement Strategies

[9]

Measurement Theory and Measure Selection

In this chapter the following topics will be discussed following the introduction of the chapter scenario and the brief literature review:

- Identifying key constructs/concepts
- Operationalizing key constructs/concepts
- Identifying existing measures
- Criteria for selecting measures
- Describing measures in a research paper/report
- Reliability and validity

CHAPTER SCENARIO

A caseworker supervisor notices that caseworker turnover appears to be increasing within the agency and is worried that this will negatively influence the timeliness of reunification efforts and morale in the foster home department. This concern is brought to the attention of the director of the program and together they begin to develop an idea for a research study of the predictors of caseworker turnover. Some research questions that they identify as of interest include: (1) What is the extent of caseworker turnover? And (2) what accounts for caseworker turnover?

BRIEF LITERATURE REVIEW: CASEWORKER TURNOVER

The problem of high turnover rates among front-line staff in the child welfare field is a longstanding one. A recent United States Government Accounting Office (1995) report found that 90 percent of states reported having difficulty recruiting and retaining child welfare workers. According to the Child Welfare League of America (2006), a quality child welfare workforce is essential to ensure good outcomes for children in the child welfare system. "No issue has a greater effect on the capacity of the child welfare system to serve at-risk and vulnerable children and families than the shortage of a competent, stable workforce." They found that in calendar year 2002, the average turnover rate in private agencies was 45 percent for casework and case management positions, 57 percent for residential and youth care positions, and 44 percent for supervisors.

Caseworker turnover is attributed to low wages, high caseloads, and generally intense, emotionally draining, and complex work. According to interviews with caseworkers conducted for a 2003 GAO report, demanding and extremely time-consuming paperwork was also a factor for many caseworkers, as well as insufficient training and supervision. There is also some evidence that the organizational climate has an effect on turnover rates (Glisson, Dukes, and Green 2006). In a similar vein, Smith (2004) found that factors positively associated with job retention included the perceptions that the employer promoted life-work balance, that a supervisor was supportive and competent, and that few other job alternatives were available. In addition, organization-level turnover rates and unmeasured organizational characteristics affected the likelihood of job retention.

When caseworkers leave their position, they create vacancies that place additional burdens and hardships on the remaining staff, who must cover these additional cases until new staff are hired. In this way, turnover is a problem that becomes compounded over time. This is especially true because of the limited pool of applicants available to fill the vacancies. In a 2001 survey of county and private child welfare agency administrators, 40 percent reported that the lack of a qualified applicant pool was the major cause of caseworker retention and recruitment problems (Child Welfare League of America 2001).

(continued)

The impact of turnover on the services provided to children and families and the outcomes for clients served by the system has been widely considered to be problematic, although empirical evidence for such a causal relationship is currently scarce. In one study, Unrau and Wells (2005) found that caseworker turnover was associated with periods of fewer services. Similarly, Pardeck (1984) found that caseworker turnover was associated with poorer outcomes such as multiple placements. While few studies have specifically assessed the effects of staff turnover on child welfare services, administrators and practitioners describe deleterious consequences of staff turnover on agency resources, staff morale, and service continuity and quality. Both the magnitude and apparent consequences of staff turnover underscore the need to explain, understand, and prevent it.

Overview of the Topic

Every study entails the measurement of constructs, either to describe the phenomenon or to assess associations between two or more constructs. Which constructs are of interest in any given study is determined by the research questions. Once the constructs have been identified, they are operationalized, exactly what manifestation of them will be measured is specified, and then appropriate measures of the constructs are selected. Usually at least one measure already exists for the constructs of interest. When that is the case, there are several considerations in selecting one of them for inclusion in the study measure.

Identifying Key Constructs/Concepts

Before measures can be selected, it is important for the researcher to know which constructs need to be measured. A construct is a concept, a model, or a schematic idea. It is a building block of the theory and bridges the gap between theory and the observable world (Corbetta 2003). If a program evaluation is being conducted, then a logic model will be developed that leads to the identification of the core study constructs (see chapter 17). If research is being conducted outside the scope of a program evaluation, then the research questions should guide the identification of the study constructs. This can happen in two ways: (1) starting with specific research questions or (2) starting with general theory. Sometimes in research studies there is a preexisting set of specific research questions that need to be answered. For example, in a study of caseworker turnover in a foster care agency, staff within the human resource department or casework supervisors might have a specific list of constructs they believe are causally related to turnover, and these will be the focus of the study. This might include marital status of the caseworker, age of the caseworker, and caseload size. The second way to identify the constructs of interest is through theory. In such a case there is general interest in understanding factors associated with caseworker turnover, but no preexisting set of constructs are thought to be especially important to study. Thus, if the general research questions were (1) "what is the extent of caseworker turnover?" and (2) "what accounts for the extent of caseworker turnover?" two superordinate constructs are identified: extent of casework turnover and predictors of turnover. The next step would be to identify through theory, prior research, and discussion with program staff a set of specific constructs that explicates "extent of caseworker turnover" and a theory of the "predictors of caseworker turnover." This theory would identify with greater specificity the constructs of interest. For example, the overarching construct of "predictors of caseworker turnover" could be further specified as sociodemographic characteristics of the caseworkers, prior child welfare work experience of the caseworkers, prior maltreatment and trauma history of the caseworkers, quality of supervision received by the caseworkers, caseworker career goals, and interpersonal relationships between caseworkers and colleagues within the agency. The researcher should aim as much as possible to identify every possible construct/predictor even though it is rarely, if ever, possible to measure all of them in any one study. But knowing what the full list is is part of the process of selecting which ones to measure. Once the full list has been identified, the constructs can be prioritized for inclusion in the study.

A major factor that will determine which constructs are to be included is whether the study will aim for depth or breadth. If depth is of interest, fewer constructs will be included, with perhaps several measures of each one. This will allow for a more thorough examination of the research question. On the other hand, if the goal is to achieve breadth of coverage, a larger number of constructs will be included, with no more than one (relatively short) measure of each. There is no right or wrong choice. It partly depends upon the goals of the study and it partly depends upon the existing knowledge base. For example, if very little research has already been conducted in a particular area, then it might make sense to start off with a broad study in which several constructs are examined. On the other hand, if several studies have already been conducted, it might make sense to look more closely at

one particular area, especially if there has been some controversy or incon-
sistency in findings across prior studies. Of course, the needs of the agency
are also a factor. If it is more likely that one set of findings can be applied to
improve practice or programs, it might make sense to focus on that area
rather than an area in which—regardless of the findings—the agency would
not be able to apply them.

Operationalizing Key Constructs

Operationalization is the process whereby the selected constructs are turned
into measurable phenomenon. The construct is the concept or idea of interest, while the operationalization specifies the observable phenomenon that
will be used as a measure of the concept. Each construct in a study needs to
be operationalized. Take, for example, the construct of "neighborhood
safety." This could be operationalized as number of crimes against persons
within a specified period of time. It could also be operationalized as an individual's perception of safety. A third alternative would be to count the number of places that meet some objective standard of danger (dark alleys, unlit
streets or parks, vacant lots, abandoned buildings, and so forth). Taking another example, "peer relationships" could be operationalized as popularity
or as maturity of social cognitive and conflict resolution skills. Even a common construct such as "school performance" could be operationalized as attendance, marking-period grades, or whether the child is promoted to the
next grade level. With rare exceptions, every construct can be operationalized in more than one way.

This is certainly true for the constructs in the proposed study of caseworker turnover within a foster care agency. For the first construct in the
set of predictors—sociodemographic characteristics of the caseworkers—
operationalization could include age at hiring, ethnicity, number of children,
and marital status. The third construct—prior maltreatment and trauma
history—could be operationalized as whether the caseworker had been physically abused as a child, whether the caseworker had been sexually abused as
a child, whether the caseworker had been neglected as a child, and/or whether
the caseworker experienced early loss of a parent as a child. Some constructs
are self-evident as to how they will be operationalized (e.g., age at hiring,
marital status), while others are complex and multifaceted (e.g., career aspirations, quality of supervision). Even a construct as simple as "caseworker
turnover" could be quite complex. For example, which types of departures from
a place of employment would constitute turnover: leaving due to pregnancy,

leaving due to family moving, leaving due to promotion within the agency, being fired, quitting, and so forth? Clearly, not all types of leavetakings are the same, although all represent a need to hire a new caseworker to replace the one who left. There is also the issue of timing. Few would argue that a caseworker leaving after forty-five years of dedicated service represents the same type of departure as someone leaving within the first three months of employment. As with most other research issues, there is no clear right or wrong approach; what is needed is consistency in definitions. It is usually advisable to collect more data than might seem necessary so that during the analysis phase decisions can be made to look more closely at certain areas. For example, if information about the reason for leaving is collected, then the analysis could report numbers for all caseworkers who leave as well as by type of leaving. Of course, the reason for leaving might also require some consideration in terms of who will provide that information. For example, if a person quit, he or she might report that the reason for leaving is discontent with the supervisor or too much paperwork, while the supervisor might report that the reason the person left was because he or she was not competent to perform the job's tasks. Again, it might make sense to collect data from both perspectives and analyze data both ways. The decision about how to operationalize the constructs in any given study should be based on theory, the specific research questions of the study, and knowledge of how the construct has been operationalized in prior studies. If one goal is to compare the findings of the current study with one or more studies already published, then it will be essential that the constructs are measured in such a way as to permit comparisons.

It might be helpful for the researcher to develop a chart of all of the various constructs in the study and how these constructs will be operationalized (a logic model can be developed if prior research and/or theory allow for an explication of the proposed relationships among these constructs as they relate to the dependent variable). Figure 9.1 presents an example of a chart of relevant constructs for the proposed study of caseworker turnover.

Only after the constructs have been operationalized can measures be selected. Thus, the next step in the process is to select the best measure for each construct. Often a measure already exists, but sometimes not, and in these cases the researcher will have to develop one (or eliminate the construct from the study). For a number of reasons explicated below, it is usually better to use an existing measure. In fact, developing a measure of a single construct (a measure of depression, anxiety, level of marital satisfaction, and so forth) is not recommended. Measure creation is an art and a science that

Figure 9.1
Chart of relevant constructs for study of caseworker turnover

Caseworker characteristics	Job characteristics
Sociodemographic factors	Job demands
Age	Perception of job difficulty
Marital status	Perception of ability to perform tasks
Ethnicity	Salary and benefits
Number of children	Salary
Prior child welfare history	Benefits
Ever in child welfare system	Importance of salary
Prior maltreatment/trauma	Importance of benefits
Physical abuse history	Quality of supervision
Sexual abuse history	Perception of helpfulness of supervisor
Neglect history	Frequency and duration of supervision
Loss of parent before age 20	Style of supervision received
Career aspirations	Social network at job
Perception of status of job	Number of friends at work
Importance of job status	Strength of friendships at work
Perception of career ladder	Extent of interpersonal conflicts at work
Importance of career ladder	Commute demands
	Length of commute
	Cost of commute
	Stressfulness of commute

many people do not have the time or resources to do well. There are entire books dedicated to item construction for measures and it is well outside the scope of this book to provide guidance about this task.

Identifying Existing Measures

Existing measures have all the benefits of having been tested and validated in the field and, often, they have norms and instructions for interpreting the results. For example, it has been established that on the Center for Epidemiological Studies Depression (CES-D) measure, a score above

16 indicates clinical depression. This knowledge has been gained through years of testing and validation studies. If a researcher used a "home-grown" measure of depression, there would be no way to determine what the cutoff score for depression would be (or whether in fact depression was actually being measured). In addition, someone else has already done the hard work of developing the items and formatting the measure for ease of administration. For these and other reasons, it is advisable to identify all the existing measures for the constructs of interest prior to developing a new measure. There are three primary sources for identifying existing measures.

The first source is the published research literature on the constructs of interest. Articles that have been published in peer-reviewed journals include a measure section, in which the specific measures utilized are described. A researcher new to a field can obtain information about the specific measures used in studies of the same construct by examining these articles. Searching for relevant articles is accomplished through searchable databases such as PsychInfo of the American Psychological Association, Social Science Abstracts, or social work abstracts (from NASW), all three of which are available in most academic libraries. Searching them will probably produce a long list of articles, many of which will mention specific measures. Once a list of measures has been identified through reading these articles, an Internet search can be conducted on these measures. Some measures even have their own Web sites providing detailed information about them. Identifying measures used in existing studies is yet another reason to conduct a thorough literature review prior to launching a study. Conducting a literature review of the core constructs in a study is an important step in theory development and knowledge building for the researcher and should not be skipped even if an existing measure has been selected.

An Internet search can be conducted on the construct as well. This will most likely reveal reports and papers that have not been published (but might still be of interest), in which various measures are discussed. Research centers and governmental agencies often prepare research reports on topics of interest that are not published in peer-reviewed journals. These reports would, therefore, not be revealed through a literature search of journals as described above. Often these reports are done well and should be included in any knowledge development activities of the early stages of planning a study. In addition, they usually contain a detailed measure section in which the various measures used in the study are described.

Finally, measurement books can be perused to identify measures. Most academic libraries have a collection of reference books that consist solely of reviews of measures. The *Mental Measurements Yearbooks* by the Buros Institute (Spies and Plake 2005) or the Tests in Print series (Murphy, Plake, Impara, and Spies 2002) are excellent starting places. For example, the *Mental Measurements Yearbook* includes up-to-date, consumer-oriented reviews of tests. A typical entry provides descriptive information about the measure along with one or more critical professional reviews and reviewer references. Likewise, Tests in Print (TIP) serves as a "comprehensive bibliography to all known commercially available tests that are currently in print in the English language." In its sixth edition, Tests in Print provides information to potential users about the test's purpose, publisher, in-print status, price, acronym, intended test population, administration time, publication date(s), and author(s). These and related books contain detailed descriptions of measures, reviews of reliability and validity information, and summaries of each one's strengths and weaknesses.

From these three steps, a list of potential measures for each study construct can be developed. The next step is to select one of the many possible measures for each construct for inclusion in the study.

Criteria for Selecting Measures

There is often more than one measure of a construct of interest in a study. The following nine criteria can be used to decide which, if any, to use in a study: (1) established reliability and validity, (2) cost, (3) availability, (4) use in the population of interest, (5) ethical considerations, (6) intrusiveness, (7) ability to detect change, (8) administration time, and (9) level of measurement.

Established Reliability and Validity

The major benefit of using an existing measure is that it has established reliability and validity. This means that—if chosen well—the measure will have been described in detail in either a manual or in a journal article as to its demonstrated reliability and validity. Researchers should be familiar with the different types of reliability and validity in order to evaluate the technical information presented about the psychometric properties of the measure. Based on this information, the various possible measures for any given construct can be compared and the one with the best reliability and validity data can be selected. If no such information is available, the measure probably should not be used. (See below for a detailed discussion of reliability and validity.)

Cost

Some measures are available free of charge while others require payments for purchasing individual copies of the measure, its manual, and/or for scoring the completed measures. While cost should not be the sole determinant of whether or not a measure is to be selected, it is a factor, and all costs should be known in advance in order to allow the researcher to keep within the study's budget.

Availability

Some measures need to be specially ordered (with or without a fee) and require special equipment that may or may not be available. Some measures are only made available to people with certain degrees or people with particular training and education. Whether any of these or other limits of availability apply to the particular measures of interest should be determined prior to selecting it.

Use in the Population of Interest

Some measures, despite being reliable and valid, have not been used in a particular population before and therefore might not be advisable for a given study. It is important to have a very clear understanding of the sample for the proposed study and to select measures that have been used with such a sample or are likely to pose no problem with such a sample.

Another consideration is whether the measure reveals any cultural or language bias that could be inappropriate for a given population. There are at least two aspects of this. The first is whether the scores mean the same thing in different cultures. In some cultures, a word might actually have a different meaning or connotation than what is normally understood to be the meaning of a word or concept. As an example, in certain cultures mothers as a matter of course refer to their babies as "mama," while in other cultures this is quite rare and can indicate "parentification" of the child. The second aspect of cultural and language bias is whether the experience of being asked something is culturally bound, even if the meaning of the word or idea is the same. For example, in some cultures it is highly embarrassing for a teenager to be asked about her age at first menstruation while in others it is less so. Familiarity with the language and cultural experiences of the potential research subjects is an important part of planning a study and selecting appropriate measures.

Ethical Considerations

Completing a measure (be it an interview, survey, or standardized form) is usually not a neutral experience. Even asking someone's age might evoke intense feelings in the person if he or she has personal issues with this topic. That being said, it should be self-evident that asking people to complete measures of parenting, depression, social support networks, and a host of other constructs relevant to research on families being served by the child welfare system can be an emotionally charged experience. Researchers have a moral obligation to be aware of the emotional impact of the measures participants will be asked to complete. Whenever possible, measures that are less disturbing for the respondent are better than those that are more disturbing. For highly charged measures (regarding sexual abuse, early loss and trauma, etc.) the researcher should believe it is vital to the study and that a serious contribution can be made to the knowledge base with the collection of that particular data.

A second aspect of ethical considerations is whether there will be any negative consequences attached to the responses to the questions on the measure. For example, asking a mother in a prevention program whether she is using illegal substances or alcohol, asking a foster parent whether she endorses corporal punishment, or asking a teen in a group home whether he or she is sexually active—in addition to being emotionally charged events—may also have negative consequences. For example, the mother admitting substance use might lose custody of her child, the foster parent who endorses corporal punishment might be mandated for immediate training on discipline techniques, and the teen who admits to being sexually active may be mandated for immediate counseling on sexuality and pregnancy. Most of the time, information collected for a research purpose is to be kept private and confidential. However, there are limits to confidentiality such that the researcher will need to share a respondent's answers with program staff and/or the authorities. Which items/measures this pertains to need to be identified in advance—through discussion with the IRB and the ethics committee—and the respondent needs to be informed of this in advance, in the informed consent procedures.

Intrusiveness

Some measures are more intrusive than others by requiring a greater degree of personal revelation than other measures. For example, one measure of depression might focus on the unique cognitive style of people who are depressed, while another measure might ask about thoughts of suicide. If both are reliable and valid for the study sample, it is probably preferable to use the less emotionally intrusive measure.

Ability to Detect Change

Some studies aim to detect change in constructs over time, such as change in attitudes, skills, or beliefs. If this is the case, then the measure must be designed for this purpose. This means that it can be administered to the same person more than one time, that the scores on the measure are sensitive to change in the person, and that in general the baseline scores will not be on the high end of the scale at the first administration. For example, if a group of six-year-old children are administered the Cooperative Preschool Inventory at baseline for a one-year study, they are all likely to score at the high end at baseline. There is little room for them to "grow" on that measure over time. At post-test they are all likely to be top scorers. With this measure, there is no opportunity to demonstrate change over time. Another factor is that some measures are only appropriate for certain age groups, and as the sample matures over time, they may "age out" of appropriateness for a given measure.

It is important to remember, however, that it is never appropriate to select a sample based on low scores on a measure. It is acceptable to select a measure on which it is expected that most of the sample will score poorly at baseline and then administer it to the whole sample at a subsequent data collection assessment in order to detect change over time. What is to be avoided is administering a measure at baseline and then only selecting the low scorers to measure again at a second point in time. This will most likely result in improvements in scores due to an artifact known as regression to the mean.

Administration Time

It is likely that a battery of measures will be administered at any given time to the study sample. If this is so, then the overall time it takes to complete the full data collection assessment needs to be considered in selecting individual measures for the study. Attention span and free time to complete the measures dictate that the whole session should not take more than 1 to 1.5 hours. Anything more and the person may feel irritated with the process and decline to participate in the next session. They also may become fatigued and pay less attention to their answers as they make their way through a lengthy set of measures. Two measures equally useful in every other way should be judged based on the time it takes for completion, with preference given to the one that can be completed in less time.

Level of Measurement

The level of measurement produced by the measure can also be a consideration. The possible types of measurement include nominal, ordinal, interval, or ratio. Nominal measurement classifies individuals into categories that have no numeric value, such as a measure of marital status (1=Currently married, 2=Currently separated, 3=Divorced and not remarried, etc.). The assignment of numbers is completely arbitrary; it cannot be said that category 1 is less than category 2. The categories in nominal measures are also discrete. An individual is either one or the other; there are no midpoints between the categories. In general, one cannot be half married and half divorced or one-fifth separated. No mathematical functions can be conducted on nominal measures other than frequency counts (how many were classified as currently married, how many as separated, etc.) and comparisons of frequencies across two or more groups (proportion of divorced in one sample as compared to in another sample).

Like nominal variables, ordinal variables are also discrete categorical variables, but in this case the values have ordered meaning, with one being higher than the next. The values are ranked such that higher numbers represent more of the property than lower numbers. The categories in ordinal scales, as with nominal scales, are discrete (there are no midpoints). One can have a score of 1 or 2 or 3 but not some point in between the categories. Examples of ordinal measures include educational degree (1=high school, 2=community college, 3=four-year college, 4=master's degree, and 5=doctorate). Each category represents an increase in the number of years of schooling, but the numbers themselves have no numeric value. Measures of satisfaction are also ordinal (0=not at all, 1=somewhat, 2=very much), in which 2 represents more satisfaction than 1, which represents more satisfaction than 0. In ordinal measures, the distance between the categories cannot be measured and is not presumed to be the same across the scale. That is, 3 is more than 2 and 2 is more than 1, but the distance between 1 and 2 is not known to be the same as the distance between 2 and 3. Because of this, it cannot be stated that a score of 2 represents twice as much of the property as a score of 1. As with nominal scales, analyses can be conducted that count the frequency of the categories within a single sample (e.g., what proportion of caseworkers had a master's degree) and compare proportions across samples (e.g., is the proportion of caseworkers with master's/doctorate degrees higher in the group who leave the agency within a year than in the group of those who stay at their jobs at least one year?). In addition, one can use ordinal measures to compare amounts across samples (e.g., do caseworkers who leave their job report lower satisfaction with supervision than caseworkers who stay?).

Interval scales have all the properties of ordinal and nominal variables and, in addition, have the added benefit of being a continuous measure in which the distance between the points on the scale is equal. That is, the distance between 1 and 2 is the same as the distance between 2 and 3. Measures of achievement and IQ are examples of interval scales. Thus, it is possible to say that the distance between a score of 100 and 110 on an IQ scale is the same as the distance between a score of 110 and 120. However, because there is no known zero point on these scales, it cannot be said that one score is so many times greater than another score (i.e., IQ scores of 100 are not twice as high as IQs of 50). In reality, many interval scales are treated as ratio scales for analytic purposes, allowing for utilization of all inferential statistics.

Only ratio scales have a known fixed zero point. Examples include age, weight, temperature, number of people in a family, and so forth. Ratio scales allow for statements regarding the differences between scores such that a score of 100 can be said to be twice as much as a score of 50. All analytic techniques can be used with a ratio scale.

The reason that the type of scale is relevant for measure selection is that certain research questions lend themselves naturally to certain types of analyses, which require certain properties of the measurement. For example, if the research question pertains to explaining the proportion of variance in a dependent variable with a set of possible independent variables, then the dependent variable needs to be measured in such a way as to produce an interval or ratio scale. One measure of the construct might produce a variable that is ordinal, while another measure of the same construct might result in a variable that is interval. Thus knowing in advance which statistics will be conducted in order to answer the study questions is important information for the planning stage, as it helps direct the selection of measures.

Describing the Measure in the Research Paper/Final Report

Whichever measure is used, the final report or paper will need to describe it in such a way that the reader understands the rationale for its inclusion in the study. The full name of the measure should be presented along with its acronym (if one exists) and a reference to the primary article or manual that presents information about it. A brief summary of its psychometric properties should be included, along with whether or not the measure has been used in samples similar to the one in the current study. Any recoding or creation of subscales should be included in the description of the measure. An example is provided in figure 9.2.

Reliability and Validity

Measure selection, as noted above, is primarily the search for a measure that is first and foremost reliable and valid. All other factors are secondary. The measure that is least expensive, shortest, most appropriate for the population, least intrusive, most available, most able to detect change, most ethical, and most appropriate for producing a certain level of measurement is useless without reliability and validity. These two topics will be explored in some detail below. The discussion provides the reader with the basic principles of what reliability and validity are and how to establish them, although this is only necessary when developing a measure (something that is not encouraged without the assistance of an expert in measurement development). This information is provided because it is essential that every researcher understand these principles and can assess the extent to which existing measures meet the criteria of being reliable and valid.

Figure 9.2
Sample measure description

THE CHILD BACKGROUND CHARACTERISTICS FORM

The Child Background Characteristics Form is an extensive child background measure. This form was completed within sixty days of admission to the foster care agency by the staff person most familiar with the youth and his/her case (based primarily on information obtained from a chart review). For purposes of describing the sample, five demographic variables were selected based on their face validity and ease of comparability across other studies: ethnicity (Caucasian, African American, Latino, mixed, or other), gender, legal status (abuse/neglect, dependent/delinquent), permanency planning goal (return to parent/relative, independent living/adoption), and age at entry to the program. In order to develop programmatic and policy implications from the data, the age variable was recoded into a categorical variable. That is, rather than being able to conclude that older children were more likely to have certain characteristics without being able to specify what age that referred to, age was recoded into a dichotomous variable (0=youth up to 11.99 years of age at admission and 1=youth 12.00 years and older at admission). The rationale underling this grouping was to differentiate preadolescent from adolescent youth.

THE CHILD BEHAVIOR CHECKLIST (CBCL)

The CBCL is a widely used measure of severity of child behavior problems (Achenbach 1991). The CBCL has been used extensively in research studies documenting extent of clinical symptomatology, change in problems over time, and comparability of different populations (Achenbach et al. 2002). In addition, the measure has been used in the field of child welfare to confirm that children being served by child welfare settings have greater problems than the general population, and that such problems tend to increase with program restrictiveness (Handwerk, Friman, Mott, and Stairs 1998). Child welfare agencies have utilized the CBCL to help decide on intervention/ placement, assess behavioral shifts over time/between environments, and evaluate intervention outcomes (Achenbach and McConoughy 1997; Hukkanen, Sourander, and Bergroth 2003; Shore, Sim, Le Prohn, and Keller 2002). Prior research has also established that for children in the foster care system, nonparental adult reporters may be more accurate than either youth self-report or parent report (Handwerk et al. 1998).

Reliability

Reliability refers to the accuracy and predictability of a measure. It means, in short, that the same measure applied to the same person at two points in time will produce the same (or very close) score in the absence of change in the person. Without reliability, it would not be possible to interpret changes in scores at two points in time because the change could be due to either unreliability of the measure or real change in the person. One needs to rule out the first possible explanation (unreliability in the measure) in order to conclude that changes in scores are due to real changes in the person. A second—and unrelated—step is to determine the cause of the change, which could be due to maturation, an external historical event, the experience of having taken the test already, and so forth. All of these are threats to internal validity of the design of a study and are explored in chapter 7. For purposes of understanding reliability, the only thing that matters is being able to ascertain that the change is not due to unreliability of the measure itself.

When the measure consists of one or more items on a paper-and-pencil measure, there are several methods of establishing reliability.

TYPES OF RELIABILITY

The first type is test-retest reliability. This is assessed by the same group of individuals being administered the same exact test at two points in time when there is no expectation of change in performance (skills, knowledge, attitudes) from one test administration to another. Typically, one or two weeks elapse between the two administrations of the measure. A correlation is than computed between the individual's scores on the two versions of the test. Correlations above .85 are considered demonstrative of test-retest reliability. This form of reliability has two very serious drawbacks. The first is that the same group of individuals needs to be available at two testing sessions, and the second is that simply taking the test could change a person's scores on that test. This could happen in a few ways. A test of knowledge could spark a person to look up the correct answer between the first and second assessment. It is also possible that a measure of attitudes could change a person's attitudes by drawing attention to the issue. Conversely, there could be greater consistency from time 1 to time 2 simply because the person remembers how he or she answered during the first test-taking session and feels obligated or compelled to provide the same answer during the second test-taking session.

An improvement on test-retest is represented by the second type of reliability analysis, parallel forms. In this case, two versions of the same measure are administered to the same individuals at two points in time—each consisting of different but comparable items. Results of the two test-taking sessions can be compared through correlation of total scores. Parallel forms eliminates some of the problems with test-retest, in which using the same exact version of the measure at two points in time could artificially inflate reliability scores simply because an individual remembers how he or she responded to the same items at the earlier administration. However, because two testing sessions are still required in this form of reliability assessment, it does not eliminate the difficulty of making sure that all of the people who participated in the first round of test taking return for the second round. Another drawback to parallel forms is that twice as many items for the final version of the measure need to be developed, so two parallel forms can exist for the reliability assessment.

A third approach, split-half, eliminates both the need for two versions of the measure and the need for two testing sessions. In split-half, one measure is administered at one point in time. One half of the measure is treated as one version of the measure and the other half is treated as a second form of the same measure. Statistical analyses are conducted to ascertain the extent to which scores on each half of the measure are comparable to each other. This is accomplished either through a correlation of total scores of each half or through a split-half reliability analysis (available on SPSS). The results are the same. It should be quite clear that this only works when every item on the measure is designed to assess the same single construct (i.e., anxiety, popularity, knowledge of child rearing, and so forth). One decision to contend with is what constitutes "half" of a measure. If the first half is compared to the second half, fatigue and boredom might alter scores on the second half—separate from issues of unreliability. A commonly used solution is to consider the even-numbered items one half of the test and the odd-numbered items the other half of the test.

Validity

Reliability establishes that the measure is accurate and consistent in what is being measured, but it does not speak to whether the measure is measuring what it is intended to measure. That is what validity refers to. The metaphor of a dartboard is often invoked to explain the relationship between reliability and validity. The bull's eye represents the construct of interest and the darts represent items on the measure. If there is neither reliability nor validity, all the darts miss the bull's eye and are hit various areas on the dartboard. That is, not only are the items not measuring the construct of interest, they are also not consistent in whatever they are measuring. If the darts all hit the same place on the dartboard but that place is not the bull's eye, the darts are reliable but not valid. That is, there is consistency in the items: they are all measuring the same construct. However, that construct is not the construct of interest. Only when all the darts hit the bull's eye is there reliability and validity. The items are all consistently measuring the same construct, which happens to be the intended construct.

Validity is important to establish because conclusions will be drawn about the constructs based on the measurements. For example, if a measure of quality of supervision is found to be statistically significantly associated with caseworker turnover, the agency could conceivably change supervision practice based on that finding. However, if the measure itself were not valid and actually measured a different but related construct, then the changes made in practice could be unresponsive to the actual cause of caseworker turnover.

TYPES OF VALIDITY

As with reliability, there is more than one way to assess the validity of a measure. The first is content validity, which entails a judgment made by designated experts that all of the necessary content is included in a measure. For example, if a new measure of caseworker knowledge of child welfare policy was being developed and a list of items were generated as possible items to be included on the measure, this list would be shown to various experts in the field of child welfare casework practice in order to determine whether all necessary content areas were included on the measure. Thus, the universe of possible topics must be identified in advance so that the content of the proposed measure can be compared to this universe to ensure adequate sampling of the universe. There is no specific statistical test to determine whether a measure has content validity.

Face validity is also based on the judgment of others, and in this way is like content validity. In fact, sometimes the two terms are used interchangeably. The difference is that face validity is established by examination of the items by those likely to be administered the measure. That is, individuals with special knowledge of or experience with the construct of interest conclude that the measure appears (on the face of it) to be measuring what it purports to measure. This is most important in research with populations who might have a negative response to items or feel alienated due to the measure being too different from what it is supposed to measure.

Criterion-related validity involves the calculation of the extent to which the measure is associated with scores on an external criterion measure. This is a data-driven form of validity analysis. As an example, if theory dictates that a measure of positive parenting is associated with a low likelihood of maltreatment, a new measure of positive parenting would establish its validity against a measure of subsequent maltreatment. Two common difficulties with this form of validity analysis is the lack of a known and valid criterion and the inability to obtain data on that measure for the same sample that has the new measure. It is also possible that associations exist between the two measures, because the first measure is a valid measure of some third construct that is itself associated with the criterion. Caution, therefore, needs to be taken when selecting the criterion measure.

Construct validity is also a data-driven form of validity assessment. In construct validity, the measure is assessed for its ability to be statistically associated with other measures that theory dictates it would be associated with. Evaluation of construct validity requires examining the statistical associations between the measure being evaluated and variables that are known to be related to the construct purportedly measured by the instrument. Associations that are consistent with the expected pattern of relationships contribute evidence of construct validity. There are two primary forms of construct validity, convergent and discriminant (or divergent). In the first, the measure of interest is statistically associated with variables that theory dictates it should be associated with, and in the second the measure is not statistically associated with variables theory dictates it would not be.

Conclusion

Every research study involves the identification of constructs of interest. Once constructs have been identified, they can be operationalized through the selection of measures. Often, more than one measure exists for any given construct, and the criteria provided in this chapter can be used to select the ones that best meet the needs of the study. The two most important criteria are established reliability and validity, which ensure that the measure actually measures the construct of interest and does so with a minimum of error. All measures used in a study should be described in the final report or paper so that others can know exactly how each construct was operationalized and measured.

Surveys

In this chapter, the following topics will be discussed following the introduction of the chapter scenario and the brief literature review:

- Deciding when to use surveys as a research method
- Defining the sample for a survey study
- Survey data collection strategies
- Designing the survey
- Developing survey questions: Improving clarity and precision
- Developing survey questions: Types of survey questions
- Piloting the survey
- Obtaining consent
- Maintaining confidentiality
- Training telephone and face-to-face interviewers
- Ensuring adequate response rate
- Reporting the results

CHAPTER SCENARIO

Agency staff begin to hear complaints about youth acting out sexually in both foster home and group home programs. A coalition of agencies from the same geographic area is formed to discuss whether this problem is widespread. This coalition convenes a working group that decides to survey all agencies about the extent of this problem. The primary research questions of the survey project are: (1) What proportion of youth served by the agencies was estimated to act out sexually? (2) Do these proportions vary by level of care? And (3) what challenges do agency staff believe these behaviors pose for the agency?

BRIEF LITERATURE REVIEW: THE PROBLEM OF SEXUALIZED BEHAVIORS OF YOUTH IN THE FOSTER CARE SYSTEM

Research on children who act out sexually is a relatively new area of empirical investigation (Pithers, Gray, Busconi, and Houchens 1998). This is particularly true for the subset of youth served by the child welfare system (Baker, Friedrich, Parker, Schneiderman, Gries, and Archer, forthcoming; Baker, Schneiderman, and Parker 2001), despite the fact that they are at heightened risk of having sexual behavior problems. Significant portions of children who have been removed from their homes and placed in foster care have suffered sexual abuse, a known precursor of sexual behavior problems (Hall, Mathews, and Pearce 2002). According to the Child Welfare League of America (1995), 13 percent of the almost 500,000 children in foster care have been sexually abused. Additionally, some parents voluntarily place their children in care because of their sexual acting out behavior. This issue is of particular concern because problematic sexualized behaviors of youth in the child welfare system have the potential to interfere with an agency's ability to keep children safe and to develop a permanency plan, the two primary objectives of the child welfare system (Pecora, Whittaker, Maluccio, Barth, and Plotnick 2000). Specifically,

(continued)

children in the child welfare system who exhibit such behaviors are likely to put themselves and their peers at risk of harm because of their provocative and inappropriate behaviors. In addition, children in the child welfare system who exhibit problematic sexualized behaviors are at risk for placement failure because foster and adoptive parents may reject children whose sexual behaviors are disturbing and excessive. This is especially true if there are other children in the home and if the foster parent has not received adequate training to understand and deal with these behaviors (Hoyle 2000). Sexual behavior in child welfare group care settings such as residential treatment is also problematic because of insufficient staff training. Crenshaw (1993) suggests that sexual acting out is one of the most difficult behavioral issues for child-care staff. Thus, a survey of agencies about the sexual acting out behaviors of youth would be a significant contribution to the field.

Overview of the Topic

Survey research involves the systematic collection of data regarding opinions, experiences, and reported behaviors (as opposed to observed behaviors) on a sample of individuals, in order to generalize the findings to a population of interest. Surveys contain primarily closed-ended items (also known as forced-choice items, because all possible response options are provided and the respondent is "forced" to choose one). Survey data tend to be primarily quantitative. Surveys can be mailed or e-mailed to people, conducted over the telephone, administered by computer, or administered to individuals or groups in a face-to-face format. Surveys tend to be developed on a study-by-study basis by the project researcher in order to meet the needs of a particular study. Surveys are one of the most common measurement strategies available to the child welfare researcher and are appropriate for correlational as well as quasi-experimental and experimental designs.

Deciding When to Use Surveys as a Research Method

Survey research is an ideal way to collect a large amount of quantitative data relatively easily and has been employed in the social sciences for many years. Lazarsfeld (see Kendall and Lazarsfeld 1950) and Stouffer

(1949) are viewed as the pioneers in the use of surveys in social science research. It is a measure that is best used to collect information on people's beliefs, attitudes, and experiences (Babbie 1990). A survey is not appropriate to gather in-depth information about people's feelings or to document people's actual behaviors or competencies. Examples of questions that could be answered through a survey study include: (1) What proportion of agency staff report satisfaction with their job and the various components of it? (2) Does the age and gender of therapists in a community-based mental health center affect the likelihood of reporting use of trauma-based therapy for foster care youth? Or (3) are youth in congregate care reported to be more likely to act out sexually than youth in foster homes? This third question was generated from the scenario at the opening of the chapter and will serve as the example for the remainder of the discussion on surveys.

As with any measurement strategy, there are advantages and disadvantages inherent in the use of surveys. The primary advantage of surveys is that the data are relatively easy and inexpensive to collect, enter, and analyze, and the findings are quantitative and appropriate for many different types of statistical approaches. The primary disadvantages of surveys are sampling problems and the risk of a low response rate. Unless a sufficient proportion of surveys are completed (ideally, at least 80 percent), the data might not be valid. Another potential drawback is that poorly developed survey questions can result in erroneous conclusions.

Defining the Sample

Identifying the Respondent

Because surveys are in large part a measure of attitudes, beliefs, and experiences (as opposed to facts), it is important to determine *whose* ideas and beliefs are of interest. That is, who should actually complete the survey? For example, if attitudes about sexual acting out in foster care is the primary research focus, this will need to be further narrowed down to determine whether it is the foster parent's experiences with the sexually acting out child and their attitudes about that or the caseworker's ideas about the foster parent's attitudes and skill in dealing with sexually acting out behaviors of youth in their care. Additional possible respondents for a survey of sexual acting out behaviors of children in child welfare agencies include the president/executive director of an agency, the directors of foster home programs within the agency, caseworker and social work staff working with the youth, or the youth themselves. Each offers a valid and important perspective, although they are not interchangeable. As with all studies, the major research questions need to be developed with sufficient specificity to guide the identification of the unit of analysis and an appropriate sampling strategy. An excellent general text to consult for further information about sampling using a survey design is *Survey Sampling* by Kish (1965). The following discussion relates to sampling in the child welfare field.

If staff within an agency is deemed to be the appropriate respondents, a multiagency study might be necessary. This is especially so if the respondent is to be the president/executive director of an agency, because there is only one per agency. Obviously, multiple agencies will need to be included in the study in order to obtain a sample larger than one. If the respondents are the directors of foster home programs, there might be more than one director per agency, but probably no more than three or four, and a multiagency study would still be necessary. If the designated respondents are caseworkers, social workers, foster parents, or biological parents, it is possible that a single agency can produce a sufficient sample size.

In surveying staff across agencies it is very important to decide in advance who is appropriate to complete the survey (e.g., what is their place in the hierarchy and how much closeness or distance to a particular program should they have?). If the survey is mailed, it is possible that the recipient of the survey will ask someone else to complete it (this is especially true when surveys are mailed to executive directors/presidents, who are likely to delegate such tasks). Therefore, the survey itself should contain items about the respondent (name, title, length of time in that position, length of time at the agency) and directions about who the possible respondents could be. These data should be presented in the final report or paper. If a specific type of staffperson is required to complete the survey, this needs to be specified in both the cover letter and on the survey itself. Qualifying variables include title, degree, working in a specific type of program, having a specific type of clientele, or working in the program/agency for a specific period of time. For example, surveys could be geared toward caseworkers in a foster home department who have been working in that program for at least twelve months and who work with children over the age of two. Or a survey could be geared toward therapists in a community-based mental health center who have provided therapy to at least one foster child under the age of eighteen years in the past twelve months.

Determining Sample Size

As noted in chapter 5, it is rarely possible to survey the entire population of interest. Thus, a subset of the population will comprise the sample of the study, the responses of which will be generalized to the larger population. With a survey study, estimating sample size is complicated by the issue of response rate. That is, first the researcher needs to calculate the desired sample size of completed surveys (see chapter 5). Following that, the researcher will need to estimate the response rate (what proportion of the sample will likely complete the survey) and then determine how many potential survey participants will be invited to participate. For example, if it is determined that a final sample of one hundred is desired and the response rate is likely to be 80 percent, then 125 participants need to be invited to participate. A response rate below 80 percent seriously compromises the generalizability of the findings. Thus, it is not advisable to maximize the chances of obtaining a sufficient sample by underestimating the response rate. For example, one could propose to invite two hundred individuals to participate in the study with the hopes of receiving one hundred completed surveys. However, the response rate of 50 percent would decrease the confidence in the findings below standards acceptable in the field. In addition, the cost involved in preparing twice as many survey packets as needed would be prohibitive for many projects. Therefore it is advisable to develop a survey that is likely to be completed by the vast majority of the participants and to develop a follow-up system that is likely to generate a high (over 80 percent) response rate.

If more than one individual within an agency participates in a survey, two forms of response rate are involved: agency level and respondent level. That is, ten agencies might have been invited to participate in a project, eight of which agreed to do so, resulting in an agency level response rate of 80 percent. Of the eight participating agencies, perhaps one hundred caseworkers were invited to be surveyed, eighty-two of which agreed to do so. This would produce a respondent response rate of 82 percent. For the integrity of the study, high response rates (at least 80 percent) are desirable at both the agency and the individual level. Both should be closely monitored and presented in the final report/paper about the project.

Sampling Agencies as the Unit of Analysis

If the agency is the unit of analysis (one survey per agency and the respondent represents the agency's perspective, not the perspective of any one individual), at least three possible approaches can be used for selecting the sample of agencies that will be invited to participate in the study. The first is to narrowly define the population of agencies and aim to measure every member. In the first option, the population is defined as every agency within a geographic range (such as every child welfare agency contracted to serve families within a particular county, or every agency providing a particular type of program within a specific region). The sampling frame is essentially the same as the population and thus there is no selection procedure, as the frame is small enough such that every member can be invited to participate in the study.

The second choice is to define the population more broadly and select a random sample of agencies to invite to participate in the study. If the population is large (say over two hundred agencies) and therefore cannot easily be surveyed as a whole, a variety of random selection procedures can be used to study a subset (see chapter 5). As long as the full list of every agency within the sample can be obtained, then a random sample can be selected. Stratified random selection might be advisable if there are key sources of variation among agencies that need to be reflected in the sample (see chapter 5).

If agency "buy-in" is perceived to be necessary prior to the delivery of the surveys, and this cannot be obtained from the full set of agencies (too much work to arrange for this, or in fact some agencies indicate they do not support the project), then a convenience sample is the likely sampling approach. In this strategy, agencies are presented with information about the project in advance and are asked to indicate their willingness to cooperate. All agencies that agree to participate will be asked to complete the survey (if the final pool is still large, a random sample can be selected from that list). A considerable drawback of convenience samples is that the agencies that choose to participate might differ from those that do not participate (i.e., are not representative of the population) in ways that would affect the findings. For example, if agencies with more sexually acting out clients were less likely to participate in the survey, the findings would underestimate the problem. On the other hand, if agencies that perceive this issue to be relevant were more likely to participate, then the findings would overestimate the problem.

Multiple Informants Within Multiple Agencies

If multiple informants within multiple agencies are required for the sample, the researcher will need to develop strategies for identifying appropriate staff within the agencies for inclusion in the study, in the event that the population of possible respondents is too large to include in the sample. There are two primary options: the agency allows the researcher to select the sample, or someone within the agency selects the sample. The primary concern with the latter option is that bias can be introduced into the process. For example, if a multiagency study is being conducted of foster parent attitudes about sexual acting out in children, and each participating agency is asked to select 20 percent of its foster parent caseload for inclusion in the study, it is quite possible that an agency will select parents who are perceived to be most likely to put the agency in a good light. Therefore, whenever possible, the participants (staff, youth, foster parents) should be randomly selected by the researcher. Ideally, the agency is willing to provide the researcher with a list of all members of the sampling frame from which to randomly select the sample. The identifiers on the list could be initials or truncated ID codes so that confidentiality is preserved. A compromise option is for the researcher to guide the agency in a step-by-step random selection strategy.

Survey Data Collection Strategies

Surveys can be sent to potential participants in the mail, conducted over the telephone, completed on a computer, or administered in person (individually or to a group).

Mail and E-Mail Surveys

Mail surveys are the most common form of survey data collection and as a strategy it has many advantages. Primary among them is that participants can complete the survey in comfort and privacy and can work on them at their own pace. Participants may be more willing to be honest if they are writing responses on a piece of paper than speaking directly to a person. Mail surveys in the long run cost less than telephone and face-to-face surveys, which require staff training and data collection time. The primary cost of mail surveys is postage (original mailing, reminder postcards, second and third mailings, and return postage for the completed surveys).

Disadvantages of mail surveys include the researcher not being able to clarify questions for the respondents or observe whether a respondent seems disingenuous or confused in his or her responses. Mail surveys also require a presentation on the page that at a minimum is not confusing or distracting and at most is attractive and appears to be easy to complete. Mail surveys require more effort on the part of the respondent, who must not only complete the survey but also take the time to mail it or fax it back to the researcher. Another drawback to mailed surveys is that some samples (which may include clients from a child welfare program) may be reluctant to open mail sent from an agency and may have limitations in literacy skills that interfere with reliable completion of the survey (errors due to misunderstanding words, checking the wrong answers by accident, and so forth). For these reasons, mail surveys are best suited to professionals as well as other individuals with known addresses who are likely to open their mail and be comfortable completing complex paper and pencil formats.

Mailed surveys require preparation of the packet of material that is sent to each potential respondent. The packet must contain the following three essential items: (1) A cover letter on official letterhead by someone briefly explaining the project and urging the respondent to complete the survey in clearly specified means (mail, fax, e-mail) to a specified address and by a clearly specified deadline. See figure 10.1 for a sample letter. This letter should be individually addressed if the survey respondents are executive directors of agencies, addressed to "Dear Colleague" if sent to professionals in the field, "Dear Foster Parent" if sent to foster parents, and "Dear Parent" if sent to biological parents. (2) The survey itself, which should be legibly printed and double sided. (3) A self-addressed stamped envelope with sufficient postage for the completed survey. The packet might also contain a small token of appreciation.

Mailing labels will need to be made up, one for each respondent and two for the researcher/sponsor of the project. One label will be used as the return address on the envelope that is mailed and the other will be used as the addressee for the self-addressed stamped envelope provided to each respondents in the packet.

E-mailing surveys instead of mailing them is a recent development in social science research. A benefit of e-mail surveys is the elimination of costs (photocopying and postage), while unique drawbacks include the researcher needing to have access to the participants' e-mail address and the participants being minimally proficient in computer technology to enable editing of Word documents and utilization of file attachments.

Computer Surveys

An even more recent development is the advent of computer-created and administered surveys. Several companies sell software specially designed to facilitate the social scientist in the creation of computer-based surveys.

Figure 10.1

Sample cover letter to accompany mailed survey

November 2005
Dear Colleague,

Your participation is being requested for an interagency study of problematic sexualized behaviors of youth in the child welfare system. The study is sponsored by the interagency coalition of problematic sexualized behaviors, which is composed of over thirty-five agencies in the (NAME GEOGRAPHIC REGION). The project is also supported by (NAME OF ORGANIZATION).

A unique ID has been placed on your survey for the purposes of allowing us to contact people who have not yet completed the survey. Once all the data has been collected, the master list linking the ID with the individual will be discarded, and there will be no way to trace the survey to its respondent. The master ID list will be stored in a locked filing cabinet until it is discarded.

The findings from the study will be aggregated across all agencies and presented in a professional scholarly journal in the field. The findings in summary format will also be made available free of charge to all survey participants. Your individual data will not be shared with anyone.

As you can see, the focus of the study is problematic sexualized behaviors (PSB) of children in the child welfare system. For the purposes of this study, PSB is defined as any sexual behaviors that cause a problem for the child and/or his or her caretakers.

Too little is known about the problem of PSB in children being served by the child welfare system. We are hoping that the results of this study can be used to help agencies better understand this phenomenon and improve services for children and families dealing with this issue.

We thank you in advance for taking the time to complete the survey. It should take no longer than twenty minutes to fill out and does not require consultation with any charts or data. It is your perceptions, experiences, and beliefs that are of importance. It is acceptable that you designate someone else in the agency to complete the survey, but it is important that this person represents you and has a broad perspective and knowledge of the agency.

Please return the completed survey to me by (DATE) in the self-addressed stamped envelope that is enclosed for your convenience. If you have questions, comments, or concerns about this survey, please contact the project manager (NAME) at (INSERT CONTACT INFORMATION).

Sincerely,

(NAME)
(TITLE)
(ADDRESS)

These programs eliminate much of the tedious work involved in formatting a Word document into a survey. These programs also offer special design features that create a more pleasing visual presentation (theme-based clip art, pleasing color schemes, interesting page borders, and so forth). These programs have the added advantage of automatically creating a database of responses and accompanying graph and chart presentation of the results. However, as with e-mail surveys, these programs require access to computers and the Internet, and the respondent must have a minimal proficiency level for completion of the survey. One unique advantage, however, is that there are often built-in checks that prevent the respondent from skipping items or making other errors such as checking two items when only one should be selected.

Telephone Surveys

Telephone and face-to-face surveys have the primary advantage of the researcher having direct access to the respondent to encourage participation, explain the items, and gauge the sincerity of the responses. In addition, less effort is required on the part of the respondent (once the questions are completed, his or her work is done). On the other hand, telephone and face-to-face interviews require considerably more effort on the part of research staff to ensure that surveyors are consistent in their survey techniques (tone of voice, warmth, phrasing of the questions, extent and nature of follow-up questions and probes, and persistence in scheduling appointments). Variation in survey technique can introduce error into the project. The cost is also greater than mail surveys, because staff need to be trained and paid for their time while scheduling and conducting the surveys. Each potential respondent might need to be contacted ten or fifteen times in order to be reached (in light of unanswered phones, busy signals, answering machines, rescheduling of missed appointments, and so forth). Even though the survey itself might only take thirty minutes to complete on the phone, at least an hour of each staffperson's time might be allocated for scheduling. In addition, surveyors need to be available to conduct the surveys during the evenings and weekends, when most people are available. If the survey is translated into another language, bilingual or multilingual surveyors will be necessary. Needless to say, telephone surveys can only be conducted with individuals who have telephones and known phone numbers.

For all these reasons, telephone surveys are best suited for potential participants who have telephones and listed numbers, who live in places that researchers are not likely to travel to, who do not readily come to a central location where researchers could recruit them, and for a variety of reasons are not likely to open their mail from an unknown person or are unable or unlikely to complete a paper-and-pencil survey on their own. In child welfare research, this best describes foster parents (who are required to have telephone numbers on record with the agency) but not biological parents (who are not required and often do not have telephone numbers on record at the agency).

Face-to-Face Surveys

Face-to-face administration of surveys can be conducted with groups or individuals. This is best when the sample is easily accessible in person, as is the typical scenario of students enrolled in an introductory social work course: the students are present and can be recruited on the spot. A comparable situation might involve recruiting child welfare program clients who are attending a workshop or training session. If the sample of interest tends to congregate in a predictable time and place, then group recruitment might be feasible (although consent would need to be obtained individually). However, group administration is not advisable if the respondents might have difficulty understanding the survey questions and/or following the survey format. All of the costs associated with conducting telephone surveys apply to individually administered face-to-face surveys as well. Surveyors need to be trained and paid for their time arranging the appointments as well as administering the surveys. Most likely there will be several attempts before each survey is completed, and although staff may not be collecting any data, they will need to be paid for their time. Cost for transportation and refreshments will increase the budget when individually administered face-to-face surveys are conducted. For these reasons, face-to-face individual surveys are probably best suited for situations in which more in-depth information is desired, there is doubt as to the potential participants' ability to complete a written survey, and there is no other means of gaining access to individuals (they do not have known telephones or addresses). An example of the latter would be individuals who attend a one-time-only event (information session, one-day training, a conference, etc.).

Designing the Survey

Surveys should be presented on the page in such a way as to be pleasing to the eye and easy to follow. Densely packed questions, frequent changes in fonts or margins, and small margins may be so confusing or disconcerting to the potential participant that it may lower the response rate. Surveys should be no more than six pages in length (three double-sided pages if mailed, in order to reduce postage associated with returning the survey)—any longer, and the recipient is likely to feel overwhelmed and unable to complete it without a significant amount of effort. Surveys should not require the participant to write extensive answers to open-ended questions, as these take much longer to think about and respond to. If there is an ID system utilized to track survey respondents (see below), the ID should be written in advance on each page of the survey, in the event that the pages become separated. Each item on the survey should be numbered for ease of data entry. Few if any "skip patterns" should be used (i.e., if respondent answers "no" then skip to question XX, but if respondent answers "yes" then proceed to next question). The same font should be used throughout (one that is relatively easy to read and not too distracting) except when presenting instructions to the respondent.

Opening Questions

The survey should begin with a set of questions about the sociodemographics of the respondent. This usually includes age, ethnicity, and gender. For child welfare program staff, highest educational degree, number of years working in the field of child welfare, and number of years at the current agency should also be included. For child welfare clients, number of months involved with the current program, number and age of children, education, employment, and marital status should also be included. There are several reasons for including these items at the front of the survey. First, answers to these questions can be used in the final report/paper to describe the sample and provide the reader with information about the study participants. The second reason to ask for sociodemographic information is because these variables may be important covariates or correlates in the analyses. That is, it may turn out that males and females answer questions differently. In such a case, gender would be entered into the analysis first in order to control for variation due to gender, allowing for an examination of the variable after the effects of gender have been removed from the analysis. Third, a research question might concern differences in attitudes based on the gender of the caseworker or age of the parent, number of children in the family, or length of involvement in a program. These "background" variables may actually be essential in the data analysis. A fourth reason for placing the sociodemographic questions at the beginning of the survey is that they serve as a "warm up," in that people are generally used to answering these types of questions about themselves. They are also almost always closed-ended and therefore easy to answer. These variables can also be used as a screening device, in that they may help the participant determine whether or not to continue with the survey. For example, if a survey is designed for foster parents over the age of fifty with kinship children in the home, questions about age and type of children in the home should be asked first, and the survey would indicate whether the respondent should stop at a certain point and return the survey or continue answering the remaining questions.

A note about including items regarding race and ethnicity: It is advisable to use the latest census coding system, both because it represents the best thinking in the field and because it produces data that can be compared with national samples. However, it is important to know the specific sample under investigation. For example, if the sample is entirely Hispanic, then it might make sense to include several possible countries of origin (e.g., Puerto Rico, Dominican Republic, and so forth), as these differences are meaningful to the clients and may be relevant for the analyses. An "other" category is always useful for coding race and ethnicity. A biracial or multiracial category might also be necessary with space to indicate which two (or more) categories the person considers relevant. Number of children in the family is a particularly complex question that requires guidelines regarding whether the children are living in the home, under a certain age, biological only, or also foster. There is not necessarily a right or wrong way to define this, but care should be taken to ensure that everyone works with the same definition. Income is also particularly tricky to ask about, because alimony, child support, food stamps, "off-the-books" income, and so forth need to specified as whether or not to be included.

Organizing Questions

The remainder of the survey should be organized into logical units or sets of questions with headers used to orient the respondent as to what to think about for the next section of the survey. These units can also be organized with questions that have the same type of response choices. This saves considerable room. In this way, the response choices are only listed once, saving space on the page and making it easier for the respondent, who does not have to learn a new set of response options for each question. See figure 10.2 for an example.

Figure 10.2

Sample survey questions with shared response options

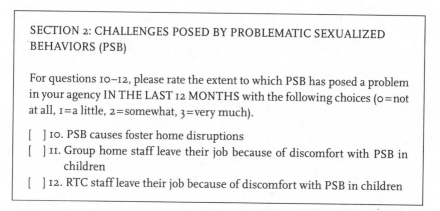

> SECTION 2: CHALLENGES POSED BY PROBLEMATIC SEXUALIZED BEHAVIORS (PSB)
>
> For questions 10–12, please rate the extent to which PSB has posed a problem in your agency IN THE LAST 12 MONTHS with the following choices (0 = not at all, 1 = a little, 2 = somewhat, 3 = very much).
>
> [   ] 10. PSB causes foster home disruptions
> [   ] 11. Group home staff leave their job because of discomfort with PSB in children
> [   ] 12. RTC staff leave their job because of discomfort with PSB in children

One caution regarding lining up the items in this manner is that it can create a "response set" on the part of the respondent such that he or she believes that a certain answer is the one that is most likely to apply to him- or herself based on choosing that response in the first question, and then the person might proceed to simply check that answer all the way down the column for the rest of the questions. One way to deal with this is to include items that break up the pattern of responses (e.g., if high scores generally indicate more problem behaviors, then add an item for which a high score indicates fewer problems).

Also note the placement of the response boxes on the far left margin. This facilitates data entry, as the eye of the data entry person does not have to scan an uneven right margin and because the answer is written close to the item number. Also note that the words "in the last 12 months" are written in capital letters (it could also be bolded or underlined) to draw the respondent's attention to that critical piece of information.

Developing Survey Questions: Improving Clarity and Precision

The quality of survey questions is critical for a study. If the questions (or answers) are ambiguous or poorly worded, the findings could be nearly useless. If the question is unclear, the answer will be unclear. Below are several ways to improve clarity of survey items.

Define Terms

All terms in the survey should be defined. If a term is critical to the entire survey or a large portion of it, the term should be defined at the beginning of the survey. For example, if foster parents are being asked to complete a survey about a foster child, they might be instructed: "If more than one foster child under the age of nineteen years is currently living in your home, please think about the one that has been the most problematic for you to control (behaviorally and emotionally) and complete all answers about this child only. This child will be referred to as 'the Target Child' for the remainder of the survey." On the other hand, if a term is used only once in the survey, define it as it is being used. In all cases, avoid acronyms, scientific terms, slang, or ambiguous phrases.

Specify Timeframes

If one timeframe is the focus of the entire survey, specify that at the top of the page and have a brief reminder at the top of each subsequent page. If the timeframe shifts throughout the survey, indicate the relevant timeframe in bold or italics as necessary throughout the survey to ensure that the respondent is aware of which timeframe applies to which questions. One option is to ask about whether something has happened ever in a respondent's life. A second option is to limit the timeframe based on the calendar year, such as "in the last six months" or "since this past Labor Day" or "since January." If a specific date is used (e.g., since January) then it will be important to ensure that the surveys are completed within a short period of time; otherwise the respondents who complete the survey later will be reporting on a longer amount of time than those who complete the survey sooner. Using a phrase such as "the last six months" could also be problematic with people who are not attuned to calendars and have only a vague sense of when things happen. A third option is to limit the timeframe to an event in the respondent's life, such as "since you started participating in the (name of program) program." Using a timeframe marked by an event solves that problem (assuming people can recall when that event happened), but introduces the problem that for some people the event happened longer ago than for others. Some caseworkers have been on the job ten years, while others joined last week. These decisions about timeframe will need to be made based on knowledge of the sample and knowledge of the phenomenon (what timeframe is relevant for the research topic).

Avoid Double Negatives

The clarity of a question can be improved simply by avoiding double negatives. If a double negative is the only or best way to phrase a question, make sure to bold or uppercase the negative so that the respondent clearly sees it. For example, an item for foster parents might be "how often do you not feel supported by the agency when talking about a foster child's sexual acting out behaviors?" and the response choices might be "Never, Rarely, Sometimes, Often, and Always." This item contains a double negative, because some parents might "never" not feel supported. If the word "not" is written in bold or capital letters, it will signal to the foster parent the need to think carefully about this question's response options.

Ask About One Thing at a Time

Questions should only ask about one event or belief at a time. Avoid "double-barreled" questions in which two or more issues are raised. A question such as "do you think staff and foster parents need more training about problematic sexualized behaviors?" lacks clarity, because a respondent might think that staff need more training but not foster parents. The best solution is to ask about only one concept or event per question. If two concepts or events are important to ask about in tandem, then the question and responses should be very clear. For example, the responses for the above example could be: "(0) No. Staff and foster parents do not need more training about PSB or (1) Yes. Both staff and foster parents need more training about PSB."

Avoid Assumptions

Clarity can also be compromised if assumptions are made, as is the case in the following question: "When children exhibit problematic sexualized behaviors, should they be removed from a foster home?" Not everyone completing the survey might think that problematic sexualized behaviors even exist in children living in foster homes. One solution is to include a "not applicable" option.

Avoid Bias and Emotionally Charged Language

Survey questions and the response options offered should not include racist or otherwise prejudicial language. As much as possible, survey language should be free of bias regarding gender, race, ethnicity, sexual orientation, religion, class, disability status, and so forth. Language that is in any way emotionally disturbing or overly personal should be avoided (unless some form of warning or explanation is offered). Slang should also be avoided because it could appear to be condescending.

Reduce Influence of Social Desirability for Sensitive Topics

In all cases, questions need to be framed in such a way as to reduce the likelihood that respondents will produce the socially desirable answer rather than their honest answer. The more specific the question and answer, the less likely it will be that the response will be pat or represent what the respondent thinks is the "right" answer. Asking for elaboration with an open-ended item can sometimes be used to elicit a more truthful answer. Another technique is to provide some introductory text that suggests to the respondent a sense of not being judged, such as: "Some children act out sexually in child welfare programs and we want to learn about your experience and your perception of this issue." Normalizing the behavior that is being asked about reduces the likelihood that the respondent will feel that he or she must conceal the truth in the survey. The following statement is an example of an attempt to do this: "Some foster parents feel frightened or upset by sexual acting out behavior in their foster children. How often, if at all, does this happen to you?" A statement such as "there are no right or wrong answers" might be useful to include in the instructions of the survey.

Developing Survey Questions: Types of Survey Questions

Open-Ended Items

Open-ended items do not offer the respondent a set of possible responses from which to choose. The answer is "open." As noted above, open-ended questions should be included sparingly in surveys because they require more space on the page; require more thought and effort on the part of the respondent; and result in data than can be more difficult to enter, analyze, and interpret. Open-ended questions should be included only under the conditions that the possible choices are too many to list, the possible answers are unknown, the researcher wants the final report/paper to include the "voices" of the respondents to add richness and texture, or the respondents' own way of thinking about something is of interest. At least two lines should be provided on the page with a note for the respondent to use extra paper if additional space is needed. Ideally, there will be space on the back of the last page of the survey for this. Open-ended questions should be phrased in such a way as to produce responses that go beyond a factual or one-word answer (yes or no), because this type of information is better obtained from closed-ended questions. Open-ended questions are best utilized for asking about "why" or "how" or "what." For example: "What do you like most about your job?" or "What, if anything, is difficult for you in having children with problematic sexualized behaviors in your home?" or "What, if anything, do you wish you had more training in for improving your job performance?"

Coding open-ended responses involves reading each respondent's answer and assigning it to a superordinate category. Ideally, no more than ten categories will be developed for one hundred survey responses. For example, a survey of youth experience in a residential treatment center included an item about what, if anything, the youth liked most about being in the center. Responses "the baseball team" and "playing football" were placed into the category "sports," while the responses "staff caring about me" and "staff helping me with my problems" were placed into a category labeled "the staff." However, if the question was narrower and asked, "what was your favorite sports activity at the program?" then the responses "baseball" and "football" would not be placed into the same category, although "being quarterback" and "helping coach the football team" would be combined into a "football" category. As can be seen, the categories depend greatly on the original question. For internal agency reports, it is probably sufficient for a single researcher to code the open-ended responses. For peer-reviewed publications, it may be necessary for two independent researchers to code the same set of responses and calculate the extent of agreement between the two raters (inter-rater reliability).

Closed-Ended Items

Closed-ended questions should be used when the response options are already known. There are two main types of closed-ended items: (1) "choose one answer" and (2) "check all that apply."

Figure 10.3

Sample "choose one" survey item with two mutually exclusive responses

```
1. Please indicate your gender [   ] Male [   ] Female
```

CHOOSE ONE ANSWER: TWO POSSIBLE OPTIONS

In these questions, the possible responses are mutually exclusive, and the respondent chooses one and only one response. An example would be asking about the gender of the respondent, where the only two possible responses are "male" or "female." Figure 10.3 presents an example of the layout of such an item. Data from such an item will be coded as a single variable (labeled Item 1 in the database) with two choices: male or female. The value attached to them (e.g., Male=0 and Female=1) is arbitrary (it could be Male=1 and Female=0) and can be decided at the data entry stage (although it could also be included right on the survey). When there are only two possible responses, the items should be coded as 0 and 1 in order to facilitate data analysis.

CHOOSE ONE ANSWER: FREQUENCY

The example of gender is a "choose one answer" question that is coded as presence/absence. Another form of a "choose one answer" question concerns the frequency of an event. Possible answer categories might be: "Never," "Rarely," "Sometimes," "Often," and "Always." Here there is some room for judgment on the part of the respondent. What one person thinks of as "rare" could be another person's "sometimes." What is of interest, though, is the frequency of the occurrence from the perspective of the individual respondent. Alternatively, frequency could be asked for with specific quantities specified: "Never," "Once a month," "2–3 times a month," "Once a week," "More than once a week but less than once a day," and "At least once a day." These data provide more concrete information about the actual frequency but less information about what that frequency means to the respondent. Choosing the type of frequency scale should be determined based on the research questions of the study. When choosing a specific frequency scale, there is no hard and fast rule about what these categories should be. The response options should be developed based on theory and prior research. For example, research on alcoholism has revealed that drinking every day is indicative of a serious problem, while for other behaviors (such as getting into physical altercations or skipping school), the relevant categories might be different.

Values will need to be assigned to these frequency labels so that the data can be entered into the database. One formula to use is to assign the value of 0 to the category that reflects no occurrence (answers such as "never," "not at all," "at no time," and so forth) and to assign integers sequentially to the remaining response options, such that "Never," "Rarely," "Sometimes," "Often," and "Always" would be coded from 0 to 4. The values have no numeric meaning except insofar as each number sequentially represents a greater degree of frequency (i.e., it is an ordinal scale).

CHOOSE ONE ANSWER: AGREEMENT

Another "choose one answer" type of question asks about strength of agreement with a statement. The commonly used response set is "Not at all," "Only a little," "Somewhat," and "Very much" (coded from 0 to 3). Possible questions include: "How important do you think it is to call before canceling a home visit?" or "How confident are you that you are helping your clients improve their parenting?" Sometimes, researchers use scales without anchors. That is, numbers are given (on a scale of 1 to 10, in which 1 signifies lack of agreement and 10 signifies complete agreement) without specifying what the other points on the scale refer to. This is not recommended, because the results cannot be translated into meaningful categories. At best, the findings can report: "On average, agencies reported that the problem of problematic sexualized behaviors was a 6.3 on a scale of seriousness that ranged from 1 to 10." This is clearly not as compelling as writing that "75 percent reported that problematic sexualized behaviors was very much a problem."

Regardless of the response format, a "choose one answer" question produces one response per question, and the possible response options are mutually exclusive. A respondent cannot be male and female, cannot do something never and rarely, and cannot think something is not at all important and very important at the same time. In all cases, the respondent will select one from a set of possible options as his or her response. In the database, the response will be allocated one column of data and the value labels will represent the possible response choices (for example, a 0 will be entered if the person checked male or a 1 will be entered if the person checked female).

CHOOSE ALL THAT APPLY

A "choose all that apply" item, on the other hand, is a question in which more than one answer might be applicable to the respondent. For example, if the question is, "Which placement services are offered within the agency?" possible responses could include foster homes, group homes, residential treatment centers, and so forth. One respondent might work at an agency that offers foster homes and group homes, while another might work at an agency that provides foster homes as well as a residential treatment center. Although some respondents might only choose one response, the response options are not mutually exclusive. In this case, the responses (not the question) form the item numbers on the survey. Figure 10.4 provides an example of how these items and the possible responses can be presented on a survey.

With "choose all that apply" items, each possible response choice becomes a variable in the data file, each of which is coded present or absent. If it is checked, then it is coded as present (1), and if it is not checked, it is coded as absent (0). For the example provided in figure 10.4, data entry will involve six variables (columns of data) in the data file. Each will be coded as 0 or 1. Thus for an agency that provides regular foster homes and residential treatment, the data file would entail the following entries into the columns for items 11 through 16: 1 0 0 1 0 0 to indicate yes to foster home, no to therapeutic and group home, yes to residential treatment center, and no to shelter and other. It is always important to include an "other" category to capture additional options that are not provided. A long line extending to the right margin of the page should be included for the person to write down what

Figure 10.4
Sample "choose all that apply" survey item

Please indicate all types of programs CURRENTLY OFFERED by your agency (Choose all that apply).

[ ] 11. Regular and kinship foster homes
[ ] 12. Therapeutic foster homes
[ ] 13. Group homes
[ ] 14. Residential treatment centers
[ ] 15. Shelter
[ ] 16. Other _____

the "other" is. In the data file, a string (alphanumeric) variable should be created in which to enter data about what the "other" category is.

Piloting the Survey

Under no circumstances should the survey be administered (given to the respondents) without being shown to several key informants for feedback and then piloted. Once a draft of the survey the researcher/research team feels reasonably comfortable with has been developed, it should be shown to several people inside the agency who can provide feedback on it. Once the draft has been revised based on the feedback received, it should be piloted. That is, the survey should be administered to someone who meets the criteria for inclusion in the sample but is not technically in the study. This person should be asked to complete the survey as if he or she were in the study (i.e., approach it seriously, item by item, trying to respond to the questions) in order to provide concrete feedback about items that are unclear or aspects of the survey that seem awkward and/or out of place. If substantial changes are made based on the initial piloting, it is advisable to pilot the survey again in order to ensure that no new problems were introduced into the second version. It may take several rounds of piloting and revising for the researcher to feel confident that the survey is ready to be administered.

Obtaining Consent

As with all research, informed consent will need to be obtained prior to completion of a survey. With a mailed survey, this usually involves a cover letter that states the voluntary nature of the survey, explains the purpose of the study, the sponsor of the study, if and how confidentiality will be maintained, and provides contact information if the person has questions. Risks and benefits of survey completion are also outlined. Completion of a mailed/ e-mailed/computer-generated survey is taken as de facto consent for participation. In face-to-face interviews, a consent form should be provided to potential participants explaining confidentiality, risks and benefits, and providing contact information. If the person agrees to participate—after having read (or been read) the consent form and after having a chance to ask all questions—then the person should sign the consent form. In telephone surveys, consent should be read over the phone and audiotaped oral consent should be obtained. Another option is to mail the consent to the person in advance and have him or her sign and return it prior to conducting the actual phone interview.

A special case occurs when the response to a survey question must be acted upon by the surveyor (or someone he or she reports to), which in turn results in negative consequences for the respondent. Examples of such responses would include a foster parent admitting to hitting a foster child, a caseworker indicating that sometimes home visits are rushed through in order get all the work done, or a parent in a prevention program admitting to using drugs. Questions eliciting information that could pose a threat to the survey respondent should not be included on the survey without careful discussion with an ethics committee and without clear indication to the respondent about what, if any, the consequences will be for providing certain answers.

Maintaining Confidentiality

With mailed surveys, confidentiality is handled in one of two ways, the first of which is for the surveys to be anonymous. No identifier is placed on the survey and there is no way to ascertain from the completed survey who the respondent was. The disadvantage to this method is that there is no way to target the follow-up postcards, reminders, and so forth to those who have not completed the survey. Thus people who actually participated will receive follow-up materials, wasting time and resources on unnecessary mailings. In addition, the people who did not participate will know that their lack of participation will remain unknown. Therefore they cannot receive targeted materials for follow-ups either. The only materials that can be sent are those that say, "If you did not complete the survey here is a second copy and we urge you to take the time to do so." This is not as compelling as a follow-up mailing that states, "We know you have not yet completed the survey and we are asking that you do so."

This introduces the second approach to confidentiality. A unique ID number could be applied to each survey and a master list could be created that links the number to the person. In this way, the surveys themselves have no identifying information, just an ID number. Yet it is possible to know who completed the survey and who did not by tracking the survey ID numbers. If this procedure is used, it must be explained to the potential participants along with a description of where the master list will be kept (usually in a locked filing cabinet to which only research staff have a key) and what will happen to the master list upon completion of the project (usually it is discarded). In this way, the identity of the survey completers is protected yet the researcher is able to enhance response rate through targeted follow-up activities. However, the people completing the survey will know that *someone* knows which survey is theirs and that a list exists linking their name to the survey. The reality and experience of confidentiality is lessened somewhat with the use of an ID system. In addition, with a small enough sample of known possible respondents, it might be possible to determine survey respondents by analyzing the responses. For example, if the sample is every agency within a particular county and an agency indicates on the survey that it serves two hundred youth in an RTC and operates over five hundred foster homes, it may be possible through the process of elimination to determine which agency that is. If this is the case, then an ID system might as well be used, because the agency staff completing the survey will realize that they can be traced by the responses to the survey questions. Telephone and face-to-face surveys can be handled the same way. An ID number can be assigned to each participant and that number can appear on the page. In this way, no one seeing the raw data (each individual interview or the rows of data in the computer) would be able to link the survey responses to the individual respondents.

Training Telephone Interviewers and Face-to-Face Interviewers

Surveys conducted over the phone and/or in person require consistency in the presentation of the questions and response choices in order to remove any variation due to the interviewer from the data collected. The purpose of the study is to measure variation that exists in the participants. This means that if more than one person conducts the surveys, the people being surveyed would provide the same answers regardless of who the interviewer was. If a team of people will be conducting the surveys, it is best to train them all at the same time so that they each receive exactly the same instructions. Instructions should also be written down such that they do not have to rely on memory (which varies from person to person) about how to do the job. Everything should be explained and described, including how to introduce themselves to the participants; how to sit in relation to them (across a table, side by side); whether to serve refreshments and, if so, what to serve; how to phrase the questions; how to read the response choices (in terms of tone of voice, length of pauses, inflection); and how to dress (professional, casual, etc.). It is not so much that there is a right or wrong way to handle the survey. The most important thing is consistency across surveyors.

That being said, a few points are worth making. First, surveyors should be attuned to the culture, class, race, age, and language of the survey participants and be respectful and appropriate. Second, the general stance in reading survey questions is one of detached warmth. That is, the person should appear to be a warm person but not a person who is keenly interested in the specific answers provided by the respondent. The surveyor should never appear alarmed, distraught, concerned, shocked, and so forth by the respondent's answers. Third, unless otherwise instructed, the surveyor should not elaborate on the meaning of the questions or response choices. In general, when asked about what something means, the person should repeat the question and then say: "Please answer based on what you think it means." If the response provided is outside the list of choices provided, the person should repeat the question and possible response options. The surveyor should also be trained to not give advice under any circumstances. And finally, it is usually helpful if the people conducting the surveys practice asking the questions and writing down the answers in order to become comfortable and familiar with the material. Also, if conducting the survey in person, the seating arrangement should be such that the respondent can see the actual survey and the responses being written down. The surveyor should not have the survey hidden behind a clipboard or concealed in any way that is likely to induce feelings of being judged, tested, evaluated, or criticized.

Ensuring an Adequate Response Rate for Mail Surveys

One key to a successful survey study is an adequate response rate. The technique for achieving this is based on one thing: persistence. If surveys are conducted over the telephone, then the research assistants conducting the interviews need to keep calling a number until someone answers and keep scheduling a time for the survey until the person completes it. Good organizational skills are a must for keeping track of who was called, when, and the results, such as "child answered and said to call back at 6:00 p.m. tonight," or "left voice message on answering machine about the project," or "no answer." Each person in the sample should be allocated a single page on which his or her name and phone number is written. A log should be kept of every effort to reach the person. This will ensure that each person is called at several different times of day and on different days of the week. If a person is reached, it is ideal to conduct the survey on the spot rather than to schedule it for a time in the future, at which point the person might change his or her mind. If it is not possible to conduct the interview at that first contact, then a time should be scheduled for as soon as possible. For appointments several days in the future, a call could be placed the night before to serve as a reminder. If the person is not available at the appointed time (does not answer, the machine comes on, the person is said to be not home or not available), the researcher needs to be understanding and flexible about rescheduling. This same strategy applies for individually administered face-to-face surveys.

Enhancing the response rate of mailed surveys also requires persistence. Dillman (1978) has developed a widely used set of procedures involving a reminder postcard sent one week after the initial mailing, a follow-up letter and additional survey sent two weeks later, and a final letter and survey sent one month after that. Careful tracking is the key to this or any follow-up approach so that each person receives the necessary follow-up materials. The use of fax and e-mail reminders can also be incorporated into this strategy. In addition, when the sample is composed of high-level staff within an agency, follow-up calls, faxes, and e-mails can be directed to the administrative assistant who oversees that person's mail and phone messages. Engaging them in the process can often facilitate response rates. Building a relationship with these people can be quite useful. Additional response rate enhancers include tokens of appreciation being sent with the original mailing as well as having a raffle for all individuals who complete the survey by the due date (this only works if an ID system is used to track survey completion). When conducting research in a child welfare setting, support of key stakeholders can facilitate response rates. If the survey is conducted within a single agency, the cover letter accompanying the survey should be signed by the executive director/president as well as necessary program directors. If the survey is conducted across agencies, then the project should be sponsored by a funder, a coalition, or the county or state government agency. Their name on the letterhead enhances the prestige of the project and serves as an inducement to participation.

Reporting the Results

When reporting results of a survey, it is very important to be conceptual in the presentation. Typically, there is an embarrassment of riches in that a single survey might contain dozens if not more items. The results should not simply present the frequency distribution of each item. The organization of the results section should follow the logic of the introduction of the paper and the research questions developed. That is, typically the introduction section of a paper or research report culminates in the identification of about three major research questions that the survey was designed to address. Using the example for this chapter, problematic sexualized behaviors in child welfare programs, the three research questions were: (1) What proportion of children are estimated to have PSB? (2) Are children in congregate care perceived as more likely to exhibit PSB than children in family care? And (3) to what extent do agencies perceive PSB to be a problem for them? These questions clearly guide the presentation of the results, which would begin with frequency distributions of PSB in all the different levels of care (question 1), then would involve the testing for differences in rates of PSB between congregate and family care (question 2), and end with a presentation of the frequency of several items asking about impact of PSB on agency work (question 3).

It is very important in presenting survey findings to remind the reader of the self-report nature of the data. Thus, a typical statement might be: "Agency staff reported that problematic sexualized behaviors was a significant problem (85 percent) that was getting worse over time (92 percent), which they felt required greater attention on the part of the agency (87 percent). Agency staff also reported that more training was needed for foster families (86 percent) and group care staff (98 percent)." The results are clearly presented as they relate to the opinions and beliefs of the respondents. There is no way to verify that in fact the problem is getting worse or that foster parents need additional training on this topic. But the fact that over 85 percent of the agencies completing the survey believed that to be the case is of meaning to the field, because the respondents are believed to be knowledgeable about the topic and not likely to make false claims about it. As noted above, surveys are a good fit when the respondent's opinions are deemed of interest.

Conclusion

Survey research is an excellent tool for collecting information about the attitudes and stated beliefs of a sample of individuals in order to generalize the findings to the population of interest. Surveys can be administered in a number of different ways, and the best approach can be selected on a study-by-study basis depending upon the sample. In all cases, a response rate of at least 80 percent is desirable in order to have confidence in the findings. Survey questions need to be carefully crafted and piloted prior to administration of the survey in order to ensure clarity and precision. Results are reported as they pertain to the specific questions that guided the study.

[11]

Case Studies

In this chapter, the following topics will be discussed following the intro-duction of the chapter scenario and the brief literature review:

- Deciding when to conduct a case study
- Defining the case
- Developing data collection strategies
- Collecting data
- Tips for researchers conducting case studies
- Analyzing the data
- Writing the report

CHAPTER SCENARIO

One specific cottage on the campus of a residential treatment center has had an extended period of what is perceived to be a positive peer culture, and it has come to the attention of the agency as a model cot-tage. Executive personnel within the agency are interested in under-standing what is contributing to this positive environment in order to

(continued)

replicate it in other cottages throughout the campus. Such a goal is consistent with the agency's strength-based approach and with its model of continuous quality improvement. The agency researcher is asked to develop a study that will illuminate the factors (structural as well as personal) that are promoting the positive climate in the cottage. Based on the interest in a holistic understanding of the cottage's climate, the researcher develops a case study project. Research questions include: (1) What are staff and youth perceptions of the climate within the cottage? (2) What do staff and youth believe are the major factors contributing to the positive environment? And (3) what other factors appear to be relevant for understanding the culture of the cottage?

BRIEF LITERATURE REVIEW: POSITIVE PEER CULTURE IN A RESIDENTIAL TREATMENT CENTER (RTC)

Children in residential treatment receive at most one hour of psychotherapy or individual-level intervention a day. Therefore, the "other twenty-three hours a day" are viewed as critical for the success of residential group care programs (Treischman, Whittaker, and Brentro 1969). As Leichtman (2006) explains, apart from the fraction of their time involved with formal interventions, youth in residential treatment spend most of their day involved in routine activities such as sleeping and waking, dressing, taking care of their personal hygiene, eating, attending school, completing chores, interacting with child care staff, and socializing with peers. It is widely accepted that for troubled children these seemingly mundane tasks can pose significant challenges. Everyday life can provide numerous opportunities for youth to learn and grow. Negotiating these everyday tasks can often lead to personal and interpersonal difficulties, as youth experience frustration and challenges that exceed their coping abilities and skill level, which have been negatively affected by the abuse and maltreatment and distorted relational styles they have been exposed to from their violent, chaotic, and abusive homes and neighborhoods. Thus, helping children navigate their daily lives is an ongoing lesson in personal adjustment and growth that can be as, if

(continued)

not more, effective than discrete formal therapy sessions. For example, the life-space interview (Redl 1959) is a tool for reshaping a youth's maladaptive behaviors as they occur in the moment of a crisis.

Another way to intervene with youth in residential treatment is through the implementation of a positive peer culture (Vorrath and Brentro 1985). According to this model, the other youth residing in the program are viewed as creating a culture and climate that can help reshape the behaviors and attitudes of the individual. This model is built on the acknowledged role that community peers have in exerting an influence on socially acceptable or unacceptable behavior. This influence is thought to also occur in the context of residential treatment as well. In essence, a youth is removed from the family and from their community peers who might have encouraged or exacerbated the behavioral problems that led to placement. Once in treatment, the youth is surrounded by a new peer group that holds (or is working toward holding) a more socially appropriate normative set of values and attributes. Once in this new peer culture, youth are encouraged to work through their interpersonal and individual adjustment problems as a group, helping to hold one another accountable and provide positive peer role models for healthy and adaptive behavior. This peer culture is based on the belief that peers can take responsibility for their own behavior and that they will model positive behavior to their peers, which will result in a positive change via peer pressure. According to Tannehill (1987) and Kapp (2000), the primary mechanism for such problem solving is a daily one-hour peer-mediated group meeting. Thus, a cornerstone of positive peer culture is guided group interaction (GGI) intervention, developed by Empey and Lubeck (1972).

Positive peer culture has been the focus of some empirical investigation, not all of which has been supportive. For example, Ryan (2006) concluded that positive peer culture may not be the most effective intervention model for delinquent-maltreated youth in residential treatment, and Kapp (2000) found a consistently critical assessment of aspects of the positive peer culture in interviews with former clients of juvenile delinquent facilities. In a qualitative study of current staff and youth in ten different programs employing positive peer culture, a range of concerns and criticisms were raised, including abuse of power, overemphasis on problem behaviors, and reliance on jargon in overly rigid and mechanical

(continued)

verbal interactions during group meetings (Brentro and Ness 1982).
Nonetheless, positive peer culture is a popular and widely used model
of residential treatment programs. For example, it was cited by 20 percent of New York State RTCs as their model of therapeutic milieu (Baker,
Fullmore, and Collins, forthcoming).

Overview of the Topic

A case study is "a method for learning about a complex instance, based on a
comprehensive understanding of that instance obtained by extensive description and analysis of that instance taken as a whole and in its context" (United
States Government Accounting Office 1990). Put another way, a case study is
a research endeavor in which qualitative data—collected from a combination
of interviews, observations, field notes, archival material, and examination of
documents—are used to develop a multiperspective, holistic understanding of
a single case or set of cases in order to generalize those findings to other similar cases. Like other forms of qualitative data collection, the case study is concerned with the "lived experience" of people (Holloway 1997) and is rooted in
the theory of phenomenology (Husserl 1990). In practical terms, a case study
entails a researcher (or research assistant) spending considerable time at the
location of the case (program site, cottage, hospital, home, etc.) conducting interviews as well as extended observations of individuals and interactions
among the relevant parties for as long as it takes to develop what is perceived to
be a valid understanding of the case. The case study utilizes a triangulated research strategy in which information collected from multiple sources and different methods converge on the truth (Yin 1984). Historically, the use of case
study research has been cyclical, in which periods characterized by active utilization are followed by periods of disuse. Tellis (1997) traces the earliest use
of this form of research to Europe, predominantly France, and concludes that
in the United States the case study methodology is most closely associated with
the University of Chicago's department of sociology from 1900 until 1935.

Deciding When to Use Case Studies

Some research questions are best answered through in-depth analysis of
documents, observations, and interviews with individuals who have had a

particular experience. This is especially true if the goal is to understand the felt or lived perspective of these individuals as it pertains to the event in question as it occurred in a specific historical and geographic context. Like all approaches, there are advantages and disadvantages to the case study methodology, and the child welfare researcher should be familiar with them. The primary advantage is that a case study develops a holistic understanding of the case from multiple perspectives and in a specific context. The researcher considers not just the voice and perspective of the actors but also the interactions between them. This means that the findings are rich, often fascinating, and can provide the researcher and the audience of the report with the "felt shared experience" of the participants located in a particular time and place. The final report is interspersed with quotes and true accounts that bring the case to life. Case studies also offer the researcher the opportunity to understand the interrelationships among events and experiences beyond the capabilities of quantitative data.

The primary disadvantage of case studies is the ease with which they can be done poorly, resulting in little or no new information being generated. At worst, inaccurate conclusions can be drawn from the data due to biases in observation style, interviewing technique, or coding decisions. Case studies also require a significant time commitment, as the researcher must immerse himself or herself in the experience of the case. Another pitfall is that the presence of the researcher can change the case so much that the information collected and observations made are no longer representative of the case itself. A common criticism of the case study methodology is that because only one or just a few instances are studied, the researcher will typically uncover more variables than he or she has data points, making statistical control impossible. This, however, may be considered a strength of the methodology, because it allows for the discovery of causal paths that might not have been included as variables in a quantitative study. Similarly, the methodology has come under attack as being anecdotal and unscientific. However, if the case study researcher uses caution when generalizing the findings, the results can provide useful information that could not be obtained from any other methodology.

Types of Case Studies

Several specific types of case studies have been identified. Three that are commonly recognized include descriptive/illustrative, exploratory, and explanatory, although other types have also been identified, such as intrinsic (when the researcher has an interest in the case), instrumental (when the case is used to understand more than what is obvious to the observer), collective (when a group of cases is studied), and critical instance (when a case study aims to understand a specific, usually negative event and its consequences), among others.

Descriptive/Illustrative

In a descriptive case study, information is collected (interviews, observations, field notes, examination of documents) in order to describe the case. Using the chapter example, a researcher would spend time at the selected cottage describing the different types of peer interactions, staff interactions, and peer-to-staff interactions that occur. A typical day might be described in detail, in terms of the activities and the emotional climate of these activities. Interviews would be conducted with the youth and staff within the cottage and perhaps youth and staff outside the cottage, in order to gain their perspective as well. The final report would provide a rich description of the social climate of the cottage.

Exploratory

Exploratory case studies are sometimes considered a prelude to other forms of social science research, as their primary purpose is to generate hypotheses for future efforts. Preliminary causal associations are identified, which are then tested in quantitative studies. Exploratory case studies provide all the detail of the descriptive case study but also make some tentative suggestions about the causal relationships between the variables (which aspects of staff behaviors and attitudes appear to account for the positive social climate in the cottage). Observations and questions would be made with an eye toward generating hypotheses, but there would be no a priori ideas about such associations.

Explanatory

In an explanatory case study, the researcher attempts to induce theory from case examples. A list of possible causes of the dependent variable is constructed through a literature review and brainstorming, and information is gathered on each cause for the selected case. Thus, data collection is more directed and theory driven. The researcher then inventories causal attributes that are common to all instances of interest (in this case, a positive climate), common only to cases high on the dependent variable (positive climate), and common only to cases low on the dependent variable (not positive climate). The researcher comes to a provisional conclusion that the differentiating attributes are the significant causes while those common to all cases are not. Explanation building is particularly compelling when there are plausible rival explanations that can be rebutted by this method. For example, a rival hypothesis might be that team staff meetings account for the positive peer climate, yet the case study might reveal that in fact these team meetings are not held consistently in the cottages deemed to have the most positive peer climate.

Identifying the Case and the Relevant Participants

There are three primary approaches to selecting a case for a case study: convenience, purposive, and probability. In a convenience sample, the case is selected because it allows for convenient and timely access to the phenomenon of interest. There are six types of purposive sampling: (1) bracketing, in which the best and worst cases are selected in order to allow the researcher to study extremes; (2) the best case is studied in order to allow the research to understand the factors associated with positive outcomes/processes; (3) the worst case is studied in order to allow the researcher to understand the factors associated with negative outcomes/processes; (4) a cluster of cases is studied in order to allow for comparison of different types of cases; (5) representative, in which a range of cases is selected for study (not necessarily proportionate to the population); and (6) a typical case is studied to understand an average case. In probability sampling, cases are selected on a probability basis to ensure proportionality to the population of cases.

Using the chapter scenario of the social climate in a cottage on the campus of an RTC, a convenience sample would involve the first cottage that agreed to participate. A bracketed sample would include the two cottages deemed to have the best and the worst social climate. The best sample would entail only the best cottage and the worst sample would entail only the worst cottage. A cluster sample would involve several of the best and several of the worst cottages while a representative sample would include some of the best, some of the worst, and some of the more mixed cottages. A sample consisting of a typical case would be chosen from a consensus opinion of an average cottage. A probability sample would involve a random selection of cottages with the goal of having a proportionate number of good, poor, and middle quality in terms of social climate. Which procedure is used depends upon the goals of the project (is more than one case necessary?) and resources (how many cases can the given project budget support?).

Determining Relevant Parties to Observe and Interview

Once the decision regarding how many and which cases to include has been made, the next issue is to identify the parties within the case(s) that need to be involved in the study itself. As much as possible, the case study should be comprehensive, as it is better to err on the side of inclusion than exclusion. Thus, for the chapter example, it would make sense to observe all of the youth and all of the staff. As discussed below, it is possible for case study researchers to get drawn into the dynamics and unspoken belief systems about who is important to talk to and observe and who is not. As much as possible, the researcher should be aware of these unspoken rules and beliefs and resist being influenced by them. For example, some youth may be unofficial leaders in the cottage. This will be important to acknowledge and perhaps even write about in the report (why do some youth appear to be given a leadership position, what benefits does that confer on the youth and staff, and so forth), but this should not result in those youth being interviewed or observed more than other youth or in their voices dominating the final report. It is important for the researcher to not replicate the power dynamics and imbalances in the sampling and data collection methods. It is also important for the researcher to be flexible and open-ended about whom and what to interview/observe. For example, it is possible that, over the course of interviews of current cottage youth, a particular former resident is mentioned several times as being pivotal for setting the emotional/social climate at the cottage (either in a positive or negative way). If at all possible, the researcher should try to interview this person as well, even if he or she is no longer actually living in the cottage of interest. Perhaps there are some individuals who have a peripheral position vis-à-vis the cottage on a formal basis (i.e., volunteers who visit once a month, parents of one youth who spend time in the cottage) but appear to play a significant role in setting the tone of the cottage. These individuals should be included in the data collection as well, if possible. Thus, it is not possible to know in advance the final set of participants in the study, because the researcher will need to listen to the information that is shared and adjust the data collection strategy accordingly in order to be responsive to the reality of the case.

Types of Data Collection

Collection of Physical Articles

While spending time at the site of the case, the researcher should make an effort to pay attention to objects that are relevant to the purpose of the case study. For example, in the study of the climate of the cottages, the researcher should collect (copies) of any materials that are relevant to the research question. Examples include informal notes written between youth, between staff, and between youth and staff that pertain to the climate of the cottage, and awards, trophies, posters, and other items that express the desired or actual climate of the cottage. It is hard to specify in advance exactly what, if any, articles would be relevant, but the observant case study researcher will recognize them should they exist.

Collection of Documents

Formal documents will also be an important component of the data collection process. These will include staff notes about youth behaviors; lists of rules of the cottage; daily reports of incidents; methods by which staff inform youth of rewards and punishments; and any standardized instruments used by staff to rate, rank, chart, or monitor youth behaviors. Again, it is not possible to specify in advance the exact list of all documents that will be of interest in a given case study project. The researcher should always be asking himself or herself what documents, if any, should be considered relevant.

Examination of Archival Material

Existing documents will also contribute key data to the case study. In the case of a study of the social climate in a cottage, it could include lists of youth served in the cottage, length of stay and reasons for leaving, and any other computerized data files on the youth served.

Administration of Open-Ended Interviews

All relevant parties should be invited to participate in at least one open-ended interview in which his or her general experiences and perceptions are discussed. These interviews should be private, confidential, and subject to all of the rigors of in-depth interviewing as outlined in chapter 13. Ideally, each participant will participate in more than one interview over the course of the case study, with the most open-ended being conducted in the beginning and the more focused interviews being conducted later in the data collection process.

Administration of Focused Interviews

As hypotheses are generated over the course of the project, these can be subjected to preliminary tests in focused interviews. Relevant parties can be asked about their perceptions and beliefs about certain plausible explanatory pathways. For example, if—based on extensive observations, interviews, and analysis of documents—a researcher concludes that one staffperson is particularly important for setting the tone of a positive peer culture and that this staffperson is able to do this primarily through force of personality (i.e., a charismatic leader) and by functioning as a role model, having been in child welfare himself as a young man, then youth and other staff could be asked questions that would help the researcher confirm or refute this hypothesis.

Administration of Structured Surveys

Standardized and structured data collection instruments can also be used to gather systematic data across the participants of the case study project. This might include a demographic form, so that the sample can be described using comparable data across all participants (age, level of education, marital status of staff, and so forth), or a standardized instrument for a key construct. For example, if a hypothesis is developed over the course of the case study that explicates that certain peers have more influence in the cottage than others, a sociometry measure could be administered to test that hypothesis.

Making Direct Observations

Direct observations of individuals and interactions among individuals are a critical component of any case study. Observations should be made at a variety of different times of day and variety of different events (staff meetings, youth meetings, social events, outings, meal times, and so forth). If interviews or other sources of data indicate that certain events are particularly important for the understanding of the study topic (in this case, social climate in the cottage), then every effort should be made to observe this event as well. No assumptions should be made that certain times or certain events will produce nothing of interest. Field notes taken during (and after) observations should be kept in a systematic fashion based on these observations. In the beginning, everything should be recorded, as it cannot be known in advance what will be of ultimate use for the project. As much as possible, the notes should be kept in a consistent format (using the same aliases for the participants, indicating clearly relevant facts such as location, time of day, all actors present, and so forth).

Carrying out Participant Observations

Unlike direct observations, participant observations involve the researcher partaking in an event as it unfolds. This might include having a meal with the youth in the cottage, attending activity night and playing games with the youth, participating in outings, and in every way being an active member of the group. By putting oneself into the event, the researcher can have access to a different type of information than is available through direct observation, including what it feels like to be with these particular individuals in that particular context. The researcher, if attuned to his or her reactions and feelings, can gain insight into subtle and unspoken interactional styles and influences that might not be accessible from other more objective sources of data.

Role of the Researcher

Explaining the Purpose of the Project

The various participants in the case should be aware that a project of some sort is underway and have some understanding of what that entails (usually, that another person will be spending a lot of time at the site, talking to people and learning about "how things are done"). It should be made clear that this is not a test or an evaluation per se, that no one is being judged, and that no one's job is on the line. The researcher should be comfortable talking about the project in relatively general terms in such a way as to not convey secrecy, deception, or hidden agendas.

Relationship to Participants

When conducting the case study, the researcher should present an "ob-server/interviewer self," a persona that is empathic and connected to the humanity of the participant while still demonstrating and respecting clearly defined boundaries. The researcher must be warm and humane, otherwise, the experience could be detrimental to the participants, yet the researcher should recognize and respect that the case study is not a therapeutic encounter nor is he or she an agent for change. Thus at no time should the researcher advise, challenge, or help the participants make connections or gain insight. Nor should the researcher break confidence or reveal information obtained over the course of the project.

The researcher also must recognize that the time spent together is not an interaction between friends or colleagues (in which personal information is shared mutually). Thus the researcher should rarely, if ever, share personal information in the context of the time spent together. Understanding how case study interactions resemble therapy sessions and informal discussions among friends without actually being either of these two types of interpersonal communications will allow the researcher to set appropriate boundaries. Obtaining ongoing supervision to discuss and process the information obtained and the impressions and experiences therein will be very helpful for maintaining appropriate boundaries.

Specific caution needs to be heeded in conducting a case study on several fronts. The first is preventing the researcher from "going native," so to speak, and becoming so enamored with the "local" culture of the case that he or she loses sight of the study and its purposes. This might entail forgetting to seek countervailing evidence or alternative explanations and generally unquestioningly accepting various myths and taboos that might exist within the culture of the case. The second area of concern is that the researcher could convey a judgmental attitude that could induce in the participants feelings of being watched, criticized, examined, misunderstood, and generally resentful of the project. The personal attributes necessary for conducting a case study do not come naturally to each and every researcher and might not be a good fit for some researchers. In fact, it might be advisable to hire a research assistant who receives ongoing supervision rather than to have a researcher who is not ideally suited conduct the case study himself or herself. Researchers should know their own strengths and weaknesses and make decisions about what role to play in a case study based on an honest appraisal of their own skills, talents, and comfort level.

Analyzing the Data

Case study data take many forms, including, but not limited to, transcripts from interviews, field notes from observations, results of structured surveys, existing current and archival documents, and informal documents and materials collected along the way. The way in which these data are analyzed largely depends upon the original purpose of the project (descriptive, exploratory, or explanatory).

A descriptive study of cottage climate would have its the main goal to describe the climate and the ways in which variation in the climate is expressed. Data from a descriptive project could be organized in a number of different ways. One approach is chronological, describing a typical day or describing key events that occurred over the course of the entire data collection period. Descriptive information can also be presented according to informants. That is, what youth said and did regarding the issue, what staff said and did regarding the issue, and what others said and did relevant to the issue.

An exploratory study, on the other hand, is designed to generate hypotheses about causal relationships. The major question would be: "What are possible explanations for why the climate in this particular cottage is positive?" The analysis would be organized around identifying these causal agents. The report/paper would define climate, describe why understanding climate is important, and then present some preliminary estimates as to what factors were found to be associated with the positive climate in the cottage.

Finally, in a report or paper resulting from an explanatory case study, the paper would present a theoretical rationale for why some factors were believed to be associated with positive climate as well as evidence regarding whether they were in fact found to be present in the studied case. Any countervailing evidence should be provided as well.

The following principles of case study data analysis apply regardless of the type of report being written.

Data Analysis Is Iterative

While data collection is occurring, the existing data are already being analyzed. This would include the transcription and coding of the in-depth and focused interviews and organization and categorization of field notes, documents, archives and so forth. Preliminary findings from the initial stages of data collection could be used to guide and inform subsequent phases of data collection to ensure that "all bases are covered."

Triangulation

Triangulation is the principle by which the researcher gains confidence in initial findings when they are supported through multiple methods and multiple sources. The truth is revealed through a convergence in the data. Thus the researcher should examine the same issue (say, the role of a particular youth or the impact of a particular reward and punishment system) from all data sources in order to determine whether there is consistency across these sources.

Consideration of Rival Hypotheses

Alternative explanations for relationships or processes are considered and ruled out in order to increase the level of confidence in the findings. Alternative interpretations of findings are developed and tested through a search for confirming and disconfirming evidence until one hypothesis is confirmed and others ruled out.

Conclusion

The case study is a research method that entails the immersion of the researcher in a single case (or set of related cases) in order to describe and understand the holistic experience of that case as it relates to a specific issue or experience. The researcher utilizes a range of data collection strategies including in-depth interviews, observations and field notes, and examination of formal and informal documents in order to create a detailed and rich understanding of the case in order to learn something about the population from which the case was drawn.

Focus Groups

In this chapter, the following topics will be discussed following the introduction of the chapter scenario and the brief literature review:

- Deciding when to use focus groups as a research method
- Defining and recruiting the sample
- Design of the focus group
- Developing focus group questions: improving clarity
- Developing focus group questions: steps in the process
- Piloting the protocol
- Techniques of the facilitator
- Focus group logistics
- Transcribing the tapes and analyzing the data

CHAPTER SCENARIO

A supervisor in a foster home program supervises a team of caseworkers who work with several families for whom concurrent planning is relevant. This means that in addition to working with the biological

(continued)

family toward reunification, the caseworker is also exploring the possibility of terminating parental rights and finding an adoptive home for the children. Concurrent planning represents a realignment of policy and practice, and it has come to the supervisor's attention that many of the clients affected by it appear resentful and frightened about the implications for reunification. From this general line of thinking, two major research questions were developed for a study addressing this issue: (1) What do biological parents who are working toward reunification understand concurrent planning to mean for them? And (2) what are their perceptions (positive and negative) about this new policy and practice?

BRIEF LITERATURE REVIEW: CONCURRENT PLANNING

A guiding principle of the child welfare system is that every child deserves a safe and permanent home. All else being equal, the preference in the system is to return children in out-of-home care to their families of origin. Thus, for the vast majority of children removed from home, the primary plan is reunification with their family, and sequential planning was the standard casework approach following the passage of the Adoption Assistance and Child Welfare Act of 1980. According to this practice, the preferred permanent plan of reunification had to be ruled out prior to the development of an alternative plan. Thus, caseworkers worked in a linear fashion, pursuing one permanency goal at a time. However, this method was believed to contribute to long lengths of stay and multiple placements in out-of-home care (Lutz 2000), as it may take years before it becomes evident that a biological family is not ready or able to provide a safe home for the child. Long lengths of stay were particularly true for infants and young children under the age of four, one of the fastest growing segments in the child welfare population (Goerge, Wulczyn, and Harden 1994).

Concurrent planning represents a new way to pursue both reunification and prevent foster care drift and thus is an approach that seeks

(continued)

to eliminate or reduce delays in attaining permanent family placements for children in the foster care system. Concurrent planning was developed in the 1990s, at Lutheran Social Services of Washington and Idaho and at the Washington Division of Children and Family Services (Katz, Spoonemore, and Robinson 1994).

Concurrent planning involves the consideration of all reasonable options for permanency at the earliest possible point following a child's entry into foster care and concurrently pursuing those that will best serve the child's needs. In concurrent planning, an alternative permanency goal, such as adoption, is pursued at the same time as the goal of reunification (Lutz 2000). As such, concurrent planning is both a philosophy and a case management method emphasizing candor, goal setting, and time limits with birth parents. It is based on the belief that foster care outcomes are determined as much by the agency's approach as by the parental situation. The Federal Adoption and Safe Families Act of 1997 paved the way for the legal sanction of concurrent planning in states and the formalization of the practice in child welfare agencies (Schene 2001).

Different models of concurrent planning can be utilized, but they all share certain core features, including expedited timelines and the providing of ongoing candid feedback to the biological parents about the expedited timeframes by which it is expected that they achieve improvement in their ability to care for their child. Ideally, this—along with support and guidance from the caseworker—will spur the parent to make greater gains in order to avoid permanency alternatives for their children. Biological parents are to be informed and involved at every step of the way about the likelihood of reunification and their role in their child's life should reunification not be possible (National Resource Center for Foster Care and Permanency Planning 1998).

According to the Children's Bureau (2004) analysis of Child and Family State Reviews (CFSR), "concurrent planning efforts are not being implemented on a consistent basis when appropriate" in a majority of states. Casework staff still considers concurrent planning a "back-up" plan should the primary goal of reunification prove unattainable. In addition, staffpeople have noted the difficulties inherent in working toward two mutually exclusive goals simultaneously and have raised concerns that concurrent planning might create anxiety and discomfort in birth and/or foster/adoptive parents, which could ultimately impede reunification.

Overview of the Topic

A focus group is a data collection strategy in which a trained facilitator leads a group discussion about attitudes and beliefs among a set of individuals who share a particular experience or characteristic. Merton, Fiske, and Kendall's (1956) seminal writing on this topic highlights three critical parameters of focus groups: (1) the participants have a specific experience of or opinion about the topic under investigation, (2) a standard question protocol is used, and (3) the subjective experiences of participants are explored.

In practical terms, a selected group of six to ten individuals, all of whom have experienced the same event or process and/or share a similar characteristic, are brought together to discuss and share their ideas, beliefs, attitudes, and experiences. It is important that they do not already know one another and that they are not likely to interact with one another in the future. Typically, a structured protocol is developed, consisting primarily of open-ended questions in which participants are guided through an exploration of their feelings and beliefs in detail. Several focus groups are conducted in order to capture the full range of experiences and beliefs about the topic. Focus group sessions typically last between 1.5 and 2.5 hours and are audiotaped. Tapes are transcribed verbatim and submitted to a content analysis in which major themes and issues are identified. The findings can be used to answer research questions as well as generate hypotheses for future studies. The premise underlying the group nature of the data collection is that the synergy of the group dynamic produces richer, more authentic, and more meaningful information than would be produced by a series of individual interviews. Krueger (1994) explains that this occurs "because it taps into human tendencies, attitudes, and perceptions relating to concepts, products, services, or programs which are developed in part by interaction with other people." Seal, Bogart, and Ehrhardt (1998) conducted both focus groups and individual interviews with the same sample of forty-four men and concluded that focus group discussions as a research method are useful and can be employed to study sensitive topics. The focus group discussions led to conclusions similar to those based on the individual interviews.

Deciding When to Use Focus Groups

Focus groups are ideal if the problem formulation phase of a project results in an interest in people's opinions and expressed attitudes or if more information is being sought about a topic in order to guide future research. With reference to the chapter scenario described above, examples of questions that could be answered through a focus group study include: (1) What do former foster care children believe were the most effective services received and what do they wish had been done differently by the agency? (2) What kinds of behavioral problems of foster care children do foster parents have the hardest time dealing with and want more training in? And (3) what are the biological parents' perspectives on and feelings about concurrent planning?

The primary advantage of focus groups is that, as with interviews, the findings are rich, often fascinating, and can provide the researcher and audience with the "felt shared experience" of the participants. The final report/paper includes quotes and true accounts that bring the issue or event to life and that can also be useful for advocacy and fundraising purposes. Focus groups also offer the researcher the possibility of being surprised by the data and of learning something genuinely new. The synergy among the participants can lead to honest and interesting findings. Another advantage is that the sample size tends to be smaller than quasi-experimental and experimental studies. Typically, six focus groups are held on a given topic.

The primary disadvantage of focus groups is the ease with which they can be done poorly, resulting in little or no new information being generated. At worst, inaccurate conclusions can be drawn from the data, due to biases in sampling, questioning technique, or coding decisions. Focus groups also require significant time and resources for the design and piloting of the protocol, arranging the time and location of the sessions, conducting the sessions, transcribing the tapes, and coding the data, contrary to the myth that focus groups can be done cheaply (Morgan and Krueger 1993). In addition, this design does not allow for inferential analyses and statistical hypothesis testing, because the data generated are qualitative.

Another consideration in determining the appropriateness of this methodology is ensuring that the individuals participating in a session do not know one another and are not likely to come into contact with one another in the future. For this reason, many potential child welfare samples are not ideal for focus groups, such as samples made up of clients served in the same program at the same time, staff working within the same agency (unless it is a very large agency), youth living in the same group home or residential program, or even administrators across agencies within the same geographic area (because they probably know one another through working on interagency committees). Further, it is essential that what people say during the session not be repeated outside the session. Thus, clients in a program must know that the program staff will not be told what was said by whom, staff in an agency must know that what they say will not be shared with their supervisors, and children must know that what they say will not be shared with their caretakers or parents. For all these reasons, the gold standard of focus group sampling is that the participants do not know one another and the person running the focus group is not beholden (and is not perceived as being beholden) to the agencies serving the clients. Only in this way can the participants be comfortable enough to share their thoughts and feelings without fear of consequences or reprisal. Following these guidelines will result in the strategic and appropriate use of focus groups in child welfare research.

Defining and Recruiting the Sample

Identifying the Population

Because focus groups are in large part a measure of attitudes, beliefs, and experiences (as opposed to facts), it is important to determine *whose* ideas and beliefs are of interest. Thus, identifying the inclusion and exclusion criteria for the study is essentially an exercise in defining to whom the findings can be generalized. To explore the notion of inclusion and exclusion, the chapter scenario will be used, in which the research question is: "What are biological parents' perceptions about concurrent planning?" In order to identify the sample for a study that addresses this question, the concept of "biological parent" will need to be defined. First, characteristics of the parent will need to be identified, including issues such as geographic location, type of foster care provided to the child (regular foster care, kinship foster care, therapeutic foster care), reason the child was removed (abuse, neglect, other), and the permanency goal of the child (reunification or other). Second, characteristics of the individual will need to be defined in terms of any special focus for the study. Characteristics to consider include age, gender, ethnicity, marital status, and income.

At its broadest, the sample could be composed of any biological parent with a child removed from care regardless of the individual's age, race, marital status, gender, income, number of children in the home, number of children removed, and so forth. A narrower approach entails defining the sample as only biological mothers of ethnic minority status whose children— age birth to ten years of age—were removed from care due to abuse or neglect within the last eighteen months. Narrower criteria tend to reduce the variation in responses and, therefore, require smaller samples (and fewer resources) but have more limited generalizability. Conversely, broader criteria require larger samples to contend with the increase in variation in responses (and greater resources) but also allow for greater generalizability of the findings.

If it is determined that parents served by one agency within a geographic region will be sampled, the population will be limited by the extent to which the population of biological parents is limited. For example, if the agency only serves low-income or minority parents or only parents from Hispanic backgrounds, these real-life constraints represent limits to the generalizability of the study.

In addition, requirements for participation in the project itself (hearing and vision, mobility, etc.) will need to be taken into account. Focus groups always occur outside the home or office of the participants and require mobility and transportation on the part of the participants. As much as possible, the extent to which these requirements restrict the sample should be limited. The focus group should be held in a central location that is wheelchair accessible, if necessary (more about location below).

Determining Sample Size

Every research study entails the collection of data on a sample of individuals in order to learn something about a larger population to which the sample belongs. It is rarely, if ever, possible to study every single member of a population of interest. Using the example for this chapter, the agency is interested in biological parents whose children were removed from care and are subject to concurrent planning requirements, perhaps at a particular agency. In the absence of a multistate study, the population will be defined as all biological parents within a specific geographic area. In large urban areas in which several programs serve parents in the child welfare system, several thousand families could be served at the same time. Clearly, it is not possible to include everyone in the population, and it is not necessary to do so. If the sample of the study is clearly defined and large enough, it is possible to generalize the findings from the study sample to the population of interest.

Because quantitative analyses will not be conducted, it is not necessary nor possible to calculate the desired sample size according to the guidelines and formula provided in chapter 5. There are two ways to think about sample size in focus groups: the size of each group and the number of groups. In general, the size of the focus groups should be between six and ten participants. If there are fewer than six participants, the group will feel too intimate and each participant may feel uncomfortable and pressured to speak. In addition, insufficient variation in perspectives will be generated with a smaller group. In groups with more than ten participants, each participant will have insufficient time to speak and may tune out or give up on actively participating. People may speak over each other or create side conversations, which can be distracting to the other participants. Groups larger than ten participants will also result in each person being seated too far away from the rest of the participants. This may create a sense of the group being too formal or intimidating. Based on extensive experience, the field has developed the consensus that between six and ten participants is ideal.

Determining the number of focus groups to conduct is more complicated. The following three issues should be considered: coverage, credibility, and saturation. Coverage relates to the need to include in the focus groups a sample of all members of the population. If the population of biological parents can be described as individuals between twenty-two and fifty-five years of age but disproportionately under thirty, of both genders but disproportionately female, from a range of cultural, racial, and ethnic backgrounds, and both married and unmarried, to the extent that these factors might influence the findings, the sample should consist of individuals with these characteristics as well. Simply ensuring coverage across these categories necessitates several focus groups.

The credibility of the study can also be used to guide the number of focus groups held. It is highly unlikely that the findings of a study that involved a single focus group would be considered credible. Even someone unfamiliar with scientific methods would probably intuitively conclude that no one group will adequately represent the population nor generate a sufficient quantity of data from which to draw valid conclusions. In order to establish credibility, the researcher should determine how many focus groups have been conducted by respected researchers in the field and conduct no fewer than that number (more might be necessary, but probably not fewer). The researcher should be familiar with published articles that have utilized focus groups as the measurement strategy and from that literature review have a sense of what is acceptable in the field. For example, O'Donnell, Johnson, D'Aunno, and Thornton (2005) conducted a study of thirty-four child welfare caseworkers who participated in five focus groups. In a study of parents with children in foster care, Kapp and Propp (2002) conducted eight focus groups with a total of forty-seven participants. The aim was to learn about effective methods for collecting consumer satisfaction information from clients served by the child welfare system. Issues of sexual intimacy were explored in five focus groups with forty-four men (Seal, Bogart, and Ehrhardt 1998). Twelve focus groups with seventy participants were conducted by Chippman, Wells, and Johnson (2002) to explore the meaning of quality care in kinship homes. This miniature literature review suggests that five focus groups is the minimum number of groups necessary, with between thirty-five and seventy participating individuals in total.

The concept of theoretical saturation is yet another basis on which to decide how many focus groups to conduct (Glaser and Strauss 1967). If possible, the audiotapes of the focus groups should be listened to by the researcher on an ongoing basis. As long as new information (ideas, beliefs, experiences) is being generated from the discussion, additional groups should be scheduled. At some point, the concepts under investigation will become "saturated," and no new groups will need to be scheduled. Krueger (1994) suggests a minimum of three groups before deciding whether to continue collecting new data.

A final factor to consider in selecting the number of focus groups to conduct within a given study is that, ideally, the same facilitator should conduct all of the focus groups in order to control for the influence of his or her personal style and skill (Albrecht, Johnson, and Walther 1993).

Recruiting Participants

Both probability and nonprobability sampling strategies can be employed in the recruitment of participants for focus groups. If the sampling frame can be identified (every member of the population can be listed), then random selection procedures can be employed to select individuals to invite to participate in the focus group. This might be possible if every biological parent in the relevant programs can be listed (perhaps by ID code or initials, so as to protect their confidentiality). Alternatively, the researcher can work with someone within the agencies to provide step-by-step guidance in developing a random selection process. (See chapter 5 for examples of random selection strategies.) If random selection is utilized, the next step will be for the parents to be notified that they have been selected to be invited to participate in a focus group. How they are contacted needs to be considered. One option is for the researcher to be provided with the names and phone numbers of the parents for direct contact. This is not likely, for reasons relating to confidentiality, unless the researcher works at the agency. Another option is for someone within the agency or agencies to notify the parents about their selection and provide them with information about how to contact the researcher. A third option is for someone within the agency or agencies to obtain parental permission to release their contact information to the researcher.

It is important to remember that not everyone selected and invited will agree to participate (this is probably more true for focus groups than surveys, because the personal nature of the interaction and greater time and energy investment is likely to dampen response rates). It is also important to bear in mind that not everyone who is scheduled to participate will actually show up. Thus, even if the invited individuals were randomly selected from the population, the final sample might not be statistically representative if response and participation rates are low.

In the event that the sampling frame is not available (one exists but will not be provided to the researcher, or one does not exist), nonprobability sampling strategies will be employed. For focus groups, this usually entails some form of a convenience sample in which individuals volunteer to participate, usually by responding to a project flyer, notice, or announcement. That is, the researcher makes known to some or all members of the population that a study is being conducted and that they are invited to contact the researcher to participate. The wider the distribution of the flyer/notice/announcement, the higher the response rate will be. The flyer should contain the following information: (1) a brief description of the purpose of the study (e.g., to hear from biological parents their ideas about whether or not their children will come home or be adopted), (2) the sponsor of the project, (3) the type of involvement and time commitment (e.g., a two-hour focus group to be held during a certain time period), (4) whether payment will be made to participants, (5) how confidentiality will be maintained, (6) anything else pertinent (refreshments, child care available, location), and (7) what interested individuals should do (e.g., contact the researcher at a specific number for more information and to schedule an appointment). Figure 12.1 provides a sample flyer.

There are at least two ways to schedule the focus groups. The first is to set dates and times in advance, inform potential participants of those dates and times, and ask them which session they can attend. This makes the most sense if the location of the sessions has a limited amount of free time (such as a group room in community-based organization or a classroom in a nearby school). The other option is to ask individuals who indicate interest which dates and times they would be free, and then schedule groups around these times. Either way, there will be some back and forth with potential participants to schedule and confirm the dates, times, and locations of the sessions. It is important to structure the groups so that similar people are in the same group, as people are more likely to reveal information about themselves when they are with people whom they perceive to be like themselves (Jourard 1964).

Figure 12.1
Recruitment flyer for focus group of biological parents with children in foster care

---

WE WANT TO KNOW WHAT YOU THINK ABOUT CHILD WELFARE

Who: Parents with children in foster care

What: Participate in a focus group discussion about your experience with the foster care system. A focus group is a small group discussion with other parents. It is not a test and there are no right or wrong answers. Your beliefs and experiences are what we want to understand.

Why: Help the (name) agency learn how to improve services for parents

When: To be arranged at your convenience

Where: At the (name) building at (location)

Fee: Participants will receive $25.00 for participating in a two-hour discussion

Contact: Please call (name) at (phone number) for more information.

- Everything said during the discussion will remain private and confidential.
- Childcare is available on location and refreshments will be served

---

Design of the Focus Group

The focus group is composed primarily of the protocol, which is the script of the "conversation" between the facilitator and the participants. Bracketing the protocol are some "housekeeping" activities. There are ten basic units to the focus group process: (1) welcome and orientation, (2) explanation of the ground rules for participating, (3) informed consent, (4) the opening question of the protocol, (5) the main questions of the protocol, (6) the closing question/activity of the protocol, (7) wrapping up the protocol, (8) debriefing, (9) completion of the participant forms, and (10) payment.

Welcome and Orientation

The focus group should start with a standardized welcome and orientation. This should be written out in full and read verbatim to the group (unless the facilitator is particularly adept at public speaking). A sample orientation might be:

Greetings everyone. Thanks so much for taking the time to come out today/tonight for this focus group. My name is [name] and I will be your facilitator. The person sitting to my right is [name]. S/he will be assisting me in running the focus group. I want to tell you a little bit about what is going to happen in the group, review some group rules, answer your questions, and then we can get started. You were all invited to come to-day/tonight because the [name of agency] wants to hear from parents their understanding of their children's likelihood of returning home or being adopted. I was hired by this agency to run these focus groups and to prepare a final report to them. In that report, no names will be used and there will be no way for anyone reading the report to know which partici-pant made which comment. There will be quotes in the report, to illus-trate specific attitudes and beliefs, but again no names will be provided that would allow the reader to know which participants made which com-ments. The [name of agency] really wants to learn about your ideas and thoughts. We urge you to be honest because that is what will be most helpful. You will receive a payment of [amount] dollars at the end of the session. Refreshments are available, so please help yourself. I am going to explain the ground rules and then ask you to sign a consent form that [name of assistant facilitator] will pass around.

Explanation of the Ground Rules

The major ground rules that need to be explained are (1) how people will be expected to answer questions (called on or spontaneously offered), (2) whether people should identify themselves before they speak, (3) issues re-lated to confidentiality (what is said in the room stays in the room), (4) being respectful and nonjudgmental, and (5) role of the facilitator. A sample expla-nation of the ground rules might be:

> We will be turning on an audiotape once you have all signed the consent form. The purpose of that is so that I can listen to the tape later and re-ally understand what is being said. So please try to speak up when you talk and try not to talk over each other. For some questions, I will ask you to go around the room and respond, but for others I will just throw out a question to the group and ask you all to respond as you feel like. You don't need to raise your hand; you can just jump right in. There is no right or wrong answer and this is not a test. We do ask that you be re-spectful of others in the room. You can disagree with what someone else

says but please do so in a respectful manner. Also, I will be master of ceremonies for tonight and the keeper of the time, so there might be times when I have to cut your comments short; please do not be offended. I want to make sure that everyone has a chance to speak and that we keep on schedule. Before we get started, does any one have any questions?

Informed Consent

Informed consent should be obtained after the project and the ways in which confidentiality will be maintained have been described. Once the welcoming statement has been made and the ground rules described, the facilitator should ask if anyone has questions about the purpose of the project or what is going to happen. After questions have been answered, the assistant facilitator should give a consent form and a pen to each person. The facilitator should read the consent form out loud, ask if there are any questions, and then ask everyone to sign. The assistant facilitator should collect the signed forms and place them in a folder. Later they should be labeled as to which group the individuals participated in.

The Opening Question of the Protocol

Typically, the first question of a focus group is a round-robin type of question; that is, the facilitator asks a question each person is expected to answer in turn. The purpose is to give every person an opportunity to speak. Once a person has spoken in a group setting, it is more likely that he or she will speak again. Thus, the round-robin question gives everyone a chance right from the start to be an active member of the group. This question should ask each person to state his or her first name and say something general about the topic, such as how many children they have currently in out-of-home care and their ages and genders. It is also helpful to ask each person to say something about why he or she decided to participate in the focus group.

The Main Questions of the Protocol

The bulk of the protocol should be composed of six general questions. If the questions are substantive enough, the conversation in response to each question could take fifteen minutes, and this would make up the major portion of the focus group. Ideally, the questions will be so thought provoking and interesting that a lively discussion will ensue.

Closing Question/Activity of the Protocol

Some focus groups include an opportunity for the participants to break into small groups and do some brainstorming, the results of which are then shared with the full group. An example would be to ask the teams to develop the ideal timeframe for reunification/adoption or a policy statement about when agencies should consider adoption as an option. This kind of activity can energize the group, lead to a freer way of thinking, and generate some very useful information. The group work can be fun, if the topic is not too depressing or threatening, and is a nice way to wind down the session.

Wrapping Up the Focus Group

The group should be informed that the session is coming to an end. If there is time, each person can be asked to make a final statement. The facilitator should thank each person for participating, let the group know that there is a bit of "housekeeping" that needs attending to, and then the session will be formally over.

Completion of Participant Forms

It is usually advisable to ask the participants to complete a background form so that the final report can provide some descriptive information about the sample. The form should be laid out in a pleasing manner that is easy to follow and takes little time to complete. It should include questions about age, gender, marital status, ethnicity, highest level of education, and so forth.

Payment

At this point participants are paid (if a fee is part of the project) and asked to sign a proof of receipt of payment.

Developing Focus Group Questions: Improving Quality

Ask Open-Ended Questions

Questions should be phrased in such a way as to elicit complex responses that provide rich and textured answers. The possible options for answering should be unlimited, and possible response options should not be offered or suggested to the participants. Take as an example the question, "do you think that the caseworker is pursuing adoption as an option for your child because she or he has to by law or because she or he thinks it is right for your child?" Such a double-barreled question suggests that there are only two answers and that they are mutually exclusive. A better choice of wording would be to ask, "what are some reasons you can think of that your family's caseworker would pursue adoption as an option for your child?" Questions that elicit one-word answers or factual answers are not the type of questions likely to produce the rich response being sought.

Avoid Asking "Why"

The word "why" is ambiguous at best and can be interpreted by each participant somewhat differently, depending upon his or her theory and understanding of motivation. Rather than asking, "why do you want your child to be returned home?" it might be better to ask, "what are some of the reasons that you want your child to be reunified with your family?"

Ask Questions That Elicit Story Telling

One type of question asks members of the group to give an example or "tell a story" about a particular experience they have had. In telling the story, people might recall additional aspects of their thoughts and feelings. In addition, the stories are very useful in writing up the final report/paper.

Avoid Making Assumptions

Questions should be asked in such a way as to avoid assumptions on the part of the facilitator. Asking "what are some ways your family has been helped by the child welfare system?" assumes that the family has in fact been helped. It would be better to ask, "what, if any, way has your family been helped by the child welfare system?"

Avoid Technical Terms, Jargon, and Questions That Assume Prior Knowledge

Avoid using terms that will not be understood by the members of the group. It is unlikely that someone will admit to not knowing what something means. For example, in the hypothetical focus group of biological parents, do not ask a question about their beliefs about concurrent planning (unless that term has been defined). In a hypothetical focus group of social work students, do not ask a question about their opinions on the impact of ASFA on social workers in the field of child welfare, because it requires knowledge of the term ASFA (which stands for the Adoption and Safe Families Act) and requires a level of knowledge about the field that, as students, they may not have.

Developing Focus Group Questions: Steps in the Process

Begin by making a list of general issues about the topic. For the chapter scenario, issues might be: (1) perceived advantages and disadvantages for children, families, and the "system" of concurrent planning; (2) the family's actual experience with concurrent planning; (3) the family's beliefs about their chances of being reunified and what they need to do in order to achieve that goal; (4) their knowledge of anyone else who has been affected by concurrent planning; and (5) the sources of their information about concurrent planning.

From this list of issues, a pool of questions can be developed. Several different options for writing each question should be explored in order to identify any hidden assumptions, biases, or lack of clarity in the questions.

The list of potential questions should be revised and refined over a period of several weeks in order to allow the researcher (and others on the team) to reflect on the questions and consider their usefulness for the project.

The final draft set of questions should be submitted to experts in focus groups and experts in the subject matter (e.g., biological parents, caseworkers with experience in concurrent planning, supervisors with knowledge about policy and practice related to concurrent planning) for their feedback. The questions should be revised and refined accordingly.

Piloting the Focus Group

Once a complete draft of the protocol has been developed, at least one pilot session should be held. The participants can be a convenience sample of individuals who are in the same population as the proposed study participants. They should know in advance that this is a pilot, and they should be aware that this is a very important part of the research process. The facilitator should take his or her job very seriously and try in every way to stay in the role of the facilitator. Only in this way can the questions be evaluated for their utility. The pilot also allows the facilitator to obtain practice in managing a group, dealing with logistics, and so forth. Any kinks in the system can be identified in advance. This phase should never be skipped unless the facilitator is an expert in running focus groups and has absolute confidence that the draft protocol will produce exactly what is of interest.

Techniques and Role of the Facilitator

Facilitators of focus groups can make or break the experience. The facilitator creates the tone, sets the atmosphere, and directs the group. If the facilitator is warm, friendly, professional, and skillful at managing group interactions, the participants will feel at ease, interested in the topic, and comfortable exploring and sharing their thoughts and feelings. A good facilitator will ensure that all participants feel supported, respected, and valued.

Managing the Group

It is important that each person be an active member of the group and that no one person dominates or intimidates the other participants. Some people will naturally be more talkative than others and the facilitator will need to monitor closely the group dynamic to even out the participation as much as possible. If one person is speaking too much, one technique is to gently interrupt that person before he or she begins to express a new thought and say something such as, "Mary, you have many interesting things to say and I want to get back to that thought if there is time, but right now let's hear from some other participants." Another option is to ask people to go around the room and comment on something. This will break up the pattern of domination by one speaker. It is vital not to hurt that person's feelings or humiliate that person, as this could sour the mood of the whole group.

Likewise, if one person seems particularly reticent to speak, he or she could be called on specifically. One way to do that without calling attention to that person's shyness or quietness is to draw on something he or she said earlier such as, "Alice, I am interested to hear what you have to say about this because earlier you mentioned. . . ."

Another common issue for focus groups is making sure that the answers provided are in depth and detailed. The facilitator should have several stock phrases at his or her fingertips in order to elicit more material from a speaker. Comments such as "can you say more about that?" or "can you give an example of one time when that was particularly true?" can be useful to probe for more information. Sometimes simply being quiet will elicit more responses, and sometimes a simple phrase such as "anything else?" will elicit elaboration.

In general, the facilitator should be nonjudgmental in response to the statements made by the participants. Comments such as "good" or "how interesting" could inadvertently shape the type of information shared, because the participants may want to please the facilitator and therefore may be inclined to produce more content like the content eliciting the "positive feedback" from the facilitator. It is much better to use neutral phrases to encourage involvement, such as "thanks for sharing that" and "I see." Head nodding (if not too enthusiastic) can help the speaker feel understood and heard without conveying value judgment about the content. It is also sometimes helpful to summarize what an individual or a group is saying in order to make sure that the facilitator understands. The facilitator can repeat a thought and ask for confirmation ("Is this what you mean?"). Sometimes it is helpful to say to the group, "some of you have mentioned feeling [a certain way]. I am wondering if some of you have also ever felt . . ." This gives participants permission to disagree with what was said and makes sure that both sides of an issue have been examined and discussed.

Focus Group Logistics

Location

The space in which the focus group takes place is very important. It needs to be a private quiet room large enough for twelve people. There should be a single table in the room or a space large enough for a circle of chairs. Everyone should be able to have eye contact with everyone else. The location should be equally accessible to all participants and in a neutral area. It should not be difficult to reach. It should be safe, well lit, and not too different from what the typical participant is used to. For example, if the participants are biological parents of children in the foster care system, it is not advisable to hold the focus group in an upscale neighborhood not accessible to them by public transportation. Likewise, if the participants are social work students in graduate school, it would not be appropriate to convene the focus group in a high-risk neighborhood late at night. Ideally, the location will not belong to an organization that has some authority over the participants (e.g., if the topic is school involvement, the focus group should not be held in the school; if the topic is client involvement in an agency, the focus group should not be held in a building associated with/owned by the agency). If people with disabilities are expected to participate, then the location should be handicapped accessible.

Refreshments

Refreshments should be served and should be equally accessible to all participants. Ideally, they will be located in the center of the table around which the participants are seated. This way, no one has to get up in the middle of the focus group to get something to drink or eat. The refreshments should be items that the participants are likely to enjoy (e.g., not vegetable crudités for a focus group of teens). The items should not be too noisy (e.g., individually wrapped cookies or crackers), as the sound can be amplified on the audiotape and be very distracting for the person listening to or transcribing the tape. Do not schedule a focus group at a regular mealtime (12–2 pm or 6–8 pm), as the participants might be hungry and resentful of not being provided with more than a snack.

Child Care

If low-income parents are the primary targeted participants, then babysitting should be offered by professional babysitters in a clean and safe environment. It is important that the sponsoring agency and the owner of the building be aware of this, as there may be liability issues.

The Role of the Assistant Facilitator

Whenever possible, the facilitator should have an assistant in the room the entire time. This person serves several important functions. First, it is useful for the assistant to be of the same ethnic and cultural background as the participants. If the focus group is composed of low-income minority women, it would be helpful to have an assistant who is a minority woman (unless the facilitator is also). Second, this person can be in charge of refreshments (replenishing cups, coffee, etc., if necessary) and can oversee the taping (testing the equipment, setting it up, turning the tape over, putting in a new tape, labeling the tape). In this way, the facilitator can devote all of his or her attention to management of the group dynamics. The assistant facilitator can also make observational notes that might be useful for the interpretation of the data or for the improvement of subsequent focus groups.

Before and After the Session

The facilitator and assistant facilitator need to arrive at least half an hour prior to the start time to set up the room (place chairs around a table or in a circle), set up refreshments, and test the audio equipment (extra batteries, tapes, and extension cords are a must). A checklist should be utilized to ensure that all necessary tasks are completed. A sample checklist is presented in figure 12.2. At the end of the session, once the participants have left the room, the assistant facilitator and facilitator should briefly discuss the session and note what needs to be modified for the next session, if anything. Major issues raised should also be jotted down while they are fresh. The tape should be labeled and the room cleaned up. Any cosponsoring agencies should be written thank-you notes.

Transcribing the Tapes and Analyzing the Data

Each audiotape should be transcribed verbatim (word for word). This can best be accomplished with a transcription machine in which the tape speed is controlled by a foot pedal. This allows for the continuous typing of the audio material, as the foot controls when to stop and start the tape, allowing the hands to remain on the keyboard. Transcribing can be quite time consuming. A good rule of thumb is about ten hours of transcription per hour of audiotape, although this varies depending upon how quickly the participants speak, the quality of the tape and the transcribing machine, and the speed of typist. Focus group transcription is particularly challenging, as people tend to interrupt each other, and it may be difficult to determine the point at which one speaker stops and another starts. As

Figure 12.2
Checklist for conducting focus groups

PRIOR TO THE SESSION

[ ] Remind the liaison to the building that it will be used for designated time
[ ] Remind participants of date and time of session
[ ] Purchase and bring refreshments to room (including paper goods)
[ ] Assure access to two tape players, extra batteries, extension cords, labels
[ ] Make copies of consent forms (two per person)
[ ] Make copies of participant forms
[ ] Make copy of protocol
[ ] Assure access to payment
[ ] Purchase/make receipt of payment forms

DAY OF SESSION

[ ] Set up room
[ ] Make coffee, set up refreshments
[ ] Test audio equipment

AFTER SESSION

[ ] Take notes about session
[ ] Label tapes, consent forms, receipt of payment forms
[ ] Clean up room and refreshments
[ ] Write thank-you notes (if relevant)

---

much as possible, the final transcript should demark one participant from another.

It is possible to hire someone else to transcribe the tapes, but it is advisable that the researcher himself or herself take on this task, as it is an effective mechanism for getting to really "hear" what was said during the interview. This process of hearing the interview, typing in the words, and seeing the words on the screen can deepen the researcher's understanding of the material. The typed transcript should be double spaced and printed on single-sided pages. Each interview will result in about twenty-five to fifty pages of text depending upon the length of the interview and how quickly the people spoke (i.e., how dense the text is).

The main approach to analyzing focus group transcripts is to conduct a systematic content analysis based on a grounded theory approach (Berg 1998; Straus 1987). The researcher reads and rereads the text of the transcripts and "discovers" or labels categories. The ability to perceive variables is termed "theoretical sensitivity" and is affected by a number of factors, including one's reading of the literature and use of techniques designed to enhance sensitivity. Practically speaking, one way to conduct such an analysis is to read each transcript and demark each unique unit of thought. A unit could be a phrase, a sentence, a paragraph, or even longer. Each unit is then literally cut off the page and taped onto an index card. This results in hundreds—if not thousands—of index cards. These cards are then read through and sorted into piles that represent some commonality. The results section of the paper/final report then presents each pile of cards as a theme. Chapter 15 presents additional information about writing up the results of focus groups.

Conclusion

A focus group represents a useful research method for collecting data about the attitudes and beliefs of a group of individuals about a common experience, issue, or event. The questions need to be carefully crafted and piloted, and the facilitator of the focus group needs to have excellent group-process skills. A major limitation in the utilization of focus groups in child welfare research is that the participants must be complete strangers at the time of the study and must be unlikely to see each other after the focus group has been completed. Thus, many samples within the field of child welfare are not amenable to participation in a focus group (such as staff or clients within the same agency). When feasible, however, focus groups can produce findings that are rich and of great use to improving programs and practice.

In-Depth Interviews

In this chapter, the following topics will be discussed, following the introduction of the chapter scenario and the brief literature review:

- Deciding when to use in-depth interviews
- Defining and recruiting the sample
- Developing interview questions: improving clarity
- Developing interview questions: steps in the process
- Piloting the interview protocol
- Techniques of the interviewer
- Interview logistics
- Transcribing the tapes and analyzing the data

CHAPTER SCENARIO

A caseworker in a foster home department in a child welfare agency notices that there is a lack of consensus among her colleagues about the advantages and disadvantages of kinship care. Some of her colleagues believe that the child welfare policy of promoting placements

(continued)

with a child's relatives (kinship care) makes a lot of sense because in most cases there is an existing relationship between the prospective foster parent and the child, making the transition to the placement less stressful to the child. On the other hand, some of her colleagues point out that in some cases these individuals do not meet the same standards that nonrelative foster parents have to meet in order to become a foster parent. Many of the kinship foster parents are the parents of the individuals from whose care the child was removed, casting doubt on their ability to be adequate foster parents of the child. The caseworker notices over time that caseworkers hold many strong and sometimes conflicting views of their work with kinship foster parents and wonders what the kinship foster parents themselves think of their role in the foster child's life and how they reconcile their potentially competing demands to be a parent to the child and to maintain a relationship with that child's mother—in many cases their own child. The caseworker thinks this would be an important topic for a research project and asks the agency to assign the agency researcher to develop a study looking into this issue. With agency support, a team is put together, including the researcher, the caseworker, two kinship foster parents, and others interested in the study. From this general line of thinking a series of research questions are developed by the team, including: (1) How do kinship parents understand their dual roles as foster parents and parents? And (2) what do they believe to be the advantages and disadvantages of kinship care? In order to answer these (and related) research questions, the team designs a qualitative research study consisting of in-depth interviews of kinship foster parents.

BRIEF LITERATURE REVIEW: ATTITUDES AND EXPERIENCES OF KINSHIP FOSTER PARENTS

Kinship caregivers are foster parents who have a preexisting biological relationship with the parent whose child has been removed from care and placed in the foster care system. Although figures vary by agency, nationwide approximately 30 percent of all children in family-level fos-

(continued)

ter care are being cared for by relatives (United States Department of Health and Human Services 2000). According to Wulczyn and Goerge (1992), kinship foster care is the fastest growing category of substitute care in the child welfare system. Berrick and Needell (1999) considered the expansion of the utilization of kinship care to be the most dramatic shift in child welfare, due in part to the 1979 Supreme Court ruling that encouraged greater use of kinship care by allowing kinship caregivers to receive payments for the support and care of the children. The vast majority of these kinship caregivers are the biological grandparents of the foster child. Thus, foster care is being provided by individuals whose own children have been deemed to be unfit parents. Because kinship care is consistent with the child welfare policy of keeping children as much as possible in a family setting, in some states the requirements to qualify for foster parenting are relaxed for kinship caregivers. Prior research has demonstrated that there are demographic differences between kinship and nonkinship caregivers, including age, race, marital status, and income. Typically, kinship caregivers are more likely than regular foster home providers to be older, African American, single, and have less education and income (Cuddeback 2004; Gebel 1996). Kinship caregivers have also been found to have different attitudes about kinship care in general (Harden, Clyman, Kriebel, and Lyons 2004) and about their foster child in particular. For example, Gebel (1996) found in a survey of kinship and nonkinship foster parents that kinship foster parents held more favorable views of their foster children: they were more likely to report them to be good natured and not difficult to handle.

Other research has found that caseworkers hold different views of kinship foster parents than nonkinship foster parents. Peters (2004), for example, found that during a training session with kinship care caseworkers, many made spontaneous negative comments about this form of foster care. Likewise, focus groups with caseworkers revealed a belief that children in kinship care were at greater risk of abuse due to increased contact with the biological parents (Chipman, Wells, and Johnson 2002). Beeman and Boison (1999) also reported that caseworkers believed that kinship care cases were more difficult to supervise. It is quite plausible that these and related negative beliefs and attitudes, if widespread, are conveyed to the kinship foster parents, affecting their attitudes toward and experience with the child welfare system.

Overview of the Topic

An interview study aims to understand in a systematic way the subject's everyday lifeworld as it relates to the topic of interest and the meaning of the issue for them, in a qualitative rather than quantitative form and with an emphasis on the description of specific experiences (Kvale 1996). This information is obtained through a sensitively conducted interpersonal exchange that, because of the deliberate naiveté of the interviewer, allows the participant to express ambiguous statements and come to new and/or changed understandings. The interview should be conducted in such a manner as to produce a positive experience for the participant.

In practical terms, a selected group of individuals, all of whom have experienced the same event or process and/or share a similar belief or attitude, are individually interviewed about their beliefs, attitudes, and experiences. Typically, a semistructured protocol is developed, composed primarily of open-ended questions and in which participants are guided through an exploration of their feelings and expression of their beliefs with specificity and in detail. Individual interviews—conducted in person or on the telephone—typically last between one and three hours and are audiotaped. The tapes are transcribed verbatim and submitted to a content analysis, in which major themes and issues are identified. The findings can be used to answer research questions as well as to generate hypotheses for future studies.

According to Holloway (1997), interviewing is concerned with the "lived experience" of people and is rooted in the theory of phenomenology as developed by Edmund Husserl (1990). According to Johnson and Christensen (2000, 315), the aim of research based on phenomenology is to obtain "a view into research participants' life-worlds and to understand their personal meanings (what it means to them) constructed from their life experiences." This method involves obtaining in-depth accounts of experiences from participants and seeking to discover the ways in which they develop and ascribe meaning to these experiences (Denzin and Lincoln 1994). Thus, a phenomenological study describes the meaning of the lived experiences for several individuals who share a specific experience. Phenomenology explores the structures of consciousness in human experiences, which, Burch (1991) posits, are essentially *constituted*. That is, meaning lies in what is made of what is lived through. The full meaning of experience emerges only from explicit retrospection, where meaning is recovered and reenacted in memory, stories, and through phenomenological interpretation. The in-depth interview is one methodology for gaining access to others' lived experiences.

Deciding When to Use In-Depth Interviews

Some research questions are best answered through in-depth discussions with individuals who have had a particular experience or hold a specific belief. This is particularly true if the goal is to understand the felt or lived perspective of these individuals. In-depth interviewing is also an ideal methodology if more information is being sought about a topic in order to guide future research. Examples of questions that could be answered through such a study include: (1) In what ways do families report that it is difficult to attend treatment planning conferences? (2) What does group home staff believe are the causes of burnout and employment termination? And (3) what do kinship parents believe to be the unique advantages and disadvantages of kinship care? This third question was generated from the scenario at the opening of the chapter and will serve as the example for the remainder of the chapter.

As with any research methodology, there are advantages and disadvantages inherent in the use of in-depth interviews. The primary advantage of interviewing is that the findings are rich, often fascinating, and can provide the researcher and audience with the "felt shared experience" of the participants. The report is interspersed with quotes and true accounts that bring the issue or event to life and that can also be useful for advocacy and fundraising purposes. In-depth interviews also offer the researcher the possibility of being surprised by the data and of learning something genuinely new. Another advantage is that the sample size tends to be smaller than quasi-experimental and experimental studies (although larger than single-system designs and some focus groups). The primary disadvantage of in-depth interviewing is the ease with which it can be done poorly, resulting in little or no new information being generated. At worst, inaccurate conclusions can be drawn from the data due to biases in sampling, interviewing technique, or coding decisions. Interview studies also require significant time and resources for the design and piloting of the protocol, conducting the interviews, transcribing the tapes, and coding the data. In addition, this design does not allow for inferential analyses and statistical hypothesis testing because the data generated are qualitative.

Defining and Recruiting the Sample

Identifying the Population

Once it has been decided that the in-depth interview is the chosen methodology for a particular study, the first task is to determine who should be interviewed. Whose opinions and experiences are of interest? Usually, there are multiple possible informants for any particular question. If attitudes about kinship foster care in the child welfare system is the primary research focus, this will need to be further narrowed down to determine whether it is the program staff's experiences and attitudes about this or the kinship foster parents' that are of interest. Additional possible participants for such a study include the president/executive director of an agency, the directors of the foster home programs, caseworkers, social work staff working with the families, city administrators, or the extended family of the program participants. Each offers a valid and important perspective, although they are not interchangeable. As with all studies, the major research questions need to be developed with sufficient specificity in order to guide the development of the sampling strategy. The major consideration, as with all sampling, is the population to whom the findings will be generalized.

Once the general population has been identified—say, kinship foster parents in a foster home program—inclusion and exclusion criteria will need to be defined in order to develop a plan for identifying and recruiting specific individuals who meet those criteria. To explore the notion of inclusion and exclusion criteria, question 3 above will be used as an example: "What do kinship foster parents believe to be the advantages and disadvantages of kinship care?" The researcher will need to decide how to operationalize this concept of "kinship foster parents." Based on theory and experience in the program (garnered from discussion with program staff as well as agency administrators), factors will be identified as relevant for defining the population. For example, how will "kinship foster parent" and "in the child welfare system" be defined? In defining the concept of "kinship foster parent," a decision needs to be made regarding whether only kinship grandparents will be included or whether other kinship caretakers (aunts, older siblings, and so forth) will be interviewed as well. In addition, the gender of the kinship foster parent will need to be considered. Will the study include women and men or just foster parents of one gender? Defining the concept of "in the child welfare system" will entail decisions regarding several factors including, for example, cause of placement in the system. That is, should the sample include only those cases in which a child was removed from home due to abuse/neglect or those who were in out-of-home care for any reason (voluntary placements, PINS, and so forth)? Further, length of time in the child welfare system needs to be considered. Should the sample include individuals who spent a minimum amount of time in the child welfare system or those who had been in the child welfare system for any length of time? Another question is whether the age of first placement in the child welfare system is important. Should the sample include kinship foster parents of children of one gender or both? Answers to these questions form the criteria for including individuals into and excluding individuals from the study. At its broadest, the sample could be composed of any kinship foster parent (regardless of age, gender, relationship to child) of a child who has been in the child welfare system (any level, at any age, for any length of time, for any reason) prior to attaining adulthood. A narrower approach, by way of example, would be to define the sample as minority women between fifty-five and sixty-five years of age (as of a certain date) who are kinship foster grandparents of one child who was removed from home due to the substance abuse problems of the parent, which led to neglect and abuse. There are nearly endless permutations. For example, age and gender of the parent could be narrowly defined while early child welfare experience could be less constrained. There is no right or wrong way to define the sample, although it is important to know that narrow criteria tend to reduce variation in responses and, therefore, require smaller samples (and fewer resources) but result in data that have more limited generalizability. Conversely, broader criteria require larger samples to contend with the increase in variation in responses (and greater resources) but also offer greater generalizability of the findings.

If it is determined that kinship parents within one agency's program are to be sampled, then the population will be limited to the extent to which the population of kinship foster parents in that one program is limited. For example, some agencies serve only families from one racial, cultural, or ethnic background, and some programs only serve families from a specific neighborhood or community district. These real-life constraints represent limits to the generalizability of the study. Unless a cross-agency study is implemented (which could round out the sample by including subsamples not available in the first agency), there is little the researcher can do other than describe these limits in the discussion section of the paper and try to explain the ways in which they might affect the findings obtained.

Competencies necessary for participation in the study also need to be considered as inclusion and exclusion criteria, such as the minimum level of cognitive functioning or reading level, vision/hearing, or mobility. Obviously, research with special-needs populations must take these factors into account in the planning stage. The interplay of these various factors will result in a specific set of inclusion and exclusion criteria that should be theoretically sound, informed by practice wisdom, and sensitive to the workings of the program as well as the needs of families.

Determining Sample Size

Every research study entails the collection of data on a sample of individuals in order to learn something about a larger population to which the sample belongs. It is rarely, if ever, possible to study every single person in the population of interest. Using the example for this chapter, the caseworker is interested in kinship foster parents. This is potentially a large population, as thousands of children are placed in kinship care each year across agencies. Clearly, it is not possible to interview everyone in the population, and it is not necessary to do so. If the sample of the study is clearly defined and large enough, it is possible to generalize the findings from the study sample to the population of interest.

Because quantitative analyses will not be conducted, it is not necessary nor possible to calculate the desired sample size according to the guidelines and formula provided in chapter 5. However, the following three issues should be considered: coverage, credibility, and saturation. Coverage relates to the need to interview a sample of all members of the population. If the population of kinship foster parents can be described as individuals between forty-five and sixty-five years of age but disproportionately over fifty, of both genders but disproportionately female, primarily from ethnic minority backgrounds, married and unmarried but primarily married, to the extent that these factors might influence the findings, the sample should consist of individuals with these characteristics as well. Ensuring coverage across these categories will necessitate a number of interviews.

Credibility of the study can also be used to guide the number of interviews held. It is highly unlikely that the findings of a study involving a single interview would be considered credible. Even someone unfamiliar with scientific methods could intuitively conclude that no one interview will adequately represent the population nor generate a sufficient quantity of data from which to draw valid conclusions. In order to establish credibility, the researcher should determine how many interviews have been conducted by respected researchers in the field and conduct no fewer than that number (more might be necessary, but probably not fewer). Thus, the researcher should be familiar with published articles that have utilized interviews as the measurement strategy and from that review of the literature have a sense of what is acceptable in the field. For example, Constantine, Anderson, Berkel, Caldwell, and Utsey (2005) interviewed twelve African international college students about their cultural adjustment to the United States. A sample of eleven professors in psychology whose families were from lower-class or lower-middle-class backgrounds were interviewed about their experience with "class jumping" by Nelson, Englar-Carlson, Tierney, and Hau (2006), and Petta and Steed (2005) interviewed twenty-one adoptive parents about their experiences with their children's seeking to reunite with their biological parents. This miniature literature review suggests that at least ten interviews are required to be consistent with standards in the field.

The concept of saturation is yet another basis on which to decide how many interviews to conduct. If possible, the audiotapes of the interviews should be listened to by the researcher on an ongoing basis. As long as new information (ideas, beliefs, experiences) is being generated from the discussion, additional interviews should be scheduled. At some point, the concepts under investigation will become saturated, and no new interviews will need to be scheduled.

Recruiting Participants

Both probability and nonprobability sampling strategies can be employed in recruitment of participants for an interview study. If the sampling frame can be identified (every member of the population can be listed), then random selection procedures can be employed to select individuals to invite to participate in an interview. This might be possible if every parent in a set of kinship foster home programs can be listed (perhaps by ID code or initials, so as to protect their confidentiality). Alternatively, the researcher can work with someone within the program(s) to provide step-by-step guidance in developing a random selection process. See chapter 5 for examples of random selection strategies. If random selection is utilized, the next step will be for the kinship foster parents to be notified that they have been selected to be invited to participate in an interview. How they are to be contacted needs to be considered. One option is for the researcher to be provided with the names and numbers of the kinship foster parents for direct contact. In light of privacy issues, this is not likely unless the researcher is on staff at the agency. The other option is for someone within the program(s) to notify the kinship foster parents about their selection and provide them with information about how to contact the researcher in the event that they want to learn more about the study. A third option is for someone within the program(s) to obtain permission from the kinship foster parents to release their contact information to the researcher.

It is important to remember that not everyone selected and invited will agree to participate and that not everyone who is scheduled to participate will actually show up for their appointment. Thus, even if the invited individuals were randomly selected from the population, the final sample might not be statistically representative if response and participation rates are low. The researcher should keep careful records of the participation rates and report this information in the final report/paper.

In the event that the sampling frame is not available (one exists but will not be provided to the researcher, or one does not exist), nonprobability sampling strategies will be employed. For interviews, this usually entails some form of a convenience sample, in which individuals volunteer to participate, usually by responding to a project announcement (such as a flyer). That is, the researcher makes known to some or all members of the population that a study is being conducted and that they are invited to contact the researcher to participate. The wider the distribution of the announcement, the higher the response rate will be. The announcement should contain the following information: (1) a brief description of the purpose of the study (e.g., to hear from kinship foster parents about their experience with the child welfare system), (2) who is being targeted for participation, (3) the sponsor of the project, (4) the type of involvement and time commitment (e.g., a two-hour individual interview), (5) whether payment will be made to participants, (6) how confidentiality will be maintained, (7) anything else pertinent (refreshments, whether child care will be available, location), and (8) what interested individuals should do (e.g., contact researcher at a specific number for more information and to schedule an appointment). A sample flyer is presented in figure 13.1.

If the identified sample is composed of clients within an agency, recruitment should be conducted according to guidelines developed with input from program staff. One approach is to ask program staff to deliver the flyer to potential participants. In this way program participants will obtain information about the project by a neutral third party (not someone invested in their participation) and they will not feel pressured or put on the spot as they might if a researcher talked to them directly about the project. Limiting the role of program staff to delivering the flyer has the added benefit of eliminating the need to train and supervise staff in what they say and how they say it, which can affect participation rates.

Figure 13.1
Recruitment flyer for interview study of kinship foster parents

WE WANT TO KNOW WHAT YOU THINK

Who: Kinship foster parents currently caring for at least one kinship
             foster child

What: Participate in an individual interview about your experiences
             with the child welfare system. This is not a test. There are no
             right or wrong answers. Your beliefs and experiences are what
             we want to understand.

Why: Help the (name) agency learn how to improve programs for
             families

When: To be arranged at your convenience

Where: On the telephone or at an agreed-upon location

Fee: Participants will receive $25.00 for participating in one two-
             hour discussion

Contact: Please call (name) at (phone number) for more information

• Everything said during the discussion will remain private and
  confidential.

Research staff then needs to follow up and contact potential participants (via telephone, in the waiting room at a drop-in center, on program location such as in a group home, etc.) and invite each person to hear more about the project. At that point, the research staff person will follow the script that was developed and approved by the agency's IRB—covering topics such as the voluntary nature of project, potential benefits and risks, limits to confidentiality, and so forth. Those who agree to participate will be scheduled for an immediate or subsequent appointment depending upon availability of space at that location for a private interview (immediate is always better because it eliminates the possibility of logistical barriers emerging later that could interfere with participation). Research staff will need to keep careful records of recruitment procedures such as whether everyone who met the criteria was invited or only as many as needed to reach the desired sample size. How many people declined and the reasons they gave for doing so need to be documented, as well as the number who agreed to participate but did not show up for the scheduled appointment. Of course, persistent follow-up and flexibility in scheduling will be important for increasing sample size and participation rates. The project manager should keep careful records of participation rates and should revise recruitment techniques if more than 15 percent decline participation. Unless a fixed sample size has been determined a priori, recruitment and administration of the interviews will occur simultaneously. When one person is conducting all of the interviews it will be possible—without transcribing the tapes—to determine when the topic has been saturated and no additional interviews are required (because that person will have first-hand knowledge of the full set of ideas being generated from the interviews). If more than one person is conducting the interviews, the primary researcher will probably need to listen to all of the tapes on an ongoing basis in order to decide when a sufficient sample has been achieved.

Design of the Interview Protocol

The interview consists primarily of the protocol, which is the script of the "conversation" between the interviewer and the participant. Bracketing the protocol are some "housekeeping" activities. There are seven basic units to the interview process: (1) welcome and orientation, (2) informed consent, (3) the opening demographic questions of the protocol, (4) the main questions of the protocol, (5) the closing question of the protocol, (6) debriefing, and (7) payment.

Welcome and Orientation

The interview should start with a standardized welcome and orientation. This should be written out word for word and read to each interviewee. A sample orientation might be:

> Thank you for agreeing to participate in this interview and thanks so much for taking the time to come out today/tonight for this interview. My name is [name] and I will be your interviewer. I want to tell you a little bit about what is going to happen. You were invited to come today/tonight because the [agency name] wants to hear from kinship foster parents on their beliefs about the advantages and disadvantages of being a kinship foster parent. I was hired by this agency to conduct interviews and to prepare a final report to them. In that report, no names will be used and there will be no way for anyone reading the report to know which partici-

pant made which comment. There will be quotes in the report, to illus-trate specific attitudes and beliefs, but, again, no names will be provided that would allow the reader to know who made what comments. The [agency name] really wants to learn about your ideas and thoughts. We urge you to be honest because that is what will be most helpful. This is not a test in any way. There are no right or wrong answers and in no way are you being judged or evaluated. We really want to learn from you about your experience. You will receive a payment of [amount] dollars at the end of the session. Refreshments are available, so please help yourself.

Informed Consent

Informed consent should be obtained after the project has been described and the ways in which confidentiality will be maintained are discussed. Once the welcoming statement has been made, the interviewer should ask if the participant has questions about the purpose of the project or about what is going to happen. After questions have been answered, the consent form should be read out loud to the interviewee and then he or she should be asked again if there are any questions. After questions have been answered, the form can be signed. See chapter 3 for a detailed discussion of the con-tent and process of obtaining informed consent.

The Opening Questions of the Protocol

The interview should begin with a set of questions about the sociodemo-graphics of the participant. This usually includes age, ethnicity, and gender. For child welfare program staff, highest educational degree, number of years working in the field of child welfare, and number of years at the cur-rent agency should also be included. For child welfare clients, number of months involved with the current program, number and age of children, ed-ucation level, and marital status should also be included. There are two rea-sons for including these items in the front of the interview. First, answers to these questions can be used in the final report/paper to describe the sample and provide the reader with information about the study participants. The second reason for placing the sociodemographic questions in the beginning of the interview is that they serve as a "warm up," in that people are gener-ally used to answering these types of questions about themselves. They are also almost always closed-ended and easy to answer.

A note about including items regarding race and ethnicity: It is advisable to use the latest census coding system, because it represents the best thinking in the field to date and produces data that can be compared with national samples. However, it is important to know the specific sample under investigation. For example, if the sample is entirely Hispanic, then it might make sense to include several possible countries of origin (e.g., Puerto Rico, Dominican Republic, etc.) as these differences are meaningful to the clients and may be relevant for the analyses. Number of children in the family is a particularly complex question that requires guidelines regarding whether the children are living in the home, under a certain age, or biological only or also foster. There is not necessarily a right or wrong way to define this, but care should be taken to ensure that everyone is working with the same definition. Income is also particularly tricky to ask about, because alimony, child support, food stamps, "off-the-books" income, and so forth need to specified as whether or not to be included.

The Main Questions of the Protocol

The protocol should be divided into major sections with headers organizing a series of related questions. In this way, the participant is not asked about disparate or unrelated topics. The headers and section breaks function as a cue to the interviewer to let the participant know that the interview will be shifting gears and moving to a new aspect of the general issue. Ideally, the questions within each section are organized in such a way that they resemble a relaxed (yet focused) conversation rather than a stilted interrogation. The protocol should have a natural and unpressured feeling to it.

The protocol should consist of questions that request specific memories ("What is one time that you were really glad that you are a kinship foster parent?" "Can you tell me about one time, if ever, when you felt particularly negative about being a kinship foster parent?") as well as opinion questions ("How do you think being a kinship foster parent is harder than being a nonkinship foster parent?").

The Closing Question of the Protocol

After the final question in the protocol has been asked and answered, the interviewer should let the participant know that the questions have come to an end. It is very important at this point to ask the interviewee whether there is anything else he or she would like to say about the topic. This can be phrased as: "Well, we've come to the end of the questions I have. I'm wondering before we wrap up the discussion if there is anything else you would like to say about this topic. Is there anything else you think I need to know in order to understand your experiences and ideas about this?"

Debriefing

When the interview is finally completed, the participant should be thanked sincerely for sharing his or her personal memories, thoughts, and feelings. Issues of confidentiality should be reiterated. If the participant is in an emotionally charged state, it is important to stay with the participant until he or she is "ok." Some small talk at the end might help the person transition from "participant self" to "outside-world self." The participant can be asked about plans for the rest of the day, plans for the upcoming weekend, and so forth. The goal is to help the person regain composure and wind down. There should be a plan in place in the event that the participant is distraught at the end of the interview. For example, a staffperson within the program or a clinical psychologist who has agreed to be on call for such an event should be notified. The informed consent form (a copy of which is given to the participant) should contain the name and phone number of someone to contact if additional debriefing is desired later in the day or week.

Payment

At this point the participant is paid the fee (if a fee is part of the project) and asked to sign a receipt for payment. Once the participant has left the room, the interviewer should briefly make notes about the session. Major issues raised should also be jotted down while they are fresh in the interviewer's mind. The tape should be labeled and the room cleaned up. Any cosponsoring agencies should be written thank-you notes.

Developing Interview Questions: Improving Quality

Ask Open-Ended Questions

Questions should be phrased in such a way as to elicit complex responses that provide rich and textured answers. The possible options for answering should be unlimited, and possible response options should not be offered or suggested to the participants. For example, in a study about kinship care, the question "do you think it is harder being a kinship foster parent because agency staff assume that there is something wrong with you because your own relative had a child removed from his or her care or do you think it is harder being in kinship foster care because there is resentment from your family that you are working 'with the system' that took a child away from someone in the family?" suggests that there are only two answers and that they are mutually exclusive. A better choice of wording would be to ask, "in what ways, if at all, do you think that social workers treat kinship foster parents differently than nonkinship foster parents?" or "how has the rest of your family responded to your working with the child welfare system to care for your kinship foster child?" Questions that elicit one-word responses or factual answers are not the type of questions likely to produce the kind of rich responses being sought.

Avoid Asking "Why"

The word "why" is ambiguous at best and can be interpreted by each participant somewhat differently, depending upon his or her theory and understanding of motivation. Rather than asking "why is the child in foster care?" it might be better to ask, "what led to the child being placed in foster care?"

Ask Questions That Elicit Story Telling

One type of question asks interviewees to give an example or "tell a story" about a particular experience they have had. In telling the story, participants might recall additional aspects of their thoughts and feelings. The examples are also very useful in writing up the final report/paper.

Avoid Making Assumptions

Questions should be asked in such a way to suggest no assumptions on the part of the interviewer. Asking "what are some of the ways you benefit from this program?" assumes that there have in fact been benefits. It would be better to ask, "how, if at all, have you benefited from being in this program?"

Avoid Technical Terms, Jargon, and Questions That Assume Prior Knowledge

Avoid using terms that will not be understood by the interviewees. It is not likely that someone will admit to not knowing what something means. For example, in interviews with kinship foster parents, it would not make sense to ask parents to discuss concurrent planning, to comment on the commissioners' new realignment plan, to talk about COA regulations, or anything else that assumes prior knowledge.

Developing Interview Questions: Steps in the Process

Begin by making a list of the general issues about the topic. For the chapter scenario, issues might be: (1) the kinship foster parent's relationship with the parent of the child, (2) the process of becoming a kinship foster parent, (3) the kinship foster parent's experience with the agency, and (4) the kinship foster parent's current relationship with the parent of the child.

From this list of issues, a pool of questions can be developed for each section. The questions should be logically related and flow naturally. Several different options for writing each question should be explored in order to identify any hidden assumptions, biases, or lack of clarity in the questions.

The list of potential questions should be revised and refined over a period of several weeks in order to allow the researcher (and others on the team) to reflect on the questions and consider their usefulness for the project.

The draft final set of questions should be submitted to experts in research and experts in the subject matter for their feedback. The questions should be revised and refined accordingly.

Piloting the Interview Protocol

Piloting the interview protocol is vital to the success of any interview project, because it is the only way to determine whether questions—designed to produce one type of response—will result in unproductive and/or unhelpful (i.e., off-topic) responses. Carlson and McCaslin (2003) suggest that the piloting phase should serve as a formal "meta-inquiry" in order to assess, modify, enhance, and focus the formal interview. As Cresswell (1998, 335) points out: "If the questions one asks are not crucial, then differences in responses are not crucial either." The quality of the questions is integral to the success of an in-depth interview study. Piloting also provides the researcher with an opportunity to practice asking the questions, so that when the study begins in earnest there is a comfort level with the text in the context of likely responses. Practicing the interview with individuals not from the sample of interest (such as one's own friends and family) will provide the interviewer with the experience of saying the questions but not with the experience of contending with the material produced as a result of having lived the experience in question. Thus, the only way to truly "get a feel" for the types of information likely to be produced is to pilot the interview protocol with individuals from the population. In doing so, informed consent will have to be obtained as with the sample proper and program staff will have to be informed and engaged in planning how to do this.

If piloting the interview results in significant changes in the phrasing or ordering of the questions, the revised version will need to be piloted as well. Piloting should continue until it ceases to result in significant changes in the protocol. At the end of each piloting session, the participant should be asked to critique both the content and process of the interview session. In this context, the participant is the "expert" and the interviewer is the novice. The participant should be queried as to whether questions need to be added or eliminated and whether certain questions were redundant, awkwardly phrased, ambiguous, or confusing. The participant should be invited to share opinions about how to improve both the process and content of the interview. Revisions based on piloting will also be necessary if the content produced was deficient or problematic. That is, even if the participant found no fault with the pilot protocol, revisions will be required if the material produced was not sufficiently rich or germane to the study's research questions. Thus, piloting and revising the interview protocol represents an iterative process that results in a final version ready for implementation.

Techniques of the Interviewer

Relationship to Participant

When conducting the interview, the researcher should present an "interviewer self," a persona that is empathic and connected to the humanity of the participant while still demonstrating and respecting clearly defined boundaries. The interviewer must be warm and humane, otherwise, the experience could be detrimental to the participant, yet the interviewer should recognize and respect that the interview is not a therapeutic encounter. Thus, at no time should the interviewer advise, challenge, or help the participant make connections or gain insight. Having some stock phrases in mind such as "thank you for telling me about that" or "oh, I see how that was for you" will be helpful for satisfying the desire to give something of oneself to the participant without actually introducing any content into the interview that could influence the participant's responses to the subsequent set of questions. The interviewer also must recognize that the session is not a discussion between friends or colleagues (in which personal information is shared mutually). Thus, the interviewer should rarely, if ever, share personal information in the context of the interview. Understanding how interviews resemble therapy sessions and informal discussions among friends without actually being either of these two types of interpersonal communications will allow the interviewer to set appropriate boundaries. Conducting the pilot interviews should help the interviewer develop the necessary skills for navigating this terrain, as will practicing the protocol with friends and colleagues (who can role-play situations likely to activate the interviewer's desire or inclination to function like a friend or therapist).

Managing the Flow of the Questions

The interview begins with the background questions and moves sequentially through the interview items (with probes and elaborating questions asked as necessary to fully capture the person's experience of the issue). Shifting from section to section can be accomplished with transition phrases to let the participant know that the topic is changing. Phrases such as "now we are going to shift gears and talk about . . ." and "now we are going to move on to section C, 'Becoming a Parent'" will help orient the participant. Prior to ending one section and beginning the next the interviewer should ask for as much clarification as necessary to "get the story." Probes such as "can you say more about that?" and "what else can you tell me about . . ." are good for digging deeper in the same topic without conveying to the participant that the first answer was unsatisfactory. Asking for specific memories or stories is also a helpful strategy for getting more substance, such as "tell me one time when that was particularly true" or "when was the first time you had that experience/thought" to probe further. It might also be helpful to repeat back to the participant some of the things he or she said as a way to probe for more, such as: "you have already mentioned several ways that you feel that your caseworker treats you differently because you are related to the parent of the child, some of which are positive, such as providing you with emotional support to deal with your own sadness and guilt over the current state of your own child's difficulties, and some of which are negative, such as pressuring you to adopt the child. I am wondering if there are other ways that you feel your role as a kinship foster parent is different because you are related to the child's parent?" This is where taking notes during the interview can be helpful, as they can be referred to later in the discussion and used as the basis of such probes.

Note-Taking

Whether the interview is conducted in person or on the telephone, the interviewer should have a paper copy of the interview protocol on hand to use as a script throughout the discussion. This form can provide space for the responses to the background questions to be written down (eliminating the need to transcribe this portion of the tape and, thus, facilitating data entry). Having the paper on hand also provides the interviewer with a reason to alternate looking at the participant and taking notes on the paper so that the eye contact does not become too intense for the participant. Since the entire conversation is audiotaped, the notes taken during the interview serve as a useful reminder of important information during the interview itself and not as the ultimate record of the interview. On-the-spot word-for-word dictation of the entire discussion is not necessary and would be a distraction for both the interviewer and the participant.

Interview Logistics

These logistics pertain to face-to-face interviews and not to those conducted over the telephone. For phone interviews, the primary logistical issues involve ensuring that the device used to audiotape the conversation is in good working order and that background noise is reduced as much as possible. In addition, deactivating call waiting might be helpful, so that the conversation is not interrupted by incoming calls. A final consideration is in regard to sharing telephone numbers. When scheduling the appointment, the interviewer should offer to place the call in order to assume the costs. However, some participants might not want to share their telephone number with the interviewer. In that case, the interviewer should be willing and able to give a phone number to the participant. Below are a series of logistical considerations for conducting face-to-face interviews.

Location

The space in which the interview takes place is very important. It needs to be a private quiet room large enough for two people to be seated comfortably. The location should be accessible to the participant and in a neutral area. It should be easy to reach, safe and well lit, but not too different from what the typical participant is used to. For example, if the participants will be kinship foster parents living in low-income neighborhoods, it would not be appropriate to hold the interviews in a luxury building in a neighborhood vastly more upscale than theirs. Ideally, the location will not belong to an organization that has some authority over the participants (e.g., if the topic is school involvement, the interviews should not be held in the school; if the topic is client involvement in an agency, the interview should not be held in a building associated with/owned by the agency). If people with disabilities are expected to participate, the location should be handicapped accessible. The chairs in the room should be reasonably comfortable and a small table for the refreshments and audiotaping equipment will be helpful.

Refreshments

Refreshments should be served and easily accessible to the participant. Ideally they will be located within arm's reach, so that the participant does not have to get up in the middle of the interview to get something to drink or snack on. The refreshments should be items that the participant is likely to enjoy (e.g., not vegetable crudités for an interview with teens). The items should not be too noisy (e.g., individually wrapped cookies or crackers), as the sound can be amplified on the audiotape and very distracting for the person listening to or transcribing the tape. Interviews should not be scheduled at regular meal times (12–2 pm or 6–8 pm), as the participant might be hungry and may resent not being fed more than a snack.

Child Care

If parents with limited incomes are the primary targeted participants, babysitting should be offered by professional babysitters in a clean, safe environment. It is important that the sponsoring agency and the owner of the building be aware of this, as there may be liability issues.

Before and After the Session

The interviewer should arrive early, make sure the space is available and clean, set up and test the audio equipment (extra batteries, tapes, and extension cords are a must), and set up the refreshments.

When the session is over, the interviewer will need to spend some time cleaning up the space, putting away the refreshments, and making sure that the tapes and paperwork are in order (e.g., that everything is clearly labeled).

Transcribing the Tapes and Analyzing the Data

Each audiotape should be transcribed verbatim (word for word). This can best be accomplished with a transcription machine in which the tape speed is controlled by a foot pedal. This allows for the continuous typing of the audio material, as the foot controls when to stop and start the tape, allowing the hands to remain on the keyboard. Transcription can be quite time consuming. A good rule of thumb is about ten hours per hour of audiotape, although this varies depending upon how quickly the participant spoke, the quality of the tape and the transcribing machine, and the speed of the typist. The final transcript should clearly demark the interviewer from the participant. One convention for doing so is presented below:

I. What was it like when you first started to think . . .
P. Well, it was really hard because . . .

It is possible to hire someone else to transcribe the tapes, but it is advisable that the researcher personally assumes this task, as it is an effective mechanism for getting to really "hear" what was said during the interview. This process of hearing the interview, typing in the words, and seeing the words on the screen can deepen the eventual analysis. The typed transcript should be double spaced and printed on single-sided pages. Each interview will result in about twenty-five to fifty pages of text, depending upon the length of the interview and how quickly the person spoke.

There are two main approaches to analyzing in-depth interview transcripts. The first is to briefly summarize each person's "story" and then devote the majority of the results section to identifying major cross-cutting themes. Each theme should be written about extensively, including what the majority of the participants had to say about the theme and what countervailing opinions were held. Examples and quotes representing all aspects of each theme should be presented such that the reader can really "hear" what the participants had to say. The discussion section should then place these themes in the context of the theory presented in the introduction section of the paper/report. This approach works well with a relatively small sample because it is possible to present each person's story.

Another technique is a systematic content analysis based on a grounded theory approach (Berg 1998; Straus 1987). Here, the researcher reads and rereads the text of the transcripts and "discovers" or labels variables (called categories, concepts, and properties). The ability to perceive variables is termed "theoretical sensitivity" and is affected by a number of factors, including the researcher's reading of the literature and use of techniques designed to enhance sensitivity. Practically speaking, one way to conduct such an analysis is to read each transcript and demark each unique unit of thought. A unit could be a phrase, a sentence, a paragraph, or even longer. Each unit is then literally cut off the page and taped onto an index card. This results in hundreds, if not thousands, of index cards. These cards are then read through and sorted into piles that represent some commonality. The results section then presents each pile of cards as a theme. One technique that should be considered when writing up the results of qualitative analyses is to give each participant a pseudonym. That way, rather than repeatedly using phrases such as "as one participant commented," it can be written, "Nancy commented that. . . ." Assigning pseudonyms allows the reader to track participant's comments throughout the report and allows them to feel closer to the people speaking. A table or appendix can list each participant by name along with some basic demographic information such as age, gender, and so forth. In this way the reader can refer to this table and learn something about each speaker as his or her quotes are interspersed throughout the presentation of findings.

An additional analytic strategy is to transform the qualitative text into quantitative data. This can be accomplished through the counting of the number of participants who mentioned a certain issue or experience, although this is only valid if the protocol consistently asked everyone or no one about this topic. If everyone was asked about a topic, the results can report, for example, "of the sample of fifty participants, all of whom were asked whether they still felt anger toward their children, 25 percent said that they did." On the other hand, if the protocol did not explicitly ask about anger, it can be written, "of the fifty participants interviewed, fully 25 percent spontaneously offered that they still felt anger toward their children."

However, if some of the participants were asked while others were not, it is not valid to count the number who reported that issue.

Another way to quantify the information is to count the number of different responses offered to a question. For example, if the question was "what are all the ways in which you feel that being a kinship foster parent has affected your relationship with your family?" and follow-up questions were asked to ensure that the participant offered all the ways he or she could think of them, then a variable can be created that counts the number of ways each person thought of. A frequency table can be created listing each way mentioned by at least one participant and the total number of participants who mentioned each way. Again, this technique is only valid if each participant was asked to list all of the ways and probed with "what other ways?" to make sure that they provided all of the ways they could think of. Also it is only valid to do this if specific ways are not offered to participants to probe their memory, for example, by asking, "what about this way or that way?" The key for quantifying qualitative data is consistency in how the questions were asked.

Regardless of which data presentation approaches are used, the researcher has the opportunity to step away from the text in the discussion section by noting contradictions within or among the participants as well as highlighting issues that are noticeably absent from the discussion. Reasons why this might be the case need to be mentioned, including flaws in the interview protocol. Linking the findings to the theory presented in the introduction section can serve as a useful guide for organizing the discussion section.

Conclusion

In-depth interviewing is a data collection method for studying the personal accounts and constructed meaning of events and experiences of individuals. Considerable skill is required to develop the interview protocol, conduct the interviews, and analyze the data. Because of this, the novice researcher may have difficulty conducting a rigorous interview study, but, when done well, the findings can be insightful and useful for understanding the experiences of the individuals and for improving policies, programs, and practice.

PART 4

Data Analysis and Writing Up and Sharing Research Results

[14]

Data Analysis Techniques

In this chapter, the following topics will be discussed, following the introduction of the chapter scenario and the brief literature review:

- Effect Size
- Data reduction techniques
- Univariate analyses
- Bivariate analyses
- Multivariate analyses

CHAPTER SCENARIO

An agency operates a respite program for children in foster boarding homes whose foster parents need a break from caring for their foster child. After the program has been in operation for several years, the agency hires a researcher to prepare some statistical data regarding utilization of the program. An entry cohort sample of all youth is identified, consisting of youth admitted to the agency's foster care program in the first three years after the respite program was created, and five research questions are developed: (1) What proportion of the popula-

(continued)

tion of foster care youth utilized the respite program? (2) How long was the average length of stay in the respite program? (3) What proportion of youth returned to their original foster home after the respite stay? (4) What child and family characteristics were associated with length of stay in the program? And (5) what child and family characteristics were associated with whether youth returned to their original foster home after the stay in the respite program?

BRIEF LITERATURE REVIEW: RESPITE FOR FOSTER PARENTS

Foster families are expected to care for one or more children who have experienced abuse, neglect, abandonment, and drug or alcohol exposure. They also care for children who have developmental and physical disabilities, who are medically fragile, and/or who have AIDS or are HIV positive. Many children in foster care demonstrate a significant amount of emotional disturbance as a result of the abuse or neglect that led to placement and from the trauma of removal from the home. Children in foster care have been found to exhibit symptoms associated with post–traumatic stress disorder as well as a wide range of other emotional and behavioral problems (Clausen, Landsverk, Ganger, Chadwick, and Litrownik 1998; Perry, Pollard, Blakley, and Vigilante 1995).

As Barney, Levin, and Smith (1994) have noted, despite the severity of these problems, foster parents are expected to provide care for their foster children without relief from the daily caregiving routine. However, like all parents, foster parents sometimes need a break from their caretaking obligations. They may need to refuel emotionally or physically or they may need to attend to other obligations apart from their foster children (their own medical appointments or family matters). The foster care system does not permit foster parents to leave their children in the care of adults who have not been officially approved (and sometimes licensed and trained) by the foster care agency. The sanctioned care of foster children by adults who are not the foster parents is known as respite care.

Due to a combination of governmental regulations as well as a lack of state and agency resources, many foster parents lack access to re-

(continued)

spite care. Thus, taking time out from the tremendous demands of foster parenting can often be difficult to arrange. The lack of respite care may make it difficult for states, counties, and private agencies to recruit and retain foster families at a time when they are in high demand. That is, the concern about lack of respite care may function as a deterrent for some prospective foster parents. Conversely, access to respite care may serve to address concerns prospective foster parents have about agreeing to take on such an obviously challenging job. Another likely advantage of respite services is prevention of placement disruption, as prior research has established that the extent of child behavioral problems reported by foster parents was associated with eventual placement disruption (Chamberlain, Price, Reid, Landsverk, Fisher, and Stoolmiller 2006). To the extent that respite care can help families manage the stress of foster parenting behaviorally challenging children, it may aid in enhanced foster home stability.

Based on the clear consensus that respite care is useful for foster parents, many governmental as well as private child welfare agencies have established formal or informal respite programs for foster and adoptive parents. The ARCH National Respite Network and Resource Center estimates that as many as twenty thousand respite programs are serving approximately one million families in the United States. Still, not all families who could benefit from respite care receive it. Many agencies have no respite services at all, or none that serve a family's particular category of need. For example, families seeking respite care for a child with mental health needs will not be able to avail themselves of respite services and its benefits if the only respite homes available are licensed to care for children with physical disabilities (Green 2002).

The empirical literature on the effects of respite care has so far focused on its benefit for families with special needs children. For example, Cowen and Reed (2002) studied parenting stress in families before and after utilization of respite and found statistically significant improvement. They concluded that foster parents with challenging children should be monitored for burnout and provided with respite as needed. Based on the quality of this intervention evaluation, respite care was deemed to be a "supported and probably efficacious treatment" by Craven and Lee (2006) in their meta-analysis of effective interventions for children in foster care.

Overview

Data analysis is the process by which the researcher uses the data collected in a study in order to answer the research questions. First, data need to be tracked, cleaned, and entered. Data reduction techniques are often explored in order to determine whether the existing set of variables can be combined in ways that are theoretically and empirically sound. Univariate analyses are conducted next in order to present frequency distributions of the variables and answer some questions about the sample and about frequency of events. Bivariate analyses are conducted to assess the relationship among two variables, and multivariate analyses are conducted to assess associations between three or more variables simultaneously. For each statistical test, certain assumptions about the size of the sample and the distribution of the variables must be met. When they are not, the variables can be transformed or nonparametric analyses can be conducted as an alternative. All statistics associated with bivariate and multivariate analyses can be converted to an effect size in order to determine the strength of the association in addition to its statistical significance.

Throughout this chapter, the assumptions underlying statistical tests necessary for making inferences are presented. When these assumptions are met, parametric analyses can be conducted, and the appropriate tests are described. In addition, the nonparametric equivalents of these tests are presented, in the event that the underlying assumptions are not met. What is presented below is a basic primer on statistical testing. It is recommended that the novice researcher seek consultation with a professional statistician in addition to reviewing this chapter. It is also recommended that basic statistical textbooks be available for reference while conducting statistical analyses of research findings, such as Lindeman, Merenda, and Gold (1980) for parametric statistics and Siegel and Castellan (1988) for nonparametric analyses.

Effect Size

As noted in chapter 5, an effect size determines the strength of a statistically significant association. Calculating effect sizes is particularly important for large-scale studies in which many statistical tests will reach the significance level (the larger the sample, the more likely it is that statistical tests will obtain significance). Thus, the reader of a research article or report will want to know the size of the effect in order to gauge the importance of the findings. Formulas are presented throughout this chapter for converting the results of statistical tests into a standard unit, effect size, also called d. In social science research, the convention is that a d of .20 is considered small, .50 is considered moderate, and .80 is considered large (Cohen 1969).

Data Tracking, Cleaning, and Entry

Prior to analysis, all raw data need to be transferred from paper into an electronic format, either a relational database such as Access or a spreadsheet such as Excel and then into SPSS (or another statistical package), or directly into SPSS (or another statistical package). If data are collected on an ongoing basis (as opposed to all data being collected at once from an agency's database), data should be tracked as it is collected in order to ensure that every case in the sample has data for each measure at each data collection point. Every piece of data should be examined carefully shortly after it has been collected to ensure that the measures are being filled out completely and accurately. Any errors in the administration of measures can be addressed on an ongoing basis through continued training of the data collectors. This is true for qualitative data (transcripts of interviews and focus groups and data collected from case studies) as well as quantitative data (responses to surveys and other structured measures).

Depending upon how many variables are collected on each case, the data may be entered into one or more data files. If more than one data file is used, it is vital that a single ID variable be created and used consistently across all the measures. That is, ID 10031 should be used for the same person or case throughout all the measures and files of a study, so that this number can be used to link multiple files across the same study. Typically, in a data file each case represents a row of data, with the variables in the columns. Decisions about missing data and "not applicable" data should be made prior to data entry. One approach is to use the same values for missing data for all variables, often 999 (except for variables in which 999 might be a valid response) for missing data and 777 for "not applicable."

Some data is relatively straightforward to enter into the computer, while some measures require the creation of a code book that allows the data entry person to see how the paper data should be represented in the electronic data file. For example, with the variable age, there are several possibilities, including age in months, age in years with a certain number of decimal places, or entering the actual birth date and letting the computer calculate age. With a large and complicated data set it is often also necessary to have a process of "cleaning" the data, in which the electronic file is printed out and compared, data point by data point, to the actual raw paper data. This is usually a two-person job, in which one person reads what the data should be (from the original raw paper data) and the second person follows along on the data sheet to ensure that this is what was entered into the computer. Mistakes should be noted on the printout and corrected in the data file at a later point.

Prior to running any analyses, frequency distributions should be conducted on all variables in order to identify "out of range" cases. That is, if age is a variable in the data file that can only range from 5 to 18 (as that is the age of the individuals in a particular study), and the frequency distribution reveals that a case is listed as 75 for the variable age, it indicates a data entry or data collection error. The ID number associated with the case with age=75 should be identified in order to access the raw (paper) data in which age was reported for that case. If 75 is listed on the raw data, then the error is a data collection error; if 15 is listed (or any other number between 5 and 18), then the mistake is a data entry mistake and can be corrected immediately. Data collection mistakes are harder to rectify, as there needs to be a mechanism for determining what the correct information should have been (returning to the subject, asking the person who completed the form what they remember the age to have been, or some other mechanism). Only after the data has been tracked, entered, and cleaned should analysis begin.

Data Reduction Techniques

In some studies, after data on several related variables have been collected, a question arises as to whether the number of variables can be reduced in order to have a more manageable set of variables with which to work. There are several ways of doing this.

Theory-Driven Data Reduction

Some variables can be combined based on theory. This is allowable when the purpose is to count how many events or experiences each individual in the sample has had. In such situations there is no expectation or statistical requirement that the items being combined are intercorrelated. For example, in a study predicting behavioral problems in residential treatment based on characteristics of children at admission to the placement, it might be of interest to create a variable that counts the number of different types of maltreatment (e.g., physical abuse, sexual abuse, emotional abuse, neglect) a child experienced. The score would range from 0 (child experienced none of the four types of maltreatment) to 4 (child experienced all four types of maltreatment). The creation of this summary score is defensible on theoretical grounds and no additional steps are necessary prior to creating and using it.

Another theory-driven data reduction approach is to create a summary score of risk or protective factors. For example, in a study of reunification from foster care in which prior theory has determined that age at first placement, gender, and reason for referral are all risk factors for a child not being reunified, it would be meaningful to count the number of these risk factors each child had at admission to the placement. Theory would be used to determine which value is considered the risk. For example, prior research might have shown that males (as opposed to females), children ten years of age and older at first placement (as opposed to children under ten years of age at first placement), and children placed due to abuse or neglect (as opposed to a person in need of supervision—PINS petition or through the juvenile courts) are all less likely to be reunified. A new variable could be created that represented the sum total of the three risk factors each youth had. PINS/JD females under ten years of age at first placement would receive a score of 0, while abused/neglected males ten years of age or older at first placement would receive a score of 3. Scores of 1 would be reserved for youth who had any one risk factor (e.g., males who were under ten years of age at first placement and were referred due to PINS/JD, or abused/neglected females under ten years of age, or females over ten years of age referred due to PINS/JD), and a score of 2 would be reserved for youth with two but not three of the risk factors (e.g., males under ten years of age at first placement referred due to abuse/neglect). What is important to remember here is that the value is not being added up across items but across the presence/absence of the identified risk. That is, if age is entered as a two-digit number reflecting the child's age in years, the variable would be recoded as (1=ten years of age or older at placement, 0=under 10 years of age at first placement), and it is determined based on theory which values are considered risks and which are not.

Missing Data

In such theory-driven summary scores, missing data can be problematic. If a case is missing data on one or more of the variables, then the case cannot have a summary score. For example, a child missing data on physical abuse cannot be included in the summary score of number of types of maltreatment experienced, because the denominator for this case is different than for the cases with data on all four variables. A general rule of thumb is to only include variables in the creation of summary scores if no more than 10 percent of the data is missing and it can be determined that the missing data is random as opposed to systematic. Random missing data means that there is no specific cause of the missing data that can be attributable to the sample. Systematic missing data occurs when a subset of the sample with a shared characteristic are all missing data. In order to explore this, cases with and without missing data can be statistically compared on other background and demographic variables in the data set to determine the comparability of samples with and without the variable in question. If certain cases are more likely to have missing data on one or more of these variables, then the sample with a summary score would be different than the sample without the summary score. This would be a problem, because all analyses in which the summary score was included would be on a sample different than the original study sample. In such cases, the summary score should probably not be used in order to allow analyses to proceed on the full study sample. For more about missing data, see McKnight, McKnight, Sidani, and Figueredo (2007).

Reliability Analysis

A second form of data reduction occurs when several items are predetermined to measure the same construct and the intention is to only use the summary score. For example, an IQ test contains a hundred items that are combined to create a single IQ score, and the Center for Epidemiological Studies-Depression inventory contains twenty items that are combined to create a single index of depression. Because these are existing measures that have demonstrated reliability, it is not necessary for each researcher using these measures to establish that reliability exists prior to calculating the summary score. However, if the goal is to combine several items from a "homegrown" measure, it will be necessary to conduct a reliability analysis to establish that the items are sufficiently interrelated to allow for the creation of a summary score. The result of such a reliability analysis is a Cronbach's alpha score. Alphas range from 0 to 1.00, with scores above .70 considered indicative of an adequate scale. An additional piece of information provided by statistical output from a reliability analysis is what the Cronbach's alpha would be if any one item were removed from the analysis. If the alpha improves with the removal of an item, then that item should probably not be included in the creation of the summary score.

In cases where the alpha is high enough to warrant adding scores across items, it is possible to deal with missing data in a way different from adding items across a theory-driven scale. If the reliability analysis demonstrates sufficient internal consistency among the items on the scale (that is, the Cronbach's alpha is above .70), then a process called mean imputation can be used to handle missing data. If missing data were not dealt with, every case with at least one item missing would lack a summary score. However, with mean imputation a case with a missing value on an item is given an imputed value for the missing item, allowing the case to have a summary score. Table 14.1 provides an example.

In table 14.1, case 5 is missing a score on the sixth variable. Without mean imputation, that case would be missing a summary score. However, imputing the mean of the previous five variables (mean=2.8) allows that case to be included in the analyses using the summary score. The general rule of thumb is that a case with no more than 10 percent of the items missing can be included with mean imputed values for the missing data. Thus, with a summary score composed of six variables, only one variable per case can be mean imputed. If case 5 had missing values on two of the variables, that case would not have a summary score. The reason for this is that a mean based on only four values in a six-item scale is not considered sufficiently reliable.

Table 14.1
Sample of mean imputation

Case	Item						Summary score
	1	2	3	4	5	6	
1	3	2	3	3	3	3	17
2	1	2	1	1	2	1	08
3	2	2	2	2	2	2	12
4	1	1	1	1	2	1	8
5 original	2	3	3	3	3	missing	missing
5 new	2	3	3	3	3	2.8	16.8

Factor Analysis

The third form of data reduction, factor analysis, is empirically driven. A factor analysis is conducted when there are many items that may or may not be combined into one or more scales. Unlike a reliability analysis, in which it is known in advance that all the items should be combined into a single scale, a factor analysis assumes that there might be more than one scale or that none of the items can be combined to create a scale. For this reason, a factor analysis tends to be exploratory rather than confirmatory. If it were known in advance which items to combine into scales, a reliability analysis could be conducted to determine the consistency of the scale, and a factor analysis would not be necessary. Because of the exploratory nature of factor analyses and the complexity of the math underlying the procedure, a large sample is required, typically twenty cases per variable. Thus, if ten variables are entered into the factor analysis, the sample should have at least two hundred cases.

As with other statistical tests, there are requirements regarding the distribution of the variables. Continuous variables should be normally distributed (see below). In order to determine whether the continuous variable is normally distributed, it is necessary to calculate the frequency distribution of this variable and request skewness and kurtosis. If each is less than 1.0, the distribution can be said to not depart from normalcy; that is, it is considered normally distributed. Dichotomous and categorical variables entered into a factor analysis must contain sufficient distribution across the values of the variable. For example, if gender is a dichotomous variable being considered for a factor analysis with two values (0=female, 1=male), it would be necessary for at least 20 percent of the sample to be in each category. If the distribution of the variable is less than 20 percent (i.e., 10 percent male and 90 percent female), there is insufficient variation in the variable for inclusion in the factor analysis.

Some advanced statistical knowledge is necessary for conducting a factor analysis, because there are several critical decisions that need to be made, including which form of extraction to use and which form of rotation to use. Advice from a statistical consultant is often advisable.

A factor analysis also requires significant finesse in the interpretation of the output. The first portion of the output to consider is how many factors the variables should be combined into. This is usually determined by the number of eigenvalues over 1.0 produced in the analysis (Kaiser 1960). An eigenvalue of 1 indicates that the factor accounts for as much variance as at least one variable in the original equation. If the output indicates that

Figure 14.1
Sample output from factor analysis regarding eigenvalues

Total Variance Explained

Component	Initial eigenvalues		
	Total	% of variance	Cumulative %
1	1.476	29.527	29.527
2	1.281	25.617	55.144
3	1.131	22.624	77.768
4	.688	13.764	91.532
5	.423	8.468	100.000

Extraction method: principal component analysis.

there are three eigenvalues over 1.0, then the variables can be combined into three factors. The scree plot of eigenvalues can also be examined in order to determine the number of factors. An "elbow" is looked for, indicating a visually recognizable drop-off point in the eigenvalues. This method has been attributed to Cattell (as cited in Lindeman, Merenda, and Gold 1980) and usually coincides with the number of eigenvalues above 1.0. Figure 14.1 provides an example of the eigenvalues. For these data, there are three eigenvalues above 1.0, and the plot indicates that there is a dramatic drop between the third and fourth eigenvalue. Taken together, it can be concluded that there are three factors evident in this data set.

Once the number of factors has been determined, the next step is to identify which variables "load" onto which factors. Coefficients above .30 are considered to load on the factor. The items that load on the same factor can be combined into a scale, which is then given a name that indicates the commonality among the items. Table 14.2 provides sample output of loadings from a fourteen-item factor analysis. Six factors were produced from the fourteen items. The first factor consists of three variables: the child's race, age, and gender. This factor could be called "child demographics." The second factor consists of the child's history of sexual abuse and neglect and could be called "maltreatment history." The variables "depression" and "anxiety" load on the third factor, called "internalizing." "Oppositional behaviors" and "anger" load on the fourth factor, called "externalizing." The fifth

Table 14.2
Sample coefficient matrix for factor analysis

	Component					
	1	2	3	4	5	6
Race	.911					
Gender	.797					
Age	.752					
Sex abuse		.984				
Neglect		.981				
Depression			−.882			
Anxiety			.882			
Opposition				−.740		
Anger				.630		
Psych hosp.						−.408
# homes					.778	
Age at first placement					.687	
On meds.						.872

factor, "child welfare history," has two variables: age at first placement and number of prior child welfare placements. The final factor, "psychiatric history," consists of prior psychiatric hospitalizations and whether or not the child was on psychotropic medication at time of admission. As can be seen, the names of the factors are based on the content of the items that load on them. There is no right or wrong name for a factor; the names are assigned by the researcher in order to provide a general indicator of what the items have in common.

Creating factor scores from the items can be accomplished in two ways. The most common method is unit weighting, in which each case's scores on each item in the factor is summed. For example, if factor 1 was created with unit weighting and case 1 had a score of 0 on race (was Caucasian), a score of 1 on gender (was male), and a score of 1 on age (was over 10 at placement), the factor score would be 3. The second way to create summary scores from a factor analysis is to multiply the score on each variable with its coefficient. A score for factor 1 would be created by multiplying .911 (score on race) + .797 (score on gender) + .752 (score on age). Using this method, the case's summary score would be .911(0) + .797(1) + .752(1) = 1.55. Both methods (unit weighting and using coefficients) are only appropriate when the individual items in the factor have the same scale (for example, all items are coded as either o or 1, all items are coded as o to 4, etc.). If the items within the same factor have different scales (e.g., one item is coded o or 1, a second item ranges from 1 to 18, and the third item is scaled from 1 to 4), it would not be appropriate to add scores across these items. In such situations, item scores should be converted to z-scores first and then summed. Regardless of the method used, once created, summary scores can be used in univariate, bivariate, and multivariate analyses in order to answer the questions that formed the basis of the study.

Univariate Analyses

In univariate analyses, information about a single variable is presented. These analyses are usually descriptive (as opposed to inferential), in that the primary purpose is to summarize the data and describe the sample. Typical descriptive statistics for continuous variables include measures of central tendency and measures of dispersion.

The purpose of a measure of central tendency is to provide the reader with information about the average member of the sample. The mean is the statistical average and is calculated as the total of all the scores divided by the total number of scores. The median represents the score in the fiftieth percentile of the distribution. The mode is the most frequent score. Measures of dispersion provide information about how much variation there is in the scores, usually known as the standard deviation. The formula for calculating the standard deviation is presented in figure 14.2.

If a variable is categorical rather than continuous, descriptive information entails the number and proportion of cases with each value. Several univariate analyses can be presented in a single table, as is often the case in the first table of a final report or paper in which background information about the sample is provided. See table 14.3 for an example. This table presents information on four variables: age, ethnicity, spell, and reason for referral. (If this table were part of a final paper or report, the reader would know by this point what these variable names refer to and how the data were col-

Figure 14.2
Formula for calculating standard deviation

$$Sd = \sqrt{1/(n-1) \sum (x - mean)^2}$$

Table 14.3

Sample table regarding background characteristics

Background characteristics of youth (n=200)

	Mean	Standard deviation
Age	07.04	04.06
	N	%
Ethnicity		
African American	78	39.0%
Hispanic	74	37.0%
White	30	15.0%
Other	18	09.0%
Spell		
First	141	71.0%
Subsequent	58	29.0%
Reason for referral		
Abuse/neglect	94	47.0%
Voluntary	66	33.0%
PINS/JD	40	20.0%

lected.) As can be seen in the table, age is a continuous variable. Thus, the information included in the table is its mean and standard deviation. The other three variables are categorical. For each of these variables, every possible category is listed in the table, along with the number and percentage of subjects in the sample with that value. It is important to note in the table whether some cases have missing data, and it is vital to calculate the proportion based on the actual denominator and not the sample size. For example, if 50 cases were missing data on spell, and 141 were first spell and 9 were subsequent spell, then the proportion would be 94% first spell (141 of 150, not 141 of 200) and 6% subsequent spell (9 of 150, not 9 of 200).

Sometimes the primary research question of a study can be answered with a univariate analysis. The first research question for the chapter scenario is such a situation: "What proportion of the population of foster youth utilized the respite program?" Table 14.4 presents a sample presentation of such data when the dependent variable is dichotomous. These data might also be presented categorically as the number of times each youth used the respite, as demonstrated in table 14.5. Exactly what data are presented in a frequency table depends upon the research question.

Table 14.4
Sample table of dichotomous frequency distribution

Proportion of foster care youth that utilized respite
during stay (n=200)

	N	%
Used respite	94	47.0
Did not use respite*	106	53.0

*Of the 106 who did not use the respite program, 100
have been discharged and 6 are still in care and might
use the program in the future.

The question regarding length of stay in the respite program can also be
answered with univariate analyses. A frequency distribution of the number
of days could be presented, along with the mean and standard deviation.
The frequency distribution would most likely entail the creation of categories to present the data. For example, if some youth stayed one day while
others had stays up to thirty days, the frequency table would be cumbersome if each value from one to thirty were represented in the column on the
left side of the page. It would be more useful to create meaningful categories
such as "1 day," "between 2 days and 1 week," "between 1 and 2 weeks," "between

Table 14.5
Sample table of categorical frequency distribution

Frequency of times foster care youth utilized respite during stay (n=94)

	N	%
0	106*	53.0
1	40	20.0
2	14	07.0
3	19	09.5
4	10	05.0
5	11	05.5

*Of the 106 who did not use the respite program, 100 have been discharged and
6 are still in care and might use the program in the future.

Table 14.6

Sample table of categorical frequency distribution

Length of stay in the respite (n=94)

	N	%
1 day	08	08.5
2 to 7 days	38	40.4
8 to 14 days	24	25.5
15 to 21 days	07	07.4
22 to 31 days	17	18.1
TOTAL	94	100

Mean=11.0; SD=9.0

2 and 3 weeks," and "up to one month." That way, there are only five possible values instead of thirty, and the categories have real-life meaning. Table 14.6 presents an example.

Length of stay is a variable that is of special interest in the field of child welfare. Concern about how long children are in care has plagued the field for decades. In short-term programs such as the respite program that serves as the chapter example, a cohort of children all of whom have left the program can be examined to provide information about the average length of stay in the program. Often, however, it is of interest to determine how long children are staying in an agency or a particular program within an agency prior to all the children having completed their stay. A time-series survival analysis can be used for such cases, as long as at least half of the youth have completed their stays.

In producing the survival analysis, three pieces of information must be decided upon in advance, the first of which is the variable denoting length of time (a continuous variable in the unit of interest, such as days, weeks, months, or years). In many studies of length of stay there will be youth whose stays are not yet over. Their length of stay should be calculated as the length of stay between admission and the date that the study is conducted. For these youth, the data indicate the length of the stay "to date." Next is the variable indicating whether the stay is over for each youth (0=stay is not over, 1=stay is over), and third is the interval of time that should be used to create the categories in the statistical output. For a study of length of stay in the respite program, the longest stay is thirty days, and the interval might

Table 14.7

Sample table of survival analysis results

Life table analysis of length of stay in the respite (n=94)

	# entering interval	# terminal events	% terminating	% surviving	Cumulative % surviving at end of interval
0 days	94	41	.44	.56	.56
7 days	53	13	.25	.75	.43
14 days	40	20	.50	.50	.21
21 days	20	16	.80	.20	.04
28 days	4	4	1.00	00	00

be seven days. The analysis, therefore, would provide information about the proportion of youth who left after seven days (one week), fourteen days (two weeks), and so forth all the way through the highest value of thirty days (four weeks). In a study of length of stay in foster care, where stays can range from one day to several years, the interval unit might be six months. Table 14.7 presents hypothetical output for a survival analysis of length of stay in the respite program. In this example, all youth have left already left the program.

As can be seen in table 14.7, 94 youth were in the sample. They each entered the first interval (which is youth who stayed in the respite program between 0 and 6 days). Forty-one of these 93 youth stayed in the respite program between 1 and 6 days. Thus 41 of 94 youth left during the first interval, between 0 and 6 days. The probability of leaving within 6 days was, therefore, 44%, and the probability of not leaving within that interval was 56%. Fifty-three youth stayed at least 7 days (94 in the sample minus the 41 who left within the first week). Of these 53 youth, 13 left during the second interval, between 7 and 13 days. Thus, there was a 25% chance of leaving within the second week. In all, there was a 57% chance of leaving within the first two weeks (54 leaving out of a total of 94 youth) and a 43% chance of surviving (not leaving) at least two weeks. Forty youth stayed at least three weeks (between 14 and 20 days). Half of these youth (20) left during that time. Thus, if a youth made it at least two weeks, he or she had a 50% chance of leaving during the third week. Of the 20 youth who stayed at least 3 weeks, 16 (80%) left during that week, and the four

Table 14.8

Sample table of univariate analysis of frequency data

Proportion of foster care youth who
returned to their foster home (n=94)

	N	%
Returned to foster home	32	34.0
Went to new foster home	20	21.3
Went to congregate care	18	19.1
Hospitalized	18	19.1
Reunified	6	06.4
TOTAL	94	100

remaining youth all left during the last week. Thus, there was a 100% chance of leaving between 22 and 28 days if the youth stayed at least 22 days.

In this example, all the youth had been discharged from the respite program. As noted above, this is often not the case with child welfare data in which length of stay analyses pertain to long-term programs. Survival analysis was developed especially for situations in which not all cases have achieved the end of their stay, although it is necessary that at least half the sample have terminal end points (end of stay). In this way, a survival analysis can help an agency estimate the eventual median length of stay of the full sample based on a study in which not all members of the sample have achieved the end of their stay.

The third question for the study, how many youth returned to their original foster home following the stay in the respite program, can also be answered with univariate analysis. This table would present the number of youth (out of the total who used the respite program) who were returned to the foster home they had been living at prior to use of the program. The table could also present some information about those who did not return to the foster home following the respite stay. Table 14.8 presents an example. Regardless of the specific data presented in the table, all univariate analyses involve information about a single variable. Thus, calculating an effect size is not applicable.

Data Analysis Techniques

Inferential Statistics and Hypothesis Testing

When associations between two or more variables are of interest, then inferential, as opposed to descriptive, statistics are necessary. All inferential statistics involve the testing of hypotheses. As noted in chapter 4, hypotheses can be directional or nondirectional. In directional hypotheses, the researcher is making a statement about the nature (direction) of the associations, while in nondirectional hypotheses the researcher is stating a belief that there will be an association, the nature of which is not specified. A nondirectional hypothesis might state that there will be an association between age of child at first placement and length of stay in the respite program, while a directional hypothesis would state that children who are older at first placement will have shorter stays than youth who are younger at first stay. Directional hypotheses require one-tail significance tests and nondirectional hypotheses require two-tail significance tests. This is because the nondirectional hypothesis is stating that the mean of one group will be different than the other but it might be higher or lower, and thus both ends (tails) of the distribution need to be examined, whereas a directional hypothesis states in advance which end of the distribution (tail) the difference will be at.

As it relates to directional hypotheses, a note about reading statistical output is in order. Using SPSS as an example (other programs may vary), the program assumes that most bivariate and multivariate analyses are nondirectional and that two-tail tests of significance should be used. For example, the output for a t-test indicates that the p-value is for a two-tail test. If the hypothesis was actually one-tail, then the p-value can be divided in half to produce a one-tail test of significance. For example, if the p-value as produced in the output was .07, then the one-tail test would be .035. This means that the p-value moves from not statistically significant (.07) to statistical significance (.035), assuming that the alpha was .05. This, of course, can only be used if the direction of the association is as expected and if the direction was stated in advance of the data analysis (a priori).

Bivariate Analyses

Many research questions can only be answered through an examination of associations between two variables, an examination known as an inferential analysis. Inferential analyses are bivariate when associations between two variables are assessed and multivariate when associations between three or more variables are assessed. Questions 4 and 5 for the respite study entail both a bivariate and multivariate approach. Bivariate analyses begin, usually, with assessing the association, one at a time, of a set of independent variables and a single dependent variable. Once the set of independent variables with statistically significant associations have been identified, they are entered into a multivariate analysis to determine their unique and combined effects. Which specific tests are conducted depends on the scales of the variables: dichotomous, categorical, or continuous. Each is examined in turn.

Two Dichotomous Variables

If the question were, "is the gender of youth associated with use of respite program?" both the independent variable (gender) and the dependent variable (use of respite program) are dichotomous. They each have only two mutually exclusive categories (male/female and used respite/did not use respite). Assessment of the association between these two variables will entail cross-tabulations (also known as contingency tables) and chi-square analysis. The cross-tabulation will determine the proportion of cases in each of the four cells (male with and without use of respite and female with and without use of respite). The chi-square will test whether the proportions in the cells are as expected (no association between the variables) or depart from expectations (significant association). An assumption underlying the use of the chi-square is that there are at least five cases in each cell. Chi-squares can be calculated with directional or nondirectional hypotheses. If the hypothesis is directional, there is an

Table 14.9
Sample table of four-cell cross-tabulation distribution

Cross-tabulation between youth gender and use of respite (n=200)

	Use respite	
	No (n=84)	Yes (n=116)
Males (n=119)	38	81
Females (n=81)	46	35

Chi-square (1, n=200)=12.25; p<.001; d=.51

Figure 14.3
Two formulas for calculating d from a chi-square

Formula A:

$d = \sqrt{(4 * X^2)/(n - X^{2+})}$

Formula B:

$d = 2\sqrt{X^2/n - X^2}$

a priori belief as to which of the two genders will use the respite more than the other. A one-tail test is used to determine whether that difference exists. If the hypothesis is nondirectional; that is, if it is hypothesized that there will be a difference but it is not specified which gender will have higher use of the respite than the other gender, a two-tailed test of significance will be used, and the conclusion will be based on which gender happened to have a higher rate. Table 14.9 presents an example of a chi-square test.

Figure 14.4
Sample calculation of d from a chi-square

Formula A:

If $X^2 = 12.25$

$N = 200$

$d = \sqrt{(4 * 12.25)/(200 - 12.25)}$

$d = \sqrt{(49)/(87.75)}$

$d = \sqrt{.26}$

$d = .51$

Formula B:

$d = 2\sqrt{12.25/200 - 12.25}$

$d = 2\sqrt{12.25/187.75}$

$d = 2\sqrt{.06}$

$d = 2(.255)$

$d = .51$

In the event of a nondirectional hypothesis, the proportion of cases within each gender that used the respite would be examined to determine the nature of the association. As can be seen in table 14.9, 81 of 119 males (69.8%) compared to only 35 of 81 females (30.2%) were in the respite program. Thus, if the two-tail test of statistical significance meets the alpha of $p < .05$, it can be concluded that males were in the respite at a higher rate than females. Chi-square statistics can range from zero to whole numbers. Although the larger the statistic, the larger the association, the number itself is not meaningful. That is why converting chi-square statistics to an effect size is important. Two formulas for calculating d from a chi-square are presented in figure 14.3. Figure 14.4 presents a sample calculation of d from a chi-square using the data in table 14.9.

One Dichotomous Variable and One Categorical Variable

If an analysis entails testing an association between one dichotomous and one categorical variable, a chi-square can still be conducted. An example would be examining the association between reason for referral (a categorical variable with three possible values) and use of respite (dichotomous variable with two possible values). The cross-tabulation would have six cells instead of four (the number of values in one variable multiplied by the number of values in the other variable, in this case, 2 times 3). Table 14.10 presents hypothetical results. If the results are statistically significant and the hypothesis was directional (it is specified in advance which group will be higher [or lower] than the other two groups), then inspection of the cells will reveal whether this was borne out. If the test was not directional (a difference was assumed but not specified as to which group would differ from the other two), then the cells will have to be examined to discern where the difference lies. Usually this is not difficult to do. For example, in table 14.10, it can be seen that two-thirds of the abuse/neglect cases (64 of 94) used the respite program while only half of the voluntary and half of the PINS cases used the respite program (31 of 66). Thus, it can be concluded that abuse/neglect cases are statistically significantly more likely to use the respite program than other cases. One aspect of cross-tabulations that can be tricky is deciding which variable to present as the row and which as the column. The computer will allow either way. One rule of thumb is to make the presumptive independent variable the row and the presumptive dependent variable the column. Then one needs to examine the row proportions of the various groups to detect differences,

Table 14.10
Sample table of six-cell cross-tabulation distribution

Cross-tabulation between reason for referral and use
of respite (n=200)

	Not used	Used respite
Abuse/neglect	30	64
Voluntary	35	31
Pins	19	21

Chi-square $(1, n=200)=7.71$; $p<.021$; $d=.40$

in this case, the proportion using the respite in each of the three referral
groups. Effect size for chi-squares is calculated the same for a 2 by 3 cross-
tabulation as it is for a 2 by 2 (see the formula in figure 14.3).

One Dichotomous Variable and One Continuous Variable

If the association between child's age at admission to the foster home and
use of respite were examined, one variable would be continuous (age) while
the other would be dichotomous (use of respite coded as yes or no). If the
continuous variable is normally distributed (skewness and kurtosis are not
greater than 1.0), then an independent t-test would be conducted to determine whether the mean on this variable is different between the two groups.
That is, it can be asked whether the mean age of those who used the respite
is statistically significantly different than the mean age of those that did not
use the respite. Put yet another way, if a nondirectional hypothesis is tested,
it can be asked whether the age of the child is associated with the use of respite. Because the hypothesis is nondirectional, a two-tail significance test
will be conducted. If a directional hypothesis had been developed, in which
it was expected that those who used the respite would be older (or younger)
than those who did not use the respite, then a one-tail significance test
would be conducted. Table 14.11 presents the results of a t-test between age
and use of respite program. In calculating t-tests, it is also important to examine the Levine's test for equality of variance. This is usually provided
with the statistical output. If this test is statistically significant, the variance
in each of the two groups is so different that a different calculation of the

Table 14.11
Sample table of t-test results

Results of T-test comparing mean age of youth who used and did not use
respite (n=200)

	Mean	SD	t	Sig	d
Did use respite	6.13	4.2	3.35	.001	.48
Did not use respite	8.27	4.4			

Table 14.12
Sample output of Levine's test of equality of variance

	F	Sig.	t	Df	Sig.
Age equal variance assumed	.03	.86	3.35	198	.001
Equal variance not assumed			3.35	178.7	.001

t-test must be used. In SPSS, the statistical output for Levine's test is provided as well as the alternative t-test in the event that the Levine's test is statistically significant. Table 14.12 presents a sample output from SPSS.

As can be seen, the F-test for Levine's test is not statistically significant
($p < .86$), and thus the top row of the t-test output can be used. That is, t
$(198) = 3.35$, $p < .001$. If, however, the F-test for Levine's test had been statistically significant, the lower row of t-test output would be used. In this case, t
$(178.7) = 3.35$, $p < .001$. Usually, the degrees of freedom for the t-test when
Levine's test is statistically significant is not a whole number. The t-statistic
can range from zero to integers well above 1. The larger the statistic, the
greater the association, but the number itself does not have meaning. That
is why it is important to convert the t into an effect size. Thus, once the correct t has been identified, and if it is statistically significant, the next step is
to calculate its effect size. Figure 14.5 presents two formulas for calculating
d from a t-test, and figure 14.6 presents a sample calculation of d utilizing
the data in table 14.11 as an example.

If the continuous variable is not normally distributed and a t-test is not
advisable, two options are available to the researcher. The first is to recode
the continuous variable into a categorical variable and conduct a chi-square,

Figure 14.5
Two formulas for converting T into effect size

Formula A:

$$\frac{M_1 - M_2}{\sqrt{(SD_1^2 + SD_2^2)/2}}$$

M_1 = mean for first group

M_2 = mean for second group

SD_1^2 = squared standard deviation for first group

SD_2^2 = squared standard deviation for second group

Formula B:

$$d = \frac{2t}{\sqrt{n-2}}$$

and the second is to conduct a nonparametric version of the t-test known as the Mann-Whitney test. Recoding a continuous variable into a categorical variable is a good option when meaningful categories can be created and there is sufficient variation within the categories. For example, age could be recoded into infancy (birth through age 1), toddlerhood (1 to 2.5), preschool (2.5–5), school age (5–12), and adolescent (13–18). Note that the number of values within each category does not have to be the same (two in the first category, two in the second, three in the third, eight in the fourth, and six in the last). If the variable that is continuous is not normally distributed and/or meaningful categories cannot be created, a Mann-Whitney test can be calculated. Nonparametric tests do not carry the same level of credibility as parametric tests, however, so one option is to run both parametric and nonparametric tests and, if the results are congruent, to report both.

Another consideration with t-tests is the situation in which there are many continuous independent variables to test against a single dependent variable. Running numerous t-tests can result in some being statistically significant by chance alone. One solution is to divide the alpha (.05) by the number of tests and reset the alpha accordingly. Thus, if ten tests were to be

Figure 14.6
Calculation of d from a T-test

Formula A:

$$d = \frac{8.27 - 6.13}{\sqrt{(4.4^2 + 4.2^2)/2}}$$

$$d = \frac{2.14}{\sqrt{(19.36 + 17.64)/2}}$$

$$d = \frac{2.14}{4.3}$$

$$d = .49$$

Formula B:

$$d = \frac{6.70}{\sqrt{200 - 2}}$$

$$d = \frac{6.70}{14.07}$$

$$d = .48$$

conducted, then the alpha for each would be .005 rather than .05. Another approach is to run a MANOVA, in which all the independent variables are assessed simultaneously. Only if the overall MANOVA is significant would the bivariate analyses be examined.

Two Categorical Variables

If the number of categories within each variable is two or three, then a cross-tabulation and chi-square can be calculated. In the event that more than three categories exist for each variable, the cross-tabulation can become unwieldy. For example, if each variable has four categories, there will be sixteen cells in the cross-tabulation. Obtaining statistically significant results becomes highly unlikely with that many cells, and interpreting the findings can also be cumbersome. Collapsing the variables is suggested. For example, if there was interest in an association between ethnicity and type of referral, ethnicity could be recoded into a dichotomous variable of minority versus nonminority, or referral could be recoded to combine abuse, neglect, and voluntary cases, which could be compared with PINS and JD cases. Determining which categories to combine should be based on knowledge of the field and prior research.

One Categorical Variable and One Continuous Variable

If the categorical variable has three or four values and the continuous variable is normally distributed, a one-way analysis of variance (ANOVA) can be conducted. Such an analysis would test whether means of the continuous variable vary depending upon the grouping of the categorical variable. If, for example, it were of interest to test whether age varied by ethnicity, an ANOVA would be run to test whether mean age varied by different categories of the variable ethnicity. Table 14.13 presents the results of such an analysis.

When a priori hypotheses are developed in advance regarding which group will be different from the others, planned contrasts are built into the analytic command language to test for these specific differences. For example, if it is hypothesized that the Hispanic youth will be younger than youth in the other ethnic categories, then contrasts are built into the analysis. However, if no specific hypotheses were developed and the F-test is

Table 14.13
Sample table of ANOVA results

Results of ANOVA comparing mean age of youth by ethnicity (n=200)

	N	Mean	SD	F	Sig	d
Black	78	6.05	4.2	13.7	.001	.93
Hispanic	74	9.40	4.4			
White	30	5.53	4.4			
Other	18	4.05	4.5			

Figure 14.7
Formula for calculating d from an ANOVA F-test

Step 1: Calculate eta^2

$\text{Eta}^2 = \text{SS}_{effect} / \text{SS}_{total}$

Step 2: Calculate r from eta^2

$r = \sqrt{\text{eta}^2}$

Step 3: Calculate d from r

$$d = \frac{2 * r}{\sqrt{1 - r^2}}$$

statistically significant, post hoc (after the fact) tests will need to be conducted in order to determine which means are statistically significantly different from the others. There are many possible post hoc tests from which to choose. Sometimes it makes sense to run more than one (say, Tukey and Bonforonni) to confirm the results. In this case, the results revealed that youth in the Hispanic group were statistically significantly different (older) than the youth in the other ethnic groups. As with all tests, an effect size should be calculated to determine the size of the difference between the groups. The formula for doing so with an F test is presented in figure 14.7, and a sample calculation using the data generated from the analyses presented in table 14.13 is presented in figure 14.8. If the variable that is continuous is not normally distributed, options include recoding into a categorical variable or conducting a nonparametric test, in this case, a Kruskall Wallis test.

Two Continuous Variables

A Pearson product moment correlation is conducted when both the independent and dependent variables are normally distributed continuous variables. If it is of interest to determine whether age was associated with length of stay in the respite program and both variables were sufficiently normally distributed, a Pearson correlation could be conducted. In addition

Figure 14.8
Calculation of d from an ANOVA F-test

$Eta^2 = SS_{effect} / SS_{total}$

$Eta^2 = 718.711 / 4138.76$

$Eta^2 = .17$

$r = \sqrt{eta^2}$

$r = \sqrt{.17}$

$r = .42$

$$d = \frac{2 * r}{\sqrt{1 - r^2}}$$

$$d = \frac{2 * r}{\sqrt{1 - r^2}}$$

$$d = \frac{2(.42)}{\sqrt{1 - .42^2}}$$

$$d = \frac{.84}{\sqrt{.82}}$$

$$d = \frac{.84}{.90}$$

$d = .93$

Figure 14.9
Example of positive linear relationship, negative linear relationship, and curvilinear relationship

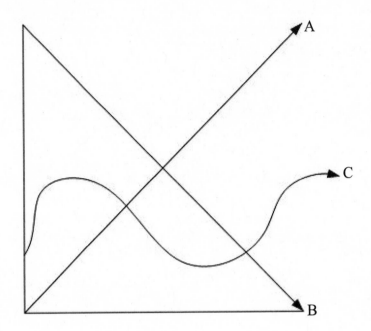

to the assumption of normal distribution, a second assumption underlying the Pearson correlation is that the two variables will be related to each other in a linear fashion. Figure 14.9 presents several different types of relationships between two continuous variables.

The line marked as A depicts a positive linear relationship between the two variables. As scores on variable X increase, so too do scores on variable Y. An example might be between height and weight. Typically, the taller a person is, the more he or she weighs. Line B presents a negative linear relationship. As scores on X increase, scores on Y decrease. The relationship between anxiety and happiness might be an example, in that the more anxiety a person experiences, the less happy he or she is. In both cases, the association between the two sets of variables is consistent. If it is positive at one end of the scale, it is positive at the other end of the scale. Line C presents a nonlinear relationship, a classic example of which—though not depicted here—is the relationship between job demands and job satisfaction. At the low end of the scale of job demands (the job is very undemanding), satisfaction is low. At middle levels of job demands

Figure 14.10
Formula for calculating d from a correlation

$$d = \frac{2 * r}{\sqrt{1 - r^2}}$$

(the job is demanding but not too demanding), satisfaction is high. At high levels of job demands (the job is too demanding), satisfaction is again low. In nonlinear associations, Pearson correlations are not appropriate. Viewing a scatter plot between two variables can help determine whether an association is linear or not. If so, it might make sense to create a categorical variable (low job demands, medium job demands, high job demands) and test with an ANOVA whether mean job satisfaction is associated with different levels of job demands.

Returning to the chapter example, if a positive linear association were hypothesized between age and length of stay in the respite program, it would mean that it was expected that the older the youth, the longer the stay in the respite. If a negative association were hypothesized, it would be expected

Figure 14.11
Sample calculation of d from a correlation

$$d = \frac{2\,(.26)}{\sqrt{1 - .26^2}}$$

$$d = \frac{.52}{\sqrt{.93}}$$

$$d = \frac{.52}{.96}$$

$$d = .54$$

that younger youth had longer stays. In either case, a single correlation is calculated. A table is not necessary when presenting the results of a correlation, unless multiple correlations are conducted. Figure 14.10 presents the formula for converting a correlation to d and figure 14.11 provides an example calculation using a hypothetical correlation as an example.

Multivariate Analyses

When the associations among three or more variables are of interest, multivariate analyses need to be conducted.

Linear Regression

In the event that the dependent variable is continuous (such as length of stay in the respite) and several of the possible independent variables are found to be significantly associated with it, it will probably be of interest to conduct a multiple regression analysis in order to determine the combined and unique influence of each independent variable. In addition to the assumptions of normal distribution of the variables and linear relationships among each independent variable and the dependent variable, an additional assumption for regressions is that the independent variables are not overly intercorrelated among themselves. The way to assess this is by examining the correlation matrix among the independent variables. In fact, many reports that utilize regression analyses include a table of the correlation matrix. If two independent variables are interrelated, one option is to exclude one of the variables from the regression equation. It is also possible to create a single variable that represents the scores on both variables. A third option is to enter the two variables as a block in the equation without the expectation of assessing the unique contributions of each.

The major questions addressed in a linear regression are: (1) How much of the total variance in the dependent variable is accounted for by the combined influence of the independent variables? And (2) what is the contribution of each specific independent variable in explaining variation in the dependent variable? Variables can be entered into a regression all at once, one at a time in an order the computer chooses, or in a specific order that tests certain hypotheses. One thing to bear in mind when conducting multivariate analyses is the sample size in relation to the number of variables in the equation. One rule of thumb is to have 20 subjects per variable. With a sample of 94, no

Table 14.14
Sample table of linear regression results

Results of linear regression of length of stay in respite (n=94)

Variable	R	R2 change	F of change	DF	Sig. of F
Age of child	.43	.19	20.89	I	.001
Gender of child	.46	.03	2.94	I	.09
First spell	.48	.02	1.81	I	.18
Ethnicity	.48	.00	.95	I	.67

more than 5 independent variables should be included in a regression. Table 14.14 depicts a standard output from a regression analysis.

If it is of interest to determine the total amount of variance in the dependent variable attributed to the combined effects of the independent variables, then the last row of the output should be examined. In this case, the total R for the four variables is .48. This should be squared to produce the answer to the question; thus, 23 percent of the variance in length of stay is accounted for by the combined effects of child's age, gender, and ethnicity. On the other hand, if the interest is in the unique effects of the variables in the equation, then the change in R square is examined for each variable. As can be seen, the first variable, age of child, accounts for 19 percent of the variance and is statistically significant. Once age is entered into the equation, the next variable, gender, is not ($p < .09$), and the amount of variance accounted for in length of stay is negligible (r square change=3 percent). The last two variables, also not statistically significant, accounted for a mere 2 percent or less of the variance in length of stay. Thus, one could conclude that only age was significantly associated with length of stay in the model.

Logistic Regression

In a logistic regression, the dependent variable is dichotomous rather than continuous. The question regarding which variables were associated with whether or not the child returned to the original foster home following a stay in the respite program can be answered with a logistic as opposed to a linear regression analysis, because the dependent variable (return to foster

Table 14.15
Sample table of logistic regression results

Logistic regression on whether or not child returned to foster home
following stay in respite (n=94)

Variable	B	S.E.	Wald	DF	Sig.	R	Exp(b)
Age of child	−.068	.25	7.21	I	.007	−.06	.51
Gender of child	.39	.19	3.99	I	.045	.04	1.47
Ethnicity	.62	.23	7.55	I	.006	.07	1.85

home) is dichotomous (the child either returned to the foster home or did
not). Table 14.15 presents an example.

As can be seen in table 14.5, three independent variables were included: age
of child, gender of child, and ethnicity. The results pertain to whether the independent variables change the odds of the outcome (dependent variable) occurring. Results are reported in terms of the odds ratio of each independent
variable affecting the dependent variable. Interpreting an odds ratio depends upon whether the independent variable is dichotomous, categorical,
or continuous. When dichotomous and statistically significant, the exp(b) is
interpreted as the odds that the dependent variable will be 1 instead of 0
when the independent variable is 1 instead of 0. For example, if the dependent variable is returning to the foster home after using the respite program
(score of 1) as opposed to not returning to the foster home after using the respite (score of 0), the independent variable is the child's gender (0=female
and 1=male), and the exp(b) is 1.47, then the odds of the child returning to
the foster home following a stay in the respite is 47 percent greater if the
child is male. If the exp(b) is below 1, then the interpretation of the odds ratio
is that the likelihood is less rather than more. For example, if the exp(b) is
0.80, then the odds of the child returning to the foster home after using the
respite is 20 percent less (1−.80=.20) if the child is male rather than female.
If the independent variable is continuous rather than dichotomous, the interpretation is based on units of that variable. If age of child (in years) is the independent variable, returning to the foster home following a stay in the respite
program is the dependent variable (1=returns to the home, 0=does not return to the home), and the exp(b) is .51, it can be said that for every one-year
increase in the child's age, the odds of returning to the foster home after using the respite decreases 49 percent. Identifying individual predictors of the

dependent variable is possible in a logistic regression, but determining the overall percent of variation in the dependent variable attributable to the independent variables—as is possible with linear regressions—is not.

Survival Analysis and Cox Regression

A special case of regression analyses is a Cox regression based on survival analysis. In this analysis, the purpose is to identify the significant factors that speed up or slow down the rate of an event. In child welfare, typically the event is discharge from a program or from care, but it could be the achievement of any other milestone (adoption, transfer to a lower level of care, release from a hospital, and so forth). Interpretation of the exp(b) is in terms of the degree to which the independent variable effects the *rate* of the dependent variable occurring. If the exp(b) is greater than 1.0, that variable is associated with faster rates, while exp(b)s below 1.0 are associated with slower rates.

As with survival analysis, Cox regression was designed for cases in which not all members of the sample have achieved the end of their stay (in whatever program the length of stay analysis pertains to). Therefore, it is important to create a variable that indicates whether or not the youth has achieved the endpoint (usually called the censoring variable). This variable should be coded as 0 (endpoint not achieved) or 1 (endpoint achieved). For youth who have not yet achieved their endpoint, the variable indicating end of spell should insert the current date. For example, if the study is of youth in the respite program and some youth have ended their stay in the respite program while others are still in the respite program at the time of the analysis, the date of the analysis should be entered as the end of stay date for the youth still in the respite. Because they are coded as 0 on the censoring variable, the analyses will take into account that their length of stay is "to date" as opposed to a final length of stay.

Conclusion

Many statistical analyses are available to the child welfare researcher, including descriptive, bivariate, and multivariate analyses, in addition to a range of data reduction techniques. In all cases, the researcher should be familiar with the statistical assumptions underlying the use of the analyses and be competent to interpret the statistical output.

Dissemination of Research Findings

In this chapter, the following topics will be discussed, following the introduction of the chapter scenario and the brief literature review:

- Writing up the results
- Presenting results to agency/program staff
- Presenting results to the academic community
- Presenting results to practitioners and policymakers in the field
- Presenting results to clients and nonprofessional stakeholders

CHAPTER SCENARIO

An agency researcher conducted a survey of prevention programs within one city. The purpose of the survey was to "unpack the black box" of prevention programs by developing detailed information about the types of services actually offered to participating families. Once the data have been collected, the researcher needs to determine which findings are relevant for which audiences and how to present the results in such a way as to ensure their accuracy as well as increase the likelihood that they will be understood and utilized.

BRIEF LITERATURE REVIEW: UNPACKING THE BLACK BOX
OF PREVENTION PROGRAMS

The child welfare system's two primary service components include
out-of-home placement services for children deemed to be unsafe at
home and prevention programs that aim to help keep children who
are at risk for removal in the family. From a philosophical point of
view, most governmental and advocacy groups have a stated preference for maintaining children in the home. For example, the Adoption
Assistance and Child Welfare Act of 1980 (PL 96–272) promotes the
use of prevention programs as a preference over out-of-home placements. Such an emphasis is consistent with family-centered social
work practice (Pecora, Whittaker, Maluccio, Barth, and Plotnick 1992).
As the national advocacy arm of the child welfare system, CWLA also
proclaims as its goal the development of services that enable families
to stay together. Removal of the children from the home is considered
a measure of last resort, when leaving the child in the home would
pose too great a risk to the child's safety.

Family preservation/prevention programs can be either short-term
intensive programs that follow a crisis intervention model for families
at imminent risk of removal due to abuse or neglect, or they can offer
long-term family support services for families struggling with a range
of concrete and social needs but not at imminent risk of abuse or neglect. Many different types of specific prevention programs exist within
each service model. In addition, many agencies develop and offer their
own mix of services. The specific content and structure of these
programs—once state and national guidelines have been met—are left
to the discretion of the individual programs. What they share is the
provision of a mix of concrete assistance to families alongside counseling and support services, with most if not all services being offered in
the home. Many of the intensive programs incorporate some or all of
the concepts of the Homebuilder's model developed by the Institute for
Family Development in Washington State. These include intervening
while the family is in crisis (as that offers a unique window for change),
providing the treatment in a natural setting (e.g., the home), providing
therapists who are on call twenty-four hours a day and seven days a
week, the intensity and flexibility of service delivery, low caseloads for

(continued)

the therapists, and on-going research to evaluate program effectiveness. The Homebuilders model has undergone considerable research and evaluation (Kinney, Haapala, and Booth 1991; Fraser, Walton, Lewis, Pecora, and Walton 1996; Kirk and Griffith 2004).

Nonetheless, agencies have tremendous latitude to develop and implement their own prevention programs. In light of this latitude, it is reasonable to assume that each agency has developed its own specific program model and implementation strategy. Although it is likely that variation exists across programs, there has been no effort to date to document the ways in which agencies provide prevention services (outside of the use of model programs). Important questions remain for the field, including: (1) What services are actually provided to children and families? (2) How satisfied are the program directors with these services? And (3) in what ways do the program directors believe that services could be improved? These issues could be examined as they relate to the three primary objectives of prevention programs: ensuring the safety of the child, improving family functioning, and avoiding placing the child in substitute care (Dagenais, Begin, Bouchard, and Fortin 2004).

Such an endeavor is consistent with trends in program evaluation studies to describe the "black box" of treatment. That is, in many early program evaluations the program itself was treated as a monolithic unmeasured phenomenon. Clients go into the "black box," receive treatment, and then emerge, hopefully improved. Because such studies could not speak to what the programs were actually doing, the findings could not be used to identify which aspects of the program made a difference, nor could they be used descriptively as a way to share practice wisdom (that is, what effective programs were actually doing). In response to criticisms of these black-box evaluations, current research has moved toward the collection and presentation of more detailed information about the process of service delivery.

Overview of the Topic

A research study is not complete until the findings have been written up and shared with the various audiences who might be able to make use of them. There are at least three major audiences for any agency-based child welfare research endeavor: (1) program staff within the sponsoring agency,

(2) program staff in other agencies as well as administrative staff within the sponsoring agency, and (3) researchers, clinicians, policymakers, and advocates within the professional community. A three-step process of disseminating child welfare research is proposed. In the first step, the findings are shared with a select group of agency staffmembers who have the most knowledge about the program. This is typically the staff within the service or program that was the focus of the research, and a few key administrative staff within the agency. This discussion should help identify nuances to the study, clarify misperceptions or misrepresentations about the program/service, and lay the groundwork for a richer and more valid interpretation of the findings. In the second step, the findings are presented in a full-length manuscript submitted for publication in a peer-reviewed journal. Acceptance by the journal provides the researcher with the assurance that the study meets the standards in the field. In the third step, agency-wide staff as well as staff outside of the agency can be informed about the findings in a brief report. Regardless of the audience, there are conventions in the field for describing the findings of research, based on the type of data collected.

Writing Up the Results

Quantitative Data

When presenting quantitative findings, one typically begins with a table of descriptive information regarding the means and standard deviations on the various scales or items of the measure(s). Table 15.1 presents an example of a table of descriptive information. For a single-sample study in which the only research questions are descriptive in nature, these frequency tables will constitute the sole presentation of the results. It is standard to present both the n (the number of subjects with a particular score) as well as the percentage (the number with a particular score divided by the valid sample size). In the case of table 15.1, seventy-five prevention programs ("program" was the unit of analysis) out of ninety valid responses reported that the educational requirement of caseworkers was a four-year college degree. This resulted in a percentage of 83.3. Results should be presented in tabular form and then described in the text of the results section, as follows: "As can be seen, at the vast majority of programs (n=75, 83.3%), completion of a bachelor's program was necessary for casework staff."

If the study included hypothesis testing, the results of these analyses also need to be presented, even if the findings did not support the hypotheses.

Table 15.1
Sample table of background characteristics

Sample Characteristics (n=100)		
Variable	N	%
Caseworker education		
Less than high school	00	00.0
High school	00	00.0
4-year college	75	83.3
More than 4-year college	15	16.7
Missing=10		

These results should be organized around the research questions of the study. Statistical significance as well as size of the effect should be presented. Cohen's (1969) conventions in the field should be used to assess meaningfulness of effect size. If only a few statistical tests were run, the findings should be presented in the text only; no table is necessary. If several statistical tests were calculated, a table should present the findings and the results should be described in the text. An example of a table presenting results of a t-test is presented in table 15.2.

The results of a t-test should be described in the following manner:

An independent t-test was conducted to determine whether programs with in-house substance abuse services were different in size (number of clients served at a time) than programs without in-house substance abuse services. Results revealed that agencies with in-house substance abuse

Table 15.2
Sample table of t-test results

Results of t-test comparing size of program and whether program has in-house substance abuse component

	Mean	SD	T	Sig	d
Has in-house	245.6	40.34	3.51	.02	.70
Does not have in-house	224.5	24.5			

services were statistically significantly larger (mean=245.6, SD=40.34) than programs that did not have an in-house substance abuse program (mean=224.2, SD=24.5), t (98)=3.51, p<.02 (d=.70). The effect size was between moderate and large.

If the results were not statistically significant, the statistical data should still be presented, as in the example that follows:

Results of the t-test examining differences between programs with in-house substance abuse services (mean=21.1, SD=13.5) and without an in-house substance abuse service (mean=19.2, SD=13.3) in number of years the program had been in operation were not statistically significant: t (89.23)=.68, p<.78.

Note that in either case, certain information such as standard deviation is presented in the text but not in the table, and note that when Levine's test for equality of variances is not statistically significant (variance is not different between the two groups), then the degrees of freedom presented in the parentheses is a whole number representing the sample size minus the number of groups (always two for t-tests). However, if Levine's test for equality of variance is statistically significant, then the degrees of freedom is smaller than n−2 and tends to be a number with two decimal places.

Also note that the exact p value is presented, rather than rounding to the nearest .05 level (.05, .01, .005). Presenting the exact p value takes up no additional space and provides the reader with the maximum amount of information. Likewise, note that the exact p value is also presented, even when the results are not statistically significant, in contrast to simply writing NS

Table 15.3
Sample table of ANOVA results

Mean differences in size of programs (number of clients) by length of program operation for new programs (n=38), intermediate length of operation programs (n=22), and established programs (n=40)

	New Mean (SD)	Intermediate Mean (SD)	Estab. Mean (SD)	F	Sig.
Size of program	246 (8.9)	201 (8.7)	244 (6.)	321.8	.001

Table 15.4
Sample table of cross-tabulation results

Cross-tabulation between and having in-house
substance abuse services and meeting OASAS
standards for recidivism

	Meet OASAS standards	
	No (n=47)	Yes (n=49)
In-house (n=58)	21	37
Not in-house (n=42)	30	12

Chi-square (1, n=100)=12.09, p<.001, d=.74

(for "not significant"). Again, this is recommended as standard practice, in order to be as informative as possible about the nature of the results. Kraemer and Thiemann (1987) also make the case for the utility of such information for knowledge building in the field.

If an ANOVA was conducted instead of a t-test, then the table should present the means and standard deviations for all the groups. Table 15.3 presents a sample table presenting the results of such an ANOVA. Results of this test should be written up in the following manner:

A one-way analysis of variance was conducted to test whether size of program (number of clients served) was associated with age of program (number of years in operation), with age of program categorized as newer programs (in operation less than 3 years), intermediate programs (in operation between 3 and 19 years), and established programs (in operation 20 or more years). Results revealed that there was a statistically significant effect of age of program on number of clients served: $f(2,97)=321.8$, $p<.001$, $d=5.2$.

In the case of a two-group analysis such as a t-test, it is immediately apparent in examining the means which group had a statistically significantly higher mean than the other group. However, with a three-group analysis, it is not always immediately apparent. Post hoc (after the fact) analyses will need to be conducted and reported on as well. For example:

Post hoc tests [insert name of test] were conducted to determine which means were statistically different than the others. Results revealed that

Table 15.5
Sample table of regression results

Results of linear regression of proportion of cases that abstain
from using (n=100)

Variable	R	R2 change	F of change	DF	Sign of F
Age of parent	.43	.19	20.89	1	.001
Age of youngest child	.46	.03	2.94	1	.09
Number of prior programs	.48	.02	1.81	1	.18
Number of years using	.48	.00	.08	1	.78
Size of program	.48	.00	.03	1	.87

programs operating between 3 and 19 years (mean=201.4, SD=8.7) served significantly fewer clients than programs that were both newer (mean=246.7, SD=6.9) and more established (mean=245.9, SD=6.0).

When both the independent and dependent variables are categorical, a cross-tabulation is conducted, followed by a chi-square test, to determine the statistical significance. The table for a chi-square analysis presents the proportions within each of the four cells. An example is provided in table 15.4. Results should be described in the text as follows:

A cross-tabulation and chi-square were conducted in order to test the association between having in-house substance abuse services and meeting OASAS standards regarding recidivism. These data are presented in table 15.4. As can be seen, 37 of the 58 (63.8%) in-house programs passed the OASAS standards while only 12 of 42 (28.5%) programs without in-house substance abuse services passed the OASAS standards. This difference was statistically significant: X^2 (1, n=100)=12.09, p<.001, d=.72.

Degrees of freedom for chi-square tests report the total number in the sample preceded by the number of groups (in the independent variable) minus 1.

Results of linear regression analyses should present in tabular form information about each step of the equation in the model, including r, change in r-square, f of change of r-square, and statistical significance of change in r-square. Table 15.5 presents an illustration. In this example, the dependent variable is the proportion of cases each year in which a parent does not test

Table 15.6
Sample table of regression results with blocks

Results of linear regression of proportion of cases that abstain
from using (n=100)

Variable	R	R2 change	F of change	DF	Sign of F
Block 1					
Age of parent	.43	.19	20.89	1	.001
Age of youngest child	.46	.03	2.94	1	.09
Block 2					
Average caseworker pay	.49	.03	10.89	1	.05

positive for substance use, and the five independent variables are average age of parent, average age of youngest child in family, average number of programs the parents had been in, average number of years the parents had been using substances, and the size of the program. The description of the results should be as follows:

A multivariate stepwise linear regression was conducted to determine the unique and combined influence of the five possible correlates of the proportion of cases in which a parent failed a drug test. Results revealed that only one of the five variables, average age of the parents, was statistically associated with proportion of cases (R=.43, p<.001).

An alternative approach to the stepwise regression is to test the strength of association of certain variables of interest after controlling for other variables. In this case the table would look a little different, as in table 15.6. In this example, two variables are entered first—regardless of what the strength of the association is between them and the dependent variable. Here the question is whether the third variable will be statistically significantly associated with the dependent variable, once the variance attributed to the first two variables is accounted for. This could be written up thus:

Looking at table 15.6, it can be concluded that caseworker salary is in fact associated with proportion of cases abstaining from drug use, over and above the effects of average parent age and average age of youngest child in the family (R-square change=.03, f of change=10.89, p<.05, d=1.1).

Table 15.7

Sample table of logistic regression results

Logistic regression on whether or not an agency has in-house substance abuse program (n=100)

Variable	B	S.E.	Wald	DF	Sig.	R	Exp(b)
Age of program	−.068	.25	7.21	1	.007	−.06	.51
Size of program	.39	.19	3.99	1	.045	.04	1.47
Serves multilingual families	.62	.23	7.55	1	.006	.07	1.85

Presentation of the results of logistic regressions are essentially the same, except that the headers in the table are somewhat different. The primary difference in writing up the results of a logistic regression is the interpretation and description of the findings. In logistic regressions, the outcome (dependent variable) is dichotomous (has two values) rather than continuous. The results pertain to whether the independent variables change the odds of the outcome occurring. For example, in the survey of prevention programs, a dichotomous dependent variable might be whether or not the agency has its own substance abuse counseling services (as opposed to referring out). Independent variables might be the number of years the program has been in operation, the number of prevention slots, and whether the program serves a bilingual/multilingual population or not. Results are reported in terms of the odds ratio of each independent variable affecting the dependent variable. Table 15.7 serves as an illustration.

Interpreting an odds ratio depends upon whether the independent variable is dichotomous, categorical, or continuous. When dichotomous and statistically significant, the exp(b) is interpreted as the odds that the dependent variable will be 1 instead of 0 when the independent variable is 1 instead of 0. For example, if the dependent variable is having an in-house substance abuse service (score of 1) as opposed to referring clients to other agencies for substance abuse counseling (score of 0), the independent variable is the size of the agency (coded as 0=small and 1=large), and the exp(b) is 1.47, then the odds of the agency having substance abuse services in-house is 47 percent greater if the agency is large rather than small. If the exp(b) is below 1, then the interpretation of the odds ratio is that the likelihood is less rather than more. For example, if the exp(b) is 0.80, then the odds of the agency having in-house substance abuse counseling services is 20 percent less ($1-.80=.20$) if the agency is large rather than small. If the independent variable is continuous rather than dichotomous, the interpretation is based on units of that variable. If age of agency (in years) is the independent variable, having an in-house substance abuse component is the dependent variable ($1=$has in-house, $0=$refers out), and the exp(b) is .51, it can be said that for every one-year increase in agency age, the odds of having in-house substance abuse services decreases 49 percent.

A very special case of regression analysis is a Cox regression based on survival analysis. In this analysis, the purpose is to identify the significant factors that speed up or slow down the rate of an event. In child welfare, typically the event is discharge from a program or from care, but it could be any other milestone. Interpretation of the exp(b) is in terms of the degree to which the independent variable affects the *rate* of the dependent variable occurring. If the exp(b) is greater than 1.0, that variable is associated with faster rates, while exp(b)s below 1.0 are associated with slower rates. For example, Baker, Wulczyn, and Dale (2005) found that children who had a psychiatric crisis while in care had discharge rates 55 percent slower per unit of time (in this case, months) than reunified children without a reported crisis. The exp(b) was .45, calculated as $1-.45=.55$, that is, a 55 percent slower rate.

Qualitative Data

As discussed in chapters 12 and 13 regarding the results of focus groups and interviews, using the grounded inductive approach organizes results around major themes. These should serve as the headers for the results section in the paper/final report and should be previewed in the first paragraph. For example:

> Four major areas of concern were identified in the interviews with prevention program caseworkers: (1) difficulty working with multiproblem families, (2) fear of not ensuring child safety, (3) concern about the balance of preserving families and protecting children, and (4) worry about becoming burned out from the job.

Each of these topics becomes a header with a lengthy discussion about the major points raised in the discussions. Each section should present the general issues. Taking the first theme as an example:

Caseworkers spoke at length about the difficulty in working with what they perceived to be multiproblem families. This took several forms including: (1) feeling that the issues were so intertwined it was difficult to know where to start or make a difference, (2) being concerned that trying to help the parent stay drug free might exacerbate other problems such as coping and stress, (3) concerns about insufficient training to work with the families, (4) sadness and guilt over the poor living conditions and general hardship, and (5) difficulty and frustration over trying to help families navigate the many systems in which they are involved.

Each of these then becomes at least one paragraph and perhaps several pages of text summarizing the points made by the respondents. First the majority point should be presented, followed by any dissenting or contrary opinions, if they were expressed. In all cases, quotes from the respondents should be included in order to add flavor and specificity to the presentation of the findings. If possible, some identifying information about the respondent should follow each quote (e.g., "thirty-five-year-old female caseworker with one year of experience"). If an interview study was conducted, it might make sense to assign pseudonyms to each respondent and then identify each quote by the pseudonym of the speaker. A separate table could list all of the respondents and provide some information about them such as age, gender, and other relevant information for the study. With focus group data, it is more difficult and often not possible to identify the speaker, and so this kind of table will probably not be included.

Presenting the Findings to Program Staff

First and foremost, staff working in a program that was part of a research study should have the opportunity to see and comment on the findings prior to anyone else within or outside of the agency. This is both to preserve goodwill with program staff as well as to gain their perspective prior to sharing the results with others. The discussion serves as a courtesy to the staffpeople in the program, who should not learn about the findings along with everyone else, and also serves to ensure that the research project did not make any mistakes that could lead to a misinterpretation of the results. One practice to consider is inviting program staff to become authors on a report or published paper if they make a substantive contribution to the study by way of feedback on the first draft of the report. It is often the case that there are nuances to the program that can only be provided by program staff, and the researcher would do well to remember that program staff-people have a wealth of practice wisdom that can add insight and depth to the understanding of results.

Thus, prior to finalizing any paper or report, the findings should be shared with program staff in such a way as to be understood by them. Usually, this takes the form of a brief report that states the purpose of the study and presents the major findings and some of the identified practical implications of these findings. This report should be a few pages at most and should include an introductory paragraph and methods section. This report should be labeled "draft" and should not be circulated outside of a small group of research and program staff. Ideally, this report can be presented to the program staff in an informal brainstorming session in which staffpeople are asked to comment on the findings. Questions that they might be asked include: (1) Which findings were surprising? (2) What, if anything, would you do differently in your program now that you have read this report? (3) What do you think we need to know about your program in order to fully understand the meaning of these findings? This would be a good time to identify unanswered questions and brainstorm future research ideas. It is very important to present findings in a way that are not unnecessarily critical of the program or its staff. If the findings are not shared and discussed in a sensitive manner it is likely that agency staff will not agree to cooperate in future research. This does not mean that negative findings should be buried or ignored, only that research staff should be aware that research can be threatening to practitioners and that findings should be presented in a sensitive manner.

One thing to think about is structuring the study from the beginning in such a way as to produce some findings that will be of interest to program staff regardless of the specific findings. For example, in the citywide survey chapter scenario, it is not likely that the findings will be threatening to the program staff within any single agency, as the findings are not a direct reflection on the program. However, a study that does collect data on one program at one agency (often the case with agency-based child welfare research) can be perceived as an evaluation or test of the program even if that is not the intention of the researchers. Therefore, building into the design some "win-win" data will be very helpful. For example, in a study of number of teens who run away from an agency's maternity shelter (the example used in chapter 5), the study might ask some questions about age of youth or weeks pregnant at program intake as predictors of running away in order to produce some data that will be of general interest and will not be seen as a reflection on the program staff—regardless of the findings. In addition, these findings, if statistically significant and meaningful, can be used by program staff in developing targeted runaway prevention efforts. This should help engage program staff in the presentation of the research findings. Based on this process, the researchers should revise their analytic strategy and incorporate the program staff's perspective into their interpretation of the results.

Presenting the Results to the Academic Community

If the findings have wide-ranging implications, they should be written up for submission to a professional peer-reviewed journal. There are several reasons to do so. First, by putting the ideas and the findings through the peer-review process, the researcher can gain the assurance that the findings pass muster in the field. Very useful feedback is often obtained through the peer-review process and can be used to improve and strengthen both the presentation and the understanding of the study itself. If the manuscript is rejected on its merits, then the researcher should seriously consider not sharing the findings with others in the field, as they have been found to be lacking in scientific rigor or in value. If accepted by the journal, the researcher can gain confidence that the study was done well and the findings meet the standards in the field. Another reason to do this is that going through the process of writing the paper and thinking through the logic of the design and the meaning of the findings can sharpen and strengthen the researcher's understanding of the project, which can be used in the presentation of the findings internally and to other agencies (see step 2). Publication in peer-reviewed journals also lends prestige to the agency-based researcher, which is useful for grant seeking as well as the development of collaborations with other researchers (who assess each other's credibility in part by the number and quality of peer-review publications).

One of the first steps in writing a manuscript for submission to a journal entails identifying the appropriate journal. Ideally, this is done at the project-planning phase, to ensure that there is in fact a journal that would be interested in this particular study. Decisions about which journal(s) should be targeted for submission should be based on the following factors: (1) their likely interest in the study's topic, (2) their likelihood of accepting the article, (3) the prestige of the journal, (4) average length of time in responding to a submission, and (5) the number of other articles any of the authors have recently submitted to the journal. To begin with, there is no point in submitting a manuscript to a journal that has no history of publishing articles on that topic. Most journals have an "about the journal" section or mission statement on their Web page and in the front or back of each issue. This should be read in advance to determine whether the journal is likely to be interested in the topic. The likelihood of a journal's acceptance of a manuscript cannot be known in advance, but there are certain factors to take into account—even after it has been determined that in general the topic would be of interest. One such factor is the rigor of the study in relation to the rigor of studies described in articles accepted by the journal. For example, in some journals the articles tend to describe the utilization of cutting-edge multivariate statistical techniques in large-sample probability designs. A small sample study using chi-squares and correlations would probably not be of interest to this journal. A journal that prefers quantitative studies would not be ideal for submission of a paper utilizing qualitative analyses. Another factor in selecting a journal is prestige. The researcher should aim to submit the manuscript to the most prestigious journal likely to accept it. Prestige is not something that can easily be quantified, but some thought should be given to this, as it helps both the agency and the researcher to be published in well-respected journals. Although response time should not be a major factor, it is also something to consider. If the agency-based researcher follows the advice provided in chapter 2 regarding not sharing findings until the manuscript has been accepted for publication, then it will be a hardship for the agency to have to wait an inordinate amount of time for an article to be accepted. Many journals take as long as six months to respond to the submission, but ones that are known to take longer should probably be avoided. Remember, it is the length of time between submission and acceptance that is important, not the length of time between submission and publication. Once the manuscript has been accepted for publication, the findings can be shared with others, because the researcher knows that they have been approved by peer reviewers. The final factor to consider when selecting a journal is the number of articles already published and under review in that journal. Many journals do not want to publish too many articles by the same author. Unless there is some compelling reason to return to the same journal, it is advisable to submit manuscripts to several different journals (though not the same manuscript to more than one journal at a time, which is not allowed).

Once a journal has been identified for a particular manuscript, the submission guidelines for that journal should be carefully reviewed. These can usually be found in the back of each issue as well as on the journal's Web site. Most journals follow American Psychological Association (APA) guidelines. The APA publication manual should be purchased and readily accessible to the researcher as a vital resource. Following these guidelines are essential for writing research papers. However, there is certain information that APA does not provide but that is standard in the field. For example, most journals accept manuscripts that are twenty to twenty-five pages in length, double-spaced. One- or 1.5-inch margins should be used and the font should be Times Roman, 12 point. The pages should be single sided. Each journal provides more specific information, such as the exact number of words the abstract should be (this varies from journal to journal), the exact layout of the title and first page, where the running head should be placed, and so forth. These guidelines should be followed as closely as possible. Many manuscripts can be submitted electronically, but not all. The researcher with an active list of papers should develop a detailed tracking system for monitoring the status of articles submitted for publication.

Most journals acknowledge receipt of submission within a month of submission date. If this has not been received, some follow-up might be necessary (including resubmitting the manuscript). That is why it is important to track the status in order to make sure that the manuscript is in fact moving through the process. The review period technically begins once the manuscript has been received by the journal. Typically, the confirmation letter will include information about average wait time. There is no point in contacting the publisher about publication decisions prior to the end of the review time, as this will only annoy the editors. However, if the time period has expired and no word has been received, it is acceptable to place a phone call and request information on the status of the manuscript.

The journal's decision regarding the manuscript always comes in the form of a written response. Rarely is a manuscript accepted with no revisions necessary (and as the prestige of the journal increases, so does the level of expertise of the reviewers and the level of difficulty of the requested changes). The three main responses are outright rejection, rejection with an invitation to resubmit if substantial changes are made, and acceptance with the provision that certain changes are made. Although the rejection with offer to resubmit might seem like bad news, it is not necessarily so. In many cases, the revisions requested are not only possible but clearly desirable, as they will improve the manuscript and are therefore well worth taking the time to implement. The first step in digesting the information provided by the journal is to read the cover letter from the editor. This letter provides information about the status of the manuscript, summarizes major concerns if there are any, and offers a timeline for resubmitting the manuscript. The second step is to read the reviewer's comments. These are offered in full to the researcher (anonymously, of course) and should be read several times to process the information. Often, there are three reviews presented and, in some cases, there is consensus and overlap among them about the major problems with a paper, but that is not always the case. The next step is to make a list of all the concerns raised by the reviewers, with an eye to determining whether these can be addressed. It is usually clear from the tone and content of the reviewer's comments which suggestions are "deal breakers" and which are merely suggestions for improvement. So it is important to determine whether these "deal breaker" suggestions can be implemented and whether the researcher agrees with them. Sometimes it is possible to respond to a review of a manuscript by arguing why a certain suggestion cannot be accomplished (for example, if the data are simply not available). But if a suggestion is clearly a deal breaker for the reviewer, then the researcher should either address the concern or not bother resubmitting the manuscript. Manuscripts should only be resubmitted if the vast majority of the suggestions are addressed. Sometimes, the researcher makes adjustments to the manuscript that are not actually deemed to be the best choice, simply to appease the reviewers. Unless the researcher believes that these changes violate the truth or the spirit of the work, they should be made.

Assuming that the vast majority of the comments made by the reviewers can be addressed and assuming the researcher agrees to these changes, then the manuscript should be revised and resubmitted. All possible changes suggested by the reviewers should be incorporated into the revised version of the manuscript. This revised version should be an exact replica of the original file with only the suggested changes made. The title and everything else should stay the same. The name of the file should be the same except for a notation that it is the revised version. The date on the cover page should remain the original submission date, with the words "resubmitted on [date]" added beneath it.

The most important aspect of submitting the revised version of a manuscript is the cover letter addressed to the editor. This letter should begin as follows:

> Thank you very much for the thoughtful and timely review of the above referenced manuscript. I was very pleased with the reviewers' suggestion that the manuscript be resubmitted after revisions have been made. I am very pleased to be able to resubmit a revised manuscript to you, incorporating the feedback of the three reviewers. Below, I outline the ways in which the manuscript has been revised. I believe that the revisions have

Figure 15.1
Sample cover letter to journal in response to manuscript review

---

REVIEWER # 1

Comment 1: The terms "children" and "youth" are used interchangeably. Only one should be used.
Response: The term "youth" is now used consistently throughout the paper when it refers to the sample for this study.
Comment 2: Page 3 (top) Sentence beginning "Specifically, children..." Could you provide a reference to evidence this point?
Response: A reference has been provided (page 3).
Comment 3: Other information would have also been informative, since we are given nothing about these children other than that they reside in out-of-home placement (e.g., abuse hx, comorbidity for other types of behavior problems, how long they have been out of the home, how long in the placement, etc.).
Response: Currently, background information are not available regarding the sample. Ideally, this can be the subject of future research efforts.

REVIEWER # 2

Comment 1: Please include the Smith and Jones (1998) reference in introduction.
Response: The Smith and Jones (1998) reference was quite relevant to the argument made in the introduction and has been added accordingly (see page 2 and 7 of the revised introduction).
Comment 2: A table of the means and standard deviations for the CSBI scale would be helpful.
Response: A table of the means and standard deviation of the CSBI have been added (see table 3, page 26).

---

vastly improved the manuscript. Of course, I would be willing to make additional revisions based on further feedback from the reviewers. Thank you again for your interest in this manuscript.

The rest of the cover letter should present all of the concerns of each reviewer and the ways in which they have been addressed. Figure 15.1 presents an example of such a cover letter. In some cases, the suggestions for improvement are not possible, especially when additional references that do not exist are suggested or additional data that are not available are asked for. Unless this is a "deal breaker" type of request, simply acknowledge that this is a valid suggestion and point out that it is not possible at this time. End the cover letter with the following statement: "Thank you again for the opportunity to revise the manuscript. The comments and suggestions of the reviewers were quite helpful and the revisions have improved the paper considerably. Please let me know if any additional revisions will be necessary." Resubmitted manuscripts sometimes are sent back to the original reviewers. Therefore, it could take another month or longer to hear whether the revised version has been accepted for publication. If the vast majority (and all of the important) suggestions have been addressed, the manuscript will most likely be accepted for publication. Sometimes, additional revisions are requested and another revised version is created and resubmitted, along with another cover letter outlining the ways in which the new revised version is responsive to these additional concerns raised by the reviewers.

In the event that the manuscript has been rejected from the journal with no invitation to revise and resubmit, it is possible to submit it to another journal. There is no rule that says that this cannot be done. However, the concerns of the reviewers of the first journal should be taken into account. For example, if the reviewers' concerns are deemed so damning that the researcher no longer has confidence in the paper, there is no point in resubmitting it. On the other hand, it is possible that the manuscript does not meet the standards of a particular journal but could still be accepted by another. This is a judgment call on the part of the researcher. In any event, the manuscript can be revised prior to submitting elsewhere, and some if not at all of the comments made by the first journal's reviewers can be used as a guide for improving the manuscript prior to submitting it elsewhere.

Presenting the Results to Practitioners and Policymakers in the Field

Presumably the findings—if statistically significant and meaningful—would be of interest to program and administrative staff throughout the agency and to program staff in similar programs in other agencies. At the same time, it is usually not feasible to hold informal presentation sessions for program staff in other agencies and, depending upon the size of the agency itself, it might not even be feasible to present the findings personally within the sponsoring agency. It is, therefore, often the case that the findings are summarized in a brief report and distributed that way. Some agencies have an internal staff newsletter, and this could be used as a format for sharing the findings of a study with staff. The report should briefly state the purpose of the study, provide some basic information about the methods, and then present the results with a few graphs, charts, and/or bulleted points. This should be followed by a listing of the practical/clinical implications of the results. If an agency has conducted a series of studies on a related theme, these could be put together in a topic-based newsletter and bracketed by a forward by the agency's president/CEO and a commentary by a notable clinician or researcher in the field. This newsletter could then be distributed to professionals throughout the field.

Presentation of the findings to program staff, agency- and system-wide staff, and the professional community will hopefully lead to the identification of future research studies, as the cycle of question formation, investigation, knowledge development, and question formation continues.

Presenting the Results to Clients and Other Nonprofessional Stakeholders

The findings of many child welfare research studies might also be of keen interest to clients and other nonprofessionals in the field. To that end, the researcher should aim to identify the general and specific nonprofessionals to whom the findings could be shared. At a minimum, this could include the specific individuals who participated in the study, and at a maximum, the population from which the study sample was drawn.

Clearly, the format and tone of reports written for nonprofessionals will need to be very different than reports to staff or manuscripts written for academic publications. Several key points should be kept in mind.

The first caution is to keep the report or presentation brief. A report written for nonprofessionals should be brief and formatted in a way accessible to the lay reader. There should be a minimum of extraneous information provided that would deter the layperson from reading the report. Second, language should at all times be accessible and not reliant on any jargon. Use of technical terms should be kept to a minimum. The goal is not to impress the reader with the researcher's vast education but rather to explain the main points in a way that can be appreciated by the reader. Additionally, the report should be useful to the reader and contain the information necessary for the reader to grasp the main purpose and findings of the study. Finally, the report should be written in unbiased and nonjudgmental language.

It is possible that a written report is not the best way to share information about research findings with clients. It may make more sense for agency staff to make presentations to clients (at events or meetings they would have attended anyway to avoid scheduling additional appointments for them) at which the findings can be shared and an opportunity for discussion and input provided.

The spirit of this endeavor must be that there can be a sharing of thoughts and feelings rather than conveying the impression that the experts have important information to impart. The clients (as in all cases) should be treated as individuals with valuable ideas to share and deserving of respect and consideration.

Conclusion

No study is complete until the findings have been shared with at least some of the study's stakeholders, including administrative and program staff within the agency participating in the study, the clients who may be affected by the study's findings, and researchers and clinicians in the professional and academic communities. Reports and papers must be tailored to each of these different audiences. Early drafts of results should be shared with key internal stakeholders to ensure that the findings are interpreted appropriately and sensitively.

[PART 5]

Special Topics in Agency Practice

Continuous Quality Improvement
in Agency Practice

In this chapter, the following topics will be discussed, following the introduction of the chapter scenario:

- What is continuous quality improvement (CQI)?
- The researcher's role in CQI
- The ten components of CQI for the Council on Accreditation

CHAPTER SCENARIO

A child welfare agency has decided to become accredited in order to obtain the prestige and credibility that accompanies approval by an accreditation organization. After considering two options, the agency decides to seek accreditation from the Council on Accreditation (COA), as this is the organization that accredits the vast majority of child welfare agencies and seems to offer the best fit (the other option under consideration was the Joint Commission on Accreditation of Healthcare Organizations, JCAHO). The agency gives itself twelve months to prepare the pre–site visit material and asks the agency's researcher to spearhead the preparation of the efforts related to standards pertaining to continuous quality improvement.

Overview of the Topic

In the current performance- and outcome-driven competitive environment, social service agencies need to achieve standards of excellence in all areas. One way to achieve and demonstrate excellence is through accreditation. Child welfare agencies that seek accreditation do so with either JCAHO or COA, with a preference for the social service model of COA, as opposed to the medical model of JCAHO (for a comparison, see Pecora, Seelig, Zirps, and Davis 1996). Agencies seeking such accreditation believe that it will confer many advantages, including prestige, credibility, and improved services. For example, a 2003 report found that COA accreditation was believed by agencies to be associated with reduced caseload size and enhanced morale among the child welfare workforce (United States Government Accounting Office 2003). Accreditation is also deemed beneficial for fundraising and public relations, and especially as more agencies seek and obtain COA accreditation, those without it will be viewed as below industry standards. As of this writing, there are about 1,100 agencies in the United States with COA accreditation (many, but not all, of which are child welfare agencies). Accreditation by COA requires complex and detailed documentation, one section of which pertains to continuous quality improvement. Standards that pertain to service delivery are called S standards and those that pertain to operations are called G standards. G2 is the set of COA standards pertaining to continuous quality improvement. Within each agency, the structure of the continuous quality improvement process and committee varies as does the researcher's role in continuous quality improvement. What remains constant is that COA has ten components of continuous quality improvement in the G2 standards: (1) stakeholder participation, (2) long-term planning, (3) short-term planning, (4) internal monitoring, (5) case record reviews, (6) outcomes, (7) consumer satisfaction, (8) feedback mechanisms, (9) information management, and (10) corrective action plans.

What Is Continuous Quality Improvement?

Continuous quality improvement (CQI) is a system of data collection and review that allows an agency to monitor, understand, and improve on an ongoing basis all aspects of service delivery and documentation. The philosophy underpinning the name is that continuous quality improvement is an ongoing process of monitoring, learning, and improving. An agency will never reach the point at which it can conclude that quality has been achieved and thus the job of continuous quality improvement is over. The assumption is that services and procedures will always need to be monitored and that something can always be improved. To begin the process, CQI committees are formed representing all service areas in the agency. The CQI committee(s) at an agency are ongoing longstanding committees that should always be in place and hold regularly scheduled meetings.

The following five factors are integral to an agency's CQI plan: (1) strong leadership and commitment to CQI at all levels of an agency to articulate a vision and ensure active participation in CQI, (2) cross-function teamwork and team-based decision making, (3) conceptual links between strategic planning goals and assessment outcome goals of the service delivery process, (4) a consumer-driven philosophy that ensures all consumers know about CQI and have several different types of opportunities to provide their perspective on both CQI and service delivery in general, and (5) an empirical orientation, in which data are collected to systematically assess quality and make decisions about how to improve it.

Strong Leadership and Commitment

CQI functions best when the leadership within an agency is committed to the process and ensures that appropriate and necessary resources are allocated to it. Ideally, there will be one or more CQI "champions" within the agency who value, understand, and push for a stronger and expanded role for CQI. CQI needs to be both "top down" and "bottom up" to function well. The "top-down" part means that agency leadership, starting with the agency's board of directors, conveys the agency's commitment to CQI. Examples of leadership commitment include ensuring that high-level staffpeople have the time and responsibility to participate in regular CQI meetings, top-level review of CQI reports and projects, and circulation of agencywide materials regarding CQI and containing messages from agency leadership indicating their support and commitment to it. The "bottom-up" component is reflected throughout the CQI process (see below), in the many ways that staff is involved in CQI activities, because they have unique insight into services and programs and are the ones that ultimately deliver the services to the consumers. Many gaps and areas for improvement in service provision are discovered first by line staff. CQI offers a continual opportunity for them to share this information with senior management and explore ways to address issues and improve practice.

Cross-Function Teamwork

CQI is a process-driven enterprise, not a content-driven enterprise. There-fore, CQI teams should be composed of staff at all levels and across all functions of an agency. This enhances the quality of the CQI work itself and sends a message throughout the agency that the entire agency is com-mitted to CQI. It also creates an opportunity for staff who usually operate within their "silos" to get to know and interact with other staff through-out the agency, creating, ideally, greater cohesion and commitment to the agency (as opposed to commitment to one's own department or work group).

Conceptual Links Between Strategic Goal and Outcomes

CQI is designed to be a seamless process, in which all the various tasks are knitted together to create a coherent quality assessment program. The start-ing place for this is the agency's strategic plan. Everything else should flow logically from this. For example, the outcome measures should be related to the short-term plans, which should be logically related to the long-term goals in the strategic plan. In this way, all aspects of CQI are working to-gether to assess the overall quality of the service delivery as philosophically developed and outlined in the agency's strategic plan.

Consumer Driven

Quality of service delivery is to some extent a subjective assessment made by the recipients of the services. Consumer and staff input into the CQI process is, therefore, a vital component of CQI. It is not enough to mea-sure length of stay or count the number of parents who attend their child's treatment conference (although these are both important components of many CQI plans). It is as important to assess consumer satisfaction with the provided services that are offered to shorten length of stay and to as-sess how parents perceive the treatment plans (perhaps along dimensions of inclusiveness and helpfulness). Thus, feedback mechanisms for client and staff input into the CQI process must be woven throughout all aspects of CQI.

Empirical Orientation

CQI involves the systematic collection and analysis of data in order to measure and assess its quality and make decisions about how to improve it. Thus, CQI is by nature an empirical process that follows as much as possible the scientific method (see chapter 2). This does not mean that every aspect of CQI should resemble a paper publishable in a peer-reviewed journal. What it does mean is that CQI projects should begin with problem formulation, then proceed with identification of the constructs and appropriate measures of them, then to the development of a meaningful sampling and data collection plan, and conclude with utilization of appropriate data analysis and reporting techniques. The results should be submitted to the senior CQI staff committee for review and decision making.

The Ten Components of COA's CQI Plan

Stakeholder Participation

The goal of this component is that representatives from all stakeholder groups, including persons served, personnel from all levels of the organization, and other stakeholders (board members, funders, other agencies) will participate in the CQI process. This goal cannot be met with a single set of activities. It is a philosophy that must support the entire CQI process. Examples of activities that would meet this requirement include (1) sharing the content and results of CQI projects with personnel in all levels of the agency, such as posting throughout agency offices flyers that explain what CQI is and how different stakeholders can be involved; (2) creating an agency newsletter or allocating a portion of an existing newsletter to CQI activities; and (3) ensuring that the committee of the agency's board of directors responsible for CQI is aware of the CQI plan and receives ongoing reports on CQI activities. At all stages of CQI, staff should be asking themselves how stakeholders can become even more involved in CQI.

Long-Term Planning

According to COA, each agency must undergo a strategic planning process every four years. The strategic plan should clarify the organization's mission, values, and mandates; establish goals and objectives; assess the agency's strengths and weaknesses; assess human resource needs; and formulate strategies for meeting the agency's goals. All levels throughout the agency must be involved in this process, including clients, service delivery staff, administrative staff, and board members. The plan must be outcome driven, endorsed by all levels of the agency, and comprehensive. Consistent with the first component (stakeholder participation), the plan should be known to all members of the agency. In particular, every staffperson should be able to explain what the mission of the agency is and what the agency has identified as its key outcome goals. Many agencies hire professional companies to oversee the strategic planning process to ensure that state-of-the-art practice is used and that no one internal staffperson imposes his or her vision onto the process. The strategic plan becomes the guiding framework for the agency and its CQI plan. The CQI committee supports and monitors the application of the plan through the other CQI activities.

Short-Term Planning

Each of the organization's programs or services annually conducts short-term planning in support of the organization's long-term plan. The short-term plans should identify short-term goals, methods for assessing progress toward goals, associated timelines, and personnel designated to carry out the tasks necessary to meet the goals. That is, each service should know what the long-term goals of the agency are and identify one or two short-term goals appropriate for their specific program and consistent with the long-term goals. Examples for an agency whose overall long-term goal is to improve the well-being of children could include preventing psychiatric hospitalization of youth in foster care, reducing disruptions of adoptions (when a planned adoption becomes no longer viable), eliminating incidents of abuse and neglect in foster homes, preventing running-away behaviors of youth in group homes, and so forth. The plans should be measurable and objective. They should—but do not have to be—linked to the outcomes measured (see below).

Outcomes

According to COA, there are five possible domains for short-term goals: (1) change in clinical status, (2) change in functional status, (3) health/welfare/ safety, (4) permanency, and (5) another life indicator. COA has identified

Figure 16.1
COA-required goals by service type

Domain	Services assessed in each domain
Clinical status	Substance abuse, group living
Functional status	Substance abuse, shelter/crisis nursery, adoption, home visitor, family preservation, foster/kinship, respite, group living, child care, prevention
Health/welfare/ safety	Substance abuse, shelter/crisis nursery, adoption, home visitor, family preservation, foster/kinship, respite, group living child care, prevention
Permanency	Adoption, foster, and kinship
Other quality-of- life indices	Substance abuse, Shelter/crisis nursery, adoption, home visitor, family preservation, foster/kinship, respite, group living, child care, prevention

certain services that must assess outcomes in one or more of these specific outcome domains. Figure 16.1 lists the goals and outcomes that need to be assessed for each different type of service area. Not every service must have every type of goal and outcome. However, for each goal developed, there must be a measurable outcome that the CQI team (or subset thereof) will assess. Usually, there is more than one way to operationalize and measure any one outcome and it will be particularly useful for a researcher to be involved in the development of these outcome studies.

Two primary approaches a researcher can consider include an entry cohort study and ongoing monitoring. Each provides a different type of information. In an entry cohort outcome study of, for example, runaway behaviors, a cohort of youth entering a particular service (e.g., group home, maternity shelter, and so forth) is followed from entry into the program to discharge from the program. An entry cohort is defined as a group of youth who enter the program during a designated period of time and are followed longitudinally until they leave the program. This entry cohort should begin far enough back in time that the majority have already left the program and should be large enough to be meaningful (e.g., a sample of ten is too small to have confidence in the findings). Using administrative data, the researcher can provide a report on the total number and proportion of the youth in this cohort who ever ran away while in the program and the number of times each youth ran away. The following year, the CQI committee could produce a replication report that looks at exactly the same phenomenon with the subsequent cohort (youth entered in the year following the year of entry of the cohort in the first outcome report), in order to determine whether runaway behaviors increased or decreased over time. In addition, even within a single cohort, it could be determined whether the agency met some predetermined benchmark or goal (such as no more than 20 percent of the group home youth will ever run away while in the program). The outcome target should be developed in advance and can be revised every year based on the CQI committee's goals for the next year. If the data consistently look good (the target is always met and the target is deemed to be meaningful), then at some point the CQI committee could decide to stop monitoring runaway behaviors in the group homes. On the other hand, if the data are so poor (a reasonable target is never met), the CQI team could request a corrective action plan (see below).

An alternative approach to the entry cohort study is to monitor the number of runaways each month within the designated program, with the short-term goal of reducing runaways. Rather than following a group of youth over time, every youth in the program as of the time of data collection would be included, regardless of when the youth entered the program. It would be important in such an approach to control for varying denominators. That is, in one month the designated program might have had 300 care days (10 beds filled for each of 30 days) while in another month the program might have had 341 care days (11 beds filled for 31 days). Because the denominator changes, a comparison should be converted into rates (number of runaways divided by the number of care days). As an example, 15 runaway episodes in the first month would result in a rate of 5 percent (15 divided by 300), while 15 runaway episodes in the second month would result in a rate of 4 percent (15 divided by 341). Note that the absolute number of runaways did not change, but the rate did.

Internal Monitoring

Internal monitoring requires that the agency regularly evaluates its own systems and procedures in order to improve performance. This includes the following five components: the agency (1) regularly monitors internal processes related to outreach, intake assessment, service delivery, and human resource deployment, training, and supervision in order to identify barriers and opportunities for better serving clients; (2) conducts annual risk management reviews including risks related to research and risks associated with compliance with licensing and mandatory reporting laws; (3) conducts quarterly risk management reviews of practice related to limits on the freedom of movement of clients; (4) conducts a quarterly review of all grievances, incidents, and accidents of staff and clients as well as review of issues associated with dispensing or prescribing medications and review of environmental risks; and (5) reviews results of all internal reviews and finds ways to integrate those findings into the CQI process.

Case Record Reviews

The COA goal is to have 15 percent of all charts reviewed each year. This can be done annually, bi-annually, quarterly, or monthly. The purpose of the record reviews is to ensure that the services are being delivered as designated and that the records include the appropriate and necessary documentation. Each agency can develop its own case record review form but must use the COA-approved methodology as defined in their guidelines. COA guidelines require that case records of 15 percent of the clients within each program should be identified and reviewed once a year, with about one-fourth of the selected cases being reviewed each quarter. COA also requires that all levels of staff within an agency participate in the record review, that both open and closed records are reviewed, and that some high-risk cases are included in the review each year.

A researcher could be helpful in designing a sampling and data collection strategy that maximizes the rigor of the process. Ideally, the selection of the charts should be overseen by the CQI team to meet COA standards of random selection. There are four complicating factors with the record review requirement: (1) selection of records, (2) honesty of reviews, (3) generality/ specificity of the review form, and (4) need for guidelines for the review form.

The first issue to be tackled is what constitutes 15 percent of the caseload of records. Unless there is no turnover in a program in a given year, counting the number of clients in a program at a given point in time underrepresents the number of cases served in a given year. One way to determine the caseload in a year is to count the number of cases in a program at a point in time (such as of January 1) and then determine how many new clients enter the program over the next twelve-month period. The sum of these two numbers closely approximates the total number of clients served each year. Fifteen percent of this number is the number of charts that should be reviewed for that the program each year. One-fourth of that number is the number that should be reviewed each quarter. For example, if a foster boarding home program serves about six hundred families at any one time, with about one-fourth being replaced each year (about 150 families leave and about 150 new families enter), then it can be estimated that the agency serves about 750 families in any given year, 15 percent of which is 112 families. That is the number that needs to be reviewed each year, resulting in about twenty-eight records being reviewed per quarter. It probably makes sense to obtain a list of all six hundred cases on the roll at any one point in time, randomly select 112, and make that 112 the list of cases to be reviewed for the entire year. Each quarter, twenty-eight should be randomly selected and assigned to the staff for review (if the whole list is given at the beginning of the year to the program staff, staff will have an opportunity to improve the records, possibly creating a false picture of the quality of the records).

The second issue to consider is who should actually conduct the record reviews. This is an issue because it is important to increase the likelihood that the reviewers will be honest about the record even if it puts the program in a bad light. COA's rule is that no staffperson involved in a case can review the record for that case. It is suggested here that an even more stringent rule be followed, in which, as much as possible, individuals completely separate from the program conduct the record reviews. That is, according to COA a caseworker in a foster boarding home program could review a record of another caseworker's foster boarding home case, or, better, a caseworker in a prevention program could review a record of a foster boarding home case for a caseworker and colleague in the next office. The more stringent standard might be that in no way will the coder feel any pressure, desire, or impetus to modify the results of the record review; for example, CQI staff or staff in one location can code records of cases served in another location (if the agency has more than one office or location). The greater distance (programmatic, geographic), the less likely it is that the reviewer will experience any conflict of interest.

The third issue for record reviews is whether the form itself should be general enough to be consistent across programs (e.g., a respite program for Office of Mental Retardation and Developmental Delay clients, a foster home program, a maternity shelter, and so forth) or specific to each program. The more general the questions, the less useful the review might be for each specific program, but the easier it will be to combine the results across programs and create one final report each quarter. The more specific the review, the more it will be necessary to create one record review report for each program or service type. One option is to have some cross-cutting items and some specific items as well. If the agency operates many different types of programs, it can be quite unwieldy to develop several different record review forms. The data will have to be entered into separate databases, analyzed separately, and reported on separately. On the other hand, the data might be or seem more useful for the local program staff who can really see how they are doing with their records.

Regardless of whether there is one universal form or multiple versions of the form, guidelines will need to be developed that provide the reviewers with specific information about how to make coding decisions. For example, if an item on the review form is "all necessary consents are in the chart," a list must be provided in the guidelines about what the required consent forms are for each program type. Without such information, it is likely that the reviewer will simply check "yes" if some consents are there, not knowing that some might be missing. This is even more true if people outside the program area review each other's records. For example, it is unlikely that a foster care supervisor would know what consent forms are necessary for a day care center or that a prevention worker would know what consent forms are required for a group home program. The guidelines will probably need to be developed with a team of front-line staff in conjunction with CQI staff familiar with funding and reporting guidelines. It is also likely that there will be several drafts of the guidelines before a complete, clear, and final version has been developed.

Someone within a central CQI committee will most likely need to take responsibility for overseeing the entire case record review process. For each quarter, there are multiple tasks, starting with selecting the cases to be assigned for review and notifying the local programs of which cases have been selected and providing them with rules about who can and cannot review the cases and current review forms and guidelines. At some point, a reminder notice may need to go out to ensure that everyone is on track. Once the reviews start to come in, they will need to be tracked and reviewed for thoroughness. Cases that were not reviewed on time should be kept track of in order to allow for a system of reminders and notices of which data have not yet been received. Once the reviews are in hand, they will need to be entered, analyzed, and written up in a brief CQI report to be distributed to the appropriate committees and teams for review and discussion. At this point, it might be time to start the process all over again. A yearly calendar of which chart review tasks need to be accomplished each month would probably be helpful.

Consumer Satisfaction

Consumer feedback is a critical component of CQI, as it is one of the key ways that clients have an opportunity to describe their concerns about the agency (there are other ways as well, including a grievance/complaint system) and share ideas about how programs and procedures could be improved. COA has developed such a form but each agency can create its own as well. COA does not have a fixed number or proportion of clients that participate in consumer feedback each year, although the guidelines require a "valid sample." Again, a researcher could be helpful in designing an approach to collecting this data that is as rigorous as possible. Issues to consider include (1) sampling, (2) general versus specific form, (3) administration of the form, and (4) who will administer the form.

Opinions about the services received probably vary widely within any given group of clients. Some will be quite pleased and perceive the staff to be competent and well meaning, while other clients may be very unhappy with the services received and have many specific suggestions for improvement. With the consumer feedback survey, it is vital that every client—the satisfied and the unsatisfied—has an equal chance of participating in the survey. If only the satisfied consumers are surveyed, the results will be glowing, but the agency will miss an important opportunity to engage the unsatisfied ones and will not have access to their opinions and ideas, which could lead to improvements in services. If only the unsatisfied clients are surveyed, then the results will be unrealistically negative, perhaps leading to demoralization among the staff. The ideal sampling strategy is one in which the satisfied and the unsatisfied have an equal chance of participating in the consumer feedback survey. This can best be accomplished through random selection of a group of clients to survey about their experience with the agency. This rules out other more convenient methods of selecting participants for a survey, including handing the survey to everyone who walks through the agency doors (unless every single client must show up within a certain period of time) or asking staff to select clients to give the survey to for completion. It is quite likely that the people who show up or the people whom staff would select would be more inclined to be positive about the agency. Ideally, a list of all current clients can be obtained from the program, from which a certain percentage can be randomly selected to participate in the consumer feedback survey. For many programs, this would be feasible, especially when the staff have equal access to all clients, such as youth in a congregate care program or parents of a home visiting program. In these cases, once the sample has been selected it is not too difficult to invite the selected clients to participate. However, in some cases some clients are much easier to access than others. This is particularly true of biological families of youth in placement or parents in a prevention program in which the primary service takes place at the agency (in which case, some parents attend more regularly and frequently than other parents). The CQI team will need to work in coordination with each program in order to develop a sampling strategy that increases the likelihood that participation is random.

As with the case record review, the issue of whether the form will be general across different service types or specific to service type must be addressed for agencies that provide multiple services or serve multiple clients (parents and children). Some issues ("the staffpeople treat me with respect," "I received a handbook explaining my rights and responsibilities," "the offices are safe") apply to all program and client types; others might be program specific. For example, a question about whether the office is convenient for clients to get to might not apply to participants in a home visiting program.

How the form will be completed is the third issue, with choices being self-report and oral administration of the form (in person or on the phone). If there is any likelihood that the clients cannot read the form or follow the instructions, it is advisable to administer the form orally rather than as a paper-and-pencil measure. It is not appropriate to ask clients if they can read and, if not, if they would like someone to read the form to them. This is potentially embarrassing and likely to produce few requests for assistance with reading. Therefore, it is possible that clients will accept the form and agree to complete it even though they cannot actually read it. This could result in low completion rates or forms completed incorrectly. For this reason, it probably makes sense to have staff administer the forms to clients individually (i.e., read the items, offer the response choices, and check the selected response).

Who will administer the form to the clients is another important issue to consider. It is vital that the clients do not feel pressured to participate or to say something positive. It is also important that their confidentiality be maintained and that there are no repercussions should the client be less than positive about the agency. For these reasons, the staff providing the service should not be asked to administer the feedback survey to their own clients. It is highly unlikely that the clients will feel comfortable being honest in such a situation. It should be clear by now that this cannot be done by someone within the program. There would be no way to protect the confidentiality of the responses and it is not likely that the respondent would be honest. If at all possible, research staff, CQI staff, other staff throughout the agency, interns, students, and other individuals who do not have a vested interest in the program should be hired to conduct the surveys.

Surveys can be conducted over the telephone or in person, depending upon ease of access. For example, youth in congregate care programs can be surveyed in person, because they tend to be easily accessible in the evening and may feel more comfortable answering in person rather than over the telephone (which might not be in a private location in the home). On the other hand, foster parents might be easier to survey on the telephone in the evening when the children are sleeping, as opposed to when they come in to the office for appointments and training. At these times they may be preoccupied with watching children and tending to other issues. Program staff should participate in the development of a program-by-program strategy for engaging participants in the survey process. The two major questions to consider at all times are: (1) Will the responses be truthful, so that the data are useful? And (2) is there any coercion or conflict of interest at play in the methods used?

Another way to assess consumer satisfaction is to administer an exit interview of clients leaving a program. This should not replace ongoing consumer feedback surveys, as the sampling is biased (the more difficult or more troubled clients stay longer, while the less needy or vulnerable have shorter stays and therefore are overrepresented in the sample of exit interviews conducted in any given year), but it can be a nice supplement to an agency's consumer feedback plan, because there is some reason to believe that clients will be more forthcoming about their experience if they know there can be no ramifications for subsequent relationships and services. It is also a time when the client can look back over the whole service experience and provide a different kind of perspective than that available to clients still receiving services. Yet another benefit is that some questions can only be asked at the time of departure from a program (such as what the best and worst parts of the program were, how the client feels about next steps, does the client feel prepared for next steps, does the client know how to recognize the need for future services and how to obtain them, etc.). In addition, an exit interview represents one last chance to demonstrate to the client that the agency cares about his or her feelings, thoughts, and experiences while in the program.

Feedback Mechanisms

COA's CQI goal is for the agency to provide clear, accurate, and timely information regarding all aspects of the CQI process to its service recipients, governing body, personnel, and stakeholders. Thus, the task is to determine how the results of CQI projects (outcome studies, case record reviews, consumer feedback surveys) are shared throughout the agency and its clients. There is no one structure for accomplishing this, and most likely each agency will develop multiple means of providing feedback to staff and clients about the CQI process. Examples of activities that would meet this goal include an agencywide newsletter reporting on results of various CQI projects, rotating members of a CQI committee who are then responsible for sharing the projects and reports within their designated area within the agency, inclusion of clients on various CQI committees, and the reporting of updated information on the agency's intranet about CQI projects. Throughout the life of an agency's CQI endeavor, staff should be asking themselves whether all relevant parties have access to information about CQI and opportunities for commenting on the findings of CQI activities as well as on the CQI process itself. It might be advisable, for example, to include a few items on the consumer feedback survey asking about CQI (such as whether the client feels informed about the agency's CQI process, whether the client is asked about how he or she thinks programs can be improved, whether the client would like more opportunities to share his or her opinions with agency staff, and so forth).

Information Management

Each agency must maintain all the information that is necessary to effectively plan, manage, and evaluate its services. Information systems must be designed to protect the confidentiality of the clients and have necessary protections (firewalls, passwords, backup mechanisms, data entry and cleaning systems) to ensure that the data are accessible and accurate. The agency should have individuals on staff who can ensure that the technology is updated, safe, and confidential. They should be able to provide the necessary assistance so that staff can perform their job functions.

Corrective Action Plans

The tenth component of CQI, according to COA, is a mechanism for developing an action plan to address any issue that indicates a problem arising from any of the other agency activities. If an outcome study indicates that a program is consistently not able to meet a reasonable target or whose

Figure 16.2

Conceptual framework for corrective action plan

PLAN, DO, CHECK, ACT:

A four-step process of continuous quality improvement

When CQI findings identify a problem, a corrective action plan is developed, with the following four components: Plan, Do, Check, and Act. These can be seen as a continuous process in which the last phase of one project (ACT) leads to the first phase (PLAN) of the next.

PLAN

Clarify current knowledge of the process

Uncover the root cause of the variation

Identify an interdisciplinary multilevel team

Develop the plan

DO

Test the proposed improvement

Collect and analyze data

Draw conclusions

CHECK

Determine if process should be

    Adopted

    Abandoned

    Adjusted

    Standardized

    Incorporated into policy

Continue to monitor gains

ACT

Analyze results of proposed improvement

    Trending of data

    Flow charts

    Run charts

    Bar graphs

    Internal benchmarking:

    Evaluate the results

Did the process improve as expected?

What do our consumers think?

performance even in one year is so far from the targeted outcome that serious concern is raised about the adequacy of the services it provides, or if the consumer feedback survey reveals consistent or pervasive discontent with one or more aspects of services (clients feel disrespected, unsafe, uncared for), or if the case record reviews indicate serious lapses in mandatory documentation that could jeopardize funding streams, a corrective action plan should be developed by the CQI team (or a subset of its members) to immediately address the problem. A corrective action plan has four steps: (1) plan, (2) do, (3) check, and (4) act. These four actions represent ongoing steps in an improvement plan and are presented in figure 16.2.

In the first phase, the team plans an intervention or remedy that addresses the problem at hand. This should come as a result of serious and focused discussion about the problem and its likely root cause. The second phase involves the implementation of the intervention (e.g., staff training to improve rapport with clients, improving the lighting and hiring more guards to increase safety at the building, and so forth). In the third phase, data are collected to determine whether the problem has been remedied. This might entail an additional outcome study, a focus group with clients or staff, or a follow-up survey in order to gauge whether there has been improvement in the designated problem area. Following analysis of these data, the team will decide how to act. If the data indicate that the problem has been addressed, the intervention might be repeated as necessary (training all new staff), established as ongoing (repeated training regarding certain documentation issues), or discontinued. It is even possible that it will be concluded that the intervention did not result in improvement, and in response a new and different intervention will be developed. In this case, the cycle of plan, do, check, and act will begin again.

The Researcher's Role in CQI

There is no one fixed role for a researcher on the CQI team. In some agencies, the leader of CQI might be a researcher; in another agency, a researcher might sit on the CQI team and provide ongoing advice; while in a third agency, a researcher might only be consulted on an ad hoc basis about a subset of discrete CQI activities. There is no one model and no clearly determined best way to incorporate a research perspective into CQI. Ideally, if the agency has access to a researcher (as a consultant or on staff), that person could assist with the development of the consumer feedback survey and methods as well as the development of the case record review form and methods. A researcher can also be helpful in developing sampling strategies for outcomes studies, consumer feedback surveys, and record reviews. There may be times when the researcher is placed in the position of having to explain why something is not feasible or appropriate when the rest of the committee does not understand or want to acknowledge that fact. It is the researcher's job to clarify what the rigors of science involve and let the committee make the ultimate decision. At the same time, the researcher needs to be mindful that CQI activities do not need to meet the standards of publishable science. For example, a literature review is not necessary for the outcome studies: a few sentences explaining what the outcome is would be sufficient. Likewise, benchmarks for targets and for consumer feedback do not need to be consistent with the field; they simply must be meaningful for the agency.

Conclusion

CQI is a process whereby a child welfare agency can monitor its programs, services, and activities on an ongoing basis in order to continuously improve the agency. CQI is a component of the two major accreditation programs for child welfare agencies, COA and JCAHO. Many child welfare agencies select COA, which has ten aspects of CQI. If done well, the ten components of COA's continuous quality improvement plan can be used to improve cohesion among various programs and departments within an agency, align practice with agency vision and mission, and monitor and improve objective services as well as clients' subjective experience of the service delivery process and outcomes. Integrating research techniques as much as possible into the CQI plan and systems can improve the rigor and quality of the data collected, as well as its utilization.

Agency-Based Program Evaluation

In this chapter, the following topics will be discussed, following the introduction of the chapter scenario and the brief literature review:

- Deciding to conduct a program evaluation
- Conducting a prospective summative program evaluation
- Conducting a prospective formative program evaluation

CHAPTER SCENARIO

An agency that operates a foster boarding home program has started providing additional home-based services to families following trial and final discharges in order to prevent failed reunifications and reentry into the system. As an innovative program model funded strictly by external foundation grants, the agency is eager to determine whether the program is effective. An independent researcher is hired to conduct a program evaluation. It is anticipated that, if positive, the findings will be widely shared with other child welfare agencies as well as family advocates in the child welfare community.

BRIEF LITERATURE REVIEW: INTERVENTIONS TO SUPPORT
REUNIFICATION

The twin goals of the child welfare system are to provide every child
with a safe and permanent home. Whenever possible, reunification
with the child's biological family is the preferred outcome for children
in out-of-home placement, even for children who have been removed
due to serious abuse or neglect by the parent (Pecora, Whittaker,
Maluccio, Barth, and Plotnick 1992). This policy preference is borne
out in the fact that of the children with established case plan goals,
over half are slated to be reunified with their birth family (Children's
Bureau 2003). Longitudinal data indicate that for the vast majority of
children removed from home, reunification with a family or relative is
in fact the likely outcome. For example, Connell, Katz, Saunders, and
Tebes (2006) reported that family reunification was the outcome for at
least 49 percent of their sample of 6,700 youth who entered out-of-
home care during a four-year period. Because 24 percent of the sample
was still in care, rates of reunification will be even higher when all of
the youth in the sample have completed their stays.

Unfortunately, previous studies have suggested that roughly 30
percent of reunified foster children reenter foster care (Berrick, Needell, Barth, and Johnson-Reid 1998; Frame, Berrick, and Brodowski
2000). Nationally, rates of reentry following reunification have been
estimated to be about 17 percent (National Clearinghouse on Child
Abuse and Neglect 2001). As Festinger (1994) pointed out, some of
the discrepancies in these rates are due to variation in sample characteristics as well as in definitions of reentry.

Factors associated with the return to foster care following reunification have been identified in previous research. For example, Miller,
Fisher, Fetrow, and Jordan (2005) found that the following variables
significantly differentiated between failed and successful reunifications: parental utilization of substance abuse treatment; child utilization of special educational services; child utilization of individual,
family, or group therapy; overall parenting skill level; appropriate use
of discipline; and quality of neighborhood. Systemic factors may also
be at play. For example, McDonald, Bryson, and Poertner (2006) studied the relationship between length of time in care and likelihood of

(continued)

reentry in thirty-three counties in Oklahoma and found that counties that routinely reunified children within six months experienced higher rates of reentry than those that reunified the majority of children after six months. The association between shorter stays and reentry was also found in other states as well (e.g., Wulczyn 2004).

There is some concern that the Adoption and Safe Families Act (ASFA), with its compressed timelines for reunification, will result in children being discharged to their families before they or their parents are really ready (Cordero 2004). Thus there is a clear need for a new slate of research on the topic of reentry rates and factors associated with reentry now that ASFA has been implemented.

Deciding to Conduct a Program Evaluation

Program evaluation has a long history, one tied to the advent of federally funded programs. In 1967, Suchman published a review of evaluation methods, and by the 1970s, evaluation had become a well-defined field (Rossi, Lipsey, and Freeman 2004). Since that time, much attention has been placed on the effectiveness of interventions and programs that are publicly funded.

Many agencies, especially in response to the recent push for "accountability," have become increasingly interested in program evaluation. There is often the belief that at the end of the day the program will be found to be "effective" and such findings can be used to encourage more program funding and support, greater utilization of the program, enhanced agency pride and prestige, and perhaps recognition of the program as a model that can be disseminated outside of the host agency. In addition, program staff and agency administrators want to know if what they are doing "works" by some objective standard. Another impetus for program evaluation comes from the funders of programs, who often attach research dollars and evaluation requirements to program grants. The funders, too, want to know if their dollars are being spent wisely. It is also believed that program evaluation can provide insight into which aspects of a program are effective and perhaps what adjustments could be made to further enhance program performance. Needless to say, there are many reasons for agencies to conduct program evaluations.

When a researcher is called in to conduct a program evaluation, there are two issues that must be addressed immediately. The first is whether the evaluation is to be formative or summative (Scriven 1967), and the second is whether the evaluation will be prospective or retrospective. The first choice pertains to the goals of the evaluation and the second to its timing in relation to service delivery.

Formative evaluations are designed to describe and analyze the process of program implementation. Information is collected about how much and which specific components of the program participants are receiving, the nature and degree of variation in service delivery, and, perhaps, how the program staff and clients perceive and feel about the program. This information is summarized and presented to the program stakeholders with information about how to improve service delivery.

Summative evaluations, on the other hand, are designed to assess the effectiveness of the program. The primary question is whether the program is achieving its intended outcomes. Questions are asked about improvement over time in key outcome domains, which can then be attributed to participation in the program. Usually, such improvements in the program participants are compared to those in a group of individuals who did not participate in the program.

Retrospective evaluations (post hoc) are conducted after the participants have completed their involvement in the program. Information is collected from existing program documents and perceptions of the program are obtained as a reflection on the entire experience rather than as an unfolding process. Program participation has occurred, whatever data can be used have already been collected, and it is the evaluator's job to make sense of the existing data to shed light on how the program service components were delivered to the participants and whether the participants improved in the identified outcome domains.

Prospective evaluations are planned prior to service delivery and are carried out simultaneously with program participation. The evaluator is involved in the design of the study from the beginning, having a hand in development of recruitment strategies, selection of measures, and overseeing the entire data collection and analysis process as it unfolds.

Based on these descriptions, it is evident that there are four potential evaluation scenarios: (1) retrospective formative evaluations, (2) prospective formative evaluations, (3) retrospective summative evaluations, and (4) prospective summative evaluations. Figure 17.1 presents a brief comparison of these four possible scenarios. In a retrospective formative evaluation, the program has already served the clients and the evaluator is asked to analyze existing program participation data (attendance sheets, staff logs, and so forth) in order to describe patterns of participation and service delivery. Us-

Figure 17.1
Four program evaluation scenarios

Type of evaluation

Timing	Formative	Summative
Retrospective	Access to program charts	Existing comparison group or normative data Existing outcome measures
Prospective	Access to program charts Creation of forms to track program participation Interviews with program staff and families	Creation of comparison/control group Administration of standardized measures at baseline and post-test Analysis of differential attrition and program diffusion

ing the chapter scenario as an example, the researcher would examine data pertaining to the number of home visits per family, the content of the home visits, the type of assessments of family members made, the number of referrals made for additional services, and the length of time families remained involved in the program. In general, this form of evaluation is subject to limitations inherent in using data collected for one purpose (internal staff forms) for a second purpose (evaluation). Also, data collected routinely by program staff are often inconsistent, ambiguous, and incomplete, especially if they are not monitored on an ongoing basis for consistency and clarity.

In a prospective formative evaluation, the researcher is involved from the beginning and can therefore play a role in developing the forms that program staffpeople complete about participation in the program. The researcher can also arrange to attend staff meetings and observe staff training, as well as accompany staff on home visits in order to observe service delivery (with staff and participant permission). Thus, the data collected can be more systematic, make use of multiple methods (logs, notes, observations), and be tailored to the goals of the evaluation. If an evaluator were asked to conduct a prospective formative evaluation of the home-based intervention program described in the chapter scenario, the evaluator might create forms for program staff to complete at the end of each visit that describe—using a standardized checklist—challenges facing the family (according to both family and program staff), strengths and supports available for dealing with these issues, services offered, and referrals made. These forms could be entered into a database on an ongoing basis to provide monthly updates on family concerns and services delivered to address those concerns.

Retrospective summative evaluations occur when an evaluator is asked to determine whether a program that has already been implemented has had its desired effect. In such situations, a preexisting comparison group or normative data are used as a basis of comparison, and whatever data have been routinely collected is used to measure outcomes. A researcher hired to conduct a retrospective summative evaluation of the home-based intervention program would aim to identify the key outcomes of the program (such as prevention of maltreatment of the children in the home, prevention of reentry into out-of-home placement of the children in the home, and more timely reunification of the children already in out-of-home placement). Using existing data, the researcher could try to determine what the citywide rates are for reentry in order to determine whether the rates for the children in the program are below these existing benchmarks. Alternatively, the agency could assess whether there were some families who met the criteria for the program but for whatever reason did not participate. Comparisons in rates of maltreatment, reentry to out-of-home placement, and timeliness of reunification of the placed child could be made between the program and these "no-program" families. Given the retrospective nature of the design, it is unlikely that a full complement of measures would be available to assess all relevant outcomes.

In contrast, prospective summative evaluations provide an opportunity for the evaluator to share in the design of the study, select the measures, and oversee the entire process, allowing for greater rigor in the methods used and, thus, greater confidence in the results. Using the example provided at the beginning of the chapter, the evaluator would help develop a logic model that would identify the key outcome areas and would select measures and a data collection strategy that would maximize the likelihood that positive outcomes, if they exist, will be revealed.

It should be clear by this point that a prospective evaluation, especially summative, represents the strongest option. It is also important to recognize that certain factors need to be in place for such an evaluation to be feasible. Not every program and not every setting allows for the implementation of a prospective summative evaluation.

Factors Necessary for Prospective Summative Evaluation

There are five factors that should be considered when deciding whether to embark on a prospective summative program evaluation: (1) financial resources, (2) time, (3) isolation of program elements, (4) existence of a comparison/control group, and (5) consensus among the stakeholders regarding the purpose of the evaluation.

Financial Resources

Financial resources need to be available to support a prospective summative evaluation. Done well, such an evaluation can cost tens of thousands of dollars a year. If an outside researcher is hired (or if a research staffperson's time is allocated to the evaluation), salary alone can be substantial. In addition, there are usually data collection costs (hiring and training research assistants to collect data), data entry costs, costs associated with purchasing measures, and payments to families for participation in data collection.

Time

Prospective summative evaluations can take several years to conduct. Many programs that intervene with families provide services over several months if not years (e.g., Head Start, Multi-Systemic Therapy, Multi-Dimensional Family Treatment). Data need to be collected at baseline and at several points of post-testing, usually at the end of the program and then again at some meaningful point after that, in order to determine whether the changes in the families have some lasting power. If multiple cohorts are required to establish a sufficient sample size, then the wait time between onset and completion of the evaluation can be even longer.

Isolation of Program

Another issue to contend with is whether the program is really a program. There is no one definition of a program, but at a minimum it should contain a discrete set of services or experiences and it should be possible to distinguish between people "in the program" and people "not in the program."

According to McDavid and Hawthorn (2006, 15), a program is "a group of related activities that is intended to achieve one or several related objectives." If the program is so idiosyncratic that each person receives an entirely different set of services in order to achieve an entirely different set of outcomes, then it probably does not make sense to evaluate the program, because a logic model could not be developed and a common core set of outcomes could not be measured.

Existence of a Comparison or Control Group

Most program evaluations entail comparing those who received the program with those who did not receive the program. Three types of "no-program" groups exist: (1) a control group randomly assigned to *not* receive the program, (2) a comparison group of individuals who happened *not* to receive the program, and (3) existing normative data that can serve as a basis of comparison. In the absence of these options, a program evaluation is probably not viable, as there is no way to determine whether performance in the program group can be attributed to the program. Without some form of a comparison group, the seven threats to internal validity described in chapter 7 cannot be ruled out as plausible alternative explanations for any improvements in the families. For example, a program designed to improve literacy in children would probably result in "improved" literacy scores between the beginning and end of the program because children's literacy improves over time even in the absence of an intervention. Using the chapter scenario, the timeliness of reunification could change over time due to any number of factors unrelated to the program (e.g., a citywide change in regulations, the agency hiring staff better able to facilitate reunification, the latest cohort of children being easier to reunify). A control or comparison group allows the researcher to rule out most if not all of the other factors likely to contribute to the outcomes, making it possible to conclude that the program itself produced them.

Consensus Among the Stakeholders Regarding the Purpose of the Evaluation

Another issue to consider in conducting any type of evaluation (prospective or retrospective, formative or summative) is what the purpose of the evaluation is and how the findings will be used. The potential evaluator should have a clear handle on who all the stakeholders in the evaluation are and have confidence that they are not working at cross-purposes. It sometimes happens that one set of stakeholders (such as the agency administrators or funders) plan to use evaluation results to reduce funding and support for the program while other stakeholders (such as staff and families) believe that the findings will be used to justify increased spending and support. These kinds of internal conflicts can undermine an evaluation and need to be resolved prior to signing on for such an endeavor.

Conducting a Prospective Summative Program Evaluation

The following ten activities form the core of any prospective summative program evaluation: (1) developing a logic model, (2) identifying key constructs to measure, (3) selecting measures, (4) creating a comparison/control group, (5) deciding on the timing of data collection, (6) obtaining informed consent, (7) paying families, (8) tracking families, (9) cleaning and entering data on ongoing basis, and (10) analyzing the data and writing the report.

Developing a Logic Model

The first step in developing a summative program evaluation is thinking through the logic of the program. According to the Kellogg Foundation's (2004, 1) *Logic Model Guide,* "a logic model is a picture of how the program works. It uses pictures and words to describe the sequence of activities thought to bring about change and how those activities are linked to the results the program is expected to achieve." The development of the logic model should be a joint venture between the researcher and the various stakeholders involved in the program's development. It is surprising how people involved in the same program can have vastly different ideas about what the desired effects of the program actually are. Using the chapter scenario as an example, it is possible that some staff believe the program is essentially a family-level intervention designed to enhance cohesiveness while other stakeholders might be primarily concerned with cost savings for the city associated with shorter stays in foster care. Likewise, there may be varying opinions regarding which program "inputs" are associated with which outcomes. While some stakeholders might emphasize the relationship between staff and program participants and believe that staff should spend most of their time providing instrumental support, others could believe that

Figure 17.2
Sample logic model of home visiting program

Resources	Activities	Outputs	Outcomes	Impacts
1. Staffing 2. Resources in the community 3. Resources in the agency 4. Materials provided directly to families 5. Money for supplies, refreshments, etc.	1. Home visits 2. Group meetings 3. Referrals to community resources 4. Developing relation-ships with parents	1. Change in parent behaviors toward child 2. Change in family cohesion 3. Change in parent-child relationships	1. Reduced reentries	1. Reduced strain on foster care system. 2. Improved long-term outcomes for children and families

the concrete opportunities for parents to learn how to engage their children in more emotionally supportive methods is vital for the program to achieve its goal. There is not necessarily a right or wrong vision of the program, but some of these discrepant ideas should be resolved prior to the initiation of the evaluation. Developing the logic model is one way to bring divergent views to consensus.

There are several different types of logic models, and no one is necessarily better than the other. Figure 17.2 provides an example of a basic logic model for the home visiting program described in the chapter scenario. This is a relatively simple model in that it does not present specific causal relationships (which service inputs are necessary for which outcomes). More complex logic models may resemble flowcharts with multiple decision points and complex feedback mechanisms. Regardless of the complexity, each logic model depicts the aspects of service delivery deemed necessary to achieve the desired outcomes. The model should also identify the key constructs that might mediate such effects so that they can be measured as well. If, for example, child's age at entry to the program is viewed as likely to dramatically affect the impact of the program, then this variable should be included in both the model and the actual evaluation.

One key issue to address at this stage is the extent to which the evaluation will be a "black box" evaluation in which participation in the program represents a monolithic and unmeasured phenomenon. In such a model, the evaluation focuses exclusively on measuring outcomes with the assumption that whatever happened "in the program" was either uniform across all participants or unmeasured variation. As an alternative, a summative program evaluation could aim to identify and measure key aspects of program service delivery in order to determine whether participants who received more or different combinations of services had better or different outcomes than those who did not. This is especially useful when participation is likely to vary considerably across participants. For example, it is possible that when the program group is compared to the no-program group, no differences emerge. This might actually be due to the fact that some of the families in the program group received little or no services. If participation in the program were measured, it would be possible to separate out those who did not receive the program and only compare the program participants who participated with the no-program group. This might be a fairer test of the program. In addition, such analyses could help determine whether a minimum amount of program participation is necessary to achieve positive outcomes.

Identifying Key Constructs

The logic model pictorially presents the major constructs relevant to the program and its outcomes. These are the constructs that will need to be measured. In evaluations of programs delivered to families in the child welfare system, constructs to consider include (1) child, parent, and family demographics likely to be related to participation and/or outcomes; (2) child, parent, and family cognitive, behavioral, social, and emotional functioning at the beginning of the program likely to be related to program participation and/or outcomes; (3) child, parent, and family participation in key components of the program; and (4) child, parent, and family cognitive, behavioral, social, and emotional functioning at immediate, intermediate, and long-term outcomes. Which specific aspects of cognitive, behavioral, social, and emotional functioning to measure should be determined based on theory as presented in the logic model. A program that aimed to prevent reentry into out-of-home placement, for example, might measure child temperament and/or fit between child and parent (children whose temperaments are more difficult for parents are more likely to be abused), parenting stress and skills, social support of the family, and the parents' own maltreatment history.

Selecting Measures

Identification of the key constructs is followed by the selection of measures for these constructs. Often there is more than one measure for each construct. For example, there are many measures of child cognitive performance; family cohesion, and parenting attitudes. Chapter 9 presents an in-depth discussion of measure selection strategies, briefly summarized here. Issues to consider in selecting one measure over another include: (1) established reliability and validity, (2) cost (some measures need to be purchased while others are available at no cost), (3) availability, (4) ethical considerations, (5) intrusiveness, (6) ability to detect change, (7) administration time, and (8) level of measurement. Whenever possible, existing measures with proven reliability and validity should be selected over "home-grown" measures, as they have greater credibility in the field.

Creating a Comparison/Control Group

One very important issue to work through is selection/assignment of families into the program and no-program group. As noted above, a group of individuals who did not participate in the program can be used as a basis for comparison with the families that did participate in the program. Without this no-program group, it can be quite difficult to conclude that any improvements in the program group are attributable to the program rather than time itself (or any of the other threats to internal validity identified by Campbell and Stanley 2005 and described in chapter 7). The primary consideration at this stage is how this group will be formed. Two primary options are (1) random assignment of families to the program and the no-program group or (2) finding a group of families that happened to not participate in the program. The first option entails random assignment and the formation of a control group while the second option does not entail random assignment, in which case the no-program group is referred to as a comparison group. Random assignment is the gold standard for program evaluation, as it dramatically increases the likelihood that the program participants and the no-program participants will be comparable in all ways that could affect the outcomes under investigation. Differences between the two groups on outcome measures, therefore, can be attributed to the program with greater confidence (there are two caveats to this, discussed below).

To achieve random assignment, every member of the sample must be known in advance and the total pool of families must be at least large enough to place the desired number of families in each group (program and no-program). Methods associated with random selection described in chapter 5 can be applied to random assignment (writing names on slips of paper placed in a container and randomly selecting them one at a time from the container, using a computer program to randomly select a certain predetermined number or percentage of families, or using a table of random numbers). Sometimes it is possible to ask everyone in the sampling frame whether they want to be included in the random assignment process, in which case the people who are selected will be notified of the results and most will likely agree to participate. Alternatively, if the names were picked prior to the notification, then there is the possibility that not everyone selected will agree to participate. A waiting list might need to be selected from the pool to replace the families who decline participation. The same process applies to the selection of the control group. They will need to be notified once they have been selected and invited into the control group (e.g., receiving payment to participate in periodic data collection sessions).

Despite its obvious methodological superiority, random assignment is infrequent in social service program evaluations. In addition to logistical constraints, random assignment appears to offend the sensibilities of program staff. It is perceived as unkind (if not cruel) to invite twice as many people to participate only to offer the program to half (relegating the other half to the control group). However, there are ways to conduct random assignment that are ethical and even appealing. For example, if there is a natural pool of potential participants that is larger than the number of program slots, inviting people to participate in a lottery to obtain admission to the program might seem (and be) more equitable to staff and families than hand-picking some families to participate while excluding others. The most important aspect, from an ethical standpoint, is to be completely clear about what it is that the family is agreeing to, participation in the program or a chance to be selected to participate in the program.

If random assignment is not feasible, identification of families to be in the comparison group will have to be thought through carefully. One common approach is to recruit into the comparison group families that are on the waiting list for the program. These families meet the criteria for program participation and will eventually receive the program. On the face of it, this appears to be an ethical and scientifically sound approach. However, it is possible that those on the waiting list are in some important ways different than those in the program. If, for example, initiative, persistence, parental involvement, commitment to the family, and organizational skills are required for early sign-up for the program (as opposed to ending up on the waiting list), then the families in the program will likely be better off than those in the no-program group. On the other hand, perhaps the parents in the most trouble or the most anxious sign up early and get a slot in the program. In that case, ending up on the waiting list would be left to the less troubled and less anxious parents. At a minimum, baseline measures should aim to assess any ways in which the two groups actually differ, in order to control for such differences in the analyses.

An alternative to the waiting list approach—which would be appropriate for community-based programs—is to recruit into the comparison group similar families who live in a similar town/neighborhood as the program families but because of geography are ineligible for the program. This would eliminate the differences that might be attributable to motivation and interest in the program.

For child welfare agencies, the primary options will be families from the same agency who did not participate in the program or families from another agency that is not providing the program. Although cross-agency comparisons are possible (as long as the families are comparable and the baseline services are comparable), they are unlikely due to natural competition and fear of having negative aspects of the agency exposed to "outsiders." Thus it is most likely that an agency conducting a summative evaluation will need to recruit a comparison group from within its own pool of clients. The most important thing to remember in doing so is that the comparison group participants should be similar to the program participants in every way that could affect the outcomes.

Regardless of the method of creating the control/comparison groups, differential attrition and program diffusion pose serious threats to the comparability of the groups and need to be understood and addressed in the design of the evaluation. Each is discussed in turn.

DIFFERENTIAL ATTRITION

Although the two groups may be comparable at group creation, it is possible that over time attrition from the study will result in two groups that are no longer comparable. Some families will drop out of the program, some will move away, others will refuse to participate in data collection. Thus, the samples with outcome data will most likely be a subset of the original samples of program and no-program families. If the attrition is equal across the groups, then the resulting subsamples will still be comparable. However, if the attrition is different in the two groups, then the resulting samples may no longer be comparable. This can dramatically affect the results of an eval-

Figure 17.3
Example of differential attrition that creates appearance of no program effects

	Scores at baseline	Score at post-test
Comparison/control group	low low low low low	
	low low low low low	
	low low low low low	
	low low low low low	low low low low low
	low low low low low	low low low low low
	hi hi hi hi hi	hi hi hi hi hi
	hi hi hi hi hi	hi hi hi hi hi
	hi hi hi hi hi	hi hi hi hi hi
	hi hi hi hi hi	hi hi hi hi hi
	hi hi hi hi hi	hi hi hi hi hi
	Mean=10	Mean=14
Program group	low low low low low	low low low hi low
	low low low low low	low hi low low low
	low low low low low	low low low hi low
	low low low low low	low hi low low low
	low low low low low	low low low hi low
	hi hi hi hi hi	hi hi hi hi hi
	hi hi hi hi hi	hi hi hi hi hi
	hi hi hi hi hi	
	hi hi hi hi hi	
	hi hi hi hi hi	
	Mean=10	Mean=6

uation. For example, if the higher functioning no-program families leave the study, the program families will outperform the no-program families on the outcomes measures, creating the appearance of an effective program. However, this superior performance might not be due to the impact of the program. Rather, it might be because the families remaining in the no-program group are the poorer functioning families. Conversely, if the "worse" no-program families drop out of the study, then those remaining as the comparison/controls might outperform the program families, creating the appearance that the program was not successful at achieving its outcomes. Figure 17.3 depicts such a scenario.

Even if the program had an effect and some of the low-performing families at baseline improved, it would probably not be enough to overcome the

Special Topics in Agency Practice

inequality in the samples due to differential attrition. The way to handle differential attrition is to compare the subsets of samples with and without outcome data on measures collected at baseline in order to determine whether the attrition was random or whether it affected the composition of the sample. If differences emerge, these variables should be used as covariates in all analyses. For example, if the home visiting program evaluation utilized random assignment to create a program and control group, with fifty families in each group, forty of which in each group participated in the outcome assessment, ten families in each had no outcome data, while forty did. Prior to comparing the forty program and forty no-program families on outcomes, several analyses should be conducted to determine whether the two groups are still comparable: (1) the program families with and without outcome data on baseline measures thought to be important for the study, such as age of child, parenting skills, and family stress; (2) the no-program families with and without outcome data on baseline measures thought to be important for the study (see list above); and (3) the forty program and forty no-program families on baseline measures thought to be important to the study (see list above). Any differences that emerge should be controlled for in all subsequent analyses.

PROGRAM DIFFUSION

The second way in which formation of a comparison/control group can become contaminated is with program diffusion. This occurs when the no-program families receive some portion of the program, in which case a comparison of the program and no-program families on outcomes might not reveal improved performance of the program families. It might appear to be the case that the program did not achieve its effect but it might actually be the case that the program helped both the program and the no-program families. Program diffusion occurs when the staffmembers delivering the program also come into contact with the no-program families. It may be very hard for them to "withhold" the program from families whom they perceive to be in need. For example, the home visiting program might add a new component of marital sessions to be evaluated in a random assignment design in which half the program families receive this new component while half do not. If staff serves both the families that are to receive the marital services as well as families that are not, the staff might accidentally (or deliberately) introduce elements of marital counseling into the home visits with the no-program families. It is clearly best to not ask the same staff to both change their behavior (introduce new program elements) and not change their behavior (provide services as usual) at the same time. Program diffusion can also occur through the program participants themselves. If the program participants and the no-program participants come into contact with one another, the program participants might accidentally disseminate the program (share materials, share referral resources, discuss new attitudes and skills). Program evaluations need to consider the various mechanisms through which the program might be delivered to the no-program families and build into the design of the study safeguards against this.

The third means of creating a no-program group is to utilize existing benchmarking data. It is possible that data have already been collected either at the agency, by the city, or by other researchers, and these data can be used as a basis for comparison with the program families. This is not the strongest design, because it is unlikely that these data are composed of all the measures of interest in the study and because there is no ability to document comparability of the program and no-program groups. But sometimes the data is so compelling (like national norms on key constructs) that it is a viable option.

Deciding on the Timing of Data Collection

Another major component of the design of a study pertains to the timing of the administration of the measures; that is, which measures will be administered to whom, when, and by whom. Typical timing of data collection includes baseline measures (before the program starts or within a certain period of time within onset of program participation, also called a pre-test), program participation measures (over the course of the program), immediate end of program outcomes, and follow-up outcomes both intermediate and long-term. Baseline data collection is critical to the success of the study for several reasons. The data collected prior to program participation can be used to (1) describe the sample, (2) determine comparability between the program and no-program groups, (3) determine preprogram levels on key outcome constructs, (4) predict program participation, (5) predict outcomes, and (6) determine comparability of the sample after attrition. The timing of the follow-up assessment should be based on the logic model and the theory underlying the design of the program. For example, there might be certain points in time in which program participants are expected to change or there might be key developmental milestones during which it would be important to document that the results have emerged or been maintained. For example, a researcher who has conducted a study of teens might want to follow up to see if the teens graduated high school, went to college, and stayed out of trouble with the law, while a follow-up assessment of a study of early intervention programs for preschool children might want to see how the children performed at the end of kindergarten.

HIRING AND TRAINING DATA COLLECTION STAFF

A major expense of a prospective summative program evaluation is payment of staff to collect the data. Often evaluations of social service programs entail staff making home visits for the purpose of collecting data. This is so for at least two reasons. First, the likelihood of participation is higher if less effort is required on the part of the program participants. Although some people are not home when they say they will be, it is easier to go to the person than to expect the person to come to where the researcher is (the costs and effort involved in arranging for child care and transportation are eliminated). Second, program participants might be more comfortable completing the measures in the privacy of their own home. Many program evaluations require administration of measures that may be of a personal nature (e.g., depression, parenting beliefs, literacy, children's behavioral problems, marital issues, and so forth). Thus, it is wise to assume that data will be collected in the home of the program participants. If data were collected at three points in time from program participants (baseline, at the end of the program, and one year later) and there were fifty individuals in the program and fifty in the no-program groups, then three hundred data collection visits will need to be scheduled, traveled to, and completed. If it takes an hour to complete each data collection visit and another hour for scheduling and traveling, this can easily become a time-consuming job. If more than one person is collecting data at any one time or over the course of the project, considerable effort will be expended to ensure that the different staffpeople are consistent in all aspects of their work (tone of voice, what they say, how they relate to the participants, how the forms are filled in, and so forth). This means that someone will need to oversee the data collectors to prepare training materials and provide training and ongoing supervision.

Data collection staff can most easily be found in graduate schools of social science, as students are often willing to accept lower-paying part-time jobs for the opportunity to work on a research project and gain experience with the types of families usually served by child welfare agencies. Such individuals should be flexible in their hours, mature in their deportment, able to develop rapport with people different from themselves, willing to travel to poorer neighborhoods, organized with their paperwork, and consistent in their administration of the measures.

Obtaining Informed Consent

Participation in the program does not de facto mean that the parents and children must or will participate in the program evaluation. It is not ethical to mandate that everyone who receives the program also complete the data collection assessments. Therefore, informed consent will need to be obtained prior to every data collection assessment visit, in which the purpose is explained, the risks and benefits are described, issues related to confidentiality are discussed, a contact name and number is provided in the event that the individual wants to talk to someone else working on the project, and the person has had a chance to ask and have answered all questions related to the project.

Paying Families

It is customary to provide a token payment to participants who complete data collection sessions. These payments should be large enough to indicate that the person's time is valued but not so large as to compel participation simply to receive payment. Many studies pay around $25.00 per session for adults and $10.00 for teens. One useful strategy is to build in a sliding scale, with the later sessions garnering larger payments. For example, if a study entails three data collection sessions, $20 can be paid for the first, $25 for the second, and $40 for the last. Because people tend to drift away or lose interest over time, the larger fees may increase participation rates. Receipts should be signed (by parent and participant with a copy for the participant and a copy for the project) for all money paid to participants, in order to have a thorough accounting of program evaluation funds.

Tracking Families

If families will be asked to participate in data collection sessions well after the program has ended or over an extended period of time during a long-term program, it will be useful to build into the project some strategies for keeping track of the families who move from one residence to another. One option is to ask the families at the beginning of the project for the names and phone numbers of people who would know where they are should they move. Another technique is to send out a mailing to families every few months, even if there is no need to schedule a data collection session. A Valentine's Day card, birthday card, holiday card, etc., can be mailed. Such a mailing serves two purposes. The first is that it creates good will on the part of the families for the data collection staff. This is especially so if a little gift is sent with the card (a coupon to a food store, stickers for the children). Second, if the words "do not forward" are printed on the envelope, then it will be returned to the research staff in the event that the person has moved. Often the post office will affix a label with the new address. This is vitally important information that allows the research staff to know well in advance of the next data collection sessions which families have moved and which have not. Address lists can be updated and plans can be made to contact the families at their new residences, if possible.

Cleaning and Entering Data

Data entry should be performed on an ongoing basis. This means that in addition to data collection staff, the project will need to hire, train, and supervise at least one person familiar with data cleaning and entry. Ongoing data entry forces the project staff to clean and organize data and ensure that data collection assistants are completing the forms properly. Any mistakes in the completion of the forms can be corrected rather than being carried forward throughout the project. A second benefit is that interim reports can be created for the stakeholders about the progress of the evaluation. Tables can be created comparing the program and no-program families and charts regarding program participation can be presented. In addition, if data are entered on an ongoing basis, as soon as the final piece of data is collected, outcome analyses can be conducted. This allows for a more timely presentation of the findings than if the data were entered only after the project has been completed.

Analyzing the Data and Writing the Report

Chapter 14 presents a detailed overview of which analyses are appropriate for which types of data. In general, program evaluations include comparisons of two groups (program and no-program) on various outcomes. One common strategy is to conduct an ANCOVA (analysis of covariance) with the covariates entered first followed by the outcome measure. In this way, any preexisting differences between the two groups are accounted for prior to the program itself being assessed. ANCOVAs allow for the presentation of the means of the two groups on the outcome measures. An alternative approach is to conduct a linear regression (with continuous outcomes) to determine the proportion of variance in the outcome that can be attributed to the program, after taking into account the effects of background variables and scores on the baseline measures. If the outcome is dichotomous, then a logistic regression can be conducted, in which the odds of participation in the program affecting the outcomes can be assessed.

As noted in chapter 15 regarding dissemination of findings, staff involved in the study (be it research or program evaluation) should be afforded the opportunity to hear and provide feedback on the preliminary findings prior to anyone "outside" the program hearing them. In fact, if possible, staff should be presented with interim reports and should be familiar with the trends and directions of outcomes, so that there are no major surprises when the final report is shared. Staff should have an opportunity to brainstorm reasons why outcomes might not have emerged, suggest additional analyses, and comment on all aspects of the draft report prior to submission of the report to the agency and/or funders. Program staffpeople have practice wisdom that can shed light on findings and it is essential that this wisdom be honored in the creation of the final report.

Conducting a Prospective Formative Program Evaluation

Conducting a prospective formative program evaluation requires the same diligence and logic as a prospective summative evaluation, but the details attended to are somewhat different. There are eight major issues to consider: (1) identifying key program implementation services, (2) identifying areas of variation, (3) development of service delivery assessment tools, (4) observations of staff training, (5) observation of service delivery, (6) interviews with staff, (7) interviews with program participants, and (8) report writing.

As with a logic model for a summative evaluation, the first step in a formative evaluation is outlining in detail the key program services being delivered to the program participants. For the home visiting program, the services might include home visits, assessment of family stressors and supports, provision of instrumental support, referrals to families, advocacy on behalf of families within the agency, family sessions, and provision of material support. It would also be important to specify the ideal (i.e., plan) for when these services are delivered and by whom.

Identifying Areas of Variation

The next step is to identify the areas in which delivery of such services may vary. If all services were delivered exactly as specified in the model, there would no need for a formative evaluation, because the program plan would be implemented in its entirety. The assumption underlying a formative evaluation is that variation does exist in the delivery of services. For example, just looking at home visits, there might be variation in how many different staff over the course of the program provide home visits to each family, overall number of visits made, length of time of each visit, who else is in the home during the visit, the content of the visit, the program participant's feelings about the visit, the staffperson's feelings about the visit, the number of times the visits were rescheduled, and so forth. Family assessments could vary in which assessment tools were used, the age of the children at the time of the assessment, the results of the assessment, and so forth. Each aspect of the program can vary in innumerable ways, and the purpose of this phase of the evaluation is to identify the sources of meaningful variation. This should lead to a clear idea of what to measure and when.

Development of Service Delivery Assessment Tools

Once the important sources of variation have been identified, report forms/measurement tools can be created to measure this variation. Most of these forms will be completed by program staff, although some could be completed by program participants. Staff will need to be encouraged to be honest (e.g., reporting on missed sessions, admitting that some issues/problems are not discussed during a visit), or the tools will not be useful. It might be necessary and helpful to build in some checks and balances regarding the completion of these forms. Examples include supervisors attending some home visits with program staff or calling families to gauge the extent to which services are actually being delivered. These forms should be examined on an ongoing basis to determine that they are being completed correctly. Interim reports can be created and shared with program staff about the service delivery process.

Observations of Staff Training

It might also be of interest to measure variation in the staff training component of the program. As long as more than one staffperson is delivering services to program participants, the staff will need to receive training and ongoing supervision. This should include discussion of family-specific issues as well as information that will increase the consistency of the delivery of the program across staff (discussion of program philosophy, sharing of ideas about how to conduct certain aspects of the program, and so forth). These staff training sessions could be observed by the evaluator in order to deepen his or her understanding of the program. Issues to assess might include staff cohesion, staff willingness to share concerns and possible weaknesses, staff openness to supervisor's suggestions, organization of the meeting, and apparent helpfulness of the training materials. These observations can be systematic or ad hoc, but either way can be built into the final report if it is useful to do so.

Observation of Service Delivery

Likewise, the evaluator might want to observe actual service delivery, that is, make home visits with the program staff and observe staff-participant interactions. It is quite likely that simply being present will change the tone or content of the service delivery process and therefore is only partially representative of actual service delivery. In addition, these visits should only be made after obtaining prior permission of the families. Even making a few of these visits can provide the researcher with a more realistic and nuanced understanding of the program. Issues to pay attention to include rapport and comfort level between participant and staff, willingness of participant to share concerns, knowledge level of staff in addressing the concerns, and apparent helpfulness of services delivered.

Interviews with Staff

The formative program evaluator will certainly want to schedule interviews with program staff. A semistructured protocol could be developed (see chapter 13) in order to systematically capture staff ideas and feelings about the program. Issues to focus on include their vision of the program and how they believe that the services produce the outcomes, their comfort with the service delivery process, their thoughts about the training and supervision they receive, the best and worst aspects of working in the program, the reasons why the program may not achieve its outcomes, their beliefs about participant receptiveness to the program, the extent to which they believe they do and do not follow the service delivery guidelines, their commitment to the program, and the ways in which the agency itself helps and hinders service delivery. The data collected from these interviews could be submitted to a content analysis and incorporated into the final report.

Interviews with Program Participants

If allowable, the evaluator will also want to schedule interviews with some program participants (without the program staff being present) in order to interview them about their thoughts and feelings about the program. A semistructured protocol could be developed (see chapter 13) in order to systematically capture their ideas and feelings about the program. Issues to focus on include what they hoped to gain from their participation in the program when they enrolled in it and whether they now believe the program has been helpful for them, their feelings about the various staff with whom they have come into contact, the different aspects of the program they have participated in and why, which aspects have they declined to participate in and why, what the best and worst parts of being in the program have been, whether they believe the program has helped them and, if not, why not, and how, if at all, they would like to see the program changed. The data collected from these interviews could be submitted to a content analysis and incorporated into the final report.

Report Writing

As noted above, staff involved in the evaluation should be provided with an opportunity to hear and provide feedback on the preliminary findings prior to anyone "outside" the program hearing them. Ideally, staff will be presented with interim reports and should be familiar with the trends and directions of findings so that there are no surprises when the final report is shared.

Conclusion

Program evaluation is an important component of agency-based child welfare research, as it offers an opportunity to secure funding and to conduct timely studies, the results of which will be of interest to the agency, the clients, and the funders. However, it is important that all of the stakeholders come to agreement about the type of program evaluation that will meet their needs as well as be feasible to conduct given logistical, time, and financial resources and constraints operating at the time of program implementation and evaluation. The researcher will be a critical resource for helping the stakeholders develop clarity and consensus and in overseeing the implementation of the evaluation itself. If done well, a program evaluation can make a significant contribution to the improvement of policy, program, and practice.

Final Thoughts

After decades of research in the field of child welfare, considerable knowledge has been accumulated. There is much that professionals have learned about child welfare and, at the same time, not nearly enough is known about the field. The landscape of child welfare practice continually changes as new public policies are put into place, new social issues evolve, and public sentiment concerning child welfare alters. Because of the changing context of practice, there are continual gaps in the knowledge base. These gaps of knowledge can become exciting research problems for future researchers to tackle. This is partly because no one study can answer every question about the topic of investigation. In fact, most studies raise more questions than they answer. This is true for several reasons. First, most studies are conducted with a nonprobability sample of cases selected from a population that is in fact a subset of the larger population of interest. Thus, the findings cannot be generalized to the entire population of interest (i.e., all of child welfare). For example, in most child welfare research, the population of interest is all families in the system—limited perhaps by a specific experience (e.g., adopted in 1999, those with goals of independent living, and so forth). However, the reality is that most research studies select cases from a subpopulation that is limited by gender, ethnicity, geography, historical context, measurement, or other variables. Any study that is based on a sample from a single agency or a single geographic area, for example, is necessarily limited in generalizability. Thus, a question always remains as to whether the same findings would be found in a different subset of the population.

Second, the results of most studies do not account for all of the variance in the dependent variable, indicating that other—unmeasured—factors are also exerting an influence. Most studies conclude that findings are significant when the effect size is moderate, say a correlation of .40 or .50. This means that, at best, 25 percent of the variance in the dependent variable is explained. The findings can be used to conclude that there is a statistical association between the independent and dependent variables, but it leaves open the question of what else is also influencing the dependent variable.

A third reason that studies are not definitive is that the population of child welfare clients changes over time. In addition, federal and state policies that affect child welfare services change over time. The crack epidemic in the 1980s, as an example, introduced new family-level issues into the system and introduced new factors that might limit the relevance of previous findings. Likewise, when significant policies and practices change, not only are new questions raised, but prior research might need to be replicated under these new conditions. A good illustration of this is the introduction of the Adoption and Safe Families Act (ASFA) and its requirement of concurrent planning. Research on length of time to adoption might need to be conducted anew in light of the revised guidelines regulating timelines for termination of parental rights.

For these reasons, the state of knowledge in the field of child welfare is always to some extent in flux. At the same time, with repeated replication and confirmation and extended examination with multiple samples and multiple measures, certain theories have become established and certain truths accepted. Research has clearly documented the negative short- and long-term impact of child maltreatment and trauma on many areas of child development (e.g., Briere 1992; van der Kolk 1994). Also, research has also demonstrated that separation from one's parents is itself a traumatic event in the life of a child (e.g., Bowlby 1972), and that there may be adverse effects on children who are in out-of-home care without a permanent home. These two truths reflect the ongoing dilemma and tension in the field of child welfare practice and research: to protect children from harm and to provide them with a permanent home without causing unnecessary additional trauma. Most research in the field has focused in one way or another on these two concerns. Much of this research has been conducted outside the direct purview of the field most affected by the results: child welfare practitioners. That is, many of the seminal studies on child maltreatment and a child's need for a permanent attachment figure have been conducted by developmental and clinical psychologists with no specific affiliation with child welfare policy and practice. Research conducted specifically with an eye toward child welfare implications is considerably more scant. Even rarer is research conducted by professionals working within a child welfare agency.

This is true for several reasons, including the many "curses" outlined in chapter 2: the lack of prestige associated with the field of child welfare, the general lack of resources for researchers working in the field of child welfare (colleagues, federal funding, access to libraries), and the problems associated with conducting research under the auspices of an agency that has its own agenda, most likely including a preference for findings that shed a positive light on the agency itself. An associated issue is that child welfare agencies are often under economic stress to remain viable entities, and thus research can be seen by agency management as a "luxury item" as opposed to a core service.

The goal of this book is to help researchers working in the field of child welfare—especially those working within a child welfare agency—conduct scientifically rigorous and ethically responsible research that will continue to move the field forward. From problem formulation to design development, data collection, data analysis, and writing up and sharing the findings, there are scientific and ethical considerations that shape every study and have implications for the utility of the findings. As demonstrated throughout this book, there is much that child welfare professionals know about how to conduct child welfare research, but there are also many new questions to be explored and many research methods that require additional refinement. The field of child welfare, although continually changing, is an exciting field for researchers to continue to build knowledge that informs child welfare practice, policy, and future research.

Directions for Future Research

As the practice of child welfare continues to evolve, research must keep apace. Information is needed to create, track, monitor, and evaluate new systems and new approaches in order to provide timely feedback to the decision makers within agencies, advocacy groups, and governmental entities. Currently, there are six issues that suggest themselves as important topics of future investigation or that require additional methodological or conceptual refinement. The next section of this chapter will briefly discuss these important child welfare topics.

Evaluation of Child Protection Services—Differential Response

The entity responsible for investigating child abuse and neglect allegations (typically called child protective services, CPS) is being reconfigured in some states to allow for a different balance between investigation and service. In the traditional model, the vast majority of the resources are allocated to investigating cases, and families who do not require investigations are relatively ignored and underserved, despite the fact that they too need services and supports. The one-size-fits-all model of CPS investigations has come under attack, and a proposed differential response model is being tested in several states. This differential response model (Waldfogel 1998) is designed to allow CPS to develop less adversarial relationships with families who need services but might otherwise be hesitant to become involved with CPS for fear of investigations and possible removal of their children. At the core of this paradigm are three building blocks: customized response, developing community-based services, and incorporating other community services or sources of support (Waldfogel 2000). In the first instance, rather than have a one-size-fits-all protective service, the differential response paradigm encourages a customized response to families based on their individual needs. Second, the differential response paradigm encourages cross-agency collaboration within the community, as one agency typically cannot address all the issues with which a family in protective services presents. Finally, the differential response paradigm looks to the family's informal and natural supports within their community as part of the family's social network.

Some important research questions require immediate attention as the use of a differential response paradigm becomes more widespread across the country. Most pressing is the question of what proportion of families with a customized response for an assessment ultimately are reassigned to the investigation track and/or regardless of reassignment what proportion of children in these families are abused or neglected. That is: how effective are the tools used to determine the needs of families? Without accurate tools (and correct application of these tools) for making the protective decisions, the differential response paradigm is not likely to represent an improvement. A second important question is whether a differential response paradigm is more cost effective (and service effective) than the traditional approach, and third, whether the differential response paradigm actually achieves its goal of establishing less adversarial relationships with families and communities. The Child Welfare League of America (i.e., Morgan, Spears, and Kaplan 2003) concluded that pilot data strongly support the effectiveness of dual-track or differential response approaches and it is suggested here that additional research continue in this area to further explore the utility of this program on a larger scale.

Impact of Increased Use of Prevention to Avoid Placement

From a philosophical point of view, most governmental and advocacy groups have a stated preference for maintaining children in the home. To that end, the Adoption Assistance and Child Welfare Act of 1980 (PL 96–272) promotes the use of prevention programs as a preference over out-of-home placements, although not when abuse or neglect is suspected. Such an emphasis is consistent with family-centered social work practice (Pecora, Whittaker, Maluccio, Barth, and Plotnick 1992). In some cities (for example, New York City), this philosophical emphasis is being put into practice with a historic shift in focus from out-of-home care to prevention/in-home care for at-risk children and families. As a result, congregate care facilities are closing, foster home/adoption programs are undergoing "right-sizing," and prevention programs have become the service of choice within the system.

The primary goal of prevention programs is to prevent the removal of children from the home and their placement into foster care. Thus, no study of prevention programs would be complete without an analysis of whether they are meeting this primary objective. Results of prior studies have proven to be mixed, especially because it is not clear what proportion of the children in families served by prevention programs would have been placed in out-of-home care in the absence of participation in the program. Some portion of these cases would have zero placement rates regardless of participation in prevention. It is not possible to assign cases to a prevention program or no-services control group, so no study has been able to answer the twin questions of what proportion would be placed without services and whether participation in a prevention program reduces those rates.

Studies that compare two prevention programs can determine whether one is more effective than the other, but not whether either program is actually an improvement over no program at all. Equally problematic is the issue of timing. Some studies define effectiveness as not being removed from the home at the end of participation in the program while others define it as not being removed three or more months following program completion. Too short a timeframe and the effectiveness data look better but may not be meaningful, while too long a timeframe and the results may be more meaningful but perhaps hold the program to too high a standard. In addition, if the timeframe for program evaluation is too long, other intervening and/or confounding variables will come into play that may render the program effects ineffective.

All of these issues must be resolved so that some key questions can be addressed: (1) Is length of stay in the program associated with outcomes? (2) Should outcomes be conceptualized as reduced placement rates, reduced abuse/neglect, or reduced risk factors for abuse/neglect? (3) Are some components of the program more important for achieving certain outcomes than other components? (4) Are some families more likely to benefit from prevention programs than others? And (5) are family and child characteristics important to identify as variables that impact a program? Conducting a study that addresses even some of these questions would need to be prospective, long-term, involve multiple programs across multiple sites, and include assessments of children, families, and program characteristics.

Analysis of Communities as a Social Network Buffer

Traditionally, child welfare has acted as an isolated service to children and families who have come to the attention of the local child welfare service because of suspected abuse and/or neglect. Child welfare services have been unconnected to the local community. Over the past few years, several states have actively reached out to communities where families live in order to begin to build a support network for the family (Chahine, Van Straatan, and Williams-Isom 2005). In this approach, the community (consisting of relatives, friends, houses of worship, community services, etc.) takes on greater importance as a necessary social support for a family at risk for potential foster care placement as well as for a child or youth who is returning from a foster care placement (to reduce the chance the child will return to foster care).

Research indicates that a family that has a stronger social network (strength of network is defined primarily by quality of interactions as opposed to the quantity of people in the social network) will be better able to contend with difficult environmental stressors such as unemployment, health issues, and so forth and be better able to cope with transitions and major changes within the family (Bain 1978; Froland et al. 1979; Greenblatt et al. 1982; Hirsch 1979). Conversely, research has also demonstrated the connection between a poor-quality social network and the potential of child abuse occurring within the family (Gaudin and Pollane 1983).

Future research on this topic could focus on the impact of a social network on families receiving child welfare services to determine at what point and in what capacity should the child welfare practitioner begin to intervene in the social network to achieve a positive result for the family. Another interesting approach would be to explore the interplay of the social network, the child welfare institution, and other systems (i.e., mental health, juvenile justice, etc.), and how the social network could potentially help a family "navigate" between systems of care. Research might also aim to uncover the signs of a poor social network and preventively enhance a family's social network in order to prevent abuse from occurring.

Rethinking Length of Stay as an Outcome in Foster Care

Child welfare agencies are under enormous pressure to measure and reduce the length of stay of children in out-of-home care. In many child welfare administrations, this is the primary way in which agencies are evaluated for effectiveness. In some cases, financial rates and bonuses to agencies are based on reduced care day utilization. This emphasis on reducing length of stay is a response to what was identified in seminal research as "foster care drift" (Maas and Engler 1959), in which children were found to spend several years in the system with no clear plan for permanency. Rightly so, these findings sparked alarm and concern for children's need for a permanent home and have helped to shape decades of practice aimed at reducing children's length of stay in the system.

At the same time, length of stay per se is a blunt tool that overlooks a child's or family's need for treatment and services offered by the system. If children are removed from their homes for cause (founded abuse or neglect and/or serious emotional problems of the child, depending upon the level of care in which the child is placed), then presumably a certain amount of time is needed to provide the child and family with mental health and support services aimed at improving child and family functioning. To measure length of stay without taking this into account is perhaps missing a critical component of the purpose of the system. In some agencies, even youth placed in care for serious emotional and behavioral disorders are measured according to length of stay as opposed to improved ability to function safely in the community. It is clearly in no one's best interest for violent and dangerous youth to have shorter lengths of stay in care if shortening stays is not accompanied by concurrent improvement in functioning. Perhaps the outcome of interest should be conceptualized as "appropriate length of stay" as opposed to shorter length of stay.

Measuring Long-Term Outcomes of Children Discharged from Foster Care

One of the thorniest methodological issues plaguing the field is what happens to youth after discharge from the system. One exception to this is the relatively rich body of knowledge about youth aging out of the system (staying in care until they attain adulthood) (e.g., Courtney, Piliavin, Grogan-Kaylor, and Nesmith 2001; Festinger 1983). However, for youth who are discharged from care prior to adulthood, little is known about how they fare. There are no resources to provide services to families, and most agencies simply fall out of touch with the vast majority of clients they formerly served. Furthermore, youth who are discharged home and then reenter the system may not be returned to the original agency serving them. Thus, at the agency level, there is no way to determine the proportion of cases that return to care following discharge (researchers working with administrative data across agencies may have access to these data but will not necessarily have access to the richer data available from charts that could shed light on the determinants of reentry). Even these data are relatively short term and do little to answer the question about the long-term impact of removal from home and the services provided on the well-being of children and families.

At the most basic level, there is scant information about whether involvement in the child welfare system improves the lives of children and family, especially once the involvement is over (i.e., following final discharge). Some important questions that require investigation include whether or not parent and family functioning has been altered in a significant way and whether child well-being and positive developmental outcomes are more likely for families touched by the system. Retrospective data suggest that former foster care youth are overrepresented in the populations of prisons, public assistance rolls, and homeless shelters, but prospective data are required to determine causality and to identify the pathways from out-of-home placement to such long-term negative outcomes. Such studies need to be longitudinal, prospective, and involve data from multiple states. Clearly such an endeavor will require a significant commitment from funding sources and from a collaborative team of researchers.

Creation of a Battery of Core Constructs

There are many core constructs in the field of child welfare for which there are no universally accepted reliable and valid measures. Too often, child welfare researchers utilize homegrown measures that lack reliability and validity, doing a disservice to the children and families participating in the research and making it nearly impossible to accumulate knowledge across studies. Key constructs such as child well-being have been operationalized in several different ways, as have family functioning. As noted in previous chapters, even seemingly simple variables such as admission to an agency can be measured in different ways. Ideally, conventions will be developed over time that allow researchers newer to the field to draw on the collective wisdom of earlier researchers. It is our hope that the next generation of researchers will take the lead in developing and validating core constructs that are widely used in child welfare research.

Conclusion

The field of child welfare is an exciting and dynamic arena within which researchers can address important and interesting questions and in turn continue to develop child welfare as a viable research field. Doing so will allow child welfare to assume greater importance and prestige in both academic circles as well as in political discourse. This is of vital importance, because the more attention provided to child welfare, the greater the resources that can be garnered, and the higher the standards will be for both research and practice.

It is our hope that with the tools provided in the previous seventeen chapters, this work can be undertaken in an ethical, methodologically rigorous, creative, theoretically based, sensitive, and timely manner. Child welfare represents a fruitful and important avenue for researchers, and we hope that the field is able to attract the nation's brightest social scientists to such a worthy area of investigation. The clients served by the child welfare system deserve nothing less.

Classroom Discussion and Activity

Chapter 1

1. Develop a research question in which the theory is *not* falsifiable.

2. Using the theme of length of stay in the child welfare system, develop a research idea from two different postpositivistic perspectives.

3. Identify some of the benefits and drawbacks to the placing-out system created by Charles Loring Brace.

4. Go to the Children's Bureau Web site and identify one piece of information that you think should be there that is not.

Chapter 2

1. Identify three advantages and disadvantages to the application of the scientific method to child welfare research.

2. Using the issue of youth aging out of care (youth who have not been adopted or reunited by the time they are emancipated), develop a research question that would be of interest to a particular agency but not to the field, and then develop a research question that would be of interest to the field but not to a particular agency.

3. Using the topic of adoption disruption (when a planned adoption does not work out after the child has been placed in an adoptive home), develop three questions

that could be answered with qualitative data and three questions that could be answered with quantitative data.

4. What should an agency-based researcher do if the results of an evaluation of an agency's program did not produce evidence of program effectiveness?

5. What are some ways that an agency-based researcher could identify other professional researchers with whom to develop collaborations?

Chapter 3

1. What would an appropriate payment be for participation in a research study for (1) a one-hour interview with an adolescent in a group home, (2) a two-hour focus group for a parent in a prevention program, (3) three one-hour assessments of a foster parent, and (4) a survey completed by agency staff?

2. What are some of the issues that might be covered in a proposal for a study that would be considered appropriate for expedited review?

3. What could some of the limits of confidentiality be for a study of pregnant teens in foster care?

4. Develop a child welfare research study in which deception is a necessary feature of the design.

5. Obtain ethical guidelines for conducting human subject research from at least three sources and compare them.

Chapter 4

1. A residential treatment center for youth (the highest level of care in the child welfare system) has experienced a large turnover in staff, and it seems that children are staying longer. Develop three research questions to investigate this issue. Should qualitative or quantitative data be collected?

2. Thinking about the topic of children with special needs waiting for adoption, create three questions that could be asked to explore this phenomenon.

3. A researcher has been awarded a grant of $250,000 from the Good Research Foundation to conduct a study entitled "The Impact of Child Ethnicity on Length of Time Waiting for Adoption for Special Needs Children." What could some research questions be?

4. Develop directional and nondirectional hypotheses for the above study.

5. Develop descriptive and explanatory/predictive hypotheses for the above study.

Chapter 5

1. Explain why "short-stayers" are overrepresented in exit cohorts and "long-stayers" are overrepresented in "point-in-time" cohorts.

2. How would a convenience sample of families served in a prevention program in New York City be generated, and what are some ways in which the sample would not be representative of the population?

3. How can a researcher determine that a sample is representative of a population?

4. Calculate sample size for a study of depression in teen mothers in a shelter with estimated effects of .20, .50, and .80.

5. What are the Type I and Type II errors associated with a study of the effectiveness of a new program to prevent recidivism in teens discharged from a runaway shelter, under conditions that the program was in fact effective and that it was not?

Chapter 6

1. Prior to beginning a single-system design research project, what would the caseworker have to do as the project leader to ensure that staff and families will understand the project and cooperate with agency staff to collect data?

2. Does therapeutic effectiveness and statistical effectiveness refer to the same thing? What are the potential differences?

3. When a caseworker collects data for the baseline and the baseline is unstable, what options does the caseworker have to stabilize the baseline? When would the unstable baseline prohibit a family from entering the project?

4. What are some of the concerns of caseworkers who do not use manualized casework methods as it relates to single-system design? Are they valid concerns? Can SSD be used with less clearly defined casework?

Chapter 7

1. In a study of the effects of a peer intervention on group home youth use of alcohol and illegal substances, how would each of the seven threats to internal validity apply?

2. How would one diagram a study of pre-test, intervention, first post-test, and second post-test? Why would it make sense to have two post-testing sessions?

3. What are some variables on which it would be important to establish comparability of groups in a study of substance abuse in teens?

4. Why does the order of the measures administered sometimes affect the data?

Chapter 8

1. Identify three research questions that could most likely be answered with data collected from agency paper records.

2. Identify three research questions that could most likely be answered with data collected from an agency electronic database.

3. Identify three questions that could most likely be answered with data collected from social worker progress notes about family therapy sessions between a child in a group home program and his or her family.

4. What should a researcher do if one of the coders on a team consistently is not reliable in the training sessions?

5. Access the CWLA NDAS and replicate the data presented in this chapter.

Chapter 9

1. Identify three frequently used measures of self-esteem for children and describe their reliability and validity.

2. If establishing reliability of a new fifteen-item measure of caseworker job satisfaction, which form(s) of reliability would be useful, and why?

3. Describe what the levels of a scale of caseworker commitment to the job would be if the scale were nominal, ordinal, interval, or ratio.

4. When would it be necessary to use the same measure of a construct that has been used in prior research and when would it be necessary to use a new measure of the construct?

5. In a study that measures caseworkers' vicarious traumatization, how could each of the criteria for selecting measures apply?

Chapter 10

1. Develop a budget and timeline for a survey study of sexual acting-out behavior of youth in therapeutic foster care.

2. What should a researcher do if the response rate is 50 percent in a survey study of RTC child care staff attitudes about PSB?

3. What are the advantages and disadvantages, if any, of administering some surveys in a study by mail and others in the same study by e-mail?

4. Develop a set of survey questions for a study of foster parent knowledge of PSB for foster parents in the same agency.

5. Develop the template in SPSS for those survey items.

Chapter 11

1. Make a list of some of the documents that could be useful for a case study of (1) recidivism of juvenile delinquency in youth, (2) success of a parent education program, and (3) depression in pregnant teens.

2. How would "going native" be expressed in a study of a prevention program for parents at risk of losing their children due to a history of abuse or neglect?

3. How does a researcher know when the data collection phase of a case study is completed?

4. Develop a budget and timeline for a case study (with a single case) of positive peer culture in a residential treatment center.

5. In a case study of job satisfaction of foster home caseworkers in a child welfare agency, what are some activities that the researcher would want to observe? Whom would the researcher interview?

Chapter 12

1. Develop research questions and possible focus group questions for a study of satisfaction of students in a social work research methods class.

2. Develop a flyer/announcement for a focus group of parents in a prevention program.

3. Develop a budget and timeline for a study of five focus groups of former foster care youth about their readiness for independent living after leaving foster care.

4. Develop some focus group protocol questions for a study of biological parents' experience with concurrent planning.

5. Identify possible locations for a flyer for a study of biological parents who are experiencing concurrent planning such that parents from more than one agency will be recruited into the study.

Chapter 13

1. Why is it not advisable for an interviewer to share personal information with an interviewee, and how should the interviewer respond if the participant tries to elicit personal information from him or her?

2. What would the major topics be in an interview protocol for a study of case-worker attitudes about kinship care?

3. What, if any, are the drawbacks to conducting "too many" interviews?

4. Develop a sample budget and timeline for an interview study of the childhood child welfare experiences of parents currently served in a prevention program.

Chapter 14

1. Create a 2-by-2 cross-tabulation using one variable as the row and the other as the column, and then switch the variables and observe what happens to the proportions within the cells.

2. What is the primary difference between linear and logistic regression?

3. What are the advantages and disadvantages of reporting effect sizes?

4. Once the data collection for a study has been completed, about how long does the data analysis phase take? What factors would affect the length of time it takes to analyze data?

5. What resources are available to agency-based child welfare researchers who need assistance with the interpretation of statistical output?

Chapter 15

1. Identify five types of requests by the reviewers of a manuscript submitted for publication that a researcher might not be able to comply with.

2. Identify five journals that tend to publish articles about child welfare populations.

3. What could a researcher do if the staffpeople within a program respond negatively to the findings of a study?

4. Find an article and—without looking at the existing abstract—write a sample abstract for the paper.

5. Find an article about a child welfare population and develop a draft report for agencies that might be interested in the data.

Chapter 16

1. Develop a long-term plan, a short-term plan, and one outcome study for families served in a therapeutic foster boarding home.

2. What are five items that could be included on a consumer feedback survey of youth in a residential treatment center?

3. What are five items that could be included on a record review form for prevention program cases?

4. Look up the COA Web site and the JCAHO Web site and identify five ways in which their CQI accreditation requirements are different and five ways they are similar.

5. What are five ways that clients in a shelter could be provided with feedback about various CQI activities?

Chapter 17

1. Develop one question for each of the four types of evaluations for a program that provides peer group counseling sessions to teens at risk of running away from a group home.

2. Analyze the seven threats to internal validity in a program evaluation of a program designed to prevent the out-of-home placement of children in families deemed at risk of abusing their children.

3. What are the advantages and disadvantages of collecting program evaluation data from participants in their own home?

4. What could a program do to address the problem that positive outcomes are found at immediate post-test but not six months later in a program designed to improve parenting skills and attitudes of foster parents?

5. List five ways in which participation might vary in a program for improving family visits for children in residential treatment.

Glossary 1:
Social Science Research Methods Terms

The following is a glossary of salient social science research methods and basic statistical terms that will help the readers as they read through this text. It is a useful tool that can be used as a reference at any time.

ACTION RESEARCH. A form of research that a team of practitioners undertakes in order to implement some action, typically a program improvement effort. The term is attributed to Kurt Lewin in a 1946 paper. In action research there is an expectation that the findings will be of immediate applicability in the context in which the research was conducted.

AGENCY CASE RECORD. All child welfare agencies maintain paper case records of clients/consumers served. The records usually contain documentation about the reason(s) for referral, background information about the clients, information about services offered, and usually a record of outcome or status at termination or discharge from service. With careful thought, these records can be used in research studies. An added benefit is that such studies usually require only expedited (as opposed to full) review from the agency's institutional review board, because the data are preexisting.

ALPHA. The probability that a statistical effect will be found by chance. An alpha of .05 (typically used in social science research) indicates that the statistically significant findings would only be found five times in a hundred by chance alone. That is, ninety-five out of one hundred times, an effect of that size would occur when there really is an effect.

ANALYSIS OF VARIANCE (ANOVA). A statistical technique for determining whether mean scores on a continuous dependent variable are statistically significantly different between three or more groups. When variables are entered as control variables, or covariates, into the analysis, then the procedure is referred to as an analysis of covariance (ANOCOVA or ANCOVA).

BETA. The probability that an effect will not be found when it really exists. Beta is calculated as 1−power. A beta of .20 (typically used in social science research) indicates that twenty times in one hundred, a finding of that size will not be found when it really exists.

BETWEEN-GROUP DESIGN. In a between-group design, the scores of two or more groups are compared for one or more measure. Research studies that assess differences between two or more groups of individuals require a between-group design. In contrast, a within-group design examines scores on two or more variables within a single sample.

BIVARIATE ANALYSIS. The calculation of associations between two variables. Examples include t-tests, f-tests, correlations, and chi-squares.

BLIND CODER. A blind coder is not aware of the hypotheses of a study nor any other key information about the variables that could influence the coding of the data.

CASE STUDY. A research method in which one (or more) selected cases (such as a school, a program, or a family) is studied with multiple methods of data collection (observations, interviews, surveys) in order to learn as much about the case as possible as it relates to a particular area of interest or research question.

CATEGORICAL VARIABLE. Scores on a categorical variable represent discrete categories in which an individual is either one score or the other. Midpoints do not exist. For example, a categorical score of marital status might be 0=single, 1=remarried, 2=married.

CHILD ASSENT. Parents/guardians provide informed consent for children to participate in research, but children can and should be offered an opportunity to agree (assent) to participate once informed consent has been obtained. In this respect, assent can be viewed as necessary but not sufficient, because consent must also be obtained.

CHI-SQUARE. A nonparametric statistic used to test for associations between two or more dichotomous or categorical variables. It is based on the cross-tabulation data in which the distribution of one variable is plotted against the distribution of the other.

CLOSED-ENDED QUESTION. In a closed-ended question, the response options are provided to the respondent in advance, who is asked to select one or all that apply. Data collected from a closed-ended question are usually reported with quantitative analyses.

CODER DRIFT. Coder drift occurs when a coder who was once reliable becomes unreliable over time, usually due to too much time elapsing since the coding training.

CONFIRMATORY BIAS. The tendency to search for or interpret data in a way that confirms preconceptions. It is a form of cognitive distortion that represents an error of inductive inference toward confirmation of the study's hypotheses.

CONSTRUCT. The theoretical concept that is of interest in a study. Examples of constructs include child well-being, depression, substance abuse, and maltreatment.

CONTENT ANALYSIS. A data analytic technique in which rich textual data are coded in order to identify common elements across several cases. Audiotapes from interviews and focus groups can be transcribed verbatim (written out word for word) and submitted to a content analysis in which the common elements and themes are identified and reported.

CORRELATION. A statistic that assesses the extent to which variation on one measure is associated with variation on another. A positive correlation indicates that as scores on one measure increase, so to do scores on the other. A negative correlation indicates that as scores on one measure increase, scores on the other measure decrease. When both measures are continuous and normally distributed, a Pearson product moment correlation is used. Other types of correlations are used when one or more of the variables are not continuous.

CORRELATIONAL DESIGN. In this design, data are collected on a single sample at one point in time. Statistical correlations may or may not be conducted with data collected in a correlational design.

COVARIATE. A variable entered into a statistical test in order to rule out or control for its influence on the dependent variable.

CROSS-SECTIONAL DESIGN. In this design, individuals of different ages are measured on a dependent variable at a single point in time. Age groups are created (such as infants, toddlers, preschoolers, and so forth) and compared on their scores in order to determine whether the dependent variable varies by age group. Tentative conclusions are made based upon how the dependent variable changes over the course of development, based on the data collected at a single point in time. Alternatively, a longitudinal design could be conducted, in which a group of individuals is studied over time to determine how variation in the dependent variable changes as the individuals in the sample age.

CROSS-TABULATION. This displays the distribution of one or more dichotomous or categorical variables against the distribution of another dichotomous or categorical variable. The presentation is usually in the format of a contingency table or matrix. Often referred to as a "cross tab."

DEPENDENT T-TEST. A special case of t-test in which the two groups are composed of the same individuals and are being compared on two different measures or on the same measure at two points in time.

DEPENDENT VARIABLE. The presumed effect. In most studies, there is at least one dependent variable. It is called dependent because presumably variation on this variable is dependent upon (affected by) variation in the other variable(s) in the study.

DESCRIPTIVE STATISTICS. Statistics that describe the distribution of a variable. Examples include means, standard deviations, and frequency distributions.

DICHOTOMOUS VARIABLE. A variable with only two mutually exclusive values. Examples include gender or any variable that is coded as presence or absence of an experience or event.

DIFFERENTIAL ATTRITION. When the subjects (families, youth, etc.) in one group of a between-group design leave the study in different patterns than the subjects (families, youth, etc.) of the other group, differential attrition has occurred. Thus, a study could begin with two equivalent groups and end with two groups that are no longer equivalent due to differential attrition.

EFFECT SIZE. A statistic (known as d) that converts all other inferential statistics (such as the t or F or r) into a standard unit that provides information about the strength (size) of the finding. An effect size of .2 is considered small, .5 is considered moderate, and .8 is considered large.

EPISTEMOLOGY. The branch of philosophy concerned with the study of the nature of knowledge and belief.

ETHICAL GUIDELINES. The federal government has developed a series of guidelines for conducting research on human subjects. These are the guidelines used by an agency's institutional review board (IRB) as the basis for review of research proposals. In addition, the researcher himself or herself may be bound by ethical guidelines of his or her professional organization (e.g., the National Association of Social Workers or the American Psychological Association).

EXPEDITED REVIEW. Some research proposals require only expedited review, which is conducted more quickly and with less scrutiny than a proposal requiring full review. In the case of expedited review, the study does not entail collection of new data. Because existing data are used in the study, the review involves primarily an examination of the procedures for ensuring the confidentiality of the research participants.

FALSIFIABILITY. The active attempt to demonstrate that a theory is not correct. The term also refers to the necessity of a theory being specific enough to be subjected to attempts to falsify it.

FOCUS GROUP. A research method in which a group of individuals who have a shared experience or belief participate in a guided group discussion about their opinions and beliefs. Typically, a series of focus groups are conducted on the same topic in order to cover the full range of attitudes likely to be expressed by members of the population of interest. Audiotapes of the conversations are transcribed and submitted to a content analysis.

FORMATIVE PROGRAM EVALUATION. This type of program evaluation aims to assess the extent and nature of the implementation of the program.

GENERALIZABILITY (EXTERNAL VALIDITY). Most research entails the study of a sample in order to learn something about the larger population from which the sample was drawn. Generalizability is the degree to which any particular study is able to do that and is determined by the extent to which the sample is representative of the population.

HUMAN SUBJECTS REVIEW. All research that involves collection of data from human subjects must be submitted for review to an institutional review board (IRB). The federal government as well as relevant professional associations (such as the National Association of Social Workers) have developed guidelines for protecting human subjects who participate in research.

HYPOTHESIS. A statement about the expected findings of a study, usually framed as an expected association between two or more variables. Every hypothesis is framed as both a null hypothesis (in which it is stated that there will be no statistical effects) and an alternative hypothesis (in which effects are expected). An alternative hypothesis can be either directional or nondirectional. If directional, the specific direction of the expected finding is explicated in the hypothesis (such as which group will score higher on a measure than the other group). If a hypothesis is nondirectional, the direction of the finding is not specified in advance (that is, the groups are expected to differ but it is not stated which group will score higher than the other group).

INDEPENDENT VARIABLE. The presumed cause in a study. In most studies, there is at least one independent variable. It is called independent because its variation is considered independent of the influence of the other variables in the study.

INDEPENDENT T-TEST. When two independent (not the same subjects) groups are compared on a single continuous dependent variable, an independent t-test is the appropriate test. The resulting t statistic will reveal whether the differences in mean scores between the two groups is due to chance or real differences between the groups.

IN-DEPTH INTERVIEW. A data collection method for learning about an individual's opinions, experiences, and attitudes. A series of interviews can be conducted on members of a population in order to identify common elements that relate to the study's overall research question. The process of interviewing usually involves following a semistructured protocol in which the interviewee is guided through a discussion involving a series of open-ended questions followed by probes as necessary to gain as full an understanding as possible. Typically, audiotapes of the interviews are transcribed and submitted to a content analysis.

INFERENTIAL STATISTICS. Inferential statistics test for associations among variables.

INFORMED CONSENT. The process of informing potential research participants about a study (orally and in writing) and then obtaining their written permission for participation. There are established guidelines for what information must be included in the informed consent procedure.

INSTITUTIONAL REVIEW BOARD (IRB). A panel of professionals in the fields of research and/or practice that makes a thorough review of all research proposals submitted to an institution (such as a child welfare agency). The members of the board are charged with determining whether the proposed study meets scientific standards in the field as well as all relevant ethical guidelines.

INTER-RATER RELIABILITY. When two or more individuals code the same data (e.g., from agency records, progress notes, responses to focus group questions, etc.) it is important to establish that the different coders agree with one another about the data collected. The standard in the field is that the coders should agree with one another enough to result in a kappa of at least .80.

INTERNAL VALIDITY. In most research, the objective is to test one or more hypotheses regarding the relationship between two or more variables. Even when statistical associations are found, however, there are often plausible alternative explanations for such associations other than that the independent variable and the dependent variable are causally related to each other. Internal validity is the extent to which the researcher can have confidence that the associations found between two or more variables are real as opposed to spurious (caused by some other factor). Seven threats to internal validity have been identified, and these should be ruled out through design and statistical controls in order to strengthen the internal validity of a study.

INTERVAL SCALE. An interval scale indicates the relative strength of each value on the scale. That is, a score of 2 is greater than a score of 1. In addition, the differences between the points on a scale are the same such that the difference between a score of 1 and 2 is the same as the difference between a score of 2 and 3. However, interval scales do not have true zero points and thus certain inferences about the values cannot be made, although they often are.

KAPPA. The statistic used to calculate inter-rater reliability (agreement between two or more coders of the same data). It is more stringent than simply being the percentage of agreement between two coders, as it takes into account the likelihood of chance agreement. A kappa of .80 is considered indicative of adequate reliability.

KURTOSIS. A measure of central tendency used to determine whether a variable is normally distributed. Kurtosis pertains to the extent to which the distribution of the scores around the mean are flat or peaked. Variables that have a kurtosis score above 1 are not considered normally distributed.

LEVEL OF MEASUREMENT. The level of measurement refers to the relationship among the values on a scale. A variable can be measured at four different levels: nominal, ordinal, interval, or ratio. The scale determines the types of statistics that can be conducted.

LINEAR ASSOCIATION. Two variables are linearly associated with each other when the relationship between them is the same across the spectrum of scores on the variables. That is, if there is a positive linear association (as one variable increases so does the other), it is true for low scores, middle scores, and high scores. Likewise, if there is a negative linear association (as scores on one variable decrease, the scores on the other increase), this holds true across all the values of the variable. A nonlinear association (positive or negative) is one in which the association between the two variables is not the same at different points on the scale.

LINEAR REGRESSION. A multivariate statistical test in which there is a single continuous dependent variable and more than one continuous independent variable, the purpose of which is to assess the unique and combined influence of the independent variables on the dependent variable. The independent variables should not be correlated with each other.

LOGISTIC REGRESSION. A multivariate statistical test in which there is a single dichotomous dependent variable and more than one continuous, categorical, or dichotomous independent variable, the purpose of which is to assess the unique and combined influence of the independent variables on the likelihood of the dependent variable occurring. The independent variables should not be correlated with each other.

LONGITUDINAL DESIGN. In this design, a group of individuals is studied over time to determine how variation in the dependent variable changes as the individuals age. Another way to study change over time is with a cross-sectional design, in which individuals of different ages are measured on the dependent variable at a single point in time. Age groups are created (such as infants, toddlers, preschoolers, and so forth) and compared on their scores in order to determine whether the dependent variable varies by age group.

MEAN. A measure of central tendency that indicates the statistically average score. The mean is calculated as the sum of all the scores divided by the number of scores in the sample. When a variable is normally distributed, the mean, median, and mode are the same.

MEDIAN. The median is a measure of central tendency that indicates the score that 50 percent of the sample scores are above and 50 percent of the sample scores are below. When a variable is normally distributed, the mean, median, and mode are the same.

MEASURES OF CENTRAL TENDENCY. The mean, median, and mode are three measures of central tendency that provide the researcher with information about the scores that are in the center of the distribution. When a variable is normally distributed, the mean, median, and mode are the same.

MEASURES OF DISPERSION. Standard deviation and variance are measures that provide the researcher with information about how the scores are dispersed around the mean. A variable with a large variance and standard deviation has a wide range of scores around the mean while a variable with a small variance and standard deviation has a narrow range of scores around the mean.

MODE. The mode is a measure of central tendency that identifies the most frequent value in a sample. When a variable is normally distributed, the mean, median, and mode are the same.

MULTIVARIATE ANALYSIS. In multivariate analyses, the simultaneous association among three or more variables is examined, usually in order to test hypotheses. Examples include linear, logistic, and Cox regression analyses.

MULTIVARIATE ANALYSIS OF VARIANCE (MANOVA). An analysis of variance in which mean differences on multiple independent variables are tested simultaneously.

NOMINAL SCALE. A scale in which the values on the scale do not have numeric value (such as 1=abused, 2=neglected).

NONPARAMETRIC STATISTICS. When the assumptions underlying the use of parametric analyses are not met (usually pertaining to whether the variables are normally distributed), nonparametric analyses can be conducted as an alternative. For example, there are nonparametric equivalents of t-tests, f-tests, and correlations.

NONPROBABILITY SAMPLING. In nonprobability sampling, there is no assurance that every member of the sampling frame has an equal chance of being selected to participate in the study. Either a sampling frame cannot be created or else it is not possible to randomly select members from the sampling frame. Examples include proportionate sampling, snowball sampling, and convenience sampling.

NORMAL DISTRIBUTION. A variable that has a normal distribution is distributed in a "bell curve" such that 68 percent of the cases reside between plus and minus one standard deviation from the mean, 95 percent of the cases reside between plus or minus two standard deviations from the mean, and 98 percent of the cases reside between plus or minus three standard deviations from the mean. Normal distribution is a requirement for most inferential statistics such as correlations, t-tests, ANOVAs, and so forth. If the skewness and kurtosis are smaller than 1.0, the variable is probably normally distributed.

ONE-TAILED SIGNIFICANCE TEST. If the hypothesis is directional, the nature of the expected finding is specified in advance and a one-tail test of significance can be conducted. It is easier to achieve significance with a one-tail test because the 5 percent (if the alpha is .05) is all at one end of the scale, whereas in two-tail tests the 5 percent (if the alpha is .05) is divided between the two tails of the distribution, with only 2.5 percent at each end.

OPEN-ENDED QUESTION. In this type of question, the response options are not provided to the respondent in advance. The respondent answers the question in his or her own words. Responses to open-ended questions are usually analyzed as qualitative data.

OPERATIONALIZATION. The process whereby a theoretical construct (such as depression, substance abuse, maltreatment) is converted into a measurable phenomenon (scores on a specific measure).

ORDINAL SCALE. A scale in which the values indicate relative degree of the variable; that is, a score of 2 is greater than a score of 1. However, it is not possible to determine the degree of difference between the points on the scale. For example, in a scale in which 1=somewhat satisfied and 2=very satisfied, the actual difference between 1 and 2 cannot be determined.

OUTLIER. A statistical outlier is a case that falls outside plus or minus three standard deviations from the mean in variables that are normally distributed. Statistical outliers can be removed from analyses (as long as doing so is described in the final report or paper).

P-VALUE. The probability of obtaining a statistic of a particular size by chance alone. When set in advance, it is referred to as the alpha. All statistical output reports the exact p-value of each statistical test conducted. If the p-value is as at least as small as the alpha, then the null hypothesis is rejected and an effect is considered to have occurred.

PARADIGM. The basic model or schema that organizes the way that a researcher views the world.

PARAMETRIC STATISTICS. Statistics that can be conducted when the variables are normally distributed.

PARTICIPATORY RESEARCH. In this type of research, all of the relevant parties are involved from the beginning in formulating the problem, designing and implementing the study, and analyzing and reporting on the findings.

PEER-REVIEWED JOURNAL. A professional publication in which the results of research studies are presented in a standardized format. Journals typically have an organizing area of interest (child welfare, substance abuse of children, child maltreatment) such that all articles in the journal relate to the overall theme in some fashion. In order to be published in a peer-reviewed journal, the researcher must submit a completed article to the editor of the journal, who then sends the manuscript to two or more professionals in the field (peers) to evaluate the content and scholarship of the manuscript and recommend whether or not the editor should accept the manuscript for publication. In most cases, the reviewers are "blind" to the authorship of the manuscript.

POPULATION. The universe of units to which the researcher wants to generalize the findings obtained from the study of the sample.

POPULATION MEAN ESTIMATE. The best estimate of what the mean of the entire population would be based on the sample mean and the error associated with the measurement (sampling error).

POSITIVISM. The branch of philosophy of science that endorses the use of the scientific method in social science research in order to test and build theory.

POSTPOSITIVISM. The school of thought that revised and responded to criticisms of positivism by acknowledging that human knowledge is conjectural, cumulative, and can be modified over time.

POWER. The strength of the study to detect a statistical effect should one exist. In social science research studies, the aim is to have a power of at least .80. It is calculated as $1-\text{beta}$.

PROBABILITY SAMPLING. In probability sampling, every member of the sampling frame (list of all members of the population) has an equal chance of being selected to participate in the study. Unless every member of the population participates in a study, probability sampling will involve some version of random selection. If random selection is not possible and not every case in the population can be included in the study, nonprobability sampling strategies will be employed.

PROBLEM FORMULATION. The stage of a research study in which the overall research topic is identified. Several sources exist for selecting a research topic, including current events, a researcher's own interests and experiences, practice needs, and prior research.

PROGRAM DIFFUSION. This occurs when the subjects (youth, families, etc.) in the control/comparison group incidentally receive a portion of the intervention designed for the program group.

PURPOSE OF RESEARCH. Research can aim to describe an experience or event, explain the factors associated with an experience or event, or aim to predict the experience or event. The purpose of the research shapes the design and type of data collected.

QUALITATIVE DATA. Qualitative data represent constructs in textual format, which allows for narrative descriptions of events and experiences in their natural context. Examples include responses to in-depth interviews and focus groups as well as the results of case studies.

QUANTITATIVE DATA. Quantitative data represent variables in a numeric format, allowing for descriptive and inferential statistics to be conducted. Examples include responses to survey questions and other standardized and constructed measures.

QUASI-EXPERIMENTAL DESIGN AND EXPERIMENTAL DESIGN. In these designs, data are collected on two or more groups at one or more points in time. In experimental designs, the two (or more) groups are randomly assigned, while in quasi-experimental designs the groups are preexisting or are assigned on a nonrandom basis (such as first come first served or based on need or some other characteristic).

RATIO SCALE. The values on a ratio scale represent both relative strength (1 is greater than 2) and equal distance between the values (the difference between 1 and 2 is the same as the difference between 2 and 3). Only ratio scales have true zero points, allowing for all statistical tests to be conducted.

RELIABILITY. The degree to which a constructed measure is free from error. Measures with high reliability produce the same score on the same measure of the same person at two points in time (or at the same point in time with two different versions of the same measure). A measure with low reliability has error in the measure such that the same person given the same measure at two points in time (or two versions of the same test at a single point in time) will have two different scores even if he or she did not actually change.

RESPONSE RATE. Not all individuals who are invited to participate in a research study actually participate. The response rate is the proportion of invited participants who actually participate. It is important for researchers to track the response rate of their study and include that information in all papers and final reports of the results.

SAMPLING ERROR. The amount of error in the sample mean that is attributed to error in measurement. It is determined by sample size and the standard deviation of the measure.

SAMPLING FRAME. A complete list of every member of the population of interest. It is usually understood that there will be some small difference between the actual population and the sampling frame (some names are left off the list by accident or misspelled, and so forth).

SCIENTIFIC METHOD. Much of social science research follows the blueprint of what is known as the scientific method. This method provides scientists with a conceptual framework for the process of conducting research. This method consists of the following five steps: (1) observation of a phenomenon of interest, (2) development of a theory that can be used to explain this phenomenon, (3) creation of testable hypotheses, (4) empirical testing of hypotheses, and (5) collection and analysis of data in order to determine whether the hypotheses are confirmed. Based on study findings, theory is either supported or refuted.

SINGLE-SYSTEM DESIGN. A quasi-experimental design in which a single case is examined for improvement using the same data collection instruments over the course of receiving a targeted intervention.

SKEWNESS. Like kurtosis, skewness is a measure of central tendency that determines whether a variable is normally distributed. Skewness refers to the extent to which scores are symmetrically distributed on both sides of the mean. A variable that is positively skewed has an elongated tail on the right side of the mean, while a variable that is negatively skewed has an elongated tail on the left side of the mean. Variables that have skewness scores above 1 are not considered normally distributed.

STANDARD DEVIATION. A statistic that measures the degree of variation in the measurement of a sample. It is calculated by subtracting the mean from each score and squaring the result. The sum of these scores is then divided by the sample size minus 1. When a variable is normally distributed all but a few scores lie within plus or minus 3 standard deviations from the mean.

STATISTICAL PACKAGE FOR THE SOCIAL SCIENCES (SPSS). A computer application that allows for data entry and analysis. Files created in other applications can be converted into SPSS files as well. SPSS must be purchased and installed. The user must have knowledge of appropriate statistical analysis and interpretation.

SUMMATIVE PROGRAM EVALUATION. Summative evaluations aim to assess the extent to which a program achieved its objectives of changing the outcomes for the participants.

SURVEY. A constructed measure with multiple items that ask about the respondent's attitudes and experiences, usually about a single overarching topic. Surveys can be mailed or e-mailed to respondents or completed over the phone, in person, or on a computer.

SURVIVAL ANALYSIS. A relatively recent advance in statistical techniques, survival analysis allows for the analysis of rates of an event even when up to half of the cases in the sample have not yet experienced the event. A survival analysis is especially useful for analyzing length of stay, an area of concern in the field of child welfare. A related technique, Cox regression, allows for an examination of the variables that influence the rate of the event occurring.

TABLE OF RANDOM NUMBERS. A chart in which a series of numbers are printed in random order. The table can be used to randomly select members of the sampling frame to participate in a study.

TRANSCRIPT. The written translation of audiotaped material produced in in-depth interviews and focus groups. The text can then be submitted to a content analysis to systematically discover and report on the results of the data collection.

TYPE I ERROR. Type I error occurs when the findings indicate that a statistical effect has occurred when one does not really exist; that is, the null hypothesis was rejected (the alternative hypothesis was accepted) when it should not have been.

TYPE II ERROR. Type II error occurs when the findings indicate the absence of a statistical effect when one really does exist; that is, the null hypothesis was accepted (the alternative hypothesis was rejected) when it should not have been.

UNIT OF ANALYSIS. The subjects of the data collection. In many studies, the unit of analysis is an individual (youth, parent, staff), but it can also be a program, a department, or some other group of individuals.

UNIVARIATE ANALYSIS. Univariate analyses report on a single variable at a time (not in relation to each other). The most common univariate analyses include means, standard deviations, and frequency distributions. Often descriptive information about the sample is presented in the form of univariate analyses.

VALIDITY. The extent to which a measure assesses the construct it is designed to measure. There are several ways to establish that a measure has validity, including face validity, content validity, and predictive validity. A measure without established validity should not be used.

VARIANCE. Variance describes the amount of variation in a sample on a single measure but is not presented in a standardized unit that allows for comparisons across measures or across studies (as is possible with the standard deviation).

WITHIN-GROUP DESIGN. In this design, there is one sample that is measured on more than one variable and/or at more than one point in time.

Glossary 2:
Child Welfare Practice and Policy Terms

The following is a glossary of salient child welfare policy and practice terms that will help readers as they use this text. It is a useful tool that can be used as a reference at any time.

AACWA. See Adoption Assistance and Child Welfare Act.

ADMINISTRATIVE DATA. All child welfare agencies are required by law to maintain a database with basic information about the clients served and the services offered. In many agencies, some or all of these data have been entered into a relational electronic database tied to the payment and reimbursement system of the agency.

ADOPTION. The process by which one or more adults who are not the biological parents of a child become the child's legal parents, following the termination of the biological parent's parental rights. Children adopted from the child welfare system are entitled to receive services and financial support.

ADOPTION AND FOSTER CARE ANALYSIS AND REPORTING SYSTEM (AFCARS). A federal data collection system that provides child-specific information on all children covered by Title IV-B and Title IV-E of the Social Security Act. On an annual basis, all states submit data to the United States Children's Bureau concerning each child in foster care and each child who has been adopted under the authority of a state's child welfare agency.

ADOPTION AND SAFE FAMILIES ACT (ASFA) (PL 105–89). This federal legislation was enacted in 1997 with the goal of reducing the length of time children wait between entering care and being adopted. In addition to allocating funds for the prevention of child abuse and neglect and for assisting families in crisis, ASFA funds specifically cover time-limited reunification services such as counseling, substance abuse treatment services, mental health services, assistance for domestic violence, temporary child care and crisis nurseries, and transportation to and from these services. Adoption promotion and support services (pre- and postadoption) are also included.

ADOPTION ASSISTANCE AND CHILD WELFARE ACT (AACWA) (PL 96–272). Federal legislation enacted in 1980 mandating states that accept federal child welfare funds to provide rehabilitative services to families in order to prevent removal of the child whenever possible and to facilitate speedy reunification once the child has been removed. AACWA was passed in response to mounting child welfare rolls and the perception that insufficient attention was being paid to reunification of children once removed from their home.

ADOPTION DISRUPTION. When a planned adoption does not work out after the child has been placed in an adoptive home, the adoption is considered to have disrupted.

ADOPTION SUBSIDIES. Families who adopt children from the child welfare system are entitled to financial support as a means of eliminating the disincentive that used to exist whereby money provided to foster parents ceased once a child was adopted. Adoption subsidies for special needs children can include medical insurance for the child, counseling services for the entire family, respite care for the adoptive parents, as well as a monthly cash stipend to help cover other extraordinary expenses and services associated with the adoption.

AFCARS. See Adoption and Foster Care Analysis Reporting System.

AFTERCARE. Services that individuals receive following discharge from the child welfare system. With few exceptions, federal and state money are not available for the provision of services to children once final discharged from care.

AGENCY SPELL. The length of time between admission to and discharge from an agency, regardless of the number or types of moves between those two dates.

AGING OUT OF CARE. The term used to describe youth who are in the child welfare system at the time they reach the age of emancipation.

ASFA. See Adoption and Safe Families Act.

BATTERED CHILD SYNDROME. Nonaccidental injuries sustained by a child as a result of physical abuse, usually inflicted by an adult caregiver. It entered the national parlance following revelations made by emergency doctors that recently developed x-ray technology was revealing multiple fractures in children, indicating intentional and persistent abuse of the child by adult caretakers.

BLOCK GRANT. Federal money provided to states in a lump sum regardless of the number of individuals who are eligible to be served under that grant.

CAPTA. See Child Abuse Prevention and Treatment Act.

CASE INITIATION DATE (CID). The date that a case first becomes involved with the child welfare system. It may or not be the same as the beginning of the child's spell.

CFSR. See Child and Family Service Reviews.

CHILD ABUSE/NEGLECT. The physical, sexual, or psychological maltreatment of a child by an adult. The federal government as well as individual states have created a set of definitions of what constitutes child abuse and neglect for the purposes of removing a child and/or prosecuting a criminal charge. These can be viewed at http://www.childwelfare.gov/can/defining/.

CHILD ABUSE PREVENTION AND TREATMENT AND ACT (CAPTA) (PL 93–247). A 1974 piece of federal legislation, CAPTA designated certain professionals to be mandated reporters who were legally required to report suspected cases of child abuse/neglect. In addition, CAPTA provided money to states for monitoring and researching the prevalence and treatment of child abuse. This act was created in response to the medical profession's recognition of the "Battered Child Syndrome," which brought public attention to the problem of child abuse, the need to protect children from harm, and the need to study this widespread problem.

CHILD AND FAMILY SERVICE REVIEWS (CFSR). In January 2000, the United States Department of Health and Human Services (HHS) announced new regulations designed to hold states accountable for being in compliance with federal requirements for child protective services, foster care, adoption, and family preservation and support services under titles IV-B and IV-E of the Social Security Act. Monitoring state compliance is accomplished with the CFSRs, a two-phase process involving statewide assessment and site visits. The results are written in annual reports shared with the HHS and the states in order to provide a comprehensive picture of the strengths and weaknesses of each state's child welfare program. Copies of the reports can be found at http://www.acf.hhs.gov/programs/cb/cwmonitoring/index.htm.

CHILD CARE WORKER. Individuals who work directly with children in a public or private agency or organization and are responsible for helping children to meet their daily needs. The use of the term includes but is not limited to individuals who work in child day care, residential treatment centers, group homes, and other congregate care settings.

CHILD PROTECTIVE SERVICES (CPS). The arm of the child welfare system involved with investigations of allegations of abuse and neglect. Based on the results of abuse/neglect investigations, a case could be referred to in-home prevention services or the child could be removed from home and placed in out-of-home care. In some states, CPS is administered through the government's child welfare administration, and in other states CPS services are provided by voluntary agencies under contract with the child welfare administration.

CHILD SPELL. The length of time between admission to care and discharge from care, regardless of the number or type of moves between those two dates—even moves from one agency to another.

CHILD STATUS. Each child "in the system" (i.e., admitted and not yet discharged from care) has a status on any given day. Options include active, on trial discharge, AWOL, in the hospital, etc.

CHILD WELFARE DEMONSTRATION PROJECTS. The federal government has allowed some states to waive portions of child welfare regulations in order to conduct demonstration projects aimed at identifying ways to improve services. The United States Department of Health and Human Services has approved projects on issues such as helping relatives obtain legal guardianship, prevention, expedited reunification programs, and restructuring of finances related to managed care. Reports are available at the Children's Bureau Web site at http://www.acf.hhs.gov/programs/cb/.

CHILD WELFARE LEAGUE OF AMERICA (CWLA). An association of nearly eight hundred public and private nonprofit agencies that together provide services to millions of abused and neglected children and their families each year. The CWLA is the nation's oldest and largest membership-based child welfare organization. Its goal is to promote the well-being of children, youth, and their families and protect children from harm. Among its many activities, CWLA publishes the premiere child welfare research journal, creates standards for the field, holds professional and lay conferences, and conducts advocacy on behalf of those served by the child welfare system. Its Web site is http://www.cwla.org.

CLOSED ADOPTIONS. In this type of adoption, the birth family and the adoptive family do not share identifying information about themselves and do not communicate with each other, either before or after the placement of the child. The adoption files are sealed and typically are not made available to the adopted child.

COA. See Council on Accreditation.

COUNCIL ON ACCREDITATION (COA). An organization that has developed a process for accrediting child welfare agencies. As of this writing, there are about 1,100 agencies in the United States with COA accreditation (many, but not all of which, are child welfare agencies). Accreditation by COA requires a complex and detailed set of documentation and site visits conducted by a panel of volunteer peer judges. One component of services pertains to continuous quality improvement (CQI). Once approved, an agency is reaccredited every four years.

CONCURRENT PLANNING. The process whereby caseworkers for foster care youth with a permanency goal of reunification simultaneously explore alternatives to reunification in the event that the child cannot safely be returned home. Concurrent planning was mandated in the ASFA legislation of 1997, prior to which alternatives to reunification were not pursued until reunification was deemed not viable.

CONGREGATE CARE. Child welfare placements in which children live in a group facility and are cared for by professional staff. This stands in contrast to foster family care, in which children live with a family and are taken care of by parent substitutes. Group homes, diagnostic reception centers, shelters, and residential treatment centers are the primary forms of congregate care. All are considered a "higher level" of care, in that there are more restrictions on the child's freedom and the setting is less like a family. In some congregate care settings, the youth do not receive services or attend school in the community, while in other congregate care settings they do.

CONTINUOUS QUALITY IMPROVEMENT (CQI). An ongoing cross-program dimension of an agency's operations aimed at improving services and outcomes for its consumers and clients. Following COA's standards for CQI would involve an agency developing ten components, including long- and short-term goals, outcomes, record reviews, and consumer satisfaction surveys.

CONTINUUM OF CARE. This concept denotes the full range of settings and placements available for youth in the child welfare system and includes family-based care such as regular and kinship homes, therapeutic foster homes, and homes for medically fragile children, as well as congregate care settings such as group homes, shelters, diagnostic reception centers, and residential treatment centers.

CQI. See Continuous Quality Improvement.

CRIMINAL BACKGROUND CHECK FOR FOSTER PARENTS. According to federal law, individuals who want to become a foster parent must have a federal background check completed in order to ensure that they do not have a criminal history. This is usually accomplished through submission of fingerprints to a federal registry.

CULTURAL COMPETENCE. The ability of individuals and systems to be respectful toward people of all cultures, classes, races, ethnicities, sexual orientations, faiths, religions, and disabilities and to function in such a way that affirms their unique strengths and dignity. Practically speaking, cultural competence is a way to broaden the knowledge and understanding of individuals and communities through a continuous process of learning about the cultural strengths of others and integrating their unique abilities and perspectives into interactions with them.

CWLA. See Child Welfare League of America.

DIAGNOSTIC RECEPTION CENTER (DRC). A diagnostic reception center is a level of care within the child welfare system. A DRC is usually a short-term facility (ninety-day stay) designed to allow professionals to assess a child's level of functioning in order to determine which level of care for a longer-term placement is appropriate. A DRC can be used at the beginning of a child's spell or it can be used in the middle to assess the need to make a change from one level of care to another.

DIFFERENTIAL RESPONSE. A recent development in child protective services is the creation of a dual-track or differential response to families who come to the attention of the child welfare system. One track is for families with children who require an investigation to determine whether children are at risk for abuse or neglect, and the other track is reserved for the provision of supports and services to families who do not require investigations.

DRC. See Diagnostic Reception Center.

EMOTIONAL ABUSE. No one definition exists that is uniformly used across states to determine founded emotional abuse that requires intervention into the family. A widely accepted definition used by researchers includes seven components of parental behaviors that when exhibited over time demean the child's worth: ignoring, isolating, corrupting, terrorizing, rejecting, overpressuring, and verbally assaulting.

FAMILY PRESERVATION AND FAMILY SUPPORT SERVICES PROGRAM (PL 103–66). As part of the Consolidated Omnibus Budget Reconciliation Act of 1993, Congress established the Family Preservation and Family Support Services Program, which provides flexible funding for community-based services to prevent child abuse/neglect and to help families who are at risk for removal.

FAMILY-CENTERED PRACTICE. A way of working with families that is designed to enhance their capacity to care for and protect their children. It recognizes that all families have strengths and aims to build on these strengths to achieve the best possible outcomes for children.

FINAL DISCHARGE. A final discharge occurs when a child has left the care of an agency and is no longer the responsibility of that agency. A final discharge can be to the family of origin (reunification), to an adopted family (adoption), to self (if the child ages out of care), to AWOL (if the youth has run away from the agency), or a transfer to another agency.

FOSTER CARE. The service provided to children who have been removed from their homes due to abuse, neglect, or other safety concerns. Children in foster care may live with unrelated foster parents (regular foster care), with relatives (kinship care), in group homes, or in residential treatment centers. Foster care was designed primarily as a temporary service while the family regains its ability to care for the child or until the child is adopted. The general expectation is that children who enter care either will return to their family of origin as soon as possible or will be provided with safe, stable, and loving families through placement with relatives or adoption.

FOSTER CARE DRIFT. The problem of children staying in foster care too long without a plan to find them a safe and permanent home.

GROUP HOME. Child welfare congregate care settings that have no more than a set number of beds (the exact number is defined by the state). Typically, group homes serve youth who are somewhat older (the age varies but is often at least twelve years of age). Professional staff provide care and support to the youth in shifts so that some staffperson is on the premises twenty-four hours a day. Youth enter group homes as a "step down" from a higher level of care, such as a residential treatment center, or as a "step up" from a lower level of care, such as a foster home. Most group home youth attend school and receive other services in the neighborhood.

ICWA. See Indian Child Welfare Act.

INDEPENDENT LIVING PROGRAM (PL 99–272). In 1986, Congress authorized the Independent Living Program as part of the Consolidated Omnibus Budget Reconciliation Act, in which funding was provided to the states to provide services to youth to help prepare them for independent living following emancipation from the child welfare system.

INDEPENDENT LIVING SKILLS. Life skills that youth in the foster care system must be taught in preparation for leaving the system and becoming emancipated adults. All youth in the system over the age of fourteen must receive training in these skills, such as food shopping and preparation, managing a budget, navigating public transportation, creating a resume, and job seeking and interviewing skills.

INDIAN CHILD WELFARE ACT (ICWA) (PL 95–608). In response to the large number of native Indian children being placed outside of their tribe, Congress passed the ICWA in 1978. According to this law, all child welfare hearings for Indian children must be held in tribal courts whenever possible. In addition, the law stipulates that tribes have the right to intervene in state proceedings. There are also specific guidelines for placement and reunification of Indian children. A separate stream of money was allocated under the Indian Child Welfare Grant Program.

INTERSTATE COMPACT ON THE PLACEMENT OF CHILDREN. The Interstate Compact on the Placement of Children is statutory law in all fifty-two jurisdictions (the fifty states, Washington D.C., and Puerto Rico). The ICPC establishes uniform legal and administrative procedures governing the interstate placement of children (children residing in one state who are placed in a child welfare home or facility in another state).

JCAHO. See Joint Commission of Accreditation of Healthcare Organizations.

JJDPA. See Juvenile Justice and Delinquency Prevention Act.

JOINT COMMISSION OF ACCREDITATION OF HEALTHCARE ORGANIZATIONS (JCAHO). An organization that has developed a process of accreditation for child welfare agencies. It is perceived to be a good fit for agencies that follow a medical or behavioral health care model of treatment.

JUVENILE JUSTICE AND DELINQUENCY PREVENTION ACT (JJDPA) (93–415). This 1974 act provides the major source of federal funding to improve state juvenile justice systems. The JJDPA was shaped by a general consensus that child offenders should not have contact with adults in jails and other institutional settings and that status offenders (youth who commit crimes that are only crimes because the individual is a child, such as skipping school, running away, breaking curfew, or possession or use of alcohol) should not be placed in secure detention facilities. Under the JJDPA and its subsequent reauthorizations, in order to receive federal funds, states are required to maintain core protections for children.

KINSHIP FOSTER CARE. Family-based foster care in which the foster parents are biologically related to the parents of the child and, therefore, to the child as well. The most common form of kinship care is provided by grandparents.

LEAST RESTRICTIVE SETTING. Out-of-home placement settings vary in the degree to which they place restrictions on youth. Least restrictive settings are those that are family-like and in which children attend school and receive other services in their communities.

LENGTH OF STAY. The number of days in care. Length of stay can be calculated as the number of days of an agency spell or a child spell, depending upon what is of interest. There is longstanding concern among professionals, policymakers, and the public that children's length of stay in the foster care system is too long.

MANDATED REPORTER. A professional who must by law report a case of suspected child abuse to the state registry. Mandated reporters include social workers, teachers, doctors, daycare providers, nurses, and other professionals who come into contact with children and families.

MEPA. See Multi-Ethnic Placement Act.

MOVEMENTS IN CARE. Children in an out-of-home placement often move from one setting to another over the course of their spell in care depending upon their changing needs. Movements can be within a level of care (for example, from one foster home to another) or between levels of care (for example, from a group home to a foster home).

MULTI-ETHNIC PLACEMENT ACT (MEPA) (PL 103–382). Enacted by Congress in 1994, this act prohibited states from delaying or denying adoption on the basis of race or ethnicity and encouraged the recruitment of foster parents from a range of ethnic and racial backgrounds. In 1996, MEPA was revised according to the Inter-Ethnic Placement Act (PL 104–188), in which routine consideration of a child's race or ethnicity was no longer permitted.

NATIONAL CHILD ABUSE AND NEGLECT DATA SYSTEMS (NCANDS). A voluntary national data collection and analysis system created in response to the requirements of the amended Child Abuse Prevention and Treatment Act (Public Law 93–247). The NCANDS consists of two components: (1) the Summary Data Component (SDC), which is a compilation of key aggregate child abuse and neglect statistics from all states, including data on reports, investigations, victims, and perpetrators; and (2) the Detailed Case Data Component (DCDC), a compilation of case-level information from those child protective service agencies that are able to submit electronic child abuse and neglect records.

NATIONAL DATA ARCHIVE ON CHILD ABUSE AND NEGLECT (NDACAN). The mission of the NDACAN is to facilitate the secondary analysis of research data relevant to the study of child abuse and neglect.

NCANDS. See National Child Abuse and Neglect Data Systems.

NEIGHBORHOOD-BASED SERVICES. Services to children and families that are provided in their home community. In the child welfare system such services are favored, consistent with the belief that safety and permanency for children and families is best served through a neighborhood-based approach that seeks to provide every child and family with culturally, linguistically, and need-driven services within their own communities.

NONKINSHIP FOSTER CARE. This form of foster care is provided by adults who are not biologically related to the child. The adults, who must be licensed and trained by an agency, receive a placement based on the agency's determination that the child and the foster family represent a good fit for each other.

OPEN ADOPTIONS. Open adoptions vary depending upon the type of relationship that the birth parents and the adoptive parents have agreed to, but, in order to be considered an open adoption, there must be some sharing of information. This could include last names, addresses, and telephone numbers. In some open adoptions, the birth parent and the adoptive family know each other and/or have ongoing communication and contact.

OUT-OF-HOME CARE/PLACEMENT. The removal of the child from his or her home due to concerns about the child's safety and the subsequent placement of the child in twenty-four-hour-a-day care provided by an agency that is contracted with the government's child welfare administration. This could be a licensed family foster home, an approved kinship foster home, or a congregate care facility. Legal responsibility of the child transfers from the family to the agency and/or the child welfare administration.

PERMANENCY GOAL. Federal law requires that every child in the child welfare system have a case plan. Part of that plan is the permanency goal, the desired outcome of the intervention and services provided to the child and family. The goal must be consistent with the health, safety, well-being, and best interests of the child. The primary permanency goals are reunification, adoption, return to relatives/family members, and independent living.

PERSON IN NEED OF SUPERVISION (PINS). Parents can file a petition in family court to have their child (of a certain age) deemed a person in need of supervision. A PINS designation is not for abused children and it is not for juvenile delinquents who have committed illegal acts. PINS is intended to be used for misguided youth who are acting out, hanging with a "bad" crowd, not complying with reasonable household rules, or who are running away from home. It was designed as a mechanism for helping families keep youth on the right track until they are able to make good decisions for themselves.

PINS. See Person in Need of Supervision.

PREVENTION. Prevention services are provided to families in order to strengthen the family and prevent the placement of one or more children into the foster care system. Depending upon the family's needs, prevention can include a range of concrete services and emotional support, including substance abuse counseling, budgeting, parent education, and so forth. Some prevention programs follow a national model such as Homebuilders, while others provide their own mix of services.

REENTRY INTO CARE. Reentry occurs when a child is placed in out-of-home care following a final discharge from care. Most agencies are not able to monitor the proportion of discharged cases that reenter care because a youth can return to care at another agency, unbeknownst to the agency from which the child was discharged.

RESIDENTIAL TREATMENT CENTER (RTC). The highest level of care within the child welfare system, placement in a residential treatment center is reserved for youth who have been removed from home due to abuse or neglect and have serious emotional and behavioral disorders. RTCs are typically large institutions serving at least twenty-five but often as many as several hundred youth at a time. RTC youth typically attend a special school on the campus of the RTC and receive a wide range of mental health services while in care.

REUNIFICATION. Reunification occurs when a child is returned to the family of origin after spending time in a foster care placement.

RISK ASSESSMENT. The systematic determination of the degree to which the home environment poses a risk to the child for abuse or neglect. Risk assessments are part of most abuse/neglect investigations as well as monitoring of families in preparation for reunification.

RTC. See Residential Treatment Center.

SACWIS. See Statewide Automated Child Welfare Information System.

SERVICE PLAN REVIEWS. All children removed from home are entitled to periodic reviews of their case. The review entails an in-depth discussion of the barriers to reunification (both child and family level) and is designed to ensure that the child and family are receiving the services necessary to expedite the child's placement in a safe and permanent home. Families are to be informed of and invited to attend service plan reviews in order to ensure their involvement in the child's treatment and planning.

SEXUAL ABUSE. Many different definitions of sexual abuse exist. One useful one is that sexual abuse is the use of any child (through coercion or persuasion) to engage in (or assist any other person to engage in) any sexually explicit conduct or simulation of such conduct.

STANDARDS OF CARE. The Child Welfare League of America (CWLA) has created a set of books outlining what the field considers to be best practice in eleven different program areas (foster home, group homes, and so forth). These standards are widely accepted as the foundation for sound child welfare practice in the United States and provide goals for the continuing improvement of services to children and their families. They can be ordered from the CWLA Web site at http://www .CWLA.org/pubs/.

STANDARDS OF PAYMENT. Federal and state guidelines for determining how much and by what formula agencies and families will be reimbursed for the care of children in the child welfare system.

STATE ADOPTION INCENTIVES. States can apply to the federal government for reimbursement of money spent with the express purpose of increasing the number of foster child adoptions and special needs adoptions. States can request these funds following submission of their AFCARS reports.

STATEWIDE AUTOMATED CHILD WELFARE INFORMATION SYSTEM (SACWIS). A computerized case management tool designed to support foster care and adoption practice. Currently, most states are involved with SACWIS either at the planning, development, or implementation phase. The Division of State Systems (DSS) provides oversight for the funding and management of SACWIS for the United States Department of Health and Human Services. The Children's Bureau Web site provides a list of resources, statutes, regulations, and other SACWIS-related policies and information: http://www.acf.hhs.gov/programs/cb/systems/sacwis/about.htm.

SYSTEMS OF CARE. This term denotes a philosophy of providing mental health services to children and families and usually involves a coordinated network of community-based services that are strength-based and culturally competent.

TANF. See Temporary Assistance to Needy Families.

TEMPORARY ASSISTANCE TO NEEDY FAMILIES (TANF). TANF was created by the federal welfare reform legislation (PL 104–193), the Personal Responsibility and Work Opportunity Reconciliation Act (PRWORA), to replace Aid to Families with Dependent Children (AFDC). States are required to use TANF funds for one of four purposes: (1) to provide assistance to needy families so that children may be cared for in their own homes or in the homes of relatives, (2) end dependence of needy parents on government benefits by promoting work and marriage, (3) prevent and reduce out-of-wedlock-pregnancies, and (4) encourage the formation and maintenance of two-parent families. However, states have broad flexibility in implementing these. For example, they are allowed to set their own income eligibility standards.

TERMINATION OF PARENTAL RIGHTS (TPR). A court order that severs the rights, powers, privileges, immunities, duties, and obligations between a parent and child. A termination of parental rights may be voluntary or involuntary. Only after the TPR has been completed can a foster child be considered available for adoption.

TFBH. See Therapeutic Foster Boarding Home.

THERAPEUTIC FOSTER BOARDING HOME (TFBH). Licensed foster homes for children in the child welfare system who have been classified as having emotional or behavioral problems that would make them too difficult for a regular or kinship foster home. TFBH parents are paid a higher daily rate to care for the child, receive additional training and support in caring for the child, and are considered part of the treatment team. Often there are specific behavioral management systems and report forms that the TFBH parents must implement and utilize. Sometimes TFBH care is called treatment foster care or specialized foster care.

TITLE IV-B. Title IV-B of the Social Security Act pertains to grants to states for aid and services to needy families with children and for child welfare services. Title

IV-B is administered by the United States Department of Health and Human Services. Part B of Title IV, child and family services, has two subparts: child welfare services and promoting safe and stable families.

TITLE IV-E. A subpart of Title IV of the Federal Social Security Act. This program provides federal reimbursement to states for the costs of children placed in child welfare settings under a court order or voluntary placement agreement. Title IV-E benefits are an individual entitlement for qualified children who have been removed from their homes. Eligibility is based on income of the family of origin.

TRIAL DISCHARGE. The reunification of a child in out-of-home placement to his/her family of origin for a set period of time in order to determine whether the child and family are prepared for a final discharge home. Unlike final discharge, the agency is still responsible for the child and can return the child to placement if necessary.

VOLUNTARY PLACEMENT. Parents can agree to have their child placed in the foster care system without a legal determination of child abuse and neglect if they sign papers stating that they voluntarily agree to do so.

References

Achenbach, T. M. 1991. *Manual for Child Behavior Checklist / 4–18 and 1991 Profile*. Burlington: University of Vermont Department of Psychiatry.

Achenbach, T. M., and S. H. McConoughy. 1997. "Illustrations of Special Assessment Needs." In *Empirically Based Assessment of Child and Adolescent Psychopathology: Practical Applications*. Developmental Clinical Psychology and Psychiatry 13. Newbury Park, Calif.: Sage Publications.

Achenbach, T. M., P. J. Pecora, and G. Armsden. 2002. "Using the Child Behavior Checklist 4–18, Teacher's Report Form, Youth Self-Report, and Related Measures in Child and Family Services." In *Assessing Youth Behavior: Using the Child Behavior Checklist in Family and Children's Services*, edited by N. S. Le Prohn et al., 7–52. Washington, D.C.: CWLA Press.

Albrecht, T., G. M. Johnson, and J. B. Walther. 1993. "Understanding Communication Processes in Focus Groups." In *Successful Focus Groups: Advancing the State of the Art*, edited by D. L. Morgan, 51–64. Newbury Park, Calif.: Sage Publications.

Allen, D. M., J. S. Lehman, T. A. Green, M. L. Lindegren, I. M. Onorato, W. Forrester, and the Field Services Branch. 1994. "HIV Infection Among Homeless Adults and Runaway Youth, United States, 1989–1992." *AIDS* 8: 1593–1598.

Alpert, L. 2005. "Research Review: Parents' Service Experience—A Missing Element in Research on Foster Care Case Outcomes." *Child and Family Social Work* 10: 361–366.

Andrews, J. A., H. Hops, D. Ary, E. Tildesley, and J. Harris. 1993. "Parental Influence on Early Adolescent Substance Use: Specific and Nonspecific Effects." *Journal of Early Adolescence* 13, no. 3: 285–310.

Babbie, E. 1990. *Survey Research Methods.* 2nd ed. Belmont, Calif.: Wadsworth.

Bailey, S. L., C. S. Camlin, and S. T. Ennett. 1998. "Substance Use and Risky Sexual Behavior Among Homeless and Runaway Youth." *Journal of Adolescent Health* 23: 378–388.

Bain, A. 1978. The Capacity of Families to Cope with Transitions: A Theoretical Essay." *Human Relations* 31, no. 8: 675–688.

Baker, A. J. L., M. Archer, and P. Curtis. Forthcoming. "Characteristics Associated with Behavioral and Mental Health Problems During the Transition to Residential Treatment." *Child Welfare.*

Baker, A. J. L., and P. Calderon. 2004. "The Role of Group Homes in the Child Welfare Continuum of Care." *Residential Treatment for Children and Youth* 21: 39–58.

Baker, A. J. L., W. Friedrich, R. Parker, M. Schneiderman, L. Gries, and M. Archer. Forthcoming. "Problematic Sexualized Behaviors in the Child Welfare System." *Child and Adolescent Social Work.*

Baker, A. J. L., D. Fullmore, and J. Collins. Forthcoming. "A Survey of Mental Health Service Provision in New York State Residential Treatment Centers." *Residential Treatment for Children and Youth.*

Baker, A. J. L., D. Kurland, P. Curtis, C. Papa-Lentini, and G. Alexander. Forthcoming. "Mental Health and Behavioral Problems of Youth in the Child Welfare System: Residential Treatment Centers Compared to Therapeutic Foster Care in the Odyssey Project Population." *Child Welfare.*

Baker, A. J. L., C. Piotrkowski, and C. Mincer. 2003. "Behavioral Predictors of Psychiatric Emergency in a Child Welfare Residential Treatment Center." *Residential Treatment for Children and Youth* 21: 51–70.

Baker, A. J. L., M. Schneiderman, and R. Parker. 2001. "A Survey of Problematic Sexualized Behaviors of Children in the New York City Child Welfare System." *Journal of Child Sexual Abuse* 10: 67–80.

Baker, A. J. L., F. Wulczyn, and N. Dale. 2005. "Covariates of Length of Stay in Residential Treatment." *Child Welfare* 84, no. 3: 363–386.

Bank, S. P., and M. D. Kahn. 1982. *The Sibling Bond.* New York: Basic Books.

Barlow, D., and M. Hersen. 1973. "Single Case Experimental Designs: Uses in Applied Clinical Research." *Archives of General Psychiatry* 29: 319–325.

Barney, M., J. Levin, and N. Smith. 1994. "Fact Sheet No. 32: Respite for Foster Parents. National Resource Center for Crisis and Respite Care Services." Retrieved December 5, 2006, from http://www.archrespite.org/archfs32.htm.

Barth, R. P. 1990. "On Their Own: The Experiences of Youth After Foster Care." *Child and Adolescent Social Work* 7, no. 5: 219–240.

Barth, R. P., and M. Berry. 1988. *Adoption and Disruption: Rates, Risks, and Responses.* Hawthorne, N.Y.: Adline de Gruyter.

Barth, R. P., M. Berry, R. Yoshikami, R. K. Goodfield, and M. L. Carson. 1988. "Predicting Adoption Disruption." *Social Work* 33, no. 3: 227–233.

Barth, R. P., D. Gibbs, and K. Siebenaler. 2001. "Assessing the Field of Post-Adoption Service: Family Needs, Program Models, and Evaluation Issues." Contract No. 100–99–0006. Washington, D.C.: U.S. Department of Health and Human Services.

Barth, R. P., and M. Jonson-Reid. 2000. "Outcomes After Child Welfare Services: Implications for the Design of Performance Measures." *Children and Youth Services Review* 22: 763–787.

Beeman, S., and L. Boison. 1999. "Child Welfare Professionals' Attitudes Toward Kinship Foster Care." *Child Welfare* 78: 315–330.

Berg, Bruce L. 1998. *Qualitative Research Methods for the Social Sciences*. Boston: Allyn and Bacon.

Berrick, J.D., R. P. Barth, B. Needell, and M. Jonson-Reid. 1997. "Group Care and Young Children." *Social Service Review* 71, no. 2: 257–273.

Berrick, J. D., and B. Needell. 1999. "Recent Trends in Kinship Care: Public Policy, Payments, and Outcomes for Children." In *The Foster Care Crisis*, edited by P. A. Curtis, G. Dale Jr., and J. C. Kendall. Lincoln: University of Nebraska Press.

Berrick, J. D., B. Needell, R. P. Barth, and M. Jonson-Reid. 1998. *The Tender Years: Toward Developmentally Sensitive Child Welfare Services for Very Young Children*. New York: Oxford University Press.

Berry, M., and R. P. Barth. 1990. "A Study of Disrupted Adoptive Placements of Adolescents." *Child Welfare* 69, no. 3: 209–225.

Bloom, M. J., J. Fischer, and J. G. Orme. 2003. *Evaluating Practice: Guidelines for the Accountable Professional*. 4th ed. Boston: Allyn and Bacon.

Brentro, L. K., and A. E. Ness. 1982. "Perspectives on Peer Group Treatment: The Use and Abuse of Guided Group Interaction/Positive Peer Culture." *Children and Youth Services Review* 4, no. 4: 307–324.

Briere, J. 1992. *Child Abuse Trauma: Theory and Treatment of the Lasting Effects*. Thousand Oaks, Calif.: Sage.

Bryant, A. L., and M. A. Zimmerman. 2002. "Examining the Effects of Academic Beliefs and Behaviors on Changes in Substance Use Among Urban Adolescents." *Journal of Educational Psychology* 94, no. 3: 621–637.

Burch, R. 1991. "Phenomenology and Human Science Reconsidered." *Phenomenology + Pedagogy* 19: 27–69.

Campbell, D. T., and J. C. Stanley. 2005. *Experimental and Quasi-Experimental Designs for Research*. New York: Houghton Mifflin.

Carlson, N. M., and M. McCaslin. 2003. "Meta-Inquiry: An Approach to Interview Success." *The Qualitative Report* 8, no. 4: 549–569.

Carter, G. W. 1955. "Problem Formulation in Social Work Research." *Social Casework* 36: 295–302.

Chahine, Z., J. Van Straatan, and A. Williams-Isom. 2005. "The New York City Neighborhood-Based Service Strategy." *Child Welfare* 84, no. 2: 141–152.

Chamberlain, P., J. M. Price, J. B. Reid, J. Landsverk, P. A. Fisher, and M. Stool-miller. 2006. "Who Disrupts from Placement in Foster and Kinship Care?" *Child Abuse & Neglect* 30, no. 4: 409–424.

Child Welfare League of America. 1995. *Child Abuse and Neglect: A Look at the States*. Washington, D.C.: Child Welfare League of America.

———. 2001. "The Child Welfare Workforce Challenge. Results from a Preliminary Study." Presented at the Findings Better Ways Conference, Dallas, Tex.

Children's Bureau. 2003. "Adoption and Foster Care Analysis and Reporting System: Preliminary FY 2001 Estimates as of March 2003." Retrieved June 29, 2004, from http://www.acf.hhs.gov/programs/cb/publications/afcars/report8.htm.

———. 2004. "General Findings from the Federal Child and Family Services Review." Washington, D.C.: U.S. Department of Health and Human Services, Administration for Children and Families. Retrieved January 5, 2004, from http://www.acf.hhs.gov/programs/cb/cwmonitoring/results/genfindings04/index.htm.

———. 2006. "Adoptions of Children with Public Child Welfare Agency Involvement by State. FY 1995–FY 2004." Washington, D.C.: U.S. Department of Health and Human Services, Administration for Children and Families, Administration on Children, Youth and Families.

Chippman, R., S. W. Wells, and M.A. Johnson. 2002. "The Meaning of Quality in Kinship Care: Caregiver, Child, and Worker Perspectives." *Families in Society* 83, no. 5/6: 508–521.

Cicchetti, D. 1984. "The Emergence of Developmental Psychopathology." *Child Development* 55: 1–7.

Clausen, J. M., J. Landsverk, W. Ganger, D. Chadwick, and A. Litrownick. 1998. "Mental Health Problems of Children in Foster Care." *Child Abuse & Neglect* 18: 923–932.

Cohen, J. 1969. *Statistical Power Analysis for the Behavioral Sciences*. 1st ed. Hillsdale, N.J.: Lawrence Erlbaum and Associates.

Conboy, A., C. Auerbach, D. Schnall, and H. H. LaPorte. 2000. "MSW Student Satisfaction with Using Single System Design Software to Evaluate Social Work Practice." *Research on Social Work Practice* 10, no. 1: 127–138.

Connell, C. M., K. H. Katz, L. Saunders, and K. Tebes. 2006. "Leaving Foster Care—the Influence of Child and Case Characteristics on Foster Care Exit Rates." *Children and Youth Services Review* 28: 780–798.

Constatine, M. G., G. M. Anderson, L. A. Berkel, L. D. Caldwell, and S. O. Utsey. 2005. "Examining the Cultural Adjustment Experiences of African International College Students: A Qualitative Analysis." *Journal of Counseling Psychology* 52, no. 1: 57–66.

Corbetta, P. 2003. *Social Research*. Thousand Oaks, Calif.: Sage.

Cordero, A. E. 2004. "When Family Reunification Works: Data Mining Foster Care Records." *Families in Society* 85, no. 4: 571–580.

Courtney, M. E., and I. Piliavin. 1998. *Foster Youth Transitions to Adulthood: Outcomes 12 to 18 Months After Leaving Out of Home Care.* Madison: University of Wisconsin, School of Social Work and Institute for Research and Poverty.

Courtney, M. E., I. Piliavin, A. Grogan-Kaylor, and A. Nesmith. 2001. "Foster Youth Transitions to Adulthood: A Longitudinal View of Youth Leaving Care." *Child Welfare Journal* 80, no. 6: 685–717.

Cowen, P. S., and D. A. Reed. 2002. "Effects of Respite Care for Children with Developmental Disabilities: Evaluation of an Intervention for At-Risk Families." *Public Health Nursing* 19, no. 4: 272–283.

Craven, P. A., and R. E. Lee. 2006. "Therapeutic Interventions for Foster Children: A Systematic Research Synthesis." *Research on Social Work Practice* 16, no. 3: 287–304.

Crenshaw, D. A. 1993. "Responding to Sexual Acting-Out." In *Children in Residential Care: Critical Issues in Treatment,* edited by C. E. Schaefer and A. J. Swanson, 19–29. Hillsdale, N.J.: Jason Aronson, Inc.

Creswell, J. W. 1998. *Qualitative Inquiry and Research Design: Choosing Among Five Traditions.* London: Sage.

Cuddeback, G. S. 2004. "Kinship Family Foster Care: A Methodological and Substantive Synthesis of Research." *Children and Youth Services Review* 26, no. 7: 623–639.

Curran, M. C., and P. J. Pecora. 1999. "Incorporating the Perspectives of Youth Placed in Family Foster Care: Selected Research Findings." In *The Foster Care Crisis: Translating Research Into Policy and Practice,* edited by P. A. Curtis et al., 99–128. Lincoln: University of Nebraska Press / Child Welfare League of America.

Dagenais, C., J. Begin, C. Bouchard, and D. Fortin. 2004. "Impact of Intensive Family Support Programs: A Synthesis of Evaluation Studies." *Children and Youth Services Review* 26: 249–263.

Dale, G., J. C. Kendall, and J. S. Schultz. 1999. "A Proposal for Universal Medical and Mental Health Screenings for Children Entering Foster Care." In *The Foster Care Crisis: Translating Research Into Policy and Practice,* edited by P. A. Curtis et al., 175–192. Lincoln: University of Nebraska Press / Child Welfare League of America.

Dance, C., and A. Rushton. 2005. "Predictors of Outcome for Unrelated Adoptive Placements Made During Middle Childhood." *Child & Family Social Work* 10, no. 4: 269–280.

Deblinger, E., and A. H. Heflin. 1996. *Treating Sexually Abused Children and Their Non-Offending Parents: A Cognitive Behavioural Approach.* Thousand Oaks, Calif.: Sage.

Denzin, N. K. 1989. *The Research Act: A Theoretical Introduction to Sociological Methods.* 3rd ed. Englewood Cliffs, N.J.: Prentice Hall.

Denzin, N. K., and Y. S. Lincoln, eds. 1994. *Handbook of Qualitative Research.* London: Sage.

References

Diego, M. A., T. M. Field, and C. E. Sanders. 2003. "Academic Performance, Popularity, and Depression Predict Adolescent Substance Use." *Adolescence* 38, no. 149: 35–42.

Dillman, D. A. 1978. *Mail and Telephone Surveys: The Total Design Method.* New York: Wiley.

DosReis, S., J. M. Zito, D. J. Safer, and K. L. Soeken. 2001. "Mental Health Services for Youths in Foster Care and Disabled Youths." *American Journal of Public Health* 91, no. 7: 1094–1099.

Durkheim, E. 1938. *Rules of the Sociological Method.* Chicago: University of Chicago Press.

Edmond, T., W. Auslander, D. E. Elze, C. McMillen, and R. Thompson. 2002. "Differences Between Sexually Abused and Non-Sexually Abused Adolescent Girls in Foster Care." *Journal of Child Sexual Abuse* 11, no. 4: 73–99.

Empey, L. T., and S. G. Lubeck. 1972. *The Silverlake Experiment.* Chicago: Aldine.

Ernest, P. 1999. *Social Constructivism as a Philosophy of Mathematics.* Albany, N.Y.: SUNY Press.

Evan B. Donaldson Adoption Institute. 2004. "What's Working for Children: A Policy Study of Adoption Stability and Termination." Retrieved November 15, 2004, from http://www.adoptioninstitute.org/publications/Disruption_Report .pdf.

Fanshal, D. 1971. "The Exit of Children from Foster Care: An Interim Research Report." *Child Welfare* 50: 65–81.

Federal Register. 1993a (December 22). "Adoption and Foster Care Analysis and Reporting System (AFCARS). Final Rule (45 Code of Federal Regulations, Parts 1355 and 1356)."

———. 1993b (December 22). "Statewide Automated Child Welfare Information System (SACWIS), Interim Rule (45 Code of Federal Regulations, Parts 1355 and 1365)."

Festinger, Trudy. 1983. *No One Ever Asked Us . . . A Postscript to Foster Care.* New York: Columbia University Press.

———. 1994. *Returning to Care: Discharge and Reentry in Foster Care.* Washington, D.C.: Child Welfare League of America.

———. 1996. "Going Home and Returning to Foster Care." *Children and Youth Services Review* 18, no. 4/5: 383–402.

———. 2002. "After Adoption: Dissolution or Permanence?" *Child Welfare* 81, no. 3: 515–533.

Fontana, V. J. 1968. "Further Reflections on Maltreatment of Children. New York State." *Journal of Medicine* 68, no. 16: 2214–2215.

Fowler, F. J., and T. W. Mangione. 1990. *Standardized Survey Interviewing: Minimizing Interviewer-Related Error.* Newbury Park, Calif.: Sage.

Frame, L., J. D. Berrick, and M. L. Brodowski. 2000. "Understanding Reentry to Out-of-Home Care for Reunified Infants." *Child Welfare* 79: 339–369.

Fraser, M., P. Pecora, and D. A. Haapala. 1991. *Families in Crisis: Findings from the Family-Based Intensive Treatment Project.* Salt Lake City: Social Research Institute, University of Utah.

Fraser, M., E. Walton, R. Lewis, P. Pecora, and W. Walton. 1996. "An Experiment in Family Reunification Services: Correlates of Outcomes at One-Year Follow Up." *Children and Youth Services Review* 18, no. 4/5: 335–361.

Friedrich, W. 2002. "An Integrated Model of Psychotherapy for Abused Children." In *The APSAC Handbook of Child Maltreatment*, edited by J. E. B. Myers et al., 141–157. Thousand Oaks, Calif.: Sage.

Froland, C., G. Brodsky, M. Olson, and L. Stewart. 1979. "Social Support and Social Adjustment: Implications for Mental Health Professionals." *Community Mental Health Journal* 15, no. 2: 82–93.

Gaudin, J.M., and L. Pollane. 1983. "Social Networks, Stress, and Child Abuse." *Children and Youth Services Review* 5: 91–102.

Gebel, T. 1996. "Kinship Care and Non-Relative Family Foster Care: A Comparison of Caregiver Attributes and Attitudes." *Child Welfare* 75, no. 1: 5–18.

Gibbs, L. E. 1991. *Scientific Reasoning for Social Workers: Bridging the Gap Between Research and Practice.* New York: MacMillan.

Gibson, T., G. S. Tracy, and M. S. DeBord. 1984. "An Analysis of Variables Affecting Length of Stay in Foster Care." *Children and Youth Services Review* 6: 135–145.

Gilles, T., and J. Kroll. 1991. "Barriers to Same Race Placement. Research Brief #2." St. Paul, Minn.: North American Council on Adoptable Children.

Glaser, B. G., and A. L. Strauss. 1967. *The Discovery of Grounded Theory: Strategies for Qualitative Research.* New Brunswick, N.J.: Aldine Transaction.

Glisson, C., D. Dukes, and P. Green. 2006. "The Effects of the ARC Organizational Intervention on Caseworker Turnover, Climate, and Culture in Children's Service Systems." *Child Abuse & Neglect* 30: 855–880.

Goerge, R. M., E. C. Howard, D. Yu, and S. Radomsky. 1997. *Adoption, Disruption, and Displacement in the Child Welfare System, 1976–1994.* Chicago: Chapin Hall Center for Children at the University of Chicago.

Goerge, R. M., F. Wulczyn, and A. W. Harden. 1994. *A Report from the Multi-State Foster Care Archive: Foster Care Dynamics 1983–1993.* Chicago: Chapin Hall Center for Children at the University of Chicago.

Goodman, L., L. Saxe, and M. Harvey. 1991. "Homelessness as Psychological Trauma." *American Psychologist* 46: 1219–1225.

Gredler, M. E. 1997. *Learning and Instruction: Theory Into Practice.* 3rd ed. Upper Saddle River, N.J.: Prentice-Hall.

Green, M. 2002. "Care for the Caregivers." Available online at http://www.cwla.org/articles/cv0205carecaregivers.htm.

Greenblatt, M., R. M. Becerra, and E. A. Serafetinides. 1982. "Social Networks and Mental Health: An Overview." *American Journal of Psychiatry* 139, no. 8: 977–984.

Groza, V., D. Roberson, B. Brindo, S. Darden-Kautz, K. L. Fujimura, D. Goode-Cross, and S. Prusak. 2002. *Minority Adoption Project: Removing Barriers and Increasing Supports to Minority Children and Families.* Final report for Bellefaire JCB, funded by the U.S. Department of Health and Human Services, ACYF, Opportunities in Adoption Demonstration Grant, # 90-CO-0884. Available online at http://msass.case.edu/downloads/vgroza/Final_Report_Minority_Adoption_Project.pdf.

Guest, K. M., A. J. L. Baker, and R. Storaasli. Forthcoming. "The Problem of Adolescent AWOL from a Residential Treatment Center." *Residential Treatment for Children and Youth.*

Guo, J., I. Chung, K. G. Hill, D. Hawkins, R. F. Catalano, and R. D. Abbott. 2002. "Developmental Relationships Between Adolescent Substance Use and Risky Sexual Behavior in Young Adulthood." *Journal of Adolescent Health* 31, no. 4: 354–362.

Guy, S. M., G. M. Smith, and P. M. Bentler. 1994. "The Influence of Adolescent Substance Use and Socialization on Deviant Behavior in Young Adulthood." *Criminal Justice and Behavior* 21, no. 2: 236–255.

Hall, D. K., F. Mathews, and J. Pearce. 2002. "Sexual Behavior Problems in Sexually Abused Children: A Preliminary Typology." *Child Abuse & Neglect* 26: 289–312.

Hall, G. S. 1904. *Adolescence: Its Psychology and Its Relation to Physiology, Anthropology, Sociology, Sex, Crime, Religion, and Education.* New York: Appleton.

Handwerk, M., P. Friman, M. Mott, and J. Stairs. 1998. "The Relationship Between Program Restrictiveness and Youth Behavior Problems." *Journal of Emotional and Behavioral Disorders* 6: 170–179.

Harden, B. J., R. B. Clyman, D. Kriebel, and J. Lyons. 2004. "Kith and Kin Care: Parental Attitudes and Resources of Foster and Relative Caregivers." *Children and Youth Services Review* 26, no. 7: 657–671.

Hartman, A. 1990. "Many Ways of Knowing." *Social Work* 35, no. 1: 3–4.

Hawkins, J. D., R. F. Catalano, and J. Y. Miller. 1992. "Risk and Protective Factors for Alcohol and Other Drug Problems in Adolescence and Early Adulthood: Implications for Substance Abuse Prevention." *Psychological Bulletin* 112, no. 1: 64–105.

Herman, J. 1997. *Trauma and Recovery.* New York: Basic Books.

Holloway, I. 1997. *Basic Concepts of Qualitative Research.* Oxford: Blackwell Science.

Hoyle, S. G. 2000. *The Sexualized Child in Foster Care.* Washington, D.C.: CWLA Press.

Hoyt, D. R., K. D. Ryan, and A. M. Cauce. 1999. "Personal Victimization in a High-Risk Environment: Homeless and Runaway Adolescents." *Journal of Research in Crime and Delinquency* 36: 371–392.

Huber, J., and B. Grimm. 2004. "Most States Fail to Meet the Mental Health Needs of Foster Children." *Youth Law News* 25, no. 4: 1–13.

Hudson, W. W. 1978. "First Axioms of Treatment." *Social Work* 28: 65–66.

Hukkanen, R., A. Sourande, and L. Bergroth. 2003. "Suicidal Ideation and Behaviour in Children's Homes." *Nordic Journal of Psychiatry* 57: 131–137.

Hunter, R. 1904. *Poverty*. New York: MacMillian.

Husserl, E. 1990. *Ideas Pertaining to a Pure Phenomenology and to a Phenomenological Philosophy: Studies in Phenomenology of the Constitution*. New York: Springer.

Johnson, B., and L. Christensen. 2000. *Educational Research: Quantitative and Qualitative Approaches*. Boston: Allyn Bacon.

Jourard, S. M. 1964. *The Transparent Self: Self-Disclosure and Well-Being*. New York: Van Nostrand Rheinhold.

Kapp, S. A. 2000. "Positive Peer Culture: The Viewpoint of Firmer Clients." *Journal of Child and Adolescent Group Therapy* 10, no. 4: 175–189.

Kapp, S. A., and J. Propp. 2002. "Client Satisfaction Methods: Input from Parents with Children in Foster Care." *Child and Adolescent Social Work Journal* 19, no. 3: 227–245.

Katz, L., N. Spoonemore, and C. Robinson. 1994. *Preparing Permanency Planning for Foster Parents: A Foster Parent Training Manual*. Mountlake Terrace, Wash.: Lutheran Social Services of Washington and Idaho.

Kellogg Foundation. 2004. *Logic Model Guide*. Battle Creek, Mich.: Kellogg Foundation.

Kendall, P. L., and P. F. Lazarsfeld. 1950. "Problems of Survey Research." In *Continuities in Social Research: Studies in the Scope and Method of the American Soldier*, edited by R. K. Merton and P. F. Lazarsfeld. New York: Free Press.

Kenny, D. A. 1979. *Correlation and Causality*. New York: John Wiley and Sons.

Kilpatrick, D. G., R. Acierno, B. Saunders, H. S. Resnick, C. Best, and P. P. Schnurr. 2000. "Risk Factors for Adolescent Substance Abuse and Dependence: Data from a National Sample." *Journal of Consulting and Clinical Psychology* 68, no. 1: 19–30.

Kinney, J. M., D. Haapala, and C. Booth. 1991. *The Homebuilders Model: Keeping Families Together*. Hawthorne, N.Y.: Aldine de Gruyter.

Kipke, M. D., T. R. Simon, S. B. Montgomery, J. B. Unger, and E. F. Iverson. 1997. "Homeless Youth and Their Exposure to and Involvement in Violence While Living on the Streets." *Journal of Adolescent Health* 20: 360–367.

Kirk, R. S., and D. P. Griffith. 2004. "Intensive Family Preservation Services: Demonstrating Placement Prevention Using Event History Analysis." *Social Work Research* 28, no. 1: 5–15.

Kirk, R. S., M. M. Kim, and D. P. Griffith. 2005. "Advances in the Reliability and Validity of the North Carolina Assessment Scale." *Journal of Human Behavior in the Social Environment* 11, no. 3–4: 157–176.

Kirk, S. A., and W. J. Reid. 2002. *Science and Social Work: A Critical Appraisal*. New York: Columbia University Press.

Kish, L. 1965. *Survey Sampling*. New York: John Wiley & Sons.

Kolko, D. J. 1996. "Individual Cognitive Behavioral Treatment and Family Therapy for Physically Abused Children and Their Offending Parents: A Comparison of Clinical Outcomes." *Child Maltreatment* 1, no. 4: 322–342.

Kraemer, H. C., and S. Thiemann. 1987. *How Many Subjects: Statistical Power in Research*. Thousand Oaks, Calif.: Sage.

Krohn, M. D., A. J. Lizotte, and C. M. Perez. 1997. "The Interrelationship Between Substance Use and Precocious Transitions to Adult Statuses." *Journal of Health and Social Behavior* 38: 87–103.

Krueger, R. A. 1994. *Focus Groups: A Practical Guide for Applied Research*. Thousand Oaks, Calif.: Sage.

Kuhn, T. 1970. *The Structure of Scientific Revolution*. Chicago: University of Chicago Press.

Kukla, A. 2000. *Social Constructivism and the Philosophy of Science*. New York: Routledge.

Kurtz, P. D., S. V. Jarvis, and G. L. Kurtz. 1991. "Problems of Homeless Youths: Empirical Findings and Human Services Issues." *Social Work* 36: 309–314.

Kvale, S. 1996. *InterViews: An Introduction to Qualitative Research Interviewing*. Thousand Oaks, Calif.: Sage.

Landsverk, J. A., I. Davis, W. Ganger, R. Newton, and I. Johnson. 1996. "Impact of Psychological Functioning on Reunification from Out-of-Home Placement." *Children and Youth Services Review* 18, no. 4–5: 447–462.

Leichtman, M. 2006. "Residential Treatment of Children and Adolescents: Past, Present, and Future." *American Journal of Orthopsychiatry* 76, no. 3: 285–294.

Light, R. J., and D. P. Pillemer. 1984. *Summing Up: The Science of Reviewing Research*. Cambridge, Mass.: Harvard University Press.

Lincoln, Y. S., and E. G. Guba. 1985. *Naturalistic Inquiry*. Newbury Park, Calif.: Sage.

Lindeman, R. H., P. F. Merenda, and R. Z. Gold. 1980. *Introduction to Bivariate and Multivariate Analyses*. Glenview, Ill.: Scott, Foresman and Company.

Locke, L. F., S. J. Silverman, and W. W. Spirduso. 1998. *Reading and Understanding Research*. Thousand Oaks, Calif.: Sage.

Lutz, L. 2000. *Concurrent Planning: Tool for Permanency: Survey of Selected Sites*. New York: Hunter College School of Social Work, National Resource Center for Foster Care and Permanency Planning.

Maas, H. S., and R. E. Engler. 1959. *Children in Need of Parents*. New York: Columbia University Press.

McCluskey, C. P., M. D. Krohn, A. J. Lizotte, and M. L. Rodriguez. 2002. "Early Substance Use and School Achievement: An Examination of Latino, White, African American Youth." *Journal of Drug Issues* 32, no. 3: 921–943.

McDavid, J. C., and L. R. L. Hawthorn. 2006. *Program Evaluation and Performance Enhancement*. Thousand Oaks, Calif.: Sage.

McDonald, T., S. Bryson, and J. Poertner. 2006. "Balancing Reunification and Re-entry Goals." *Children and Youth Services Review* 28: 47–58.

McDonald, T. P., J. R. Propp, and K. G. Murphy. 2001. "The Post-Adoption Experience: Child, Parent, and Family Predictors of Family Adjustment to Adoption." *Child Welfare* 80, no. 1: 71–95.

McKnight, P. E., K. M. McKnight, S. Sidani, and A. J. Figueredo. 2007. *Missing Data: A Gentle Introduction.* New York: Guilford Press.

Merton, R. K., M. Fiske, and P. L. Kendall. 1956. *The Focused Interview.* New York: Free Press.

Miller, K. A., P. A. Fisher, B. Fetrow, and K. Jordan. 2005. "Trouble on the Journey Home: Reunification in Foster Care." *Children and Youth Services Review* 28, no. 3: 260–274.

Monette, D. R., T. J. Sullivan, and C. R. DeJong. 2005. *Applied Social Research: A Tool for the Human Services.* Belmont, Calif.: Thomson/Brooks/Cole.

Morgan, D. L., and R. A. Kreuger. 1993. "When to Use Focus Groups and Why." In *Successful Focus Groups: Advancing the State of the Art*, edited by D. L. Morgan, 3–19. Newbury Park, Calif.: Sage.

Morgan, L. J., L. S. Spears, and C. Kaplan. 2003. *Making Children a National Priority: A Framework for Community Action.* Washington, D.C.: Child Welfare League of America.

National Association of Social Workers. 1999. "Code of Ethics of the National Association of Social Workers. Retrieved November 28, 2006, from http://www.socialworkers.org/pubs/code/code.asp.

National Child Welfare Resource Center on Adoption. 2004. "Adopting Older Children." Available online at http://www.nrcadoption.org/resources/prac/OlderChildAdoption.pdf.

National Child Welfare Resource Center on Adoption. 2002. "Sibling Placement." Available online at http://www.nrcadoption.org/resources/prac/SiblingPlacement.pdf.

National Clearinghouse on Child Abuse and Neglect. 2001. "Child Maltreatment 2001: Summary of Key Findings." Available online at http://www.calib.com/nccanch/pubs/factsheets/canstats.cfm.

National Resource Center for Foster Care and Permanency Planning. 1998. *Tools for Permanency: Tool #1: Concurrent Planning.* New York: Hunter College School of Social Work.

Nelson, J. C. 1981. "Issues in Single-Subject Research for Non-Behaviorists." *Social Work Research and Abstracts* 17: 31–37.

Nelson, K. E., and M. J. Landsman. 1990. "Three Models of Family-Centered Placement Prevention Services." *Child Welfare* 69, no. 1: 3–21.

Nelson, M. L, M. Englar-Carlson, S. C. Tierney, and J. M. Hau. 2006. "Class Jumping Into Academia: Multiple Identities for Counseling Academics." *Journal of Consulting Psychology* 53, no. 1: 1–14.

Newcomb, M. D., and M. Felix-Ortiz. 1992. "Multiple Protective and Risk Factors for Drug Use and Abuse: Cross-Sectional and Prospective Findings." *Journal of Personality and Social Psychology* 63, no. 2: 280–296.

New York State Children and Family Services. 2001. *The New York Statewide Assessment. Child and Family Service Reviews.* Rennselear: New York State Children and Family Services.

North American Council on Adoptable Children. N.d. "High Risk Definitions of Special Needs." Available online at http://www.nacac.org/subsidyfactsheets/ highriskdefinitions.html.

O'Donnell, J. M., W. E. Johnson, L. D'Aunno, and H. L. Thornton. 2005. "Fathers in Child Welfare: Caseworkers' Perspectives." *Child Welfare* 74, no. 3: 363–386.

Office of Applied Studies. 2005a. "The National Survey on Drug Use and Health Report: Substance Use and Need for Treatment Among Youths Who Have Been in Foster Care." Rockville, Md.: Substance Abuse and Mental Health Services Administration. Available online at http://www.oas.samhsa.gov.

———. 2005b. "Results from the 2004 National Survey on Drug Use and Health: National Findings." Rockville, Md.: Substance Abuse and Mental Health Services Administration. Available online at http://www.oas.samhsa.gov.

———. 2004. "The National Survey on Drug Use and Health Report: Availability of Illicit Drugs Among Youths." Rockville, Md.: Substance Abuse and Mental Health Services Administration. Available online at http://www.oas.samhsa.gov.

Pardeck, J. T. 1984. "Multiple Placements of Children in Foster Care: An Empirical Analysis." *Social Work* 29, no. 6: 506–509.

Park, J. M., et al. 2004. "Public Shelter Admission Among Youth Adults with Child Welfare Histories by Type of Service and Type of Exit." *Social Service Review* 78: 284–303.

———. 2005. "Childhood Out-of-Home Placement and Dynamics of Public Shelter Utilization Among Young Homeless Adults." *Children & Youth Services Review* 27: 533–546.

Pearce, J. W., and T. D. Pezzot-Pearce. 1997. *Psychotherapy with Abused and Neglected Children.* New York: Guilford Press.

Pecora, P. J., R. C. Kessler, J. Williams, K. O'Brien, A. C. Downs, D. English, et al. 2005. "Improving Family Foster Care: Findings from the Northwest Foster Care Alumni Study." Seattle, Wash.: Casey Family Programs. Available online at http://www.casey.org/NR/rdonlyres/4E1E7C77-7624-4260-A253 -892C5A6CB9E1/300/nw_alumni_study_full_apr2005.pdf.

Pecora, P. J., W. R. Seeling, F. A. Zirps, and S. M. Davis. 1996. *Quality Improvement and Evaluation in Child and Family Services: Managing Into the Next Century.* Washington, D.C.: Child Welfare League of America.

Pecora, P. J., J. K. Whittaker, A. N. Maluccio, R. P. Barth, and R. D. Plotnick. 1993. *The Child Welfare Challenge: Policy, Practice, and Research.* New York: Aldine de Gruyter.

Perez, D. M. 2000. "The Relationship Between Physical Abuse, Sexual Victimization, and Adolescent Illicit Drug Use." *Journal of Drug Issues* 30, no. 3: 641–662.

Perry, B. D. 2000. "The Neurodevelopmental Impact of Violence in Childhood." In *Textbook of Child and Adolescent Forensic Psychiatry*, edited by D. H. Schetky and E. P. Benedek, 221–238. Washington, D.C.: American Psychiatric Press.

Perry, B. D., R. A. Pollard, T. L. Blakley, and D. Vigilante. 1995. "Childhood Trauma, the Neurobiology of Adaptation, and 'Use-Dependent' Development of the Brain: How States Become Traits." *Infant Mental Health Journal* 16: 271–291.

Peters, J. 2004. "True Ambivalence: Child Welfare Workers' Thoughts, Feelings, and Beliefs About Kinship Foster Care." *Children and Youth Services Review* 27, no. 6: 595–614.

Petta, G. A., and L. G. Steed. 2005. "The Experience of Adoptive Parents in Adoption Reunion Relationships: A Qualitative Study." *American Journal of Orthopsychiatry* 75, no. 2: 230–241.

Piotrkowski, C. S., and A. J. L. Baker. 2004. "Predicting Discharge Disposition of Adolescents in Residential Treatment." *Residential Treatment for Children and Youth* 21: 69–88.

Pithers, W. D., A. Gray, A. Busconi, and P. Houchens. 1998. "Children with Sexual Behavior Problems: Identification of Five Distinct Child Types and Related Treatment Considerations." *Child Maltreatment* 3: 384–406.

Popper, K. R. 1971. *The Open Society and Its Enemies*. Princeton, N.J.: Princeton University Press.

Prawat, R. S., and R. E. Floden. 1994. "Philosophical Perspectives on Constructivist Views of Learning." *Educational Psychologist* 29, no. 1: 37–48.

Redl, F. 1959. "The Concept of a 'Therapeutic Milieu.'" *American Journal of Orthopsychiatry* 29: 721–736.

Reed-Ashcraft, K., R. S. Kirk, and M. W. Fraser. 2001. "The Reliability and Validity of the North Carolina Family Assessment Scale." *Research on Social Work Practice* 11, no. 4: 503–520.

Reilly, T. 2003. "Transition from Care: Status and Outcomes of Youth Who Age Out of Foster Care." *Child Welfare* 6: 727–746.

Rodgers-Farmer, A. Y. 2000. "Parental Monitoring and Peer Group Association: Their Influence on Adolescent Substance Use." *Journal of Social Service Research* 27, no. 2: 1–18.

Rogoff, B. 1990. *Apprenticeship in Thinking: Cognitive Development in Social Context*. New York: Oxford University Press.

Rohr, M. E. 1996. "Identifying Adolescent Runaways: The Predictive Utility of the Personality Inventory for Children." *Adolescence* 31: 605–623.

Rosenthal, R. 1991. "Replication in Behavioral Research." In *Replication Research in the Social Sciences*, edited by J. Neulip, 1–30. Newbury Park, Calif.: Sage.

Rossi, P. H., M. W. Lipsey, and H. E. Freeman. 2004. *Evaluation: A Systematic Approach*. 7th ed. Thousand Oaks, Calif.: Sage.

Rotheram-Borus, M.J. 1993. "Suicidal Behavior and Risk Factors Among Runaway Youth." *American Journal of Psychiatry* 150: 103–107.

Rotheram-Borus, M. J., and C. Koopman. 1991. "Sexual Risk Behaviors, AIDS Knowledge, and Beliefs About AIDS Among Runaways." *American Journal of Public Health* 81: 208–210.

Rotheram-Borus, M. J., K. A. Mahler, C. Koopman, and K. Langabeer. 1996. "Sexual Abuse History and Associated Multiple Risk Behavior in Adolescent Runaways." *American Journal of Orthopsychiatry* 66: 390–400.

Rutter, M., and L. A. Sroufe. 2000. "Developmental Psychopathology: Concepts and Challenges." *Development and Psychopathology* 12: 265–296.

Ryan, J. 2006. "Dependent Youth in Juvenile Justice Programs: Do Positive Peer Programs Work for Victims of Child Maltreatment?" *Research on Social Work Practice* 16, no. 5: 511–519.

Sacks, J. G. 1985. "Specific Strategies of Problem Formulation: A Gap in Our Methods?" *Smith College Studies in Social Work* 55, no. 3: 214–224.

Schene, P. 2001. *Implementing Concurrent Planning: A Handbook for Child Welfare Administrators.* Portland: University of Southern Maine, National Resource Center for Organizational Improvement.

Schmidt, D. M., J. A. Rosenthal, and B. Bombeck. 1988. "Parents' Views of Adoption Disruption." *Children and Youth Services* 10, no. 2: 19–130.

Scriven, M. 1967. *The Methodology of Evaluation.* AERA Monograph Series on Curriculum Evaluation 1. Chicago: Rand McNally.

Seal, D. W., L. M. Bogart, and A. A. Ehrhardt. 1998. "Small Group Dynamics: The Utility of Focus Group Discussions as a Research Method." *Group Dynamics: Theory, Research, and Practice* 2, no. 4: 253–266.

Seelig, W. R., and P. J. Pecora. 1996. "The Changing World of Services for Children and Families: Reinventions for the Twenty-First Century." In *Quality Improvement and Evaluation in Child and Family Services: Managing Into the Next Century,* edited by P. J. Pecora et al., 5–25. Washington, D.C.: Child Welfare League of America.

Shore, N., K. Sim, N. S. LeProhn, and T. E. Keller. 2002. "Foster Parent and Teacher Assessments of Youth in Kinship and Non-Kinship Foster Care Placements: Are Behaviors Perceived Differently Across Settings?" *Children & Youth Services Review* 24: 109–134.

Shuster, E. 1997. "Fifty Years Later: The Significance of the Nuremberg Code." *The New England Journal of Medicine* 337, no. 20: 1436–1440.

Siegel, S., and N. J. Castellan. 1988. *Nonparametric Statistics for the Behavioral Sciences.* 2nd ed. New York: McGraw Hill.

Sixteenth Mental Measurements Yearbook. 2005. Edited by R. A. Spies and B. S. Plake. LC 39–3422.

Smith, B. D. 2004. "Job Retention in Child Welfare: Effects of Perceived Organizational Supervisor Support and Intrinsic Job Value." *Children and Youth Services Review* 27, no. 2: 153–169.

Stouffer, S., et al. 1949. *The American Soldier.* Princeton, N.J.: Princeton University Press.

Straus, A. L. 1987. *Qualitative Analysis for Social Scientists.* New York: Cambridge University Press.

Suchman, E. 1967. *Evaluation Research.* New York: Russell Sage Foundation.

Sudman, S. 1976. *Applied Sampling.* New York: Academic Press.

Tannehill, R. L. 1987. "Employing a Modified Positive per Culture Treatment Approach in a State Youth Center." *Journal of Offender Counseling, Services & Rehabilitation* 12, no. 1: 113–129.

Tapert, S. F., G. A. Aarons, G. R. Sedlar, and S. A. Brown. 2001. "Adolescent Substance Use and Sexual Risk-Taking Behavior." *Journal of Adolescent Health* 28: 181–189.

Tellis, W. 1997. "Introduction to Case Study. The qualitative report." Available online at http://www.nova.edu/ssss/QR/QR3–2/tellis1.html.

Testa, M. F. 2001. "Kinship Care and Permanency." *Journal of Social Science Research* 28, no. 1: 25–43.

Tests in Print. 2002. Edited by L. L. Murphy, B. S. Plake, J. C. Impara, and R. A. Spies.

Treischman, A. E., J. Whittaker, and L. Brentro. 1969. *The Other Twenty-Three Hours.* New York: Aldine.

Tyler, K. A., D. R. Hoyt, L. B. Whitbeck, and A. M. Cauce. 2001. "The Effects of a High-Risk Environment on the Sexual Victimization of Homeless and Runaway Youth." *Violence and Victims* 16: 441–455.

United States Department of Health and Human Services. 2000. *Report to Congress on Kinship Foster Care.* Washington, D.C.: United States Department of Health and Human Services.

———. 2006. *Administration for Children and Families, Administration on Children, Youth and Families, Children's Bureau.* Available online at http://www.acf.hhs .gov/programs/cb. Preliminary estimates for FY 2005 as of September 2006.

———. 2004. HHS News. Press release October 14, 2004. Available online at http://www.acf.hhs.gov/news/press/2004/adoption_03.htm.

United States Department of Health and Human Services, Office for Protection of Research Risks. 1993. *Tips for Informed Consent.* Washington, D.C.: United States Department of Health and Human Services.

United States Government Accounting Office. 1990. *Case Study Evaluations.* Washington, D.C.: U.S. Government Accounting Office, Program Evaluation and Methodology Division.

———. 1995. *Child Welfare: Complex Needs Strain Capacity to Provide Services* (GAO/ HEHS-95-208). Available online at http://www.gao.gov.

———. 2003 *Child Welfare: HHS Could Play a Greater Role in Helping Child Welfare Agencies Recruit and Retain Staff.* GAO-03-357. Washington, D.C.: United States Government Accounting Office.

———. 2002. *Foster Care: Recent Legislation Helps States Focus on Finding Permanent Homes for Children, but Long-Standing Barriers Remain* (GAO-02–585). Available online at http://www.gao.gov/new.items/d02585.pdf.

———. 2003. *Foster Care: States Focusing on Finding Permanent Homes for Children, but Long-Standing Barriers Remain* (GAO-03–626T). Available online at http://www.gao.gov/new.items/d03626t.pdf.

United States House of Representatives Committee on Ways and Means. 2000. *2000 Green Book.* Washington, D.C.: U.S. Government Printing Office. Available online at http://www.acf.hhs.gov/programs/cb/dis/cwdata.htm.

Unrau, Y. A., and M. A. Wells. 2005. "Patterns of Foster Care Service Delivery." *Children and Youth Services Review* 27, no. 5: 511–531.

Urquiza, A., and C. Winn. 1994. *Treatment for Abused and Neglected Children: Infancy to Age 18.* Washington, D.C.: U.S. Department of Health and Human Services, Administration for Children and Families, Administration on Children, Youth and Families, National Center on Child Abuse and Neglect.

Van der Kolk, B. 1994. "The Body Keeps Score: Memory and the Psychobiology of Post Traumatic Stress." *Harvard Review of Psychiatry* 1, no. 5: 253–265.

Viera, A. J., and J. M. Garrett. 2005. "Understanding Inter-Observer Agreement: The Kappa Statistic." *Family Medicine* 37, no. 5: 360–363.

Vogel, C. A. 1999. "Using Administrative Databases to Examine Factors Affecting Length of Stay in Substitute Care." *Child and Youth Services Review* 21, no. 8: 677–690.

Vorrath, H., and L. Brentro. 1974. *Positive Peer Culture.* Chicago: Aldine.

Waldfogel, J. 1998. *The Future of Child Protection: How to Break the Cycle of Abuse and Neglect.* Cambridge, Mass.: Harvard University Press.

———. 2000. "Reforming Child Protective Services." *Child Welfare* 79, no. 1: 43–57.

Weick, A. 1987. "Reconceptualizing the Philosophical Perspective of Social Work." *Social Service Review* 61, no. 2: 218–230.

Wells, R. 2006. "Managing Child Welfare Agencies: What Do We Know About What Works?" *Children and Youth Services Review* 28: 1181–1194.

Whitbeck, L. B., D. R. Hoyt, and W. N. Bao. 2000. "Depression Symptoms and Co-Occurring Depressive Symptoms, Substance Abuse, and Conduct Problems Among Runaway and Homeless Adolescents." *Child Development* 71: 721–732.

Wills, T. A., J. A. Resko, M. G. Ainette, and D. Mendoza. 2004. "Role of Parent Support and Peer Support in Adolescent Substance Use: A Test of Mediated Effects." *Psychology of Addictive Behaviors* 18, no. 2: 122–134.

Wulczyn, F. 2004. "Family Reunification." *The Future of Children* 14, no. 1: 95–113.

———. 1996. "A Statistical and Methodological Framework for Analyzing the Foster Care Experiences of Children." *Social Service Review* 70: 318–329.

Wulczyn, F., and R. M. Goerge. 1992. "Foster Care in New York and Illinois: The Challenge of Rapid Change." *Social Service Review* 66: 278–294.

Wulczyn, F., J. Kogan, and B. J. Harden. 2003. "Placement Trajectories and Movement Trajectories." *Social Science Review* 77, no. 2: 212–236.

Yin, R. K. 1984. *Case Study Research: Design and Methods.* 1st ed. Beverly Hills, Calif.: Sage.

Yoder, K. A., D. R. Hoyt, and L. B. Whitbeck. 1998. "Suicidal Behavior Among Homeless and Runaway Adolescents." *Journal of Youth and Adolescence* 27: 753–771.

Index

LONGSCAN, 162
LOS. *See* length of stay
Lubeck, S. G., 217
Lutz, L., 200, 231
Lyons, J., 253

Maas, H. S., 7, 384
Mahler, K. A., 80
Maluccio, A. N., 9, 188, 313, 354, 382
mandated reporter, 9
Mangione, T. W., 139, 141
maternity shelter, as example of
    sampling, 82–100
Mathews, F., 188
McCaslin, M., 267
McCluskey, C. P., 125
McConoughy, S. H., 182
McDavid, J. C., 359
McDonald, T. P., 57, 354
McKnight, K. M., 264
McKnight, P. E., 264
McMillen, C., 126
mean: calculation, 289; differential
    attrition, 367; directional hypotheses,
    74–75, 295; imputation, 285; outlier,
    51; reporting results, 315–319; sample
    mean, 82–87; testing differences,
    128, 299–304, 307, 373; univariate
    analyses, 289–292
measurement, 27; ethics, 50–51, 177;
    theory, 167–186
measures, 28; describing, 181–182;
    identification, 173–175; selection,
    175–181
measures of central tendency, 289–290
measures of dispersion, 289–290
median, 289, 294
Mendoza, D., 126
MEPA. *See* Multiethinic Placement Act
Merenda, P. F., 280, 287
Merton, R. K., 232
methods section, 30, 324
Miller, J. Y., 126
Miller, K. A., 354
Mincer, C., 149, 158
mixed method design, 27, 29
mode, 289
Monette, D. R., 16
Montgomery, J. B., 80

Morgan, D. L., 233
Morgan, L. J., 381
Mott, M., 182
movements in care, 20, 156–157,
    164, 343
Multiethnic Placement Act, 147
multistate studies, 7–8, 235
multivariate analyses, 26, 72–73, 129,
    280; linear regression, 308–309,
    319–321, 373; logistic regression;
    309–311, 321–322; of variance; 302;
    survival analysis, 8, 292–294, 311,
    322
Murphy, K. G., 57
Murphy, L. L., 175

National Association of Social Workers
    (NASW), 37, 39, 113, 174
National Child Abuse and Neglect
    Data Systems (NCANDS),
    160–161
National Child Welfare Resource Center
    on Adoption, 145–146
National Clearinghouse on Child Abuse
    and Neglect, 354
National Data Archive on Child Abuse
    and Neglect, 161
National Longitudinal Survey of Child
    and Adolescent Wellbeing, 162
National Resource Center for Foster Care
    and Permanency Planning, 231
Needell, B., 8, 253, 354
Nelson, J. C., 117
Nelson, K. E., 8
Nelson, M. L., 259
Nesmith, A., 11, 385
Ness, A. E., 218
New York Children's Aid Society, 5–6
New York Foundling, 6
New York State Children and Family
    Services, 63
Newcomb, M. D., 126
Newton, R., 8
nominal scale, 180
nonlinear associations, 307–308
nonparametric statistics, 280, 301, 304
normal distribution, 25, 75, 129, 286,
    299–301, 303, 304, 306, 308
norms, 27–28, 173, 369